Josiah Proctor Walton

Pioneer Papers

Comprising a Collection of the Recollections of Early Events of Bloomington

Josiah Proctor Walton

Pioneer Papers

Comprising a Collection of the Recollections of Early Events of Bloomington

ISBN/EAN: 9783337132668

Printed in Europe, USA, Canada, Australia, Japan

Cover: Foto ©ninafisch / pixelio.de

More available books at **www.hansebooks.com**

PIONEER PAPERS,

COMPRISING A COLLECTION

—OF THE—

RECOLLECTIONS OF EARLY EVENTS OF BLOOMINGTON, IOWA, NOW MUSCATINE, AND ITS SURROUNDINGS, BEING A SHORT HISTORY OF THE BUSINESS MEN, THE SCHOOLS, THE CHURCHES, AND THE EARLY POLITICS OF THE ...PIONEERS...

—BY—

J. P. WALTON,

Who has been a resident of Iowa for more than sixty years, and President of the Old Settlers' Society for fifteen years. He is the author of the following works: Scraps of Muscatine History; History of Trinity Church; Masonic History 1841–1896; Records of the Walton Family, etc.

MUSCATINE:
1899.

APOLOGY.

———·———

Knowing that many important events are fast passing into oblivion, we have been induced to try and preserve a few of them for future reference, under the head of "RECOLLECTIONS," that have recently appeared in the SATURDAY MAIL. In preparing this collection of historical sketches, we have used the names and acts of many of the early builders of Muscatine and its surroundings whose names or deeds have not appeared in any other former history.

We have tried to make our "RECOLLECTIONS" readable, and have aimed to have them correct as they were known to have occurred at the time. We hope no offense has been given from the failure to say that all of our different characters were saints, (which perhaps they may be,) for they were not all so considered by those who knew them; nevertheless they helped to develop the country and should have a place among its pioneers.

J. P. WALTON.

Recollection of Business in the Early Days of Muscatine.

Published in the Muscatine Saturday Mail January 16, 1897; written by J P. Walton.

Fifty years ago Bloomington, now Muscatine, had more marked characters per capita than any city or town in Iowa at this time. In the first directory published in 1856, our city had fifteen places where dry goods were sold, Gen. J. G. Gordon, not being included, made sixteen. At this time we have but seven Some of their stocks of goods were quite large.

J. G. Gordon, whose name we have mentioned, came here near the year 1845, and brought a general stock of goods, much better than any one else had at the time. He opened in the frame, two story building that stands adjoining on the west of the street car office on east Second street. The building then stood where now stands the west room of Batterson's store.

Gordon's stock of goods was fine; he was affable, and of course he soon secured a good trade. The svtem of doing business in those early days, was to lay in a stock once a year, so as to get it here when the river was high—for everything had to be brought here on steamboats. When the river was low the large boats had to lay up or go some where else. Of course, large buildings had to be erected for storage. Gordon soon found that out, and, in 1851, he built the largest store in the city, it is the one now occupied by G. W. Dillaway, it having been enlarged and beautified since Dillaway owned it. In the rear across the alley he put up a warehouse to store goods in, and as the goods were sold out it was filled with grain, mostly wheat.

At that time there was very little money in circulation. The farmer handled very little of that, all he had to buy with was his farm products, which, like the merchandise, had to go down the river when it was high. Grain cut in July never reached a market until the following spring or summer.

While Gordon dealt in all kinds of merchandise when he commenced, he soon came near dropping all but dry goods and hardware. Both articles seeming to suit him better than anything else. He was very close and exacting in all his dealings and he expected clerks to be the same. His old bookkeeeper, Frank Thurston, had things about his own way.

Gordon had a fair share of the commission business. Business was done in this way largely.

The wholesale merchants of St. Louis or other places would lay in large stocks of goods for this county, and knowing that they had to reach here during the high stage of the river, they would load them on boats and send them up the river, while freights were low, to the merchants to be sold on commission. Frequently the steamboat officers would take a lot of heavy articles, such as sugar and coffee, salt and molasses, and bring them up and leave them for sale on commission. Advertisements of these goods would frequently read this way: "Received by steamer Osprey on consignment, 50 barrels of salt, and must be sold at once." This salt could be purchased much cheaper than salt could be in the winter time when the farmers wanted it. The best merchants were selected for handling the salt, and Gordon got his share of that kind of business.

As before stated, the farmer had no money. If he sold his produce for merchandise enough for his wants he was fortunate. His produce was shipped south and more goods bought and sold again to the farmer. There was a little trade that brought money. The river trade was the best.

All the lumber brought down was rafted. It required from twelve to twenty men to run a raft, and when the raft was landed they were paid off. Of course the money went into the hands of those that had the goods they wanted. Gordon got quite a share.

There was another class of men that traded with him—the woodchoppers. All of the great flotilla of steamboats had to have wood for fuel; coal was not in use. This made employment for a great number of men. Gordon was quite popular with them; they traded largely with him. They never had any money until boats run in the spring. He furnished supplies for a large number. At one time a gentleman from Pittsburg, an acquaintance of Gordon's, a very refined looking man, was in his store, when in came Old Stuttering Jim Humphreys (the wood king) who had a great many men working for him. He left a big order to be taken down to his wood boat at the wharf. Gordon and his men set about getting up his order, while old Jim kept them amused with his mixture of stuttering and swearing that no human being could imitate if he wished to. After Jim had gone out Gordon turned to his Pittsburg friend and said: "You see the kind of men we sell your goods to on credit!" It surprised the man a little and upon examining the book accounts it showed that he received more money from him than any other customer.

Gordon continued in the mercantile business until his death. During a few of his later years he had his brother-in-law by marriage, O. P. Watters, associated with him. Politically he was a democrat and did not go to war, but he always contributed his share to its support. On one occasion a few furloughed soldiers of the Mad Creek Rattler kind came home. After stowing away a few drinks of whiskey they started out to make the democrats all loyal. They called on Ed. Thayer, editor of the democratic paper, and walked him up to the justice's office and made him take the oath of allegiance. (which he was quite willing to do) and I think one or two others with the same success. They then started for Gordon's, walked into the store and informed Gordon what they wanted. He stepped for his hat, and in getting the hat he secured a big butcher knife and started for them, ordering them out of the store and threatening to disembowel them if they did not go at once. They went.

Gordon attended the Episcopal church, was one of its best supporters and one of its vestrymen for many years. He was a jovial good fellow and liked to enjoy life as well as almost any one. He was a stockholder in a local insurance company and in the gas company, and probably a director in both. Whenever they had a meeting he and some of the others always insisted on having a supper. It was all the dividends they received.

We always had a military law. On one occasion there was a vacancy in the office of brigadier general. Some of the b'hoys started a petition and got the appointment for Gordon, who always appreciated it.

In the year 1849 Gordon built a one story cottage on Front street above Cedar. His family was quite large and as it increased he would add an addition. Before he left it he had a four-story house all on the ground. After covering his lot with all the additions it would well stand, he bought the large house now owned by Mrs. Cora Weed on the corner of Cherry and Second streets, where he made one of the loveliest places in Iowa.

Recollection of Business in the Early Days of Muscatine.

Published in the Muscatine Saturday Mail January 16, 1897; written by
J P Walton.

No. 2

The steamboat landing at Bloomington, now Muscatine, in early days was not good, especially at a low stage of the river. In the year of 1840 a Yankee by the name of E. B Kinson, came along and built a wharf-boat for steamboats to land at. I think that W B. Fish was interested with him in the boat, and after Kinson went away Fish had the whole control of it. The boat was about sixteen feet wide and seventy feet long, and was roofed over. The upper end had a room 20 feet long, then an open space for a passage-way from the shore to the steamboats; the lower 30 feet was used for a butcher shop and for storage. They had an ice box in this room and would frequently sell a lump of ice to the bar tender on the steamboats to use in his juleps. The boats did not carry ice for general use for several years after the erection of this boat-house. The room at the upper end was used for a boat store where bread, milk and provisions of all kinds used by the passengers on the steamboats were kept for sale.

In 1840, or about that time, the largest part of the passengers traveled on deck. They had to furnish their own meals, hence the need of boat stores. The first sign we saw at Pittsburg was "boat store," and at every town or village along the the entire length of the Ohio river and all the way up the Mississippi this was the most prominent sign.

The boat trade in this city was not confined to the wharf-boat, for most of the stores on Front street had that sign stuck up over their doors.

The old wharf-boat was in use for several years and was used by different persons If I am not mistaken Henry Funck had it for a while.

Another sign quite prominent on Front street in early days, was "Forwarding and Commission." The forwarding business was done about this way: The country merchant bought goods at Pittsburg, Cincinnati, or St.

Louis, shipped them here on the steamboats, and the freight had to be paid. The forwarding merchant stepped in, paid the freight, stored the goods, and sent them forward to the country merchants the best way he could. The system adopted by the railroads of allowing the freight bill to accompany the goods and be paid at the place of destination was not in vogue at that time.

When the new comer got on shore he started up Chestnut street, the most commonly traveled one. On his right was a boat store and bake shop kept by Henry Funck; on the left was the first hotel, built in 1836 by Robert Kinney. It had the common round hotel sign of the times, it was about three feet in diameter, mounted on a post out in the street, and had the words "Iowa House" painted on it.

When John G. Steine purchased this hotel he had the sign painted yellow with a dark horse painted on it, and called it the "Pennsylvania House." The boys dubbed it the "Pennsylvania Horse." Later it became known as Steine's hotel. When Kinney built the house in 1836 and 1837 he mounted a bell on it, that bell is yet in use on the Scott House. It is the oldest bell in the city, having been in use sixty years, it is the first bell brought here for use and should be kept as a relic.

The old hotel has been so thoroughly described by the old settlers, we will not say anything about it. Mr. John G. Steine took it in charge in 1847, and one of his old advertisements reads thus: "Steine's Hotel, John G. Steine proprietor, Water street, corner of Chestnut. This is one of the first hotels in city, the present proprietor has kept it nine years. Reference to his old patrons is all the recommendation he wants." Well, we should think it was enough, for his table was loaded with good wholesome food, and the word was "pitch in," there was plenty for all. In the basement of the front part was his "bar room" where his old patrons did their loafing. The ceiling was not more than six and a half feet high, and the atmosphere was frequently blue with the fumes of tobacco, etc. The proprietor was a large and heavy set man, he came from Pennsylvania and he generally wore a low cut vest with a shirt that was white in the morning, but being an inveterate chewer the shirt acquired a buff color before night, he also sported in sight a red bandana handkerchief. He was a leader among the democrats, who had the ascendency at the time, and they elected him mayor of the city in 1855. Mr. Steine was a kind hearted man, but scarey. In the time of the cholera, it was said, he hardly slept for fear it would break out in his hotel. He did a good business, but when his wife died the hotel soon went down, and it never did any good afterwards.

On the west corner of the alley and Chestnut street, stood a large two story frame building that had been used for a saloon and restaurant for considerable time. I think Dan Ball, John Cobb, and Cyrus. Spring had occupied it. When it went into the hands of William Spring it was taken down and the present brick building now standing at the place was erected. Along the west side of the street to the building on the corner was a row of small wooden buildings, called Shanghie Row. One of these buildings was occupied by John Shafer for a lager beer saloon. Shafer was somewhat excitable and easily teased. Some of the wags among his patrons would practice all kinds of jokes on him, finally it got so bad that he could not stand it any longer and he punished some of them, and they in turn tore down his building. I have been told that one of the leaders of the mob was afterwards elected mayor of the city. It was said that during the time of this riot the mayor, John A. Parvin, went out with a lantern in his hand and said "This is a bad house and should be torn down, but you must desist." He had only made this remark when a brickbat struck his lantern and knocked it out of his hand. His Honor retired.

I think this building and one on the southeast corner of Fourth and Orange street, that was torn down by the soldiers from Camp Strong during the early days of the war, were the only ones that were ever torn down in our city by mobs.

John Shafer with others built the present three-story brick buildings on Chestnut street below Second, and the town was the gainer by the riot.

An effort was made by D. C. Cloud, on the part of Shafer, to collect damages from the city, but they could find no law at that time to make the city liable.

On the west side of Chestnut and south side of Second street, stood a small one-story building that was occupied at one time by John Lemp, who came here with a choice stock of goods and brought Luke Sells here with him. The firm soon became known as Lemp & Sells. They moved into No. 5, Union block, after it was built. They bought grain and had a warehouse on the southwest corner of Iowa Avenue and Third street, where they stored their grain until the river was high in the spring before shipping it. They kept a good stock of carpets, boots, shoes, crockery and hardware. Their stock of dry goods was too fine for the market, and the result was a great number of "stickers" that were sold at almost any rate when the winding-up day came.

When Mr. Sells left and went to St Louis to live, Mr. Lemp had a very extended trade. If I am not mistaken he had a branch store at Fort Dodge. He did considerable jobbing and at one time he was considered worth several hundred thousand dollars. The resumption of specie payment or the decline of goods from war prices proved too much for him, and he did not clean up with as much as he wanted. Mr. Lemp now lives near Chicago.

The Union block spoken of before, is the buildings on the north side of Second street east of Chestnut street. It was built by several owners under the supervision of J. A. Green. When built it was considered the most desirable property in the city for business purposes.

From 1852 to 1857 was the age of building brick blocks in Muscatine. We then built enough to do ever since. I conclude so from the fact that the name has "gone out." The word "block" is not now in use, every thing of any size is called "buildings." Many of the old tablets are yet to be seen, for instance Cedar block on Second street west of Mulberry street. In this block the postmaster, John A. McCormick, located the post office for some four years much to the annoyance of the down town patrons. Protests were made, but the postmaster claimed it near the center of the population, if not of the business. John kept it there till his term expired, or someone else took his place and moved it down town.

Recollection of Business in the Early Days of Muscatine.

Published in the Muscatine Saturday Mail January 30, 1897; written by J P. Walton.

No. 3.

Forty years ago we had four drug stores in our city, they were J. B. Dougherty, Fay & Stone, C. O. Waters, and J. E. Graham. J. B. Dougherty was the oldest druggist in the business, his drug store (now called the Pioneer drug store) was started by W. H. Holingsworth in the year (1492) or possibly in 1842, and sold to Mr. Dougherty shortly after his arrival. He came here March 10, 1842, a young man. He soon married and settled down in business. He was quite gregarious and he always had a few friends that stuck to him through thick and thin. In the rear room of his drug store could be found some of them at almost any hour, such as Gen. J. G. Gordon, Dr. George Reeder, E. Klein and others, to the number of six or eight. This trait has descended to his son the present owner of the store, Colonel J. B. Dougherty. The store has been kept nearly all the time on the lot it now occupies. It never burned out, but it was washed out and fell down, and was rebuilt.

Mr. Dougherty was not satisfied with looking out for himself alone, which he did quite well. He was willing to exert himself for other people's benefit, and I think I am safe in saying that he occupied more places of trust and importance when little or no pay was to be had, than any other man in our city. He served on the city council, the city school board, and the board of county supervisors. He was also one of the vestrymen of the Episcopal church, an officer in the Masonic order and in the Academy of Science, was director in one of the banks, and I do not know how many other minor offices he held. He was one of the principal managers in the gas company, and one of the leading spirits in securing the railroads to this city. He was not so much of a dasher as some, but he was a constant worker for the public good. We wish his mantle had fallen on his descendants, for it is sad to think that the example of such a man will be lost in two generations.

Fay & Stone started in the drug business shortly after Mr. Dougherty. If I recollect right, Edward E. and Pliny Fay started the store and when Edward's health failed Fred Stone took his place. This firm did a good business and both were very honorable men. They were New England men who had ventured west "to the very front" early, coming here in 1838 or 1839, and when the Congregational church was organized they both joined it. Pliny Fay soon acquired the name of being the most devout man in the town, which he was honestly entitled to. Fred H. Stone was an educated man, having graduated from Dartmouth college in 1835, and not wishing to follow a profession he came west, bought a stock of goods and opened a store in company with H. Q. Jennison near where the oat meal mill now stands. Fred Stone claimed to have bought the first raft of lumber ever sold in this market. It was hard lumber which had been sawed at Maquoketa. He filled the office of county recorder and was surveyor for one or more terms.

Mr. Fay's health failed and he retired from the business and went to California.

Dr. C. O. Waters opened a drug store somewhere near the middle of the block on the north side of Second street, east of Iowa Avenue, but I think it was moved to the corner of the avenue, though, perhaps, not until after the store had changed hands, possibly to Wm. De Hues.

Dr. C. O. Waters was associated with Dr. George Reeder in the practice of medicine for a long time. After giving up the drug business Dr Waters went to Chicago and went to preaching, becoming Rev. C. O. Waters. He was on the editorial staff of a Presbyterian paper.

J. E. Graham opened a drug store and his brother Dr. I. L. Graham soon became associated with him in the business. Some years ago J. E. Graham withdrew, later the doctor died, leaving the business in the hands of his son who is running it in the same locality it started in more than forty years ago.

There is one thing a little remarkable that forty years ago we had four drug stores, while now we have one-half of them running under the same name in the same locality and by the same families, one of the houses having run for fifty-five years.

Away back in the forties a tall slim Vermonter, made his appearance here and opened a store under the name of Green & Enders. The firm soon changed to Green & Stone—Jos. A. Green and George C. Stone. They kept a general store, sold goods and bought grain and pork. They soon found out that buying wheat and packing pork were different lines of business, and they turned their attention to the pork packing especially. In the winter time they cut and packed pork in the brick warehouse on the corner of Front and Pine streets. Under the management of J. Green they did very well, and the year following the opening of the packing house, they built a slaughter house on the bank of the slough, about 200 feet west of where the Hershey mill now stands. This was the first slaughtering house erected for killing hogs in the town, as all the pork packed previous to that time was killed by the farmers and hauled to the city. After the slaughter house was built, for some years the fat hogs were driven in, and it was no uncommon thing to see droves of 200 to 300 hogs go through the streets every day for a month or so during the late fall and early winter. Some of these droves of hogs were driven thirty to forty miles, at an average of four or five miles a day, but after railroads were built they were shipped on cars and hauled in wagons, as at present, to the slaughter houses. The hogs were killed and the grease steamed out at the slaughter house. the dressed hogs were hauled up town for packing. This old slaughter house was owned by Green & Stone until it was sold to S. O. Butler. Before selling the pork business they closed out their store and went into the banking business, Mr. Green doing the outside work and Mr. Stone attending to the bank. The bank was opened in a small one-story wooden building where F. W. Swan's store now stands. It was the first banking house in the city and was started about the year 1851. I recollect the first business I did with them, I was building a house for F. M. Cummins in the country, when Saturday night came he gave me a check on the bank. I went in and cashed it, it was a new way of doing business. Their room was not over fifteen feet square and they had a very common safe with a key lock on it, to keep their cash in—combination locks were not then in use. They soon afterwards erected the brick building now occupied by McBride & Cope, on the south side of Second street, between Iowa avenue and Chestnut streets. For this new building Green & Stone went to St. Louis and bought a large fire and burglar proof vault. This vault is now used by the Cook-Musser State Bank and Trust Co.

After giving up packing Mr. Green engaged in the real estate business and bought and sold land. This was at the period that the railroad was being built, and there was large emigration and everything booming. He dealt largely in real estate and prospered, he was one of the principal men who laid out Wilton and Ononwa (now Letts) and he erected the first frame building in the town of Letts. In the autumn of 1856 and winter of 1857 he owned several farms near there. He built several business blocks in Muscatine and kept a stock of trotting horses, and was a prominent man in the city. When the panic of 1857 came, it found him with obligations considerably extended, and his business about closed up, so far as large operations were concerned

At the breaking out of the war Mr. Green went into the army as quartermaster and served some three or more years. After returning he engaged in raising horses, he became the owner of the famous horse known as Green's Bashaw. The horse was sold after Mr. Green's death to a gentleman living in Illinois.

Mr. Green was a member of the Episcopal church and during his membership he stood at the head of the list on contributions. He was a blunt, outspoken man, but if an offence was given without a cause, which was frequently the case, he was willing to make any kind of reperation needed.

Recollection of Business in the Early Days of Muscatine.

Published in the Muscatine Saturday Mail February 6, 1897; written by J P. Walton.

No. 4.

At one time our currency was largely county orders; they were valued from 40 to 60 cents on the dollar. The first order ever drawn on the treasurer of the county was for $27 on Oct 5, 1837, to T. M. Isett for surveying a county road, to Mr. Isett was a young man when he came here and followed surveying, teaming and doing almost anything. He had some money and good health, both of which most of the old settlers were deficient in. He entered some very choice lots of land, and got hold of some of the choice town lots and had money to loan where the security was good and the interest 2 per cent a month. How Mr. Isett became colonel I cannot tell; I never heard of his doing military duty. He was the most successful business man we had in our early days. In those days county orders were worth 40 or 50 cents on the dollar. Isett operated in them considerably. They were used to pay county taxes and it was no uncommon thing for the county to be sued.

The court house was sold on one occasion for debt. The commissioners let the time of redemption run out, and the only way they could clear up the title was to get Isett to redeem it as a judgment creditor. A law was soon passed exempting county property from execution.

When the city commenced to pave their streets it was a question about their right to collect the cost from the property, by common consent T. M. Isett made a contest in the courts, and took it to the supreme court. The city gained the suit and no contest has been made since then.

Along in the fifties he associated with him a young man by the name of William C. Brewster, in the banking business. They occupied the room, 114 Iowa avenue, where J. H. Munroe now does business. At the time they opened business was brisk; money brought big interest. I have paid 1½ per cent a month for a great many dollars. At the breaking out of the war they unloaded their paper money and got all their funds into gold, which went up to $2.50 premium. They felt as though Muscatine was too small a place for them. Isett went to Wall street, New York, and commenced business in the name of Isett, Kerr & Co. Isett, Kerr & Co. soon failed. Isett went to Canada and stayed until the limitation act let him out of Wall street debts. He had considerable property around this city that seemed to be overlooked by his creditors; perhaps it was in some one else's hands, for as soon as the time of limitation expired he returned and sold it. As a man of integrity Mr. Isett stood No. 1, none better; he never forgot a contract, even if he should lose by it. Those who had dealings with him sympathized with him in his losses.

We usually had three banks. J. W. Dalton & Co. run a private banking house. When business settled down after the panic of 1857, the Muscatine branch of the State Bank of Iowa was started on the southeast corner of Second street and Iowa avenue, with A. O. Patterson, president; J. W. Dalton, cashier; A. O. Patterson, Chester Weed, J. B. Dougherty, S. D. Viele, W. F. Brannan, C. Healey, J. W. Lucas and A. Farnsworth, directors. The bank bought and sold land warrants. On one occasion the accountant found a shortage and soon another. The directors met and the shortage was investigated. It was soon found that the president and cashier had bought a great number of soldier warrants and had located them in different parts of the state and had them deeded to the president, using too much of the bank's money. Some one had to step in and take the land, or the bank would have to suspend, a thing that no one wanted. One or two of the directors undertook to relieve the bank, but it finally settled down on Chester Weed to furnish the money and take land. Mr. Weed was very reluctant to undertake it, but by having good eastern credit he pulled through and the land soon began to advance in value, and Weed made considerable money out of the forced deal. Before the bank got out of the difficulty they had a law suit with Jacob Butler and beat him; then Butler applied for stock and on the 30th of December, 1864, a National Bank was organized, with J. B. Dougherty, president; Chester Weed, vice president; J. Richardson, cashier; Jacob Butler, J. G. Gordon and S. D. Viele, directors, with a capital of $100,000. They had two others associated with them—T. B. Dobbs and Gilman, Son & Co., of New York, as stockholders. On one occasion the bank had a draft raised from $14.00 to $3,700 by a forger, Mr. Piper, who got the money and left; a reward was offered for his arrest; the man was secured somewhere east, perhaps in Indiana, and was brought back and kept in jail for some time. All at once the man was gone, said to have broke jail: he was not followed; it soon turned out that he was never arrested by any legal warrant; he had returned without a requisition. The outsiders concluded he must have fixed it up with the bank in some way. When the bank surrendered the National organization, it was succeeded by G. A. Garrettson & Co. and later by the Hershey State Bank.

The year following the organization of the first National Bank an application was made for another National Bank. Butler of the first National Bank, fought it, and he being a man of considerable political influence he succeeded in getting it defeated. Not being disposed to give it up, the defeated parties started out and canvassed and got up a popular bank. They got a great many of the business men to take stock, if only a small amount, and commenced business on November 1, 1865, under the name of the Merchants' Exchange National Bank, with but $50,000 capital, no dividends being made until a surplus of $50,000 had been acquired. In the meantime many of the small stockholders had sold or were squeezed out. The first officers were: S. G. Stein, president; H. W. Moore, vice president; Peter Jackson, cashier; S. B. Cook, teller; A. G. Butler, book keeper.

When the first National Bank closed up their business, or transferred it to G. A. Garrettson & Co., the Merchants' Exchange Bank changed its name to the First National Bank. Previous to changing their name they organized the Muscatine Savings Bank, with about the same officers.

In 1870 a private banking house was organized, consisting of Jacob and Charles Silverman, Henry Funck and S. B. Cook, under the name of Silverman, Cook & Co. Later, the Silvermans having sold out to P. M. Musser, the name was changed to Cook, Musser & Co. They have recently organized under the state law as a State Bank, and occupy their old quarters, southwest corner of Second street and Iowa avenue, under the name of Cook-Musser State Bank and Trust Company.

A CORRECTION.

A note from Mr. P Jackson informs me that "the first officers of the Merchants' Exchange bank were P. Jackson, president; S. G. Stein, vice-president; W. C. Brewster, cashier, and the bank paid a dividend right along." J. P. W.

Recollection of Business in the Early Days of Muscatine.

Published in the Muscatine Saturday Mail February 13, 1897; written by J P. Walton.

BY J. P. WALTON.

No. 5

The recent dedication of the Rescue Hose company's quarters calls to mind the fire department of thirty years ago, which consisted of the Bucket Brigade and comprised everybody who went to the fire. It was usual when the alarm was given for every one to secure a bucket and start to the fire; when there two lines were formed from the water to the fire, the men on one side to pass the buckets filled with water from one to another to the fire, the other line was composed of women who passed the empty buckets back to be filled again, and so one bucket after another was passed, and in that way more buckets could be kept going than there were persons standing in the line. Frequently some strong-minded women would insist on standing in the line with the men. In this case their rights were granted to them.

After the fire was over, every one who had taken a bucket with them, got a good one to take home. There were generally plenty for it was customary for the merchants that kept buckets for sale, to count them and set them out on the street to be taken to the fire. If needed they were taken. A bill was made out against the city for the buckets and it was paid at the next council meeting.

The breakage of buckets was often considerable if the water had to be passed on the roof of the burning house, which was generally the case, and after the bucket was emptied it was thrown to the ground, and frequently no one was there to catch them. A few rounds of that kind would demolish an old bucket leaving its place to be supplied by a new one.

At one time the city council started the scheme of having each house in the city supplied with rubber buckets, and actually bought a dozen or so. They soon disappeared, no one could tell what became of them. The city also had a lot of fire ladders made, they were huge, all oak and very large. I don't recollect where they stored them; perhaps in the rear of Stein's hall. These ladders were soon stored with the brick layers and other mechanics about the town. The city had a big hook made with a chain attached to it and a socket to put in a pole to stick it into a house on fire and tear it down. To get that big hook with a rope attached to the chain, hooked on to the post of a house and a hundred men surging on the rope the post always came out. A balloon frame with no large post was the most difficult house to tear down in a hurry. When a house got well on fire we did not expect to put it out; if it was where we could keep the fire from spreading we let it burn down, if not we tore it or the adjoining one down to stop the spread of the fire.

We had for water supply the Mississippi river on the front, Seiler's pond in the center, with Pappoose creek running through the middle. If a fire occurred on the hill the large cisterns which were abundant furnished the supply of water.

There is one epoch in the city's fire history that should not be forgotten. Along somewhere about 1875 the Babcock fire extinguishers were advertised all over the country. They were made of all sizes from 30 pounds up to two tons; while the 30 pound one were strapped on a man's back, the two ton ones were drawn by two fiery horses that made a beautiful picture.

Soon along came an agent to sell a large one to the city. "He sold the city" one of the large ones. A fire company had been formed, the old Champions, on January 7, 1875, who took the extinguisher in charge. A trial was had down on the river bank, a house was built and filled with inflamable material, the "Soda Fountain" was brought to a proper position; thousands of spectators were out to witness the trial; the fire was lighted, and at a proper time the soda fountain was turned on; the fire burned on; the soda fountain soon run out of soda and had to be recharged, while the fire kept getting in its work and eventually devoured the house. The fire department gave as an excuse for their failure that one of their principal men, Theodore Grosheim, sr., whose business it was to attach the hose to the soda fountain, had made a mistake and tried to attach it to one of the hubs of the wagon on which the fountain was mounted.

This trial occurred on Saturday afternoon, and on the following Sunday night a fire was discovered in one of the store rooms on Second street opposite Armory hall. The fire laddies went and got the extinguisher and put out the fire, and they undoubtedly saved the building. When the council met to decline to take the extinguisher, the owner said "No, you took the machine without my consent and used it, and you must keep it and pay for it." The city kept it rather than have any trouble over it. The agent did not neglect to hang up an extinguisher in hall of some of the influential men of our city. The Babcock Extinguisher was good for inside fires but for one on the outside it was a failure.

The city had to have a place to keep it where it would not freeze, so they built a wooden building on the lot on the Avenue, about opposite the Methodist church, and made it double, filling in the walls with sawdust like an ice house. Previous to building this house the machine was kept for a while in Connell's barn opposite the Episcopal church.

I think this was the worst failure offered the city, it kept the Bucket Brigade from doing its work and did not take its place. The "soda fountain" cost the city somewhere near $3,000. It was sold to the city of Atlantic, Iowa, for $1,000. The "boy's" took it out and made a very successful trial.

After the water works were put in and the present companies of Muscatine's fire department were organized, fires were quite scarce for a while and the boys became somewhat impatient to show their strength. On one occasion an alarm was given, one of our mills was on fire, and the men at the mill put it out. I went to the Champion hose house to find out about the fire just as they were returning, one of the boys remarked that they would not give the firemen any chance. It was not very long afterwards before Cadle & Mulford's mill at the mouth of Pappoose creek took fire; then the boys got more than they could handle, which they hated to own up to. They have since found, as is the case in all other cities, that fires frequently occur that are too much for the city fire departments. This city has been very fortunate in not having many such fires as the lumber yard and mill of the Muscatine Lumber Co.

The first fire company dates its organization on January 7, 1875. They were organized in the Mayor's office, which at that time was in the second story of a building on the south side of Second street, between Chestnut street and Iowa avenue. Gus. Schmidt was the first president. The temporary building built on Iowa avenue served as a place for their hose cart until the new rooms were fitted up in the city hall.

The room for the Champion Hose Co's. cart and a room for

the Relief Hook and Ladder Co's. truck were put in the city hall in 1876, and the houses for the Rescues and Excelsiors were built shortly afterwards. The Excelsiors in their earlier days occupied the temporary house that was erected for the Champions on the avenue after it was moved to Reservoir square.

Previous to the purchase of the present city hall from the Methodist society, the mayor's office as it was called was the city headquarters, which was changed about to suit the convenience of the mayor, who acted as a police judge and justice of the peace in many cases. For some years before occupying the present quarters one of the front rooms of the second story of Stein's Music hall was used for a police headquarters. They had a calaboose about ten feet square on the alley in the rear of the hall. In the moderate or warm weather the "plain drunks" were put in there to sober off. This calaboose was without any furniture than perhaps a chair to sit on. The occupants would frequently wake up early in the morning suffering for a drink of water. A lady of my acquaintance who lived near the calaboose, says she has gotten up many and many a time and carried water to quench their thirst. The county jail was used when the weather was too cold for this calaboose to be used, then the suffering was not so severe.

The city hall was purchased and fitted up, I think, in 1876, but the "cooler" as they call the drunkard's waiting room, was not added at that time.

Recollection of Business in the Early Days of Muscatine.

Published in the Muscatine Saturday Mail February 20, 1897; written by J P. Walton.

No. 6.

While the term "business" is usually applied to the men who buy and sell for an occupation, we are not disposed to be confined to so narrow a bound. We consider any honorable means of earning a livelihood "business;" so the mechanic can look for a share of notice. Mechanics' unions are no new thing in the world. We have in our possession the bill of prices of the first Carpenters' Union ever organized in this city, and I think the first in the state. Here is a copy of the preface and agreement:

PREFACE.

The importance of having at command a bill of prices, in which the various descriptions of Carpenter's work are fully described, and a relative standard of charges given, has long been felt by both employers and contractors.—This volume, compiled and revised to fully meet the demands of this region, it is believed, will supply what is so much needed.

It is not expected that these prices will be adhered to—they are given only as a standard, and to show the relative value of one kind of work to another. The contractor may fix his own rate of charges, by the bill—for instance, he may take contracts at 50, 60, or 75 per cent on the bill, or the locality. Disputed bills may, also, be adjusted by making them conform to the bill, at the rate per cent usual for the season and locality.

AGREEMENT.

MUSCATINE, Oct. 31st, 1851.

At a meeting of the Carpenters and Joiners of the City of Muscatine and vicinity, Iowa, held on the above date, it was unanimously agreed to adopt the following Bill of Prices, as a standard of charges for work in this City and vicinity. (Signed.)

A. F. Hoffmeyer,
B. F. Low,
S B. Hill,
D. H Lower,
J. S. Lakin,
J. P. Walton,
J. T. B. Martin,
G. W Martin,
G. D. Magoon,
J. C. Irwin,
H. H. Hine,
T. T. Scofield,
M. Goddard,
W. Davidson.

E. W. Hayman,
S. R. Burr,
T. A. Aeueys,
W. Gordon,
S. Hale,
R. Cadle,
J Heller,
J. Kingsbury,
J. J. Hoopes,
L. C. Hine,
P. Stine,
C. A. Buscherf
R. H. Hoopes,

This organization had its origin way back in England in "The Worshipful Company of Carpenters of London," founded in 1477; who established a "Book of Prices" which is retained to the present day. In 1724 the Carpenters' Company of the City and County of Philadelphia was organized; a "Bill of Prices" was established which was said to be equal to the London "Bill of Prices." Carpenters' Hall was erected by this company in 1770.

At the return of prosperity after the Revolutionary war the carpenters of Philadelphia came west, stopping at Cincinnati, there re-adopting the Bill of Prices. Later when the Hoopes', Irwins and others who had worked under it at Cincinnati came to Muscatine, they got it adopted. It was never much in use here, from the fact it was adopted about the beginning of the German immigration, who never took kindly to it. For my part, I found it quite valuable in estimating the cost of carpenter work.

In the year 1872 the great Granger movement crystalized in an agricultural implement manufactory in the city of Muscatine. They were incorporated with what appeared to be sufficient capital to do business in good shape. Hon. S. McNutt was the first president; a man by the name of Price was the first superintendent with a board of managers consisting of S. McNutt, Isaiah Davis, John Idle, R. C. Jewett, Lindley Hoopes, and perhaps some others. They secured the ground and built their building on Mulberry street east of the court square. It was a part of the building now occupied by the Barry Manufacturing Company. There was but one man among them that knew anything about the business; he was the blacksmith. Their foreman was a common carpenter who could talk his share but did not know what the business required. They went ahead and put in several thousand dollars in putting in machinery for manufacturing everything but what they wanted, even to a gun-stock or an ox yoke, and laid in a stock of material. I think the Granger stockholders must have paid up pretty well, for their credit was good. They got all ready for starting; it was done with a celebration held in the Fair Grounds on October 9, 1872. Hon. S. McNutt was the presiding officer and made the main speech; some 3,000 people were present. The understanding was that this was a farmers' manufactory and the farmers would confine their patronage to this factory, which, if they did, it would prove a success and would produce articles much cheaper than the ordinary dealers would sell them. They commenced work, mostly on plows and wagons, which with their machinery, they made quite rapidly. An agent was put on the road to sell; he also had no experience; his business was to sell, which he did. Now in all communities there is a class of men who always buy of the new men, that are not always desirable by the old ones, especially if they sell on credit. The agent found these fellows and the result was he sold a great amount of stuff for which he took notes that he could not sell or collect money on. There was doubt about the material used in many of the wagons being properly seasoned; hence many of the farmers bought elsewhere, although from loyalty they advised their neighbors to buy at the factory.

Soon the manufactory began to get hard up. More money had to be raised, and a proposition was made to mortgage the plant, which was objected to, and several of the officers withdrew, the president was one of them.

Finally three or four of the prominent ones stepped up and endorsed their obligations individually. This put the concern on its feet again, and it struggled along for three or four years, but finally closed up.

The only man that made anything out of it was the blacksmith, he had done his work by the piece and kept his pay well collected up. He built a shop of his own presumably out of the profits made in the factory.

When the affairs of the concern were closed up it was found that not only the stock had all been used up but the organization was many thousand of dollars in debt. Most of this debt was paid by the endorsers, Isaiah Davis, John Idle and R. C. Jewitt. The latter paid the greater part of it, and it is said that the grangers elected him sheriff a time or two as pay.

Recollection of Business in the Early Days of Muscatine.

Published in the Muscatine Saturday Mail February 27, 1897; written by
J P. Walton.

No. 7.

In October, 1839, Joseph Bridgman opened a store on Front street in the name of Bridgman & Patridge. Joseph Bridgman was here representing his brother who lived in Burlington.

Mr. Bridgman says he handled a small raft of pine lumber in the summer of 1840; it being the first ever brought here for sale from the northern pineries. In the winter of 1839 and 1840 he bought and packed pork, having secured the services of Charles Fish as packer. This pork he kept until the following summer and sold it to a merchant in Iowa City. In 1841 or 1842 Mr. Bridgman and the store moved to Burlington. It the store was not a success Mr. Bridgman was, for he succeeded in marrying Miss E. A. Weed on the 4th of June, 1840. They celebrated their golden wedding fifty years thereafter in 1890.

In October, 1839 (two years after the arrival of Mr. Bridgman in Bloomington, now Muscatine) Dr. Benjamin Weed came with his family consisting of his wife, a son, Dr. James Weed, and a daughter, Miss E A. Weed. The doctor secured a log-cabin that stood not far from where Mr. Bridgman now lives, on the south side of Second street between Chestnut and Pine, and commenced practicing medicine. Dr. James Weed, his son, commenced the practice of dentistry which he followed for three or four years. He then purchased the Barkalow farm where he now lives. The old log cabin standing on the south end was the old claim cabin built by Mr. Barkalow not later than 1836. Dr. James Weed soon commenced improving the farm, he started a nursrey and propagated fruit trees. He called it the Horticultural and Pomological Garden of Muscatine. He probably raised the first fruit trees in Iowa north of Burlington, where Comstock & Avery were in the business.

In the spring of 1841, the younger son of Dr. Benjamin Weed, Chester Weed, came here from Connecticut, when but 21 years of age. He had been a clerk in the Colins axe and cutlery factory at Colinsville While in the store he had a chance to learn business habits, and. strange to say, within a brief space of two years after the invention of the daguerreotype in Paris he had become familiar with the art, and he brought a camera here with him and opened a gallery in this place and in Iowa City also. I have seen several of his pictures taken with an exposure of four minutes; some of them were quite fair ones. He sold his camera and other parts of the out-fit to Arthur Washburn and went to clerking for Joseph Bennett. In the year 1845 or '46 he left Bennett and went into business with his brother-in-law, Joseph Bridgman, under the name of Bridgman & Weed. The firm continued under that name until 1851, when the business was carried on under the name of C. Weed. Mr. Bridgman went on the river as head clerk on the steamer Golden Era, Captain H. Birzee. He did not like the river and soon came back. The firm was re-organized under the name of C. Weed & Co., and later changed to Weed, Bridgman & Kent. The business was closed up at the death of Mr. Weed, December 7, 1874.

Along early in the forties Mr. Weed bought a farm of 320 acres, afterwards the Hunt farm, now Park Place. This was known at the time Mr. Weed got it as the Warfield place. Mr. Charles A. Warfield was the first owner, he built the old frame house now standing. I think the big brick chimney was put in afterwards.

When the older brother, Dr. James Weed, got married to Miss St. John in March, 1847, they commenced housekeeping in that house and lived there for some ten years. During that time Chester spent his Sundays with them.

While the old firm of Bridgman & Weed was in existence they wrote the first insurance policy ever written in this city, it was for the old Ætna Insurance Co., of Hartford, Conn., and it was dated May 1, 1846. Mr. Bridgman says that Mr. Ogilvie was the first insurance agent in this city, although he never wrote a policy for some reason, and the agency was turned over to them. On the first day of May, 1896, the Ætna company presented a testimonial in the shape of a loving cup to Mr. Joseph Bridgman as a reminder of a full half century's service.

In 1852 or '53, I commenced to insure my house with them; the rates were 75c on the $100 per annum. I insured with them at that rate for a period of fifteen years, after that other companies represented by Mr T. D. Smith came here and wanted to insure at 60 cents. Mr. Weed found out the offer and he said at once that he would do it for 60 cents and take work for it. After a run of ten more years I succeeded in getting the same house insured for 45 cents on the $100. Since the time of the combine arrangements under Ross and his successor the price has been raised to 50 cents. When I read in the newspapers that the Muscatine agency had to its credit over $50,000 above expenses I had no doubt of its truth, at least my early experience looked that way.

Chester Weed was in various branches of business outside of his mercantile pursuits. He was president of the Muscatine Gas Light and Coke Co. that was organized in 1857. The bravest work he ever done was when he saved the Muscatine branch of the State Bank. It came about in this way, the president and cashier had used the funds of the bank to purchase land and had the deeds made to the president in person, leaving the bank short. Mr. Weed stepped up and said he would take the land and furnish the money. The land was deeded to him, he raised the money and saved the bank, which if it had closed up would have been a great calamity to the public as well as the stockholders. Mr. Weed eventually cleared $16,000 out of the deal.

In January, 1864, several companies of Muscatine soldiers sent considerable money home to be distributed among their families. Chester Weed and James Jackson were the ones selected to distribute it.

At one time Mr. Weed was the owner of the Commercial Hotel. He tried to get his brother-in-law, Mr. Bridgman, to run it for him, but Bridgman declined. He then sold the hotel to Reuben Baker, but before making the deed he wanted to back out and offered $1,000, but Baker declined to take it.

In 1856 he went into the pork packing business in company with Silverman, Cook & Co., and Henry Funck, Fred Daut and Martin Bartlett. They packed considerable pork and done well.

The following year, 1857, he went in with Mr. Bartlett and a Mr. Harris and rented the old pork house close to the Hershey mill. They got all ready to commence work on a Monday morning, the house took fire and burned down on the Sunday night before. Of course, that stopped that packing company.

A few weeks previous to his death he entered into a partnership with a gentleman named Felix and rented the Bennett mill, intending to buy wheat, run the mill and make flour. His death stopped that deal.

At the time of the explosion of the Nevada mill, on October 1, 1864, he was either owner or agent, as he went to work and refitted it for operation.

Chester Weed handled a great

deal of stock, kept his farm running and was generally quite successful. At one time he had raised a large number of well bred horses, he made a sale and sold them off, took the money and made a trip or two to Europe. His letters to the local papers were read with considerable interest.

In connection with their mercantile business the firm of Weed, Bridgman & Kent kept and sold agricultural implements. They brought the first reaper here. I helped set it up; we took it down to Shepard Smalley's farm and tried it. They bought Shuttler wagons and sold them, very much to the disgust of the Aments, who were manufacturing and selling a much poorer wagon.

For thirty years previous to his marriage on July 31, 1873, to Miss Cora Chaplin, Chester Weed was a noted society man, pleasant and affable. For years he was considered the best dancer in the town, and as a good talker he had no superior, and withal was one of the best informed men of our community.

Mr. Bridgman is here with us yet; any remarks on his grace as a dancer in his earlier days, or his genial habits, are uncalled for at this time.

Recollection of Business in the Early Days of Muscatine.

Published in the Muscatine Saturday Mail March 6, 1897; written by
J. P. Walton.

No. 8

There has recently come into our hands the first account book of the Iowa Democratic Enquirer, published in Muscatine by Mr. H. D. LaCossitt, and later by W. B. Langridge. LaCossitt came here with his paper in June, 1848, from Hamilton, Mo., and issued the first number on July 4.

In looking over the old accounts in the book we find a great many very interesting items. We will venture to give a few of them.

The first account was with J. A. and W. McCormack, commencing July 4, 1848. One of the items was a charge of $49 for amount subscribed for paper, there is also $2 for one subscription of the Enquirer. We don't understand the $49 unless it was a bonus given by the democrats to have a paper started in this city. The McCormacks were leading democrats and probably wanted a paper of their political faith. The Herald, then published here, was a Whig paper.

The firm of J. A. & W. McCormack dissolved March 24, 1849, J. A. going to California and William continued the store alone.

The second account in the book is with John G. Stein, one of the items being a credit of $45 for nine weeks board for LaCossitt and wife, at $5 per week for both of them. This board bill was settled by LaCossitt giving Stein a due bill drawing 10 per cent interest. They then went and boarded with George W. Humphreys for thirty-two weeks at $4 per week. March 1, 1851, J. G. Stein is charged with $1 for the Iowa Emigration Society. I don't know what this Emigration Society was, neither do I recollect hearing of it before.

On December 14, 1850, Peter Jackson was charged with $7.50 for a $10 county order. County orders were below par for a number of years. About the same time J. B. Dougherty was advertising "John Bull's sarsaprilla." I haven't heard of John Bull's sarsaprilla for a long time—it must have gone out of use.

In 1848 D. C. Cloud commenced an account, and during the season of 1848, according to the book,

Cloud seems to have made more cash payments than any other of the paper's patrons. The facts were that most of the business was done in trade those days.

Nathaniel Halleck, the county clerk, was credited with a county order, we presume a part of his salary. This Nathaniel Halleck while county clerk lived in his office in the court house; had his bed and board there. On one occasion he was cooking onions during court time, the effluvia went through the court house greatly to the annoyance of His Honor the court. The boys after that called the clerk "old onions."

We presume Mr. LaCossitt must have gone to housekeeping, for we find that on April 9, 1849, Kelley, Horn & Co. sold "queensware" to him—a name that has become almost obsolete.

On February 25, 1851, M. Block was charged one dollar for an announcement of his candidacy for office. I presume it was for a city office, as it was the first year the city acted under the special charter and held its election as now on the first Monday in March. Block was not elected at that time. Then and for many years after we held no party caucuses, anybody could run if they had a dollar to pay the paper for announcing them as candidates. Frequently three or four would run for the same office at the same time. Before election day the contest usually settled down to two men, one for each party, but when the Know-Nothing party came into existence which it did shortly afterwards it played smash with the other parties.

In 1850 there appeared what would now be considered a very unusual advertisement, it was Ogilvie & Johns advertising "cash paid for wheat."

In July, 1851, county orders sold for 85 cents on the dollar. We give these prices to show the financial standing of the county.

We notice three places in the Enquirer's book where $4 was charged for printing 200 funeral tickets. This in the start looked a little tony, but after thinking it over it could hardly be considered so, for in those days we had no daily papers to notify friends of the deceased, funeral tickets took the place.

March 17, 1849, T. S. Battell was charged five dollars for an advertisement of the steamboat Oswego for the season. Mr. Battell came here in 1840 or '41, built the American hotel, run it for seven or eight years, made considerable money, sold out and bought the steamboat Oswego. He run the boat until July, 1851, when it was sunk somewhere below here. Joseph Bennett says he had an interest in the boat by which he lost some $3,000. Battell saved enough to get to California.

On March 31, 1849, Sarah L.

Watham advertised a school. I don't recollect her or where she kept her school.

In March, 1849 Mrs. John A. McCormack is charged with 41 week's board, for herself and son, at $3 per week, $123. I suppose that this was while Mr. McCormack was gone to California. Sixty-seven dollars of this was applied on an old debt due to McCormack

In 1859 Hare, Day & Fimple, ferry comyany, were charged with printing 600 circulars. I presume these were circulated through the country to the east of us as most of the ferrying was emigrants going west. I had forgotten that Col. Hare was in this partnership but he must have been as he paid the cash for the work. In this account $32 is placed to their credit for lot 4 in block 101. Also in the book is an old tax sale deed signed by W. A. Drury, collector, for the taxes on the same lot. In the book is also another tax sale deed dated April 6, 1852, signed by G. S. Branham, deputy marshal, and T. M. Isett, mayor; the amount was $2.67½. There is also a receipt from Cloud & O'Connor for $100 for a warrantee deed to the same lot. According to the account and these documents the lot cost $140.10. I think La-Cossitt built his house on it in 1853; it is the one now occupied by N. Neyens, 213 east Fifth street.

In the lids of this old book are several quite interesting papers. One is a certificate of payment of $25 for one share in the capital stock of "The Iowa Female Collegiate Institute" at Iowa City, dated November 2, 1853. Another is a certificate No. 72, for one share of the capital stock of the "Muscatine, Washington and Oskaloosa Road & Bridge Co.," signed by Joseph Bennett, president, and Stephen Whicher, acting secretary. This is a nicely gotten-up certificate and was printed in Philadelphia. It is dated March 27, 1851.

In 1849 Dr. James Weed was charged with 500 milk tickets. This reminds us that Dr. Weed was the principal milk man of our city at that time. He owned a fine herd of red Devon cattle which he had brought here and which took the premiums at our county fairs.

On page 46 of the old book occurs a charge for advertising the acts of the Muscatine and Linn County Grade Road Co., incorported by the legislature March 1, 1849. There are also several notices of assessments and election of officers of the company, the last one appears May 17, 1851. The grade road was a scheme started by Dr. James Weed. A pretty fair grade was made about ten or twelve miles, it was then abandoned and most or all of it is now used as a public highway between this city and Wilton.

On page 48 the different temperance organizations have their accounts, such as "The Hawkeye Section No. 3," "Cadets of Temperance" the "Rochester Division, No. 35, Sons of Temperance," "The Wapello Union of Daughters of Temperance," "The Daughters of Temperance of Muscatine," and "The Union Division of the Sons of Temperance." We mention the foregoing temperance bodies to show the fact that they are all extinct. At one time they were quite strong in members, most of the prominent men belonging to them.

In 1849 S. R Drury, of Drury's Landing, had bills-of-lading printed. At the present time one would naturally ask what would a man at Drury's Landing want with bills-of-lading? We will say, at that time, Drury's Landing was quite a place and did a large shipping business by river. It was the only reliable landing between New Boston and Rock Island, and while the business was done in a kind of a back woods style, nevertheless there was considerable business done until the ralroads spoiled the river traffic.

We very frequently had private schools opened here to run a short time at least. On August 18, 1849, Mrs. Stocker advertised her school with Suel Foster as a reference. Mrs. Stocker was the widow of the Rev. John Stocker, the pioneer preacher of our city.

We find on page 56 an account with the Iowa Western Railroad company; the company is charged with advertising notices of organization, of meetings of directors, blanks, etc., to the amount of $22, but no credits. I think the printer must have considered that a "dead horse" railroad. The first charge was made in 1851 and the last one in 1853.

In 1849 the price of fuel did not seem to be very high. I find where a load of wood was charged one dollar, and two instances where twenty-five bushels of coal are charged $2.50 each.

Recollection of Business in the Early Days of Muscatine.

Published in the Muscatine Saturday Mail March 13, 1897; written by J. P. Walton.

No. 9

In reviewing the account book of the old Iowa Democratic Enquirer we find the price of subscription to be $1.50 if paid in advance, or $2 if not. In looking over fully one-third of the book we noticed but one subscriber to have paid $1.50; that was John Zeigler; $2 was the price charged to most of the customers, although the balance was in their favor. I guess that was good financiering, but John Zeigler did not seem to have taken it that way, although his accounts were quite large.

The Democratic Enquirer seems to have had some special friends to call on when in trouble. In October, 1848, is a list of persons furnishing money to buy paper; Peter Jackson seems to be the only survivor. The amount raised was $49 cash.

In August, 1849, there were 900 democratic tickets printed, for which $9 was charged. The credits were as follows: Cloud paid $1, Ayers $1, Parvin $1, Burdic 50 cts. The other $4.50 was not paid. At the same election there was a Deming ticket printed; $2.50 charged on it and but $1 paid.

March 7, 1860, Jacob Rubelmann advertises his tan yard. We recollect that tan yard well; it stood where the Hershey Lumber Co. stable now stands. Mr. Rubelmann erected his building in the pure German style. He bought a raft of hewed pine timber and built it with this timber, putting his posts about three feet apart and filling the sides of the posts full of small pegs, then filling the openings between the posts with small stones and mortar, then covering the whole with a coat of mortar. After Rubelmann gave up tanning here and moved away the old building went into the hands of B. Hershey, who used it for a stable for awhile. This Jacob Rubelmann was the father of the one we had here some twenty years later.

In 1852 Miss Corcoran advertised her school, another private school that I don't remember. In 1857 another school entered as Young's school is advertised. This Young was connected with J. H. Wallace in some manner. On Feb. 22nd, School District No. 1 has an advertisement. I suppose it was for the spring meeting. This is the first public school notice I have seen.

In May, 1850, Joseph Bennett was credited with $6 for a barrel of flour. This would be equal to $1.50 a sack. Sacks were not in use for flour at that time. The first flour offered in market in sacks was in 100-pound cotton sacks. Fifty pound paper or cloth sacks did not come for some time, I think about 1870. I think they had no newspaper in Cedar county in 1851, for the Cedar county election tickets were printed in Muscatine.

On page 113 occurs La Cassitt's account with his devil, who commenced on July 21st, 1851, and served his calling faithfully until January 1st, 1852, when he got a case. During this time his wages were $68, of which he received only $25 in cash; two dollars of this was paid as a tribute to the preacher, the Rev. Calhoun of the Episcopal church. He stands charged with two dollars and a half for a New Year's ball ticket; he is also charged with paying another tribute to S. C. Dunn. We never knew where Sam got his early support. But enough; that once devil is now a printer on the News-Tribune, working at a case, as "Slug 2."

In 1852 flour got down to $4.25 per barrel.

December 15th, 1852, 1,000 blank deeds were printed for the Mississippi & Missouri railroad company, and ten dollars charges for the same. This was the old Chicago & Rock Island road.

On October 27th, 1852, another charge is made for advertising the organization of the "Muscatine, Iowa City, Cedar Rapids & Northwestern Iowa Rail Road Company." This was one of the many paper companies we have organized in our city.

On page 169 of this old book occurs the name of J. C. B. Ward, who probably opened here in 1852. He was the most singular man that ever visited our city. Tall, of good form, well educated and well dressed. I think he went into partnership with Hon. W. G. Woodward in the law business. I am of the impression that he came from the center or western part of Massachusetts, perhaps Springfield. He soon commenced to look up property and bought two or three lots on the top of the hill, and commenced the erection of the large building that now belongs to Mrs. Cora Weed (the Eyrie). He got it under roof, boarded up the windows and went away without giving any notice. When the mechanics began to compare notes, it was found that he had paid but very little on its construction. Then the fun began;

every one was on the run to get in his attachment first. The old adage of "Bad luck to the hindmost" was their motto. Notices had to be served by advertisements in the paper. D. C. Cloud is charged $6.50 for one of these notices. The great mystery was why an intelligent man would start to build such a house as that with as little money as he appeared to have spent on it, and then go away and leave it so abruptly without letting any one know that he was going, or where he went to. Rumor—on what authority we don't know—solved it this way: He (Ward) was engaged to marry a very rich lady as soon as his house was built, and all at once she took sick and died, thus leaving him in the lurch. He had no use for the house, neither had he money to pay for it, so he departed, and let his creditors dispose of it as they could. Gen. J. G. Gordon became the purchaser and finished it off for his own use. Since then it has stood on the brow of the hill, a landmark for all travelers on the river to admire.

I see among the list of subscribers the name of a man that did the county and city a great good and a great injury. The name is Hon. James Grant, of Davenport, Iowa. He was our District Judge and presided with more business-like determination than any judge did before or since. If court was to be called at 9 o'clock, it was called at 9, not at 10. If the attorney was not on hand his case was dropped, not continued, as is the case now. Well, the effect was, that the attorneys soon found that they had to be prompt and on hand, and they were during his term of office. The docket was cleared and kept clear. We had only one judge at that time; he could not shove his work off to the next one, as is now said to be the case.

But the good name of Judge Grant does not stand unsullied in the estimation of many old settlers. In the early days the county and city were persuaded to issue a lot of railroad bonds. In the use of them most of the tax payers felt that they were defrauded and objected to paying them. The state courts held that they were not valid; United States courts said they were. This was in "state rights" time and the United States court had no available way for enforcing their orders unless the states would agree to it. Hence we expected to beat them on the execution. They had the judgment but could not collect. Grant and Smith, of Davenport, were the attorneys for the bond holders, took the bonds to collect on shares, but had made no progress until after the war was over and state rights had "gone up." The collecting occurred in about this way, if I am correct in my recollections, and I think I am: At the breaking out of the rebellion the southern merchants owed for goods purchased of New York parties and refused to pay. The New York parties went to congress for relief and secured the passage of a law ordering the United States marshals to collect all judgments of the United States courts irrespective of state laws or courts; hence when we whipped the soutnern states we took some two or three hundred thousand dollars from our city and county that was not collectable before the war. So far as the city was concerned there was another point that the state courts adhered to; that was: Our special charter says that not more than one per cent of tax shall be raised for all purposes. The state courts decided that we could retain as much of that one per cent as was necessary for maintaining the city; if any was left it was then attachable by the bondholders for their judgment. At this time bonds were cheap, 25 cents on the dollar. When congress knocked the bottom out of our state laws Grant was heard to say that he would now collect on the bonds. The United States courts at once decided that our debt should be paid; if one cent would not do it we should levy more. Previous to that time our assessments were made on a fair valuation. After that time we dropped them down to about one-third or one-fourth to lighten our taxes. The courts would not order us to pay too large a per cent in any one year. After the bonds were refunded then the taxpayer wanted the assessment kept down for his benefit. There would not have been so much kicking if the railroads had given us stock in the road, which was the agreement when the bonds were voted. In place of giving stock that was good for anything the company sold out to the Rock Island railroad. We believe Grant and Smith made a good thing out of it if Muscatine does have to suffer a little. This ruling of the United States courts took away all the security that the tax payers had. If more than one per cent could be levied to pay a railroad bond tax it could be for other purposes and is levied without paying any heed to that special charter, which is worse than nothing as a protection to the tax payer. For our part we fail to see any special good in it.

Recollection of Business in the Early Days of Muscatine.

Published in the Muscatine Saturday Mail March 20, 1897; written by
J. P. Walton.

No. 10

In noting down our recollections of men or events in early days it is not our object to write a biography or an obituary, it is simply to give an account of them as they occurred, according to our recollection. We are well aware that the actors of the earlier times would not like to have us suggest or write them different from what they were, or what they appeared to be, to accommodate some one's ideas of propriety.

Among the first Germans that came to this city were two who attained considerable notoriety. Henry Funck, and Henry Molis, both could speak English and German. The new comers invariably drifted toward them; their names were known in Germany, the emigrants were directed to look them up and get any information desired, which was freely given.

They both knew that the German rule "was pay your debts" which almost all the newcomers adhered to, and they would lend them money when needed at good interest. We have often noticed that among those old Germans that came at an early day, 99 out of a hundred always paid their debts. Funck and Molis always looked after the new-comer and advised him to become naturalized and vote the democratic ticket which most of them did without ever learning what they were doing. We presume that Funck and Molis were educated in the same school, or at least studied politics in the same manner, from a single standpoint.

Mr. Funk was engaged in the grocery business which also included a bakery and boat store on Front street, corner of Chestnut, and on the old wharf boat while steamboats were running. After Funck had accumulated considerable money in 1851 or '52, he concluded to go into the distillery business and erected a distillery which he run for a few years, that finally went into the hands of Page & Crane, who had a large stock of whisky on hand when the war broke out, the rise in which made them wealthy.

Funck remained in the money loaning business, bought and sold notes. He served the city as mayor and councilman at different times. Funck was one of the stockholders in Cook, Musser & Co.'s bank; he was connected with M. Bartlett, C. Weed and F. Daut in the pork packing business at one time.

Henry Molis was engaged in the gun business; he as well as Funck was a political leader among the Germans. He had no superior. He served as mayor and councilman and filled many offices of trust,—was county collector and treasurer. He was never considered a leader in any new undertaking, but on the contrary a good, conservative man in everything but politics

Molis' little gun shop stood, in early days, on the north side of Third street east of Cedar, and later on the south side of Second street, between Cedar and Sycamore streets. It was a one-story frame, about 16 feet square and stood on posts to bring it up to the grade of the street. Not long after coming here he associated Barney Bieal with him in the gun business, and strange to say, they had no competition for many years, Their principal work for the first few years was changing flint-lock guns to cap-lock and stocking long barrelled rifles. They kept a stock of guns, pistols, powder and shot on hand for sale. They were considerably annoyed with burglars, as once or twice a year they would break into the little shop by either prying open the door or window; finally Molis resorted to setting a spring gun to be discharged when the door opened. We recollect going to the shop with Mr. Molis one morning, when he unlocked the door he run his hand in the crack and disconnected the combination in some way before opening the door. The burglars soon "got on to that" and cut through the floor and got in. Molis & Co. were compelled to move to the house they are now in to get clear of the burglars.

While Funck and Molis were our German Emigrant commissioners, it required one more to fill out the trio. He came in the personage of Marx Block who was a native of Baden. If a quartett was necesary Ed. Hoch was on hand, and although not a German, he spoke German and had the habits of a German.

With Mr. Block's early mercantile life we are not much acquainted. He came here in 1842 in company with a man by the name of Sherman; they packed pork together for a year or so in the Isett brick building on Front street, below the oat meal mill. They shipped a large lot of pork to St. Louis. Mr. Sherman went down there and collected the money and left Mr. Block in the lurch. If I mistake not he then tried merchandising alone. In

1845 he opened a store on the south side of Second street, east of Chestnut. Later he was in partnership with William McCormick under the name of Block & McCormick in the building now owned by J. A. Bishop, north side of Second, east of the Avenue. There they handled all kinds of merchandise for the country trade. When this new building was "warmed" the other merchants about the town had a glorious time, some of the very solid ones were quite joyful on that occasion and wagons were used in getting them home. After the dissolution of the firm some of the eastern creditors came and attached the building; McCormick lived upstairs and claimed it as a homestead; the suit was taken to the supreme court where a decision was rendered establishing the homestead claim on all of the building and lot, excepting the room used for a store which was sold for the payment of the debts.

We find in 1856, Marx Block was in the Forwarding and Commission business, occupying No. 49 Water street. Previous to this time Funck had given up the wharf boat and it left the place open for Block who by close attention and genial ways had succeeded in getting a good business.

We find that sometime prior to 1856 the name was M. Block & Co., R. T. Wallace having joined the firm.

In 1869 the name stood Marx Block. Wallace had gone to Chicago. After Block's death, Aug. 5, 1881, W. G. Block managed the business.

When the Northern Line company of steamboats was organized, Marx Block was appointed their agent, and was one of the popular agents along the river. Block liked a joke and the steamboat men soon found that out. When ever a boat got clear of St. Louis the officers would commence to study up a scheme to catch Block. Some amusing games were played on him, but he always took them good naturedly and took delight in relating them to his cronies.

The German trio loved to visit the German places of resort—the saloons. They did as the Germans did, played cards and drink beer, and here the fourth number was annexed, Edward Hoch, he could play his part with any of them.

Molis was conscientous and would not play for beer while he was mayor of the city. He was strictly honest, even at card playing. The result was Molis had to pay for the beer most of the time. After playing a few rubbers, frequently the game would lag a little, when Funck would lead off in true Gambrinas style, "The Duch Componee" or some similiar air, the others joining in. The music would have charmed a disciple of George Fox.

The story goes that on one occasion Block was up before the grand jury. The question was asked, "Who did you play cards with?" "I played mid Funck, Molis and Hoch;" again, what game did you play. "Seven up." What did you play for? "I plays for the jack." I don't think any bills of indictment were found against this quartette.

In looking over the Records I find that the four men served the city in some official capacity as follows: Funck, 5 years; Hoch, 6; Block 7, and Molis 8 years.

Recollection of Business in the Early Days of Muscatine.

Published in the Muscatine Saturday Mail March 27, 1897; written by J. P. Walton.

No. 11.

The early settler considered getting married a part of the business that had to be attended to. From 1840 to 1860 Iowa was supposed to be the best matrimonial exchange in the world. The energetic young men of the Eastern states had followed Horace Greeley's advice of "Go west, young man; go west," and came west to secure fortunes. A few years of successful efforts laid for them the foundation for a compentency.

But the young man had no wife and had no time to go for one; while plenty were to be had in the Eastern states, though they were scarce here. These wants of the Western man soon became known, and as a result the more intelligent young ladies of the east soon began to come west. There was a great opening for school teachers here, the wages were good, and the teacher went in the best society. In many cases the lady who had any qualifications for school teaching, and most of them had, would borrow the money to come west on, and they would pay it back out of their wages. They rarely earned much more for school teaching than enough to pay their debts, as they had better offers.

The school teachers were not the only ones that ventured west to better their condition.

Ladies of all callings came west; a man with a large family of girls would get the western fever—we can call to our mind several such cases. Many of the girls are here yet, but we hardly feel warranted in mentioning them. At that time we did not have any sewing machine, the sewing was done by hand; along our streets could be seen signs of "dress making", by Miss ——— ———, and "millinery" by Miss ——— ———. Those signs did not remain long in position, the owners were here but their occupation was changed, and some other Miss from the east would take the place, and she too would soon change her name and turn the business over to another Miss. In those days the bonnets were bought of the merchants and taken to the milliner; hence a lady with little capital other than taste, could succeed in the millinery line until their services were wanted in other pursuits.

The matrimonial market was never over supplied until the war broke out, since then cupid's business has changed somewhat.

Now we are celebrating the golden weddings that had their first date in those stirring days of fifty years ago. At one of these celebrations the question was asked, "Did you attend Grace Burgis' dinner party?" The answer was, we did. Of course that dinner party had to be explained. On Christmas day of 1846 Grace Burgis had a dinner party at which just twelve people sat down to. Grace was one of those young ladies who had an eye to business and came west with her brother John, and kept house for him. They moved in good society. At the Chiristmas dinner she invited five young ladies and five young gentlemen, she and her brother making the twelve that sat down to the table. There was nothing very particular about that, only that all the parties were married within one year, with the exception of Grace; she was married within two years, although several of the parties had never met before. Of the gentlemen who married ladies that were present on that occasion, we have the names of Dr. James Weed, Suel Foster, Samuel Sinnett and John Burgis. Of the ladies, but one of them had parents in Iowa, the others were generally staying with relatives. The business of supplying the young men with wives was not confined to our city, it extended all over the settled part of Iowa.

On another occasion, in the spring of 1840, old Dr. Fairchild came here with his daughter Kate; the doctor was not very old but he was generally known by that cognomon, because he was so much older than the other men in the village. They came by river from Cincinnatti. It became known some way that the doctor and daughter were coming; I think his agents, Lowe & Deshler, had purchased property for him. The steamboat landed in the morning, we had no hacks at that time to haul the passengers to and from the boats, and they had to walk; as a result the doctor and Kate walked up to the hotel on Second street, where the Cook-Musser State Bank and Trust Co. now are. It was customary when a steamboat landed for a great number of people to go down to the river to see the boat, that morning a larger number of young men went down than usual, the street was a little muddy, Kate knew that her feet were not very large, and of course she had to hold up her dress to keep it out of the mud. The result was that one of our citizens became so infatuated that he proposed the following night. It was business. How many proposals the young lady received we can't say, at all events she married Fred H. Stone the following July. On the night after the wedding came the infair, the society of the town was invited; George Humphreys, who afterwards bought out the store that belonged to Fred H. Stone, had been very attentive to a young lady who was at the infair that night. Some one proposed that they have a mock wedding and that George and Miss —— be the couple for the occasion; they stood up, and the county clerk or some one authorized to marry people was about to proceed with the ceremoney, when the uncle of the young lady stepped up and whispered to her that if she stood there a minute longer she would be married whether she wanted to be or not. She withdrew and the marriage was off. The young lady married shortly afterwards.

In the year 1840 the population of the town of Bloomington was 507, and during that year there were nineteen marriages; perhaps leap year may have helped them along. Such statistics as these show that the marriage business was lively.

———

Since writing the above we find the following going the rounds, and think it quite likely correct in the main as most of the early settlers of Oregon went from Iowa, this county alone furnished more than a hundred:

"There are plenty of women in Oregon now," observed a prominent politician, who is in Washington to see that his state is not forgotten in the matter of patronage, "but it is within the memory of many of us when women were scarce there. We gave it out that we wanted them for school teachers and the like, and encouraged them to come out there, but the truth was the men wanted them for wives. I remember once we sent a young man to Massachussetts, where he was acquanited, with orders to collect one hundred young women and escort them back to Oregon. We guaranteed every one of them one year's employment. The active man in the matter was a fine-looking young man, who afterwards served two terms in congress from our state. He spent two months in selecting the party and started west with them. On the trip out he courted one of the school teachers on his own hook and actually got her consent to a marriage on the arrival of the train at Portland. The boys howled considerably about it, claiming that he had treated them unfairly in having the first choice, but there was a lot of fine, marriageable material left. Some of those women are today the leading ladies of the society of the state. More than three-fourths of the hundred were married inside of three years, and many in less than one year. A few of the lot, however, are teaching school there today, not that they did not have any offers, but because they would not accept any of the fellows that offered themselves."

Recollection of Business in the Early Days of Muscatine.

Published in the Muscatine Saturday Mail April 3, 1897; written by
J P Walton.

No 12.

The book business assumed an independent place in the business in our city in 1848, when John Hinds and James A. Humphrey opened a little book store on the south side of Second street, west of Iowa Avenue, under the name of Hinds & Humphreys; they run the store until 1852, when they sold out to R. M. Burnett. Previous to the sale to Burnett, John Hinds sold out his interest in the store to James A. Humphreys and went to California. Humphreys made the business go quite slowly, as he lacked capital to make it succeed. When Burnett came here he bought the old stock of goods and put in a new line of books which he brought from the east with him, and in a short time opened up where he remained in business until he transferred his stock to his son, L. G. Burnett, in 1876. The cause of this transfer was the loss of his eye sight. Mr. Burnett had the front of the building rebuilt and made general repairs to it. The store has remained in the same room in which Mr. Burnett started it in 1852. In 1886 we find that Mr. A. F. Demorest had charge of it; in 1891 Neidig & Leysen took charge of the store; now it is the charge of F. A. Neidig. A business in one place for forty-five years is no common occurence in the west. We don't recollect of any other business being conducted in the same building with as little change to the building as this book store.

The historical part was during its control by R. M. Burnett, who was an out-spoken, candid man. He came here a "free soil democrat," but arrived to late to take much part in the election of 1852 He acted with the Whigs in that last effort of the Whig party, and when the Republican party was organized he with several others signed the call for a Republican convention for organization in this county. I recollect meeting Hon. Henry O'Connor in Burnett's store, O'Connor presented the call; I asked what he proposed to do? Burnett explained what they were at. The signers on that call so far as I recollect were

R. M. Burnett, Henry O'Connor, Stephen Whicher, H. H. Hine, J. P. Walton, and probably a dozen others. This was undoubtedly the first call for the Republican party within the state of Iowa. I always understood that Burnett was the main mover in starting it here. We felt that the Wnig party was handicapped by the name, and that some name that the newly arriving Germans could comprehend would be much more popular, which proved to be the case. While Mr. Burnett was a strong party man he was liberal to his political enemies, more so than some of them were worthy of. When he had any political move on hand he was usually there on time, though on one occasion he came too late. He had served two terms in the House of Representatives and wished to go to the Senate, and had secured a sufficient number of delegates to nominate him; his opponent from the country, knowing the feeling of the delegates, got his force in early and at once nominated himself before Burnett could get there. Nothing but the honor of Burnett saved the party from going to pieces that election. His opponent was elected to the Senate. Then he has since been pleased to be elected a justice of the peace. The store of Burnett's could justly be considered the literary headquarters of the city. The best informed men of the place called in to chat on literary as well as political subjects. Among his clerks we recollect seeing Samuel L. Clemens (Mark Twain), and W. B. Langridge, who was one of the best read men I ever met. I once asked Burnett how he liked Langridge; his answer was: "That Langridge always wanted to find out all there was in a book, which he almost always did before he sold it." Here could be found John Underwood for many years. While John Underwood was considered a crank by a few of those with whom he did not associate, he nevertheless was a remarkably well informed man. The question that John Underwood could not give an intelligent answer to was hardly worth answering. For years after Burnett's blindness the two men, Burnett and Underwood, could be seen walking out together. For the last fifteen years of Burnett's life he could be found in the rear part of the store being read to by a young lady. During this time he read most all the books of our city. The library of over 2,000 volumes belonging to the Academy of Science were all read through. Mr. Burnett's death occurred at the store on Dec. 23d, 1891. Some might say that we had said too much for Mr. Burnett, but we consider that one can hardly say too much for so conspicuous a man if he is worthy.

Muscatine was not confined to one bookstore. In the year 1852 or 1853 Smith & Lord brought a very fine stock of books here and opened in Cedar Block on the corner of Second and Mulberry streets. They run it awhile and it proved an unfortunate venture, or perhaps unfortunately located; at all events when it passed into the hands of Palmer & Demorest it was moved to one of the rooms under Stein's Music Hall, now occupied by the McColm dry goods house. When the war broke out, Palmer got up a company and went to the war, staid his time out, came back and was elected a Republican alderman from the Second ward, a thing that had rarely occurred before. In 1866 we find that Demorest & Coe had it in charge, Alf Palmer having gone to Dubuque. It appears as though J. E. Coe must have purchased Palmer's interest. J. E. Coe had recently returned from the war. Although "Jud" Coe spent several months in Andersonville prison, he pulled through. In 1866 we find that Demorest & Coe had moved the book store to No. 3 Olds' Block. In 1891 we find it in 111 east Second street, with J. E. Coe as proprietor. For the past two or three years R. L. Thompson has been the proprietor.

We find that the book concern of G. Schmidt & Bros. appears in 1866 in the name of Schmidt Bros. at the corner of Iowa Avenue and Second street, and later in 1883 in their present location and under the present name. They are now carrying on book binding in connection with their other business. At different times others have started in but did not succeed. In 1859 Raymond, Orr & Eystra opened a book bindery; perhaps a little before that William Butler started in at the business; but left it for a more noble calling—a tiller of the soil. Later, in 1876, the Muscatine Journal started a bindery with a man by the name of H. F. Turner as binder. All of them but Schmidt seemed to consider the business as unprofitable.

Recollections of Business in the Early Days of Muscatine.

BY J. P. WALTON.

No. 13.

The business of keeping ready-made clothing is almost without a date in our mercantile circles. In looking over an old copy of the Bloomington Herald, I find the following advertisement:

"New Store; the subscriber offers for sale a large assortment of Dry Goods, consisting in part of Ready Made Clothing; also Groceries, Hardware, Cutlery, Glassware, Boots and Shoes, Window Glass and Sash. All of which will be sold for cash or exchange for dry hides, deer skins, etc.   JOHN ZEIGLER.
Bloomington, Oct. 26, 1840."

I am inclined to think that Mr. Zeigler was the first merchant who kept ready made clothing. Up to 1849 most of the merchants kept ready made clothing in a limited way, and as late as 1856 we had nine places that kept that class of goods. Among those advertising ready made clothing were Barrus & Crocker, Drake & Stewart, L. D. Palmer, Rothchild & Bro., Rocup & Randolph, Waters & John, and C. Weed.

The first parties to open an exclusive clothing store in this place was Heilbrun & Silverman, in 1849. In the spring of 1850 Stix & Oppenheimer followed, and during the same year G. W. Kelley opened a clothing house in connection with tailoring. The firm of Stix & Oppenheimer disolved and Jacob Oppenheimer remained in the business until 1876 when he left the city.

The firm of Heilbrun & Silverman after a few years changed its name to Silverman & Bro., and this firm and Oppenheimer remained the two rival clothing houses for some time.

In 1859 there were four clothing houses, Block & Bro., Jacob Oppenheimer, Silverman & Bro., and L. Thurman. I don't recollect much about the latter. Ten years later, 1869, the names of Sam. Cohn, Jerome Crocker and C. Scheuer were added to the list. At the end of five years, in 1874, the list had reduced down to Block & Bro., S. & L. Cohn and Jacob Oppenheimer; while at the end of five more years, in 1879, the name of Jacob Oppenheimer was dropped from the list, but three new firms were advertising as being in the business, the names then being Block Bros., S. & L. Cohn, F. A. Drake, F. J. Mark & Co., D. Rothschild & Co In 1885 we find there had been some changes in the firms and the number increased, the list being Bach & Friedmen, Block & Hoffman, S. & L. Cohn, L. Hayum, J. G. Jackson and Wolf Kaufman. In 1891 there were 8 firms in the clothing busines to more or less extent: D. H. Block, Borger & Bliven, S. & L. Cohn, Hine Bros., J. G Jackson. Wolf Kaufman, H. S. Springer and the Sterneman Clothing Co.

If the reader will pardon us for so long a list of names we promise not to be guilty of doing so any more, but we must review them a little. The first real clothing dealer that identified himself with us was Jacob Silverman. His brother Charles soon became connected with him in the business; they had their store in a building on the south side of Second street east of Iowa avenue. Their competitors in the business, Stix & Oppenheimer, were located in a small building on the south side of Second street west of the avenue. When Stix left, Oppenheimer run the store alone, and he bought the building which the Silverman Bro's. occupied, thus forcing them to get other quarters. Of course they did not like this, but Stein & Hill had fitted up some new rooms under the music hall where the McColm Dry Goods Co. now are. Silverman Bros. leased one of the rooms and moved into it at once. They had a lease on their old room which did not expire for some months which they declined to surrender to Jacob, though he wanted it very badly. They were not satisfied to let it remain idle, so they hired a kind of a rough and tumble man and give him some of them bad or old stock and set him there to sell and insult every one that ventured in there to trade—the sales were not large but the effect was terrible on the successor, Jacob. He soon found out how he was being worked, but he could not help himself. The Silveman's claimed they were paying him off for the mean trick he had played on them. Jacob finally got possession and staid there until he left the city. He was a little unfortunate, though he made considerable money, but, as report said, his family spent it for him quite as fast as he made it.

Sam. and Louis Cohn were brothers of Jacob Silverman's wife and came here and learned the clothing business as clerks. Jacob Silverman generally took things easy and tried to enjoy himself as well as he was capable of doing. On one occassion he and his wife fitted up and attended a masquerade ball; of course he knew his wife's costume and masque, but while the dancing was going on he observed his wife sitting down resting, so he went up to her and commenced talking to her; she nodded all right to suit him; he advised her not to dance so hard and get heated up, and one hardly knows how many injunctions he gave her. It happened that another lady was dressed in in nearly the same costume as Mrs. Silverman, and Jacob had made a mistake and found he had been talking to Mrs. Ed. Hoch instead of his wife.

In the course of time Sam. Cohn concluded he wanted to do something for himself, so he launched out on his own hook; he opened a store on the south side of Second street west of Iowa avenue, and then there was trouble between Jacob and Samuel, but the matter was finally fixed up by the Silvermans selling out to the Cohns.

There are now ten places advertising clothing, one-half of the number learned, or partially learned, the business with S. & L. Cohn; any one of these half dozen are just as liberal dealers as their old employers and are sharing the patronage with them. After the young clothing houses had been fitted up with new store fronts, the Cohn's thought they were forced to put in a new front; they scoured the country from Chicago to Des Moines to secure a plan for one that would "knock the others out on the first round.' Well an elegant front was put in —one that is very hard to beat, but in order to make it more noticeable they hung the front door left handed and almost every one who goes there notices it and but few bless it. It has worked the charm to perfection.

A word about the senior member, Sam. Cohn. He is the most noted of any clothing dealer in our city, and perhaps the oldest one. He came here and learned the business with Jacob Silverman, who was a democrat; of course he educated Sam to be a democrat. Sam. attended the conventions and was usually a delegate, and frequently to the state conventions; he always paid his part of the expenses. He was made committeeman for this congressional district, and was one of the political magnets during the Hayes and Johnson time, and we have no doubt but that he could have had an appointment to Maricaybo or Liberia, or some similar point, if he had desired. Sam. lived for a long time in the 2nd ward, when the ward rarely gave anything but a democratic majority. On one occasion he was elected alderman; he moved out of the ward, and of course had to resign. Not long after that he got the democratic nomination for mayor, or some other office but was badly beaten at the election. He took his defeat quite hard, and since then his politics have been somewhat problematic. It is generally believed he voted for McKinley. Sam. has always had an eye to making money; on one occasion during the last campaign while Mexican dollars were worth but 54 cents, he noticed a merchant in another place was selling 50c worth of goods and giving a Mexican dollar for one United States dollar and was doing a thriving business. Sam. concluded to try it here and accordingly secured a stock of Mexican dollars and opend up, they went finely for one or two days, when he was waited on by the silver men and informed that he must stop it or they would boycot him. Sam had to stop and send his remaining Mexican dollars elsewhere.

Recollection of Business in the Early Days of Muscatine.

Published in the Muscatine Saturday Mail April 17, 1897; written by
J P Walton.

No. 14.

A lengthy notice in the News-Tribune of a recent date of the intended repairs on the gas holder, or perhaps a new holder or two, calls to mind some of the former owners of the gas works in this city. The company was originally oganized on February 19th, 1857, under the name of the Gas Light and Coke Co. of Muscatine, with a capital stock of $50,000, one-third of which was owned and paid in by citizens of Muscatine; this was used in putting in the main pipes and fitting up the works, and it is quite likely that this money was about all that was used in its construction. Mr. Peter Jackson says he carried the list around and got the signers, and was the secretary of the company. The first published officers were Chester Weed, president; E. Klein, secretary; G. C. Stone, Jacob Butler, Peter Jackson, W. C. Brewster, John G. Gordon, John B. Dougherty and Chester Weed directors, and Edward Hobart, foreman. The gas works were erected by a company of men from Cincinnati, who made a business of going from one place to another putting in gas works, a man by the name of Paine represented them while here. They put up the works, put down the mains, put up the gas posts, and made house connections and done fitting. Their price for piping, putting pipes on the outside of the plastering was 30 cents per foot. They rarely put up pipes any other way than top of the plastering. I could get any amount of pipe put up at the present time and have it concealed under the plastering for 10 cents per foot. Their prices for fixtures were equally as large.

When the Episcopal church people wanted to put in gas they got the pipes put in and wanted to use a lot of small brackets, the company would not let them have them for less than $1.00 each; the church people got one of the hardware merchants to get the brackets in Philadelphia for 12½ cents each, then the company refused to let the church have gas, but they had do it. They had too many good customers in the church who made to much noise.

To return to the beginning of my story, after the pipes were laid, the lamp posts put up and a few connections made with private consumers, the company and the citizens held a celebration of the introduction of gas in Muscatine, at Stein's hall on August 18, 1857. This was about the time that the worst money panic we ever had begun.

Well the company did not start out with any fancy price, one informant says $6 per thousand, another $4.50, with an additional charge of 25 cents per month for meter rent. Of course such prices were not much of an inducement for new consumers and so they did not have many.

Mr. Nicholas Barry tells me that when he came here to take charge of the works in 1866, he found them in charge of Robert Lincoln, with Douglas Viele as cashier and manager. They were in a bad condition every way and largely in debt. When Mr. Viele died Mr. Alex. Jackson took his place. Jackson surprised the executive board by ordering a car load of coal from Pittsburg, bought his lime in large quantities and managed things on a business basis. He soon got the company out of debt and made valuable improvements, although it never paid a dividend, only in one way, when the annual meeting occurred or when a few of the knowing ones attended and elected their officers and closed up with a banquet which was charged to the gas company's expense. When the water works were put in Mr. Barry left the gas company and went into business for himself, which was the start of the Barry Manufacturing Company.

In 1877, likely about the time the articles of incorporation of the gas company expired, along came Mr. Coverdale, of Cincinnati, and bought up the stock, most of it sold for 20 to 30 cents on the dollar, although a few cranky stockholders got 50 cents on the dollar. Mr. Coverdale was a gas man in every particular; he brought his son-in-law, Childs, here for a superintendent. Mr. Coverdale put the plant in first-class order and brought Mr. James Hannan here to operate the works.

The plant finally passed into the hands of Truman Cowell with Mr. Hannan as manager. Mr. Cowell took hold of the works under apparently good circumstances, he extended the mains, had a good many more street lamps put up, and got more consumers. He reduced the price of gas, cut off the annoying meter rent, and made it an inducement for consumers to use gas. He only got fairly to work when along came an electric lighting company and secured a lot of Muscatine citizens to help them, and they undertook to put out the gaslights. Of course, Mr. Cowell had to defend himself by putting in an electric light plant, which he did. After a short experiment the electric light company went under. Then another one was started by a Davenport company; they "bucked" Cowell awhile and went under.

A series of circumstances with which we are not familiar have placed both the electric light and gas plants into the hands of the Seevers', who have recently connected them with the street car service. They appear to be pushing the business for all there is in it, and in some cases have attached the meter rent that in days of yore caused so much trouble.

Since the gas company have commenced repairing the gas is superior to any produced for years - so much so, one considers it a luxury. We hope they will continue to make repairs.

Recollection of Business in the Early Days of Muscatine

Published in the Muscatine Saturday Mail April 24, 1897; written by
J. P. Walton.

No. 15.

The pine lumber interests in the early days began in a limited way. The first saw-mill built here was erected by Cornelius Cadle in 1843; it stood on lot No. 2, block No. 18. Mr. Cadle came here from the east, bringing his machinery with him. The log-way was on the back end of the mill; the logs that were rafted here in the river were run up in Mad creek for a harbor, the log-way running down into the creek. The creek was deep enough to float logs in the lowest stage of water, the ground where lumber is now piled was so low that it was used for storing logs that were floated in when the river was up, to be rolled in when it left. We have seen acres of logs on the lots north of Front street. Cadle kept his little mill running a greater part of the year, either on pine logs that were rafted here in a small way, or on hard wood logs that were hauled in from the timber land around here.

In the year 1844 parties brought the old Geneva saw-mill and located it near where Huttig's office now stands. I think the parties that put this mill up were Colonel John Vannatta and John G. Deshler. They started it under favorable circumstances at the time, but they did not agree. Col. John Vannatta was a very stout man and not quarrelsome, but like most of the pioneer men, preferred to settle his difficulties without resorting to the tedious aid of the law. J. G. Deshler was a large sized, long armed, bony man, in fact a skilled boxer, although not near as heavy or as stout a man as Vannatta. They disagreed about something, Vannatta started for Deshler who fell back to his early training, which he used to great advantage not allowing his antoganist to touch him. He punished Vannatta so severely that it stopped the mill. The mill then passed into the hands of Robert and Sam Kinney; they did not do much with it; in fact not much work was done with either of the mills until the spring of 1847, when the Chambers Brothers brought a lot of logs. In the autumn of 1846, the brothers William, Anderson and Isaac Chambers took their ox teams and went into the pineries on Black river and cut and brought down two log rafts with about a million feet in them. They rented the two mills and sawed the logs up, and carried on the business. The name of the firm was A. & I. Chambers until January 11, 1849, when the name changed to W. & A Chambers. In February 1853, Douglas Dunsmore joined the firm when it was known as Dunsmore & Chambers and they connected the meranetil business with that of lumber.

In 1858 they associated Cornelius Cadle with them under the name of Chambers, Cadle & Co. They took down the old Cadle mill and rebuilt it. (The other mill had stopped sawing and was converted into a stave factory.) Isaac Chambers having died, John Chambers took his place in the firm. The new mill had a much larger capacity, and they connected it with a furniture manufactory; they made turned rail bedsteads a speciality, which was a very popular bedstead at that time and sold large quantities. Turned rails and bed-cords are a thing of the past.

Chambers, Cadle & Co. run the saw-mill and Dunsmore & Chambers the store. The store was situated on the north side of Second street between Sycamore and Cedar, and occupied two buildings, one for merchandise, the other for furniture.

How long Cornelius Cadle remained with them I am unable to say, but things settled down to Dunsmore having charge of the store, William attending to the mill, Anderson doing the outside business, and John attending to running the lath and shingle machines and the planing mills. They furnished employment for over two hundred men, those in the furniture department worked the year round. They were very successful in business while they stuck to the lumber business.

In 1862 the business was rearranged, Vincent Chambers became a member of the firm, and a large packing house and grain elevator were added. The pork house was completed in 1864 and during the fall and winter they packed 27,300 hogs; many of the hogs cost the firm 8 to 10 cents per pound gross weight. The late war closed in the spring of 1865, and with it's closing, down went pork and other produce; this decline left the firm more than $100,000 short of what they expected.

This pork house burned down in 1870 or '71. In 1860 the Chambers Brothers built an elevator at the foot of Oak street. This elevator burned down on December 22, 1869; the loss was $40,000, the insurance being $22,000. This elevator had handled more than a million bushels of grain in its short existence.

In 1870 a new saw-mill was erected above the mouth of Mad creek, which was afterwards sold to Dessaint and later to the Musser Lumber Co., and on the 12th of June, 1881, it burned down. The Muscatine Lumber and Box Co. now have their factory on the ground.

On August 25, 1874, the lower Chambers' saw-mill and Baker's boiler shop burned down. A new planing mill was soon erected, it started operation on December 11 of the same year.

In 1876 the Chambers Brothers attached a stone saw-mill to the planing mill. It was not profitable and was soon discontinued.

In November, 1878, Vincent, William, John and Anderson Chambers all started for Texas with a view of carrying on the milling business in that state. They had no success there, neither did they make any attempt to regain their lost prestige here. The Chambers Brothers were very honorable men; they could be relied on in any occasion. Anderson was a little visionary, his operations did not always foot up successfully. Vincent could be classed in the list, while William was very conservative, and John managed to keep the others within bounds.

During the period of say twenty years from 1852 to 1872, no business concern figured more conspicuously than did the Chambers Brothers. There was one member of the firm that should not be forgotton, Douglas Dunsmore He was a native of Scotland; was genial, affable, and a sharp, quick business man, but always ready to enjoy a joke. I recollect calling in the store one day, when Dug. said "Hello, Walton, come here." He lead the way out into the back shed in the rear of the store, where he had a barrel with a hen in it sitting on a nest filled with China eggs. He said she had been there six weeks and had not complained, and he did not know how much longer it would be before she would "come off."

All the different members of the firm are now dead, and their children have mostly left Muscatine.

Recollection of Business in the Early Days of Muscatine

Published in the Muscatine Saturday Mail May 1, 1897; written by J P. Walton.

No. 16.

In the year 1841 James Brentlinger came here and opened a tinner's shop and stove store. Previous to this time the merchants handled all the tin cups and coffee pots, etc., and likely stoves; at all events Brentlinger was the pioneer. The first exclusive hardware store was opened by Brent & Miller in 1852. This was the first one that was confined to hardware. Moore & Ament opened a store and tinshop, and H. W. Moore an iron and hardware store.

In 1856, when the first directory was published, it claimed five places where stoves and tinware were kept, and three where hardware was on sale. Of those we are able to enumerate, were H. W. Moore, Brent & Miller, J. G. Gordon, Moore & Ament, James Tritch & Co., George G. Mahan and Charles and W. R. Stone. Previous to 1859 the following changes were made: George G. Mahan had sold to David Hoyt. Hugh Wallace and Wm. A. Brownell had gone into the business; and by 1866 the hardware and tin store men had made the following changes: David Hoyt had transferred his stock to J. Daniels & Co., W. A. Brownell had sold to J. J. Smith; W. C. Clapp, and Beach & McQuesten had entered the field, and the firm of Charles & W. R. Stone had changed to Charles Stone.

During the next three years to 1869, Benjamin Beach had sold out his interest to Wm. McQuesten; W. C. Clapp had taken in Jacob Fisch as a partner and the firm name was Clapp & Fisch; C. W. Fisher, John O'Donnell, and W. S. Parvin had opened tin shops and stove stores.

Previous to 1874, J. J. Smith had retired and transferred his stock to a Mr. Connell, who lost it shortly afterwards by fire; C. W. Fisher and John O'Donnell seem to have retired. Within the next two years R. T. Thompson Son & Co. had embarked in the business, J. G. Gordon was dropped from the list. Before 1879 McQuesten had taken in S. P. Sawyer under the name of McQuesten & Sawyer.

In 1883 the list of dealers in hardware as they appeared in the directory were H W. Moore, Jacob Fisch, McQuesten & Sawyer, and Thompson Bros. In 1886 the list stood the same. In 1891 G. C. Clapp, W. S. Parvin, Thompson Bros., Jacob Fisch & Sons, McQuesten & Sawyer, and C. W. Wells were the dealers in that line.

In 1895 the list stood, Jacob Fisch & Son. M. N. Bond, McQuesten & Sawyer, Jordan & Klein, Thompson Bros., Geo. S. Clapp, and Bartemier & Fulliam. The latter firm having taken the stock of goods that belonged to H. W. Moore. At the present time those engaged in the business are George B. Fisch. J. A. Bartemier, Thompson Bros., Jacob Fisch & Sons, McQuesten & Sawyer, N. M. Bond, and George S. Clapp.

We will venture a few remarks on some of the different individuals that have sold stoves and tinware in this city. I think J. G. Gordon was the first merchant of the number here, but he did not confine himself strictly to those lines of goods. Mr. H. W. Moore came here sometime during the forties; he opened an iron store and gradually added hardware. When the firm of Moore & Ament closed out H. W. Moore took the stock of stoves and tinware, and in 1868 he sold the stoves and tinware to Clapp & Fisch, after which he went more exclusively into the hardware and wagon material, which business he continued until his death.

Mr. H. W. Moore was a native of the state of Maine; he came west in 1838 or '39, went into business in Burlington but was not successful there. He closed out his store in that city and came to Muscatine where he commenced anew. He always attended closely to his own private affairs. During business hours he could always be found in his little office keeping his own books which frequently took way into the night to keep them up. He was very close and frugal, for instance all the old and used envelopes in his office were cut open and laid in a pile on the back of his desk for figuring on, none went into the waste basket until they had served that purpose. He made it a rule that every customer should settle up every six months and if any thing was due and not paid a note should be given for the account, if payments were made at different times the interest at the rate of 10 per cent would be calculated to that date and added in. He was strictly honest in all his dealings. When he came here he was an old whig, when that political party went under and the republican party started he affiliated with it until the presidential covention in 1860 that nominated Lincoln. Mr. Moore and myself were both

Seward men, and we were both disappointed in the convention not renominating him. I know, for I associated and discussed politics with him at that time; he never forgave the republicans for leaving Seward out; on the contrary he worked with the Douglas democrats.

At that time Mr. Moore had an almost unlimited credit, the country had not fully recovered from the effects of the panic of 1857, and goods in his line were very low but advancing; he bought heavily and most of the goods sold at retail for double or trible their first value, and this advance made Moore rich. He became connected with many of our public improvements, such as water works, railroads, banks and served on the school board, also in the honorable office of alderman; in fact, movements of public interest could rarely be found where Mr. Moore was not a prominent man. He was one of the very few mercantile men who began poor and continued in business for a long time, and died rich. He was a prominent member of the Episcopal church and was one of its wardens for many years.

Brent & Miller brought a stock of goods here in 1852 and commenced business, they run perhaps two years when Miller went away taking the goods with him; he left his brother-in-law behind in the person of Rev. R. W. H Brent—Father Brent as he was requently called. Brent remained here and farmed and preached around at the school houses near the city. In 1865 or '66, after the soldiers came home from the war of the rebellion, the office of postmaster became vacant; the soldiers thought that they had saved the country and had a right to all the offices. The worst trouble was that too many wanted the office and in place of leaving it to the congressman to select a post master they all wanted to vote on it. Father Brent knew that a vacancy would occur, and having an eye to business while he was preaching around through the country he was electioneering for the office. When it came election time he got his forces in and voted them O. K. Among the soldiers there were eight or ten candidates and each of them got some votes but Father Brent got more than any one, so he got the office, greatly to the annoyance of the soldiers and politicians. Since then no election for post master has been held in this city, the leaders don't want any more of that kind.

The firm of James Tritch & Co. did not last long in the hardware and stove business. I have been informed that Tritch went to Denver and embarked in the banking business and became very wealthy. George G. Mahan dealt in pianos and other musical instruments, and I presume he was the first one to bring pianos here for sale. He was a first rate man socially; he transferred his store to David Hoyt, a relative, and went on the road traveling for a St. Louis house, if I am correct.

Recollection of Business in the Early Days of Muscatine

Published in the Muscatine Saturday Mail May 8, 1897; written by J P. Walton.

No. 17.

In our review of H. W. Moore there was one item we intended to mention, his dislike of a law suit. There was no one in our city better posted in commercial law than he was, and no one kept away from it any better than he did. On one occasion he had rented one of his Front street store rooms to a couple of young men for a shipping and commission business; the young men did not agree, and each decided to go into business on his own account. After dividing their effects, the question of who should retain the old stand came up, both wanted it and both claimed it, and both started for Moore's store to secure the refusal of the room—one went out the front door, and the other out the back door. They both arrived at Moore's office at the same time; each claimed the room, and each threatened to go to law about it if they could not get it without. Moore said, "Boys take the advice of an old man, settle your difficulties without going to law." They took his advice and one retained the room. We never heard of Moore commencing a law suit or of getting into but one. When the Muscatine Western railroad was built, Mr. Moore was one of the board of directors; a tax was voted by the city to aid in its construction; a majority of the taxpayers paid up but a large minority refused to pay. They secured legal service and commenced suits to prevent collection. In one of their moves they commenced a criminal prosecution against the directors for fraud in some manner, but nobody was convicted. This so effectually disgusted Mr. Moore that he declared he would never take any part in any public improvement after that, which promise he kept. When the high bridge was built across the river he would not take any stock, but he made the company a liberal donation, however. When the bridge was completed the stockholders found that they had a surplus and divided it up among themselves, not sharing with Moore or any other donors.

The firm of Moore & Ament, stove and tinware dealers, was closed up somewhat suddenly. It came about in this way, in the summer of 1853 or '54, the tinner Moore, as we called him for a distinction from Henry W. Moore the iron dealer, took a young lady of our city on a steamboat excursion somewhat to the annoyance of a blacksmith who lived here by the name of John Lower. John made some remarks about them that Moore thought to be derogatory to the lady. Moore being a southern man he thought it was necessary to avenge the wrong, so he armed himself with a "Derringer" and walked up behind Lower while he was drinking a glass of soda at Adam Reuling's counter, and shot him in the back at short range. The shot was thought to be fatal, so Moore had to go to jail and while there some of the enthusiastic women of the city carried flowers to him in abundance. It soon became evident that Lower would not die at once, and Moore had an examination. It turned out that there was no cause for the shooting, so Moore was held in bail to appear at court, but before court convened he went off and left his bondsmen to settle with the state. The bond was found to be imperfect and was never paid. The effects of the firm were sold to H. W. Moore. Ament went into business with a Mr. Murry in manufacturing wagons.

In the year 1854 or '55, Charles and W. R. Stone opened a hardware store. Charles retained the store a long time, if I am correct, he closed it out and went to farming. Sometime previous to 1860 W. R. Stone had withdrawn and, I think, went to Chicago; he is now in business in Duluth, Minn. Bill Stone was certainly a wag, who was hard to equal; any joke or rig that was going around the town which could not be traced to Bill Stone was flat. The puns were too numerous to mention at this time.

Previous to 1860 William A. Brownell, now a banker in Keokuk, opened a stove store and afterwards sold it to his brother-in-law, J. J. Smith, who did not make it pay very well.

The trouble with the stove business at that time was the decline in the price of gold, which frequently was one or two per cent a day, and when resumption did come goods had declined to a panic price, in some instances to near one-half their first cost, while a man's note which he gave for money to purchase goods with did not decline any, and it was a fact that while everything was flourishing the merchant was going under, the hardware business suffering the worst if pushed.

We cannot well quit this subject without mentioning the names of Clapp and Fish. They went into business in 1868, Clapp sold out to Fisch in 1878 and George Clapp entered in the place of his father, the firm name continuing to be Fish & Clapp until 1880 when George Clapp withdrew and opened a store for himself. Jacob Fisch commenced with H. W. Moore in 1859 and in 1868 he left Moore and went in partnership with Mr. Clapp. He is now in company with two of his sons, Charles and Henry.

George B. Fish, a son of Jacob Fish, is doing business on the north side of Second street east of Sycamore; Jacob Fisch & Sons are located on the south side of Second street near Iowa avenue; McQuestion & Sawyer, and Thompson Bros. are both on the north side of Second street east of Chestnut; George Clapp at the corner of Second and Sycamore streets; J. A. Bartemeier on the south side of Second street, west of Cedar, at H. W. Moore's old stand, and N. M. Bond on the south side of Second street east of Cedar. While some of the hardware and stove men have not been successful we think it has been the most prosperous of any mercantile business in our city.

Jacob Fisch is the senior hardware dealer in our city; he is a native of Germany, came to America when young and settled in Moscow with his father, where he learned the hard work of a pioneer life. S. W. Stewart in his history of Moscow makes the following mention of the family:

"In 1844 there was a good run of sugar water. South of the city, near Sugar creek, there were two camps. One, owned by George Hunt, was run by J. B. Yeager and his boy; the other by Aurk and Jacob Fisch. On one nice Saturday, near the close of the season, some of the boys happened in the bottom hunting a bite for Sunday, and found by accident that the day's boiling would not be "sugared off" until Sunday or Monday. About larger places, like Moscow, there are apt to be some who neither fear God nor regard man, and Moscow was no exception. Five of Moscow's hoodlums suddenly developed an intense appetite for maple syrup. When darkness sufficiently intense had settled on the landscape, they quietly left the cosy streets of Moscow. Upon close inspection they found nearly a barrel of syrup about ready for the final process of "sugaring off" at each place. The camps were about three hundred yards apart. A large walnut log was selected midway between the camps; a kettle from each camp was brought up; a fire was kindled; the syrup placed in proper position to make maple molasses; a sharp ear was kept for approaching footsteps; nothing worse than the hoot of an owl was heard; the hoodlums had an immense appetite for maple syrup; paddles, spoons and skimmers were kept in constant use. By two o'clock their appetites were somewhat relieved, and the syrup had given out. It may seem strange that five persons should get outside of sixty gallons of syrup in one night, but such is the tradition in this case. A description of the five will come in order now: Two of them were six feet high but rather slim; they had the appearance of having been stretched by some special process; they extended up but not wide out. One of the others was a rather large man with a good capacity for holding. The remaining two were boys about twenty years old; their capacity for hiding syrup was enormous.

"On Sunday the Yeager boys came down to "sugar off" their Saturday's work, but it was gone, barrel, kettle and all. It is of no use to talk; what they said would have been altogether out of place at a prayer meeting or a tea party. On Monday morning Fisch and Aurk came down. Well, the boys could not tell what they said; they talked in "dutch;" only they could hear it for a month when they went into the woods."

Recollection of Business in the Early Days of Muscatine

Published in the Muscatine Saturday Mail May 15, 1897; written by
J P. Walton.

No. 18.

In 1839 as the village of Bloomington, now Muscatine, began to grow, the demand for milk became a fixed fact. To meet that demand, although small, our own father, Amos Walton, who lived on the farm where the tile works is now located, fitted out his boy, Josiah, with an old Indian pony and a couple of jugs to peddle milk. The jugs were put in a sack one at each end and swung across the pony's back, and the boy mounted on top. This trip was made six times a week but never on Sunday. We would get up early in the morning, ride to town, deliver our milk and by the time we got started home it began to get warm, the pony got lazy and we got sleepy. I don't think we ever fell off, but came very near it many times. The road crossed Mad creek near the Warfield mill where the Ninth street bridge now spans the creek. This mill was run by water from the creek; the old dam and mill race can be seen at the present time from the bridge, they having been located just above the bridge. After crossing the bridge we took the right hand road that leads up by the old log cabin, now standing on Dr. James Weed's farm, from there the road bore a little to the left and followed the top of the bluff until it nearly reached Mr. Giesenhaus' farm, when it went down over the point of the bluff. This road was among the big oak trees—every tree along the route had three notches cut in their sides. I used to notice them every trip and wondered how they came there. I have since learned that they were road markers probably put there by the surveyors when the road was surveyed. We have wandered somewhat from our subject. We continued the horse-back milk business for the season of 1839. In the spring of 1840 we moved up to Geneva proper and occupied the house erected by Harvey Gillett, and secured a one-horse wagon, and added garden vegetables to our business. We had only gotten fairly started until we had competition in the person

of Miss Cad Fish, she hauled in it.
her "garden fruck" around in a one-horse cart. I had a one-horse wagon not near so clumsy. We lived at Geneva and run the milk and vegetable wagon during the years 1840 and 1841.

In the spring of 1842 we moved down onto Muscatine Island. After that time most of our peddling was melons, the milk trade was dropped, others took our place. Old Tommy Morford followed the vegetable and fruit business, for the Muscatine Island was not at that time considered a suitable place for vegetable growing. The Smalleys, John especially, grew great quantities of pie-plant, they also raised other garden truck. There were several along down the slough who made a business of supplying our local market—a Mr. Huber for one.

After Mr. John Barnard came here in 1851, and bought out Mr. Walliker, he had his share in the "truck and fruit" line. Dr. James Weed manipulated the milk trade for, say, 1850 to 1860. He brought here a fine herd of Devon cattle, which were the premium herd of the west for fine milkers, but they were not good stockers. When the milk business stopped the Devon cattle disappeared. We are not going to follow up the milk and vegetable business for after the groceries commenced handling "truck" there were but peddlars engaged

About 1870 Benjamain Middleton settled on the island and commenced to raise vegetables on quite a large scale for the city; he did not ship any vegetables until about 1872, when T. B. Holcomb and Wm. H. Hoopes joined in the business. Hoopes had been in a grocery store and knew what could be done shipping. The three formed a partnership to raise and ship vegetables, sweet potatoes and melons under the name of Middleton, Hoopes & Holcomb. This firm lasted for a number of years; Middleton died, then Hoopes & Holcomb managed the interest. In the meantime the Vails began to operate, especially in melons and sweet potatoes.

At the present time there are several leaders in the line of garden vegetables. We make the following estimate of the probable acreage of this year: The first article in open air cultivation to sell is asparagus of which as near we can ascertain there is about 100 acres. J. E. Hoopes & Co., W. H. Hoopes & Sons, C. B. Vail, T. B. Holcomb, M. A. Smith and Hahn Bros. are the principal raisers and shippers. The firm of J. E. Hoopes & Co. in one day cut and shipped 240 boxes containing 24 bunches of asparagus in each box or 5,760 bunches. About 80 acres are in early radishes; early peas and beans, 40 acres; early cabbage,

60, and early tomatoes 45 acres. This amount of vegetables find a market all over the northwest from Chicago to the Rockeys.

But few Irish potatoes are raised on Muscatine Island. Sweet potatoes are a specialty, last fall all the storage houses were full, they having a capacity of 60,000 bushels. It is quite likely that more than that amount was sold before putting up time, making at least 120,000 bushels raised last year. This year the acreage will not be as large

Of the melons, last year there were some 500 carloads shipped, and it is probable that 200 carloads were sold otherwise, making 700 carloads or 700,000 melons.

Muscatine Island has one very serious drawback, it is the most nothern point for raising melons for market to any extent; it makes the season very short, and when they ripen they ripen all at once, and if not disposed of quickly the cold weather sets in and stops the sale of them.

There is a question frequently asked, who shipped the first carload of melons from the island. We will answer James Wiggins, probably in 1862.

Recollections of

THE WHOLESALE

Business in the Early Days of Muscatine.

BY J P. WALTON.

No. 19.

One of the earliest mercantile houses in our town was Jennison & Stone. These two gentlemen first met at Lafayette, Indiana. Mr. H. Q. Jennison was a civil engineer and was engaged in surveying for a canal. Mr. F. H. Stone had just graduated and came west to teach school; he did not succeed well at that business, and gave it up. He applied to Mr. Jennison for a job as chain carrier. Mr. Jennison soon found him to be a very worthy and talented man, and knowing of a stock of goods for sale cheap, proposed to Stone to purchase the goods and bring them to Iowa. Jennison had probably been here before. They brought the goods to this place in the spring of 1839, and opened in a small building on Front street, near where the Oat Meal mill now stands. During that year Mr. Jennison's family came west, his wife having relatives living here.

At that time Bloomington had but little of anything to sell, so their sales were not so much on the trade order as they were afterwards. Jennison & Stone sold out their interest in the store to George Humphreys, another unmarried man, who moved the stock of goods into a building on the southwest corner of Chestnut and Second street.

Mr. Stone went to clerking for Mr. Joseph Bennett where he remained until he was elected treasurer and recorder of the county. He then gave up the mercantile business for a term of five years. Previous to selling out to Humphreys, F. H. Stone went into partnership in a small way with Jack Richman and packed pork; the pork was dry salted in bulk, and what part of it was salted well was sold, but a portion of the pork spoiled and the venture proved to be unprofitable.

We spoke about George Humphreys being a bachelor. So was Fred Stone and most of the men here in the year 1840. Fred H. Stone married the daughter of Dr. Fairchild. After serving five years in the court house as county treasurer and recorder, he went into the drug business with Mr. Pliny Fay. When Mr. Fay's health gave out and he went to California, Mr. Stone bought his interest in the store. After the death of Mr. Stone, Mr. Theodore Krehe bought the stock of goods.

WHOLESALE BUSINESS.

From 1848 to 1858 Muscatine was the most important distributing point in Iowa. Situated on the bend of the Mississippi river, the "apex" as it was afterwards called, this city was the most accessible of all the river towns. Here a good wholesale business was done, especially in the grocery business. The leading house in that line was J. S. Hatch & Co., composed of J. S. Hatch and Seth Humphreys. They occupied two of the lower rooms of the Ogilvie House block, Nos. 75 and 76, Water street. They also had out a sign as commission merchants, and they did an immense amount of business. Some years ago I met a man that was one of their shipping clerks; he said they would frequently receive a barge load of coffee at a time. We doubt very much if any of our wholesale merchants at the present time receive a carload at any one time. Hatch & Co. built the large brick house at the west end of Second street, now owned by the Vail Bros., occupied by the Commercial Club. The room on the east side was built and finished off for a wholesale clothing room. The name of the firm was changed to Hatch Humphreys & Co., consisting of J. S. Hatch, Seth Humphreys and Wm. S. Humphreys. I don't think they ever handled much, if any, clothing. When the panic of 1857 came on and all the wild cat money, about the only currency we had, went under, the firm had a great amount due them from country merchants which was impossible to collect. They went out of business not much richer than when they went in.

Recollection of Business in the Early Days of Muscatine

Published in the Muscatine Saturday Mail May 29, 1897; written by
J. P. Walton.

No. 20.

The change of the name of Bloomington to Muscatine is a question that is being agitated at the present time. Through the kindness of Henry Jayne, who has been overhauling the old papers at the Court House, I am in possession of the original petition to the court for the change. It is a rare old paper of autographs of the early settlers of Bloomington; there are some two hundred names signed in their "own proper hand." We give below the petition and other papers, together with the signatures; those marked with * are supposed to be living, 20 in all. The decree was granted on the 7th of June 1849, by Hon. James Grant. Following is the petition:

The State of Iowa, Muscatine county, ss; District Court of the State of Iowa, within and for the county of Muscatine, June term, 1849:

The undersigned land holders in the vicinity of the town of Bloomington, in the county of Muscatine in the state of Iowa, think it desirable to change the name of the town to that of Muscatine for the following reasons:

1. Frequent miscarriages of letters by mail occur by reason of there being towns in Missouri, Kentucky, Indiana and Illinois of the same name.

2. Burlington is sometimes mistaken by postmasters for Bloomington, and mail matter is carried to and lies at the former place that is destined for the latter.

3. The reason for adopting the name of MUSCATINE is obvious—it is the name of one of the most noted and conspicious land marks on the Mississippi river, a name co-eval with the first discovery of the course of the river by La Salle, at the head of which the town is situated, and is the name of the county of which the town is the seat of justice. There is no other town within the knowledge of your petitioners of the same name.

L C Hine,
Moses Couch,
Suel Foster,
Henry Reece,
J Williams,
Geo Reeder,
James Swem,
Stephen Whicher,
W G Worsham,
*D C Cloud,
Ed Olmsted,
*J Scott Richman,
Jas A Humphreys,
William Sherwood,
*John Lemp,

Thos M Isett,
Adam Ogilvie,
Pliny Fay,
H H Hine,
F H Stone,
Richard Cadle,
Nath Hallock,
John B Dougherty,
B Bartholomew,
A Jackson,
Wallace & Breading
John M Beaumar,
Thos Wood,
Jas Borland,
Thos W Moore,

Lucian Chatfield,
*Luke Sells,
G L Branhams,
T G F Hunt,
A O Warfield,
B F Howland,
H W Moore,
Jacob Butler,
Chas O Waters,
Geo D Stevenson,
John H Dayton,
T M Barlow,
J S Fenimore,
J G Gordon,
J A Green,
*Wm A Drury,
Jas P Kelly,
W H Appler,
W Binna,
Lyman Smith,
D Dunsmore,
C Browning,
Michel Greeno,
A H Smith,
James B Foushee,
M Block,
M M Berkshire,
D R Warfield,
J Blake,
— Becke,
Erwin Will,
Geo Stroup,
Henri Felchmann,
H Q Jennison,
Robert Tillard,
David K Waters,
Jacob Way,
Devore Parmer,
E Stewart,
J C Webler,
E Plummer,
J W Richman,
John Dawson,
Jeremiah McMin-
  ony,
John Seiler,
W D Ament,
G W Parmer,
Lemuel L Purcell,
Z Washburn,

Samuel Anderson,
Horace Deming,
James S Aller,
I N Hudson,
N L Stout,
Chas Fowler,
Chester Weed,
Jos B Messick,
Andrew Fimple,
A T Boon,
E Hatch,
Luther H Wreys,
Alexander Fulton,
W S Ayrs,
I C Day,
E H Albee,
D G McCloud,
John Reed,
G C Harvey,
Jackson Benidger,
W H Lilly,
J Bennett,
H Matthews,
C L Phelps,
*Wm Gordon,
*John C Dietz,
G W Humphreys,
*L D Parmer,
F Thurston,
P L Washburn,
J S Lakin,
G W Willmering,
Johann Achter,
Charley Williams,
James Strong,
John L Cummins,
*Adam Reuling,
Cyrus Spring,
J W Kane,
T M Homlbs,
David H Shupe,
*Chas Norman,
Mark Kirkpatrick,
I McCullough,
W Williams,
Ansel Humphreys,
A P Arkin,
N S Dunbar,
D J Parvin,
*James Brisbine,

G A Springer,
J H Dunn,
G M Kinsley,
*J P Freeman,
Henry Molis,
*Barnhardt Beil,
Conrad Stahl,
John P Fulton,
A B Goldsberry,
John Rukee,
*Franklin Mormon,
Oliver Brisbine,
Joseph Brisbine,
*Wm L Browning,
*Peter Jackson,
Jas M Jarboe,
H D LaCossitt,
Jacob Hagan,
L C White,
P Downy,
Thos Graham,
B Cullin,
A Washburn,
Henry Fowler,
*John Roth,
Carl Kierck,
*Wm Butler,
Patteison Simpson,

Wm Leffingwell,
A Fisher,
C Hastings,
Jim Dorman,
Jacob Mahin,
A B Robbins,
G H Terry,
H W G Terry,
*Abram Smalley,
Joseph Crane,
Malen Brown,
John Fyock,
Joseph R Reece,
Thos Crandol,
S G Stein,
X P Feifer,
C H Grand M D,
Robert Douglass,
W F White,
John J Lucey,
Noah M McCormick
*Jos Bridgman,
Lewis Peterson jr.
John J Huber,
A T Banks,
John Zeigler,
H H Garnes,
Alfred Purcell.

The township officers whose names appear on the back of the petition are:

President—E Overman.

Trustees—W St John, J G Gordon, J. Butler.

St Com—C Kegel.

The State of Iowa, Muscatine county, ss:

Lyman C. Hine, sheriff of Muscatine county, Iowa, on oath, states that there are the names of at least twelve land holders in the vicinity of the town of Bloomington.   L. C. HINE.

Sworn and subscribed in open court this 4th of June, 1849   D. C. CLOUD,
                  Justice of the Peace.

The State of Iowa, Muscatine county, ss:

The undersigned citizens of Muscatine county and Bloomington, Iowa, being duly sworn, say that they are satisfied that more than three-fourths of the inhabitants of said town desire the name thereof changed to that of "Muscatine," and they further say that they know of no other town or village in this State of the same name with that which is prayed for in the petition.

    Andrew J Fimple,
    J Scott Richman,
    Stephen Whicher,
    I C Day.

Subscribed and sworn to before me this 5th day of June, 1849.
    D. C. CLOUD,
    Justice of the Peace.

The petition and papers were filed June 6, 1849, Richard Cadle being county clerk.

Recollection of Business in the Early Days of Muscatine

Published in the Muscatine Saturday Mail June 5, 1897; written by J P. Walton.

No. 21.

In the spring of 1837 Adam Ogilvie brought a small stock of goods here and opened a store in a log cabin on Front street, in company with a man named Abbott. Ogilvie soon commenced to build a new store building on lot 4, block 11, on Front street, where Gobble's wholesale grocery now is located. It was some 22 by 40 feet, two-stories high; the second story he used for a dwelling. This building had but little sawed lumber in it; the posts and studding were hewed, the lath and siding boards were split out of timber growing on the lot, or near by. This building was afterwards moved to the north side of Third street east of Iowa avenue, on lot 3, block 55, and was veneered with brick. While occupying this store Mr. Abbott died, likely in 1838.

Ogilvie sold out to Harvey Gillett and John A. Parvin in the spring of 1840. While Gillett was the principal owner the store stood in the name of J. A. Parvin. In the spring of 1841 Ogilve took the store back and associated Peter Jackson with him. Mr. Jackson had been clerking in the store since 1839. The store then stood Ogilvie & Jackson. They packed pork, made bacon of it and were not particular about their smoke house, as the skippers got in it and they lost most of the bacon.

In 1845 Jackson bought Ogilvie's interest in the store. Ogilvie then went to building his large brick residence on Ogilvie hill, now occupied by Col. C. C. Horton, Ogilvie's son-in-law.

After completing this house, which he did in a couple of years, Ogilvie wanted to go in the store again with Jackson, but Jackson had got to running alone and wished to continue so; he had built a brick store on Front street about the middle of block 11, between the Avenue and Chestnut street; he had married and lived up stairs, and had things his own way.

Mr. Ogilve then took William St. John in with him in the mercantile business. They did a smashing business for two or three years.

Ogilvie's next adventure in the way of building was the hotel (the Ogilve House) now the Commercial Hotel. This was too much for the times. He associated a man by the name of Brinton Darlington with him in the building, a man who had no definite idea of what was needed for a hotel. They built a four-story building, using the lower story for store rooms. They succeeded in getting the roof on, when the foundation began to settle and the side walls crack. They commenced to tinker with the walls one time and another, until they have been mostly removed. The west wall along the Avenue is about all that remains of the first foundation and that should be taken out.

But to go back to the mercantile business, they had the lower rooms finished off, in which they opened a store. Ogilvie & St. John bought the Nevada mill, put up the building where the Knight of Pythian's hall is, and moved their store up there. They did an immense amount of business, but the same difficulty hit them that did others in like business—the railroads cut off the grain and pork trade. The result was that Ogilvie & St. John got heavily in debt, and they sold out to Waters & Johns, two young men who had been clerking for them. Ogilve remained at the head of affairs as usual. When the war broke out Johns went into the army as captain and was killed. Waters went in company with J. G. Gordon, the firm name being Gordon & Waters. Then the stock of goods had E. P. White and White & Convers as owners. Ogilvie still stayed around the store; he died on Feb.

5. 1865, with little or nothing left for him in the store, so the proprietor said.

Mr. Ogilvie was one of the most genial and affable men we had; he was liberal to a fault. I have been informed that he was the most liberal donor for the erection of the Presbyterian church, of which he was a member; he was more widely known than any other man in our town. He should have been a rich man, he had every advantage to be be so, if he had embraced them. He was the principal commissioner to sell the lots on the commissioner's quarter section, which embraced the most popular part of the town. Ogilvie bought a good many lots for himself. Lot 8 in block 146, on which I live, was bought from the commissioners by Mr. Ogilvie, and he sold it to me. At one time a tract of land adjoining the city, owned by D. R. Warfield, containing 131 acres, was put in the hands of Peter Jackson as trustee, to secure the payment of $250 that Warfield owed Ogilvie for merchandise. Jackson held it as long as the time agreed upon and then offered it at public sale, Ogilvie bid it in for the amount of the claim, $250, and got it. Of course such dealings as that forced Warfield to take advantage of the bankrupt law and square off, which a great many did about that time. There was absolutely no money at all here then, what little stuff we had to sell was taken to St. Louis and bartered for goods. No money came back from the sales of it.

Mr. Adam Ogilvie was the first merchant here, he worked hard, was strictly honest, handled a large amount of merchandise, and like a majority of our early merchants he was not wealthy when he died, but he was respected and missed by all.

Recollection of Business in the Early Days of Muscatine

Published in the Muscatine Saturday Mail June 12, 1897; written by J P. Walton.

No. 22.

The first harness manufacturer in the town of Bloomington was John M. Kane. He kept a harness shop in a one story building on the north side of Second street, west of Chestnut, near where Jas. St. John now has his grocery store. Kane kept "bach," and, I think, H. H. Hine bached with him. I sold milk to them. Kane was the first saddler and harness maker in the county; he followed that business for twelve or fifteen years; when he got ready he got married and bought a farm and settled down to raising hogs. He died many years ago, his widow is yet living although married a second time.

In the spring of 1843, a young Scotchman came here and opened a shop in a little building on Front street, between Iowa avenue and Chestnut street; he made saddles and harness and kept a wholesale leather store in a small way. We have a practical knowledge of what he kept, as we commenced farming that spring on Muscatine island, and we were in close circumstances, and being out of shoes, we went to the merchant we had been trading with, Peter Jackson, and wanted a pair on credit; he declined to accomodate us. I have often thought that he did us more good in the refusal than he did for himself, for he taught us independence—a good lesson for a young man. We scratched around and gathered together money enough to purchase leather of our then wholesale Scotch leather dealer, Mr. Alex. Jackson, and made our own shoes. Their fashion was not like others had, but they answered the purpose.

Mr. Alexander Jackson started in the harness and saddle business in the spring of 1843 and he soon commenced to increase his business. He had at times a dozen or more men working for him, and perhaps twenty or thirty. Many of the present harness makers were then boys learning their trades.

In 1856 Mr. Jackson sold out to Mr. W. H. Taylor, who kept the shop, which was then located in the store room east of the Hershey State Bank, for about a year; he sold out to Bell & Wilson. They in turn, after a year or so, sold to F. M. Erwin, then after, say two years, Harry Loffland became its manager. He in turn sold to H. S. Compton, who occupied a building on the north side of Second street, east of Sycamore.

During Compton's management the war broke out. Harry got very patriotic, and he was made a commissary or quartermaster, or something that made him quite conspicuous in his own estimation. He had several men working for him; on one occasion three of his men entered into a written agreement if either of the number volunteered the other two would. They went up to the enlisting office and Thomas J. Melvin wrote down his name, then William Fessler followed and Joseph Bilkey had to. They were among the three month's men, and after their term of service was over Bilkey and Fesler bought out Harry Compton. After Harry left for parts unknown to most of us Bilkey and Fesler did not succeed to Bilkey's satisfaction, so he sold out to Fesler and went to farming. Fesler in turn sold to Rublemen & Co., the wholesale men from whom he got his supplies.

Thomas Melvin then went in with Fesler. It is presumed they worked together until Fesler's death.

Joseph Bilkey farmed for a year or two when he returned to the city and bought an interest in a shop run by Martin Herwig on the west side of Iowa avenue, south of the alley beween Second and Third streets. After a short time Bilkey bought his partner out and took his son in with him. The son now deals in that line of goods.

In 1869 J. Rublemen & Co. were wholesale dealers and were under that name for ten or twelve years, when the name was changed to W. H. VanNostrad. At his death the business was closed. Later a new company was organized under the name of the VanNostrand Saddlery Co. This company now runs a large factory on Front street, between Sycamore and Cedar streets, and is doing a large business, all on Muscatine capital.

A brief review of the character of some of the old saddlers will not be out of place. J. M. Kane was a pioneer in every sense of the word; coming here before 1840 a young man, although he had been previously married and had a son, one would suppose he would adopt habits of a new country, whiskey drinking, etc., but he did not. He was always genial and courteous, his shop was a kind of a loafing place—a club room as it would be called now—and John enjoyed it. His rival in business, Alex. Jackson, had no loafing around him; he was in business for the dollar, anything that would not pay he took but little interest in; he married shortly after coming here and stayed at home, taking but little interest in the loafers' quarters, the club room of the times; he is here now much the same as of yore. Mr. Jackson was a great trader, he traded his goods for almost anything he could turn around to his interest. One winter he got about traded out of stock, he had several men men working for him and didn't know how to keep them at work, and he was studying pretty sharply about it when Abijah Winn drove up to his store and told him he had a load of leather to be unloaded, that he had hauled it from Chicago, and that he had a letter from parties in Chicago who had sent the leather cut to be sold on commission. This hit Jackson just right; he loaded Winn with a load of hides which he had traded for and sent him back to Chicago for another load of leather. He got his supplies that winter from Chicago and kept his shop running, making more money than at any previous season. The spring found him with two hundred saddles on hand, they all sold right away to the farmers through the country. This was before the days of cheap buggies; then top buggies were worth from $200 to $250; saddles were popular.

J. Rubleman was very likely a native of Germany, he came here with his father when a small boy, I thing in 1844. His father built a tannery where the Hershey team stable for the mills now stands, and ran it for a few years; he found getting bark cost to much money, and he sold the land and old building and went to Tennessee where bark was plenty and started again. We changed the old tannery building over into a stable for the Hershey Lumber Co. It was afterwards taken, or burned down, and the present barn erected.

We had all forgotten the old tanner, but all at once the son who had grown to manhood appeared and opened a wholesale leather store, for awhile bringing his stock from Tennessee, where his father had lived. He afterwards associated W. H. Van Nostrand with him, and in turn sold out to Van Nostrand and went to Des Moines and went into business. Where he is now or what he is doing I am unable to say.

Mr. W. H Van Nostrand came here with plenty of capital and in connection with the wholesale business he established collars and strap work. and likely saddles. He had several men on the road and did an extensive business which was brought to a speedy end by his accidentally falling down the cellar stairs at his dwelling and dying before relief reached him. Mr. Van Nostrand was a generous and an up-to-date man, although he never married; he was the principal financial man in the Episcopal church to which he belonged; he gave the church more money in recent years than any other two of its members. He had nothing to do with the present Van Nostrand Saddlery Co., it was organized since his death, they using the name.

In our next we will mention the present saddlers and harness makers.

Recollection of Business in the Early Days of Muscatine

Published in the Muscatine Saturday Mail June 19, 1897; written by J. P. Walton.

No. 23.

In our last we wrote about Tom Melvin and William Fesler being in business. William Fesler came here in the forties and worked for Jackson; he married a Miss Crandol and enjoyed himself as well as a harness maker or any pioneer usually did. He got his pay promptly and was equally prompt in spending it. He probably earned money enough if he had only had the disposition of his boss to keep money, to have been a rich man. His later partner, Tom. Melvin, was much the same in his youthful days; neither of them left large estates to be squandered by an executor.

There seemed to have been three leading manufacturing establishments here at different times. The first was A. Jackson from 1843 to 1856 or '57, then came Pratt & Co. If we recollect aright, Harry Compton went in with Pratt or bought him out and run the business as Compton & Co. and did some business during the dull times that preceeded the war. After Compton left, J. Rubleman came, he did not manufacture much if any; he was a wholesale dealer.

Most of the later harness makers either learned their trades of Jackson or of Compton, or at least worked for them, yet a few did not.

Henry Hagerman opened a shop away up on Mulberry street to far away from business to succeed and did not. A man by the name of Andrews opened a shop at the lower end of Second street; he was here in 1856, how long he staid I can't tell. Two other firms were here awhile, during or after 1866, C. Renck and R. Burl. I think they did not remain here very long.

Henry Weisse came here and started a harness shop in A. Jackson's old stand in company with W. G. Taylor, in 1876. Weisse afterwards erected a building and occupied it, on the north side of Second street, between Cedar and Walnut. He was a close, saving man and accumulated considerable property before his death, which occurred quite recently. W. G. Taylor left here and went to Mt. Pleasant, Iowa, where he became wealthy, so I have been informed.

Harry Loffland was one of Jackson's old hands, who afterwards went into business on his own account, or perhaps with some one else. He finally gave it up and went on a farm on the Island, later on the road as a canvasser for the tombstone business, in which he was very successful, but not very particular about his habits and saved but little money and died poor. He is remembered by the old settlers as a prince of good fellows.

Harbaugh & Coover opened a harness shop about the close of the war; how long they staid in the business I can't say. L. W. Harbaugh worked a while for Compton, previous to going in on his own hook. He finally sold out to Father Brent who conducted the business a year or more.

In 1879 Adam Hartman was in business on Second street near Sycamore street. He is still working at his trade, being employed at Bilkey's shop.

In 1883 P. B. Speeer went into the business on the south side of Second street, a few doors east of Cedar, and remained in it for five or six years, with what success I don't know. He died a few years ago.

J. H. Herwig came here, worked awhile for the old shops, and finally started in business for himself; he built a fine new shop on the south side of Second street, east of Sycamore, where he did business until his health failed, when he retired and rented his building for other purposes.

Of the present harness makers now in business in this city whose names we have not mentioned are: Joseph Bilkey, jr., son of Joseph Bilkey previously mentioned, at No. 212 Iowa avenue; John Freyermuth, 421-23 east

Second street; Quandt & Otto, 304 east Second street, and Jacob Hess, at 212 east Second street.

Jacob Hess is one of the old setlers and one of A. Jackson's cubs; he learned the trade and worked at it till the war broke out, when he enlisted and served a full term, came back and went into business with Giesler; for a long time he was foreman of the harness department in W. H. Van Nostrand's manufactory. He now owns the building he occupies and is one of our popular dealers.

While writing up the business of saddles, harness and the like, there is one firm we must not miss, the Hampe Bros. They are the oldest continuous dealers in our city, having learned their trades of Alex. Jackson. They commenced on their own hook in 1865; they came to Muscatine in 1854 and in 1855 commenced to work for instruction. When they started in business they had but a small capital, but went on the principal that a small profit and a quick sale would bring the answer in the long run. This principal they have followed up to the present time, as we conclude from the fact that they have accumulated more wealth than any other one dealer in their line in this city, Mr. Jackson included. They can now sell their goods cheap if they want to, they do not have to borrow money to do business on, and judging from the amount of patronage they are receiving we think they have struck the right way to do business. They are now located at No. 126 west Second street.

Recollection of Business in the Early Days of Muscatine

Published in the Muscatine Saturday Mail June 26, 1897; written by J. P. Walton.

No. 24.
THE SMALLEY PARK

Frequently known as the "old fair grounds," it is situated at the northeast end of Second street; was a part of the old Barkalo claim purchased by Abe Smalley and entered by him or for his father. After the death of his father the land was divided up among his heirs. The most prominent part at the end of Second street is now owned by Sheprad Smalley, a man amply able to donate it to the city for a park. We hope he will.

This park was turned out for a common cow pasture for many years. After that thoroughfare known as the "graded road" was cut through, the land on the west was divided up into lots and sold. The place now occupied as a garden by Joseph Bennett was used for a fair ground from 1852 to 1855. The fair was then moved to the Island to the land now belonging to T. B. Holcomb and Barney Kemper and used as market gardens.

In 1856 a company was organized and purchased this 40 acres of Muscatine Island land. The state fair was held here for two years, 1856 and '57. After that the county fair was held on the Island until the war broke out, when agricultural fairs had to suspend all over the the country. The company's affairs were wound up, and the fair was then moved to John Barnard's farm along the Iowa City road, as Mulberry street extension was then called; here it remained for two or three years, but was found to be too far out from the city. So it was moved to the Smalley grounds—Smalley's Park. Here it remained for a number of years. The improvements finally became very much out of repair; the main building had burned down, and as a desirable purchase could not be reached, the present fair grounds on Mulberry street extension was secured. But for some reason the agricultural fairs have not been successful at the present quarters.

But we will return to the old fair grounds; the Smalleys have pretty much devoted them to the public use, and they have not received much or anything for the use of the ground. The big circuses have paid well when here. The agricultural society only released the grounds from taxation while they used them.

These grounds have been used for Fourth of July celebrations and public gatherings. We recollect a Fourth of July celebration in 1861 when 10,000 was a small estimate for the number of people present on the occasion. All the big speakers were on hand, there was one important fellow from up in Cedar county who did not indorse such coercion sentiments as were uttered; he succeeded in getting a chance to be heard in a small way; he soon found he was in the wrong crowd and had to leave with a thousand after him. I think he got away without any serious injury. On this occasion a rebel flag was displayed. This flag had been captured somewhere in Missouri by the First Iowa boys. It had only been fairly hung out until some one reached for it and it got into the crowd. It was torn into shreads and we secured a piece of it. The party who displayed it did not expect to have it destroyed. It was a valuable trophy, the only excuse was the people were mad.

On these grounds the large political meetings were held. On one occasion Weaver and Kasson were to have a discussion. Weaver had the lead and worried the crowd so long that when Kasson's turn came dinner interfered with his audience. The people "got onto him" and knew what he was at and did not all vote as Jim told them to. Weaver had been stopping at Rev. Davidson's but when Davidson found what he was at he "fired him," and Weaver had to take quarters at the hotel. Kasson stopped at Mrs. Cora Weed's home and was well treated.

On these same grounds the democrats held their barbecues. The first one we recollect was under the supervision of William Chambers, sr., some forty years ago, as chief cook. He had a hole three feet wide, twelve feet long and three feet deep dug in the ground; a fire made of hard wood was kept burning for a day and a half so as to get the bottom filled with coals. The beef in place of being roasted whole as was promised, was cut in pieces and placed on bars of iron over the fire; it had to be occasionally turned over and after an all night's cooking it was ready for serving. It may have been very good but it did not look very inviting. It was removed to a table and underwent the process of cutting; anyone wanting a piece pushed his way through the crowd and secured it if he could.

The democrats have had another barbecue since then, managed on a more modern system, but it did not suit them near as well as the first.

In these old fair grounds Major Shipley distinguished himself as a pyrotechnicst by presenting a fine display of fire works in a hard shower of rain.

On these grounds one of the earliest state firemens' tournaments was held which ended in a rumpus among our fire boys that has lasted till the present time, and the recollection of which will last as long as any of the old ones are living.

In this same park, if such we could call it, was held one of the early encampments of the second regiment of the Iowa National Guard, under the command of Colonel Lyman Banks. As a whole it was one of the most "toney" encampments of the state.

The Patrons of Husbandry held a big meeting at the old fair grounds with Farmer S. McNutt as orator. This was the last big meeting the Patrons ever held in this county, and on that day they started their manufactory which proved too much for them.

Here the Thirty-Fifth Regiment held one of their reunions. They encamped on the grounds, spun their yarns and stole the officer's rations and the amnunition for the sham battle that was to take place the following day. The battle came off all the same and the party that was short of amnunition was defeated. On this occasion Captain Wiles with his veteran artillery won praises from the "stay at homes" who were out there to be treated to a taste of war.

We hope the foregoing recollections, although but a limited number of the public events mention as taking place at the old fair grounds will call up some pleasant recollection to the reader. We also hope the Commercial Club will secure the grounds for a public park for our city.

Recollections of

Business in the Early Days of Muscatine.

BY J. P. WALTON.

No. 25.

Early in the forties, likely 1843, an enthusiastic young man with a young family of three or four children dropped down in our city. I said dropped down, for but few knew "from whence he came" or for what he come for. He worked some of the time at the carpenter business and got drunk some of the time for a variety. Shortly after his arrival the Washingtonian Temperance Society came; he, Zephaniah Washburn, joined this society and became very enthusiastic in the work. For a good many years it was supposed this society was named after Zephaniah, but such was not the case. Zephaniah became a great Methodist exorter and could always be found in the amen corner.

Our acquaintance with him began in 1844 or 1845; he, like all generous men with small means, was usually hard up, and had to work to school his children and keep the wolf from the door. Zeph. could almost always be found at all public gatherings and was always loaded for an offhand speech, these speeches were not usualy very short, if Zephanah was around the Methodist class meeting was always supplied with a talker. He became acquainted with almost every one in our city, and while not very popular was not objectionable to any one. After he became aged he attended the Old Settlers' meetings; it was no uncommon thing for him to be reminded that he was taking too much time.

As a carpenter he was not a first class mechanic, so had to turn his attention to anything that would pay. For quite a while, about 1850, he acted as engineer at Barlow's flouring mill, which stood near where Stein's Music hall now stands. While acting as engineer, in March,

1851, he was elected as the first mayor of our city, which position he kept for a short time; he found he was not suited for the place and resigned. We believe that if many of his successors had followed his precedence and resigned the city would have been better for such a rash act. I think he was the only mayor of Muscatine who ever resigned. After reaching an advanced age he went to California and lived until his death with his son, L. H. Washburn, of whom we will venture a few remarks. He is now living in Los Angeles. When a young man he lost his arm and then turned his attention to the law, was admitted to the bar, although he did but little in that line. He was a better real estate man; was full of imaginary schemes, especially railroads. If any one had dropped into his office he would have seen a large map of Iowa marked all over with "blue lines"—Washburn's railroad routes. He probably did more real work to secure and locate the Muscatine Western railroad than any one else. He was out early and late and saw the line constructed, but when the divide came, if any did come, Hart. was not in it. I think he was elected as justice of the peace awhile, at all events, he served on the city council in 1867 and 1868. During his time and through his efforts macadam was introduced as a permanent street pavement, the first the city had ever built.

He saw the necessity of having some moderate system of sidewalks; he got a law passed by the legislature allowing cities to fill that need by building second-class sidewalks, four feet wide, irrespective of the grade. Before that, when the streets were graded the city would require a ten-foot pavement put down. All smaller walks were put down by private enterprise, or by subscription. The result was, not many were laid—they were few and far between. The second-class sidewalk was one of the grandest improvements for the new cities that was ever adopted, but the originator never got the credit he should have had. During war times, L. H. Washburn took the lead in many patriotic schemes. He was the chief enrolling officer for this county. We recollect helping him enroll Bloomington township, which then embraced this city, Fruitland township and the present Bloomington township. I enrolled the Fruitland part of the township for army work. He was so zealous for the Union cause that he neglected his own town, as it afterward proved. He allowed it to raise more than its quota of men, a thing that may have looked well to those who were not subject to military duty. But not so to everyone. For instance, a man in Bloomington township was drafted and had to pay $800 for a substitute. I was not in this list, for I joined with some 20 or 30 others and paid $100 each to keep our ward ahead of the draft. After the war was over we frequently heard it bragged of, that our quota was always ahead of what it need to have been. Well, we paid for it, as before stated. After the war Mr. Washburn went into the real estate business and caught the railroad fever, as all real estate men apparently do. J. H. Munroe and S. Emerson Whicher have both had it, Kemble and Horton were seriously threatened with it, but G. M. Titus and Henry Jayne have it bad. We hope they will do as well as Washburn did and get a road and make more money out of it than he did. We have not as much fear about the latter part of the proposition as we have over the former, which we most desire.

We occasionally see a communication from Mr. Washburn, which we read with great interest and wish he were here with us.

Recollection of Business in the Early Days of Muscatine

Published in the Muscatine Saturday Mail July 10, 1897; written by
J P. Walton.

No. 26.

The question is often asked, "What is the commisioner's quarter?" and it is often spoken of as such. Our town, Bloomington, was first claimed by George Davenport. He built a trading house here and claimed a half a mile square—a quarter of a mile above, a quarter below and half a mile back from the house. He sold his claim to Col. John Vannatta, who took Suel Foster, Capt. Clark, sr., of Buffalo, and perhaps some others, and laid out the town, had a plat made and had it recorded with a plat to accompany it, or to be the record. It was lost for a great many years, but it has recently been found and restored to the Recorder's office. This plat was laid off without regard to the government lines, it was nearly square to the river. The lots were sold —that is to say, the claims on the lots were sold, but before a perfect title could be secured they had to be entered from the government by some one and a deed made to the claimer.

The government passed a law allowing any organized county to enter any quarter section of land it thought proper, irrespective of the claimers, and sell the same at its own price, the proceeds to be applied in building a court house, or perhaps court house and jail. Our Muscatine County Commissioners selected the south-west quarter of section 35, embracing the best part of the city, and appraised the lots so as to raise some $15,000. They valued them from $5 to $100 each, or perhaps more, according to location. They gave a reasonable length of time to a claimer of a lot to come forward and prove his claim and pay the assessment and get a deed. If no claimant appeared within the allotted time, the lot was subject to purchase by any one at the appraised value. A great many lots were sold this way. Adam Ogilvie was the commissioner to attend to the sales and make the deeds. This gave him a good chance to make good selections for himself, which he did; he probably bought more lots than any one else. Where he got the money to pay for them was a mystery for some time. But they were all paid for. There was a question raised about the validity of the title, as it was a deed from Ogilvie to Ogilvie, the same man. As everything was all straight and no fraud, and no one to complain but the county, and they did not, the lawyers never succeeded in making anything out of that question.

The upper part of the town of Bloomington was purchased of the government by Charles F. Warfield and deeded to the claimants. I never heard of any misunderstanding with this transaction. The lower part was bought by Suel Foster, who deeded the lots to the claimants and the streets to the city. In deeding Front street Foster claimed he only deeded a street sixty feet wide; the city claimed to the water's edge. A suit was commenced by Foster, with S. C. Hastings as his attorney, for possession. The citizens held an indignation meeting, talked very hard of Foster and Hastings, and secured Stephen Whicher to defend the city's interest. In the meantime Hastings decided to go to California, and Foster went with him. The case was dropped. We have often thought that Foster had the title, and would have held it in spite of the city if the case had been tested in the higher courts.

But to return to the "Commissioner's Quarter," as it was called. These lots were all sold to raise money to build the Court House, and the money applied to the purpose. In the spring of 1840 it was commenced. W. A. Brownell had the contract to build it for $15,000, and employed a Mr. Truesdale as his builder. I think the plans were furnished by a Capt. Frierson, a graduate of West Point, although not in the U. S. service at that time. The plan was a good one; no better court room exists in Iowa. It has been taken as a model several times by other counties for court rooms. The building is now standing essentially as it was when first completed, 56 years ago, the oldest public building within the state. The inside burned out, but the wall never bulged a bit. The wood work of the interior and the roof was restored in a short time. The fire originated from an imperfect flue and burned quite slowly. All the records and other property were removed to other quarters, mostly to the jail. During the time that the building was not usable the court met in Hare's Hall (now Armory Hall). In the restoration of the roof a larger dome was put on, surmounted by a statue of Justice, that from disgust or some other cause concluded to come down, the commissioners having a little doubt about the execution of her calling while up there, they concluded to fence her out; hence the iron cresting on the top.

This old Court House is the Fanueil Hall of Iowa. Within its walls have occurred more startling events than in any other building in the state. We will not venture to enumerate any of them at this time. There is one thing we wish to condemn, and that is the disposition to destroy old buildings. We hear it hinted that it is about time to take down the old Court House and replace it with another. We hope that time will not come for the next five centuries at least. Long before that time this restless class of people will give place to a more permanent class. Talk about taking down Fanueil Hall, the North Church or the old State House, all Boston would revolt. So would Philadelphia at an attempt to remove Carpenters' Hall or the old State House. That disposition will sooner or later reach Iowa, and if our old Court House is allowed to stand our children will call us blessed.

If more room is needed, add to it, as the people of Boston have to their old State House until the additions are much larger than the original. Keep the old Court House is our request.

Recollections of the Early Hoosier Settlers Near Muscatine.

Published in the Muscatine Saturday Mail July 17, 1897; written by J P. Walton.

No. 27.

On page 758 of McClure's Magazine for July, 1897, appears an article entitled, "The Grindstone Question," by Robert Barr. This short article of only eleven pages contains all that Edward Eggleston used a whole book to accomplish. The article has displayed more talent than the "Hoosier Schoolmaster" did, without taking so much time. While both "The Grindstone Question" and "The Hoosier Schoolmaster" were works of fiction, cases of a similar nature do occasionally occur. The environments of Muscatine are not without a parallel.

Drury township, the southern one of Rock Island county, Ill., was originally largely, if not entirely, settled by Hoosiers. They came there in 1833 and '34, and many did not leave, as the earliest settlers frequently did. As a result the county was quite primitive for a number of years, and it is yet twenty years behind its neighbors on the west side of the Mississippi river.

But to our story. Some six or eight miles east of the city stood an old school house. Among the Hoosiers of the second or third growth were those that followed the custom of turning or barring the teacher out when it suited them, and especially in the holidays. The penalty to be paid was a treat from the teacher. This was not always convenient, as teachers never got their pay until the term was out, and not much at that. In one of the winters in the early sixties, one teacher had been barred out and left, another was turned out, and as a result a vacancy occurred. A young man of our acquaintance who had previously had some experience at school teaching applied to the school director, the late Hon. Err Thornton, for a "job" The director informed him that he could have the place upon one condition, and that was that he should teach the term out or get no pay for what he did teach. This our young friend, Mr. Jones, agreed to, the director doubting his ability to fulfill the contract.

Mr. Jones was a wayward son of a Quaker. He was a native of New Hampshire, had acquired a good early education, but not being suited with the staid habits of the Friends, he wandered away from home and had fallen in company with the sporting men of New England and became quite expert in the practices of the prize ring. His parents came west and settled near our city. Of course our pedagogue followed. He was about 24 years of age, a small, heavy set fellow; hence the doubt of the school director about his ability to take care of himself.

In the school there were some three or four large girls and as many large boys, any one of the boys larger than the teacher.

The girls admired the teacher, and the boys did not like it, so they "allowed to take him down a bit." Of course a small provocation was sufficient to bring on an encounter, headed by the largest boy, and followed by two others. Contrary to the expectation of the leader he received a blow on the nose that landed him on the floor, the second one was soon lying by his side; the third concluded not to venture any further alone and went to his seat. After that event the school moved along smoothly until the end of the term. Jones got his pay.

We are indebted to the late Frank E. Jones, the teacher, for this story.

Another School Teacher Story.

Published in the Muscatine Saturday Mail July 24, 1897; written by
J P. Walton.

No. 28.

When we first commenced this series of Recollections some six months or more ago we expected to confine our recollections to the business interests, but as this is the dull time of the year we have concluded to change the subject for a few issues, expecting to "resume as business revives."

Sixty years ago it was very common for an author to collect a few facts, weave them into a romantic story with a title, A Romance, "Founded on facts." This can be safely said of our story. We were personally acquainted with its main characters, but are indebted to the late Hon. G. W. Van Horne for a portion of it, which we give in his own language. The facts in the sequel, which will appear in the next number of the MAIL, we collected from other sources:

Among the passengers up the river on board the Gipsey in 1839, was a young lady from Ohio, who was accompanying her relatives in their emigration to Iowa. Muscatine or Bloomington was the destination, and here in fact the family came ashore. Jerusha stayed aboard. No, sir; I have given her Indian name; her United States name must remain sub rosa. It happened that on board the Gipsey, Jerusha and two other members of the emigrant's family, became acquainted with a gentleman who was largely interested in the prosperity of Rockingham, a thriving town of four or five houses on this side of the river three miles below Davenport. There was some special work to be done there which suited the disposition of two of Jerusha's relatives, while our heroine herself was wanted to serve the town as schoolmarm. It was decided that the three should proceed at once on the Gipsey to the place then threatening the very existence of its rival—Davenport.

Rockingham was reached in due time and our friends began their work. But it was not long before Jerusha was transferred to another scene. There lies in the middle of the river about three miles this side of Davenport, an island two miles in length and from an eigthth to a quarter of a mile in width, and here resided in this year, 1839, a branch of the Davenport family. You might be pardoned for thinking that I am about to describe in this island something that shall bring to your mind the beautiful island blissful home, which, under the name of Blennerhassett, has given so much romance, nay, so much sad history to the famous island of the Ohio. Much to my regret I find nothing but two or three homely log cabins on this island, and as for the "grounds," suppose we say that the little land cultivated was mostly given to wheat. But occupying these rude cabins, standing near the southern extremity of the island, lived Adrian Davenport, his wife and father, and quite a family of children. Home is home, be it ever so humble; and a Davenport was a Davenport, whether living in the ancestral halls of old England, or in the log hut of the American pioneer. Adrian Davenport saw his children growing up like weeds, promising neither beauty nor worth to the world, and he determined upon getting this smart young Rockingham schoolmarm into his family. I don't know what special inducements were offered to our heroine, but such as they were, they were effective, and she became an inmate of the Island home.

Among the notable events transpiring on this island were the frequent visits made by Indian chiefs upon old Mr. Davenport. He had formerly filled the office of Indian Agent for a long time, and though now retired and quite feeble with age, the Indians did not forget that here was their friend, and their wants often brought them to Credit Island, as it was called. Turkora was the son of an Indian chief. His father was the first warrior of his tribe, and Turkora was regarded as the immediate heir to the thrown upon the old king's decease. Poor Turkora; the black eyes of Jerusha proved his ruin! On his first visit with his father and other warriors to the island, he could scarcely conceal the emotions of a "first love." He lingered long after the chief's departure and was only persuaded to go at all by Davenport's commands. On the next visit of the chief, Turkora was one of the number. A few days after this second departure, Turkora reappeared on the island, and this time he would not be driven away. He became a member of the Davenport family, and whenever the Indians were to visit the island Turkora would appear to be forewarned and nothing would be seen of him until the tribe had left; then he would come bounding back with all the antics of a dog returning to a long lost home.

Among the duties which fell to Turkora's lot was the rowing of Mrs. Davenport or Jerusha to the Iowa shore whenever those ladies wished to visit Rockingham. I am told that Davenport expressed at times some apprehensions for the safety of the ladies, more particularly of Jerusha, while thus in charge of the Indian boy. But no great degree of uneasiness could have been felt, as Turkora was pretty constantly employed at this task.

One soft autumnal evening Jerusha put on her shopping attire, and calling for Turkora, requested his arm for a row to the shore. The boat is entered by the maiden, Turkora springs in after her with the paddle, and off they go upon the current of the Mississippi. The beautiful calm of the evening was conducive to reverie, and Jerusha sat for some moments unconscious of the outer world. Then awaking to her situation, she discovered that instead of ferrying her to Rockingham, Turkora was fast plying the boat down the stream! For a moment fears overcame her. Turkora was no longer the useful errand boy, but a frightful savage, hurrying to where he could escape with her to his home in the wilderness. Could this be possible! Was this horrible fate in store for her? She throws her glance toward the shore—and above, just starting from the Rockingham bank, came two boats in pursuit. She is safe and she knows it. And Turkora feels the lessening distance between his canoe and those in pursuit and knows that he has lost.

"You'll only make trouble for yourself, Turkora," says our heroine. "Turn your course before they come further."

The Indian boy smiles the smile of despair, drops his paddle into the drifting current, seats himself in the drifting canoe and awaits his pursuers.

And Jerusha did her shopping in Rockingham that day.

THE WAY JERUSHA GOT MARRIED;
A SEQUEL TO NO. 28.

Published in the Muscatine Saturday Mail July 31, 1897; written by J. P. Walton.

No. 29.

After Jerusha's adventure with Turkora, her Indian admirer, as mentioned in No. 28, she returned to Bloomington and lived with her uncle. This uncle was one of the prominent men of the place. His house was the center of the best society. Evening parties were quite common. The lawyer, doctor, judge, sheriff, county clerk, and justice of the peace, were frequent visitors on such occasions; the minister was not usually one of the guests, as one of the amusements for the evening were mock marriages, which were frequently practiced, and it was no uncommon thing to hear of their proving real. On one occasion a majority of the society in the town were present. Jerusha and a young man present were selected as a suitable match—perhaps at the suggestion of the young man himself. Jerusha stood up with him, the justice of the peace officiating. When the ceremony was through all but pronouncing them man and wife, the county clerk interfered by asking the almost bride if she knew the marriage would be legal. This question was a stunner. Taking the advantage of woman's common or last resort for getting out of a bad scrape, she fainted. This of course stopped the wedding. When the county clerk interferred he may have been thinking of Miles Standish. Not long after this, the clerk and Jerusha were walking together. Upon the spur of the moment he proposed to go to the preacher's and get married. She consented. So they stopped at the Court House, and he made out a license. (It would seem as though our present incumbent was not the first clerk who had to issue a license to himself. Could not wait until their successors were qualified.) They then went to Rev. John Stocker's home and were married. After the wedding she went home to her uncle and the clerk back to the Court House. On the following day he called on his bride to take her buggy riding. Her aunt interfered and claimed to have charge of her niece. The clerk presented his wife to his newly acquired aunt, much to her surprise. In the course of time, her husband's death left Jerusha a widow, still young and fascinating, with some property at her disposal. Proposals for a second marriage were abundant, a young widower seeming most likely to win the prize. He had secured her promise several times, but no date could be fixed for the marrige. Jerusha had an uncle, we will call him George, who lived in the country who was a justice of the peace. Upon one occasion when the widower and Jerusha were out at Uncle George's on a visit, a promise was secured from the uncle to marry them if the time should ever be arranged. The uncle lived so far in the country that he frequently stopped at Jerusha's over night when he came to town. The widower hearing the uncle was expected on a certain night, went to the county clerk and procured a license with the understanding that if it was not used it should be returned and no record made of it. In due time the uncle arrived. The widower proposed that the long deferred marriage should be solemnized. Jerusha knowing that the clerk was out of town and thinking that a license could not be procured that night, consented. The uncle performed the ceremony and pronounced them man and wife, afterwhich the bridegroom saluted the bride as Mrs. ———, which cognomen she declined to acknowlege. She claimed only to have been married in fun, as no license was issued; which mistake the uncle set all right by producing the one handed to him by the now happy man, and declaring his niece to be a married woman, and that she could not get out of it. Jerusha, still supposing it to be a joke, spent the evening in a very joyful manner. When leaving time came the bride bade her leige lord goodnight as she had done before. He objected, and claimed he was married and that it was not his wish to play the part of a single man any longer, but he was compelled to return to his former quarters. For the next two or three days but few persons knew of the marriage; however, the story soon got out through the town. Both parties received many congratulations upon their good luck. In the course of three or four days they took a ride in the county, stopping at a friend's, where the matter was satisfactorily arranged.

Twenty-five years after this last and unexpected marriage, it was our good fortune to be present at one of the most pleasant and extensive silver wedding parties held in one of our suburan residences, that the city ever witnessed. On that occasion Jerusha had both children and grand-children present. She has since gone to her long rest. Her children and grand-children are among our best citizens, occupy prominent positions and are highly esteemed.

Recollections of Early Settlers.

S. W. STEWART, OF WILTON.

Published in the Muscatine Saturday Mail August 7, 1897; written by J P. Walton.

No. 30.

Mr. S. W. Stewart was born on December 16th, 1816, in the southern part of Ohio. He married Hulda M. Reynolds on August 3d, 1837, and came to Iowa in 1838 and settled at Moscow.

Mr. Stewart and his wife are fine examples of the pioneer. They came to Iowa in 1838 and settled in the town of Moscow. In 1839 they built their cabin and moved into it and opened a "wood shop," where chairs, spinning wheels and household furniture were manufactured. It is probable that wagons and plows were repaired when needed. Mr. Stewart soon became one of the prominent men of the town. We give a description of the place, it being contributed to the Wilton Review by Mr. Stewart some years ago:

"By this time we were very well started in the world; we had the tavern, the whisky, a wood shop, a blacksmith shop, a broom shop; a horse was kept in town during the season; we had three doctors; we had no preacher; there was no great use for them only on Sunday and then the town was full of them and running over. For amusements we hunted, fished, lay round the town and yarned and bragged, pitched horseshoes, shot at a mark for beef, or to keep our hand in, filled in the time with a horse race or a fight. The usages of horse racing have been improved; the standing bet then for a quarter race was a gallon of whisky; for half mile or mile it sometimes went at five gallons. The whisky was to be drunk on the ground. If any was left over it was to be kept for a rainy Saturday. It was against the rules to carry it home before drinking. When a barrel of whisky was first tapped it was usually worth 50 cents per gallon, but after being exposed to the rains and the Cedar river until it was somewhat water-soaked it could be had for 25 cents a gallon.

"Moscow was not a great place for fighting. There was some very stout men about the place. When they got mad they acted as if they wanted to hurt some one. If you wanted a fight, some whisky mixed with a little lip would bring it as a rule. Rochester was the place to get the nice fight, where you were neither kicked, struck, scratched or bit; they would sometimes tear each other's clothes and get some sand in their mouths after fighting several days. They often came to Moscow to shooting matches and other occasions where whisky was likely to be plenty; while they were sober they were well behaved, but whisky would bring out their lip. While it was possible to stand the barking fits, no attention was given them, but when it came too thick some Moscow man, who had more whisky than patience, would put his mark on them and send them home for repairs. The Rochester men could talk long and loud; that was their best hold.

"We had another game that was was very fascinating when we had a little money; it was seven-up. The stakes were a cent a corner, and we would work away at it all night when our blood was up. We came out sometimes as much as ten cents ahead, and oftener came out behind, but our misfortune was we had no money, and they would not let us play more than a month on tick."

Those were the pioneer days of Iowa. Our first acqaintance with Stewart was after he had left Moscow and come to Muscatine. Here he worked at carpenter work for several years. He was always known to be an outspoken and fearless man.

He used to love to argue on any question or anything that might come up; the question that he could not hold an interesting conversation on was not very easy to find. I think much of his information was gained that way. During the year 1852 or '53, S. M. McKibben had a lumber office on Second street west of Walnut street; here a number of our citizens met and spent their evenings until 9 or 10 o'clock. Questions of all descriptions were discussed. Rev. Henry Clay Dean, S. W. Stewart, A. J. Fimple, J. P. Walton, S. M. McKibben and some four or five more made what would now be considered a literary club. Stewart sometimes got the name of being contrary. We never thought so. We always thought that with proper reasoning Stewart would change his views. To illustrate. We had a man by the name of Levi Goldsbury who had much the same habit as Stewart; he loved to argue. It was said that on one occasion they got seated on a log, and commenced an argument, before they quit each had converted his opponent. They did not change places on the log, they simply changed views on the subject of discussion.

Mr. Stewart was generous to a fault. Where there was sorrow and sickness he could be found, lending a helping hand. His contributions were of a personal nature, that is to say, if he could help any one he was always willing to do so. He rarely gave money, for he had but little to give. He gave something more valuable - his personal labor and attention.

On one occasion in the year 1855, during the cholera time, a young man came to our city and took lodging in a house near where Mr. Stewart lived, and soon took quite sick. A doctor was called, who prescribed for him but pronounced his case hopeless and declined to come any more. Within the previous twenty-four hours two or three deaths occured from cholera, one of them in an adjoining house. The boarding house keeper and wife left in fright, with no one to care for the young man. Stewart visited him and said it was too bad to let that young, strong Irishman die for the want of care; so he went to nursing him. He procured ice and applied to his head and cooled off the fever. By his attentive care, without much medical assistance, the young man pulled through and has ever been grateful for the nursing he received from Mr. Stewart.

The then young man is still living in our city, although quite gray. I met him one day last week and informed him that Mr. Stewart and wife were going to celebrate their sixtieth wedding anniversary and that a few of his old acquaintances were going to make a little presentation to him, and if he wished to we would include him in our number. He did not seem to comprehend what we were doing and went off. He soon returned and responded to a share with the others, together with more thanks than any of the others had expressed.

On Tuesday, August 3d, 1897, Mr. and Mrs. Stewart celebrated their sixtieth wedding day at their beautiful home in Wilton. Several from our city visited them and found them enjoying good health, and to all appearances the chances were good to celebrate many more wedding anniversaries. One of our prominent old bachelors pronounced it a wonderful celebration. We thought so too, for we have no data of more than two occurrances in our county.

Gambling in the Forties.

BY J. P. WALTON.

No. 31.

In the first half of the present century the undesirable population of the older states largely went to the new or frontier part of the country. Texas got more that its share. It used to be a saying in the eastern states, about persons that had left in a hurry, that they had gone to Texas. That was not always the case. In the early times the Mississippi river got its share. During the forties when most of the traveling was done on the river there was a class of men that traveled on steamboats and gambled for a livelihood. It was frequently said that the owners of the steamboats were interested in their profits; at all events they were there all the time. They traveled in pairs or triplets. You could hardly go into the social cabin in the evening without seeing gambling going on. As journeys were usually long and tedious the passengers frequently took a hand in the game to pass away the time, but before they got through they were generally worsted. There was always some one looking on and watching the games. Of course the players were liberal and were willing that outsiders should share with them. The check system was not in use, so the money had to be put down or no game. It was astonishing the amount of money that was in sight. Gambling was carried on openly without any fear of interruption while on the boats, and there was but little restriction on the land. This habit of gambling was not confined to the river; all the towns along the river had places for gambling.

Bloomington had its share of gambling houses early in the forties. John Cobb kept a saloon on the south corner of Second street and Iowa Avenue, where Cook, Musser Co.'s bank is now located. This was one of the principal places of meeting for the sporting men. On one occasion a lumberman from the north, while waiting here to sell his lumber and get it measured, stopped in at Cobb's and got to playing poker with one of our citizens. This citizen knew that the lumberman had money, and "put it up" for him. The lumberman was unsuccessful and lost some $60, but concluded to try it the next night with the same parties. In the meantime he had secured his friend. They played with a deck with five aces in it. After playing a while they arranged it so the citizen had four kings and an ace, an invincible. The lumberman had four aces and a queen. Then the betting begun. The lumberman had received the pay for his lumber in $20 Missouri bank bills (the best money in circulation). The $20 bank bills of the Missouri State Bank of St. Louis passed all over the west and were more to be desired than a five pound note on the Bank of England. The citizen used gold. After putting up some $300 on a side the citizen ran out of money. The lumberman went $100 more. The citizen pulled out his gold watch and chain and offered to put it up for $100 to call the lumberman. The lumberman placed the $20 bills in a pile and wanted to see if the citizen had put down as much money as he had. In counting over the gold he placed it on top of the bills. He then says, "What have you got?" "An invincible," says the citizen. The lumberman showing his four aces and a queen said, "Here is a hand that will take that," at the same time grabbing the money. The citizen and a friend grabbed him to take the money away from him, but the lumberman was a stouter man than both of them and they could not do it. The citizen grabbed his watch and chain and secured that, but lost some $300 in money.

The citizen began to talk about getting the sheriff and having the lumberman arrested, but the sheriff, then as now (?), never visited these gambling places, and of course could not be found. There was quite a number of a certain class of sporting men who learned that the game was on and drifted in to see it. Among the number was a liveryman whom the lumberman knew; and not wishing to be delayed with an arrest, he asked him what he would charge to take him to Salem, now Fairport.

He offered to do it for $5, which he paid, and they started at once, the liveryman's brother driving the team. When he arrived at Salem he was still within the county. He then hired the driver to take him to Davenport and gave him as pay two town lots, one on Front street opposite the Rock Island freight depot, the other on Fourth street near Chestnut. The first mentioned lot the driver traded for nine barrels of whisky to a man that lived near Black Hawk in Louisa county. Of course the whisky was sold for the money.

We occasionally hear of gambling nowadays, but it is not so common as it was in the early days.

The Islands in the Mississippi.

Published in the Muscatine Saturday Mail August 21, 1897; written by J. P. Walton.

No. 32

The local names of some of the islands in the river are quite old. Island No. 335, the first island below the city, has always been known as the "Towhead." It had better be known as Moving island, from the fact it has moved from the state of Illinois to Iowa. In 1838 when Iowa was organized as a territory it was in Illinois. The state never exercised any jurisdiction over it or attempted to. Iowa was the first to lay claim to it. The law then defined the boundery as being the middle of the main channel of the Mississippi river. At that time the west channel was the main one. The east channel at low water was not deep enough to permit steam boats to go through The channel commenced to change about 1840, and so did the island. The river washed the earth off from the east side and filled in on the west side. I am well satisfied that the island has moved within my recollection in this manner more than the width of itself and is the same "Towhead" yet, although it is quite likely that not a foot of the same earth is there now that was there sixty years ago. Moving Island is a very appropriate name. It is quite probable that if Mr. T. D. Smith, the owner, lives another sixty years he will find his island moved clear to the shore on the Iowa side.

Island No. 337, known as "Blanchard Island," got its name from Ahimaaz Blanchard, who owned a farm on Muscatine Island opposite its head. Blanchard used to cut considerable wood there in the winter and haul it across the river on the ice and sell it to the steamboats in the spring and summer. The name was applied about 1840.

The next island below was known as "Barcus Island;" it is No. 345 and is on the Illinois side of the river eight or nine miles below Muscatine. It got its name from Mr. Thomas Barcus, who dealt in wood and had a cabin on the island where he lived. In the winter time he cut steamboat wood, likely in the winters of 1846 and '47. In 1848 he lived in a cabin on the Iowa shore, and was bitten by a rattle snake and died.

Island No. 446 or Bogus Island is the largest island between Muscatine and New Boston on the Illinois side. The name of this island originated in this manner: A man by the name of John Sidles came along, no one knew from where, and built a cabin on the Illinois shore on section 16 and cut steamboat wood. The timber got short and Sidles became afraid the state of Illinois would be after him for tresspass, so he moved over to the big island, as it was called at that time. From 1845 to 1850 steamboat wood brought cash and the wood dealers were looked after by the merchants. The wood had to be cut in the winter and held until the following season to sell. The wood dealer would go to town and arrange with the merchant for goods for his wood choppers and pay when the wood was sold. Mr. Sidles had been in business some two or three years, he was supposed to be all O K and could get all the goods he wanted. One winter he went in heavy and cut a great lot of wood; the following season steamboats were very abundant. Sidles sold all his wood and left for parts unknown without calling on his creditors to settle up his indebitness. Word was soon circulated about town that Sidles had left. One of his principal creditors, Gen J. G. Gordon, was looking for him; he happened to meet old stuttering James Humphreys, another man in the wood business, when the following coloquy is said to have occured: Gordon says, "What sort of a man is Sidles?" Humphreys replied, "b-b-b-by dad, he's bogus." "Where did he live?" "On Bo-Bo-Bo-Bogus island" was the reply. That reply of Humphreys changed the name of the island from "Big Island" to "Bogus Island."

Island No. 351 on the west side of the river some sixteen or eighteen miles below Muscatine, is called "Turkey Island." It had a great crop of acorns growing on it in early days and was a famous place to hunt wild turkeys.

The small island on the Iowa shore just above the city, is known as "Burdet's Island." It got its name from the man that owned the farm along the Iowa bank of the river. In 1838 or afterwards he purchased the island.

"Geneva Island" was called after the town of Geneva which was located on the Iowa side of the river some four miles above Muscatine. It was covered with heavy, large Burr oak trees. I recollect measuring one that was 6½ feet through the body at cutting height. Most of those trees were stolen off, as it was called at the time, for the government owned the land, and no one had any claim on it. The timber was used for making clapboards and rails from 1837 to 1844.

"Long Island" and "Hog Island" are of quite recent date; I don't know how the names originated.

"Nye's Island" probably got its name from Benjiman Nye, the first settler in this county, who settled at the mouth of Pine Creek in 1834. It is quite probable that Nye may have owned or had some claims on the island. It has had the name of Nye's island for fully fifty years.

The Early Hotels.

No. 33.

The Address of President J. P. Walton at the Forty-First Reunion of the Old Settlers' on Friday, August 27, 1897, at the Fair Grounds in Muscatine.

Published in the Muscatine Saturday Mail, August 28, 1897.

Old Settlers, Ladies and Gentlemen—Our old settlers society is one of the most democratic societies in existance. There is but one requisite to become a member, that one is to be or to have been a resident of this county, or of the state of Iowa, previous to or during the year 1860, or being a descendent of such a resident.

We as Old Settlers have had our annual gatherings to greet our old acquaintances and tell stories of our early days. The one that could tell the best story was frequently considered the best fellow. The president has not had that honor as yet, and is not liable to have it soon.

We have selected for the subject of our talk to-day "Taverns," as they were called in early days, and hope the recollections of them will be pleasant to our hearers and will prove an interesting subject for our meeting. They were a class of buildings of which most of the Old Settlers have some recollection, and most of the Old Settlers had to patronize them to a certain extent.

The "Iowa House, or Bob Kinney's hotel," as it was frequently called, was the first one built. It stood on the west corner of Front and Chestnut streets; the rear part was erected in the autumn of 1836 by Robert C. Kinney, who, Suel Foster once said "was the first landlord to put up a sign and keep a tavern in our town, now Muscatine." He was a native of St. Clair county, Illinois, in the great American bottom opposite St. Louis, where they raise the biggest, fattest, largest, drollest, oddist, good-for-nothing, yet one of the very best men we ever had here. He kept tavern, boarding house and hospital. This hotel was 16x30 feet and one and a-half stories high; it was divided into three rooms below and three above. It was the first frame building erected in the city. The first ten years the building had a very remarkable record if it could be compiled. We may mention later in our recollection, in the SATURDAY MAIL some of the events that occurred.

"Reed & Bare's Tavern." In the winter of 1837 or in the spring of 1838 John Vannatta erected a building on the south corner of Iowa Avenue and Second street and rented it to Reed & Bare for a tavern. They kept it until 1839, when Josiah Parvin came here and occupied it. Mr. Parvin was from Cincinnati and had an accomplished family. They set a good table, and as a result got the best customers, and all that could be accommodated. Parvin had not enough rooms so he built a part of the Kemble house, now standing on the west corner of Second and Walnut streets. It was then but two stories high. When Second street was graded it became necessary to put a lower story under it. At that time Mr. T. M. Isett owned the building and he added a rear part to it. Later Mr. A. Smalley built on an addition on the west side. But to turn back to its earliest occupant, Mr. Josiah Parvin; he was a very marked character, as unlike Robert Kinney as was possible for two men to be. He was kind hearted, social, courteous, and was considered one of our best men. He was very excitable, during those times of excitement, and he would do a great many laughable things which afforded the old settler a great fund of amusement. This hotel was too far up town to do the kind of business Mr. Parvin wished to do, so he gave it up and went away. Since then it has been occupied most of the time and by a dozen different landlords, many of them going away without paying the rent. Since the bridge was erected and business appears to be moving up town the hotel seems to be better patronized.

The third tavern open was the "American House" by T. S. Battell; it was erected in 1841 on the west corner of Iowa Avenue and Second street, it was a large two-story frame building and took the lead in the hotel business; the stage passengers stopped there over nights. During the winter season it was no uncommon thing to see a dozen stages start out in the morning for the different routes to Burlington, Iowa City, Tipton and Davenport. When this house got to running Robert McKiney rented his "Iowa House" and gave up tavern keeping. Captain Fry, his successor, did not live very long after renting it.

Battell's "American House" took the lead and maintained it for several years and accumulated considerable money for him.

His wife dying, he married her sister, "Auntie," sold out the hotel and went into the steamboat business. Bought the "Oswego," a good freight boat but "dead slow." He run it a short time and sunk it, taking about all his wealth down with it. He managed to secure enough to take himself and family to California. He died quite recently.

In the spring of 1840 an old style Pennsylvanian, Frederick Miller, commenced to build what he was pleased to call the "Muscatine Hotel." It stood at the west corner of Fourth and Mulberry streets. He leveled the ground and burnt a kiln of brick on the lot, of which he built his house. The building is standing, although it has changed in appearance. There has been a story built under it and the larger half added to it. At the time of building the streets were some twelve feet higher than at present; when the grading was done a story was put under.

Miller was a Pennsylvania Dutchman, and kept his hotel in Pennsylvania style, with plenty of substantials to eat, at moderate prices. The farmers soon found this out. He was located on one of the main entrances to our town, so he got more than his share of the farmer patronage. On the rear end of the lot he erected a large stable. One cold winter night in 1855 or '56 this stable took fire and some twenty horses perished. Shortly after the destruction of this stable the prosperity of Miller seemed to decline. When Mulberry street was graded some two or three years later Mr. Miller had gone. I think a man by the name of Freeland owned it and undertook to under-build a part of it, but not being skilled in the work, he let a portion fall and killed one or two men. Of course the city was sued, and had to pay some twelve or fifteen hundred dollars damages. The building is now owned by Martin Bitzer and used as a tenement house.

Along in the fifties, say fifty-one, Jonathan Neidig came here and erected a fine three-story building on the east side of the Court House Square and called it the "Park House." This was a bad investment for some reason; it did not run very long before it changed hands. When Mulberry street was graded it became necessary to have a basement put under it; hence the fourth story that it had a while. We put the basement under in 1857, just before the panic came on, which closed up business so effectually that it was some years before we got our pay.

This hotel went into the hands of Mrs. Hess, who had good success. Mr. Matthews was the owner. He was a mechanic by occupation, but had gone to farming; was not very successful at that business, and concluded if Mrs. Hess could run it successfully he could, and gave up farming and took charge of it himself. Mrs. Hess rented the present Kemble House and took most of her customers with her. Mr. Matthews run the hotel until he lost his farm and hotel and had to go to work at carpenter work by the day.

There was another tavern we had almost forgotten—the "Capt. Jim." It was run by Capt. Jim Palmer. Here is an extract from his advertisement that appeared in the Bloomington Herald of 1841: "Whereas, I, Capt. Jim, long a dispenser of food to the hungry and a couch to the weary, as well as a 'horn' to the dry, having taken possession of that large and commodious house on Second street, Bloomington (the former name of Muscatine), Iowa, formerly the residence of the Hon. J. Williams, do hereby make known to the world that I am now prepared at the sign, 'Capt. Jim, to accommodate those who may call upon me in a satisfactory manner, otherwise they go scot free," etc., etc. The building stood on the north side of Second street mid-way between the Avenue and Chestnut street. He kept a bar that was well patronized by the "boys," they all went there for a good time. I think he did not tolerate gambling. He was a pioneer tavern keeper in every sense of the word.

We will venture a story told by the great showman, Dan Rice, that was connected with his first visit in 1842. He exhibited in the hotel. The place in which he held forth was lighted with tallow candles furnished by the landlord. The latter was suspicious of Dan's financial standing wished him to pay in advance, but Dan, to secure his host, deputized him to sell tickets. But it happened that the landlord knew everybody around and everybody knew him, and being of an unusually accommodating disposition he did not have the heart to charge his friends any admittance fee. The result was that after the show was over he owed Dan $6 without anything to show for it. While Capt. Jim kept this house it was quite a loafing place. For the early settler who wanted to smoke, tell a story or get a drink it was quite convenient.

In 1851 James Latta, of Grandview, erected a block of buildings on the west side of the Avenue south of Third street. The second and third stories were used for a hotel. When the high school was first organized, or during its early years, the third story was used for school purposes. It was never a success as a hotel until its present landlord, J. K. Scott, took hold of its management. I think I am safe in saying that he has made more money there than any other hotel keeper in the city.

The present Commercial House (formerly the Ogilvie House) was started in 1849 by Adam Ogilvie and Brinton Darlington. It was not completed and opened until 1851. After the opening of the Ogilvie House and the completion of the railroad the hotels changed their system of doing business.

Nothing has changed so much as the sleeping accommodations. From 1840 to 1850 the hotels were comparatively new; but two or three beds were placed in a room. The mosquito was a great annoyance at that time. Then every bed had a mosquito bar over the entire bed. One would go to bed and tuck in the bar and go to sleep listening to the hum of the villainous insects. If the sleeper turned much in bed, when he waked up in the morning he would usually find a dozen or more that had secured their fill, hanging around on the inside of the bar. Now wire screens at the windows saves all that trouble.

BOB. KINNEY,
Muscatine's First Landlord.

Published in the Muscatine Saturday Mail September 4, 1897; written by J. P. Walton.

No. 34.

In our last, No. 33, we promised to relate some of the events that occurred in the Iowa House, or Bob Kinney's hotel. A little more definite discription of the building and its surroundings would perhaps be in order. The rear part was 16x30 feet, or near that size, and a story and a half high; it stood well back on the lot so when the front was erected it filled out to the street. The rear part was built in 1836, the front in 1838. The front was about 30x40, two stories high, being "L" shaped to the front. It had a two-story veranda along the entire front. This was up some four feet from the ground; under it and under the corner of the house back of it was the bar room, not to exceed six feet and a half high in the clear.

The rear part was the first

frame building in the city. It was almost made without the aid of the saw mill. The floors, doors, and window frames were made of sawed lumber; where the lumber was sawed I cannot tell. All the framing timbers, including studding and rafters, were split timber growing nearby; the siding, shingles and lath were split from large oak trees that may have grown on the lot. The front part had more sawed lumber in it, and was a more pretentious building.

It was nicely located on Front street at the west corner of Chestnut street, within sixty feet of the steamboat landing at an ordinary stage of water.

The town site was originally covered with large timber. When we first saw it in June, 1838, the timber was cut off in the immediate vicinity of the Iowa House and a few other buildings were erected along Front street. The river bank was nearer than the railroad track is now. I don't think Front street at the foot of Chestnut street was more than forty or fifty feet wide, and where trees were not growing big stumps were left standing that made very convenient seats for our town people to sit on while viewing the boats and river. The boats usually landed in front of the hotel.

The landlord, Robert C. Kinney, was a very pleasant, social, jolly old fellow, but quite excitable. At his hotel he had nearly all of our most prominent men boarding with him, for instance, S. C. Hastings, J. S. Richman, Suel Foster, David and Asbury Warfield, T. M. Isett, Dr. C. O. Watters, Dr. George Reeder, Dr. McKey, Dr. Blaydes—in fact about all the unmarried doctors, lawyers and merchants of our town boarded there. Robert set as good a table as the condition of the country would permit. They had no stove or range to do their cooking on, it was all done in a large stone fire-place and a baking oven located in the back yard.

Asbury Warfield boarded there from 1837 to 1840, and said that they had a very common quality of iron knives and forks in use at the table. If a fork got a tine short some one would jab it up under the bottom of the table top and let it stick there. The table was a stationaay one never moved and no one would think of looking up under there to find a missing fork. The "boys" would call for another one. When Bob found the forks were getting scarce he used to ejaculate, "Gor Almighty, Meriah, what got all the forks," not aware that they were sticking under the table.

Here let me make a mention of the change in the use of the knife and fork at the table. Previous to 1840 I never saw anything but a two-tined fork; then the food was passed from the plate to the mouth with the knife. Since four-tined forks (silver) have came into use, the habit of changing the fork from the left hand to the right to pass the food to the mouth has been adopted by most every one, the old settlers excepted, they are very slow about making the change.

When Kinney was in his glory there was a class of young men who used to practice jokes on him. One day they caught his dog and tied a tin can to his tail. The dog started for home at a rapid rate, making a tremendous noise; on arriving at home Bob. opened the door, and in rushed the dog much to Bob's disgust. He had to remove the can to save the house or its contents from destruction. The boys hid themselves fearing the indignation that might be vented on them.

Whenever a traveling preacher of any denomination came along Bob. always opened his doors for meeting. It is a disputed question who held the first meeting in the county, the Methodists or the Baptists. They both held their first meetings at the Iowa House, kept by Robert C. Kinney.

After the town had began to grow and we had other and better hotels, Kinney concluded he would go out of business, and a man by the name of Fry (Captain Fry) came along who rented the Iowa House. Kinney went to one of his legal boarders, Hon. S. C. Hastings, and got a lease drawn up; he said he wanted a very strong one. Hastings copied one of the old English forms which occupied several pages of paper, and read it over to Kinney, who was satisfied. Hastings paid a $25 board bill in this way. Kinney then went into the saw mill business with his brother Samuel, but did not like that very well and he concluded to go west. One night he was taken very sick and sent for Dr. C. O. Waters. The doctor went and found that there was nothing the matter with Kinney; he wanted to find out what Watters knew about Oregon, having sent for him to come and tell him in a professional manner. The charge was credited on an old board bill. In the spring of 1843 or '44 Kinney started for Oregon where he became a prominent man, was a member of the legislature and accumulated considerable property. He died a few years ago. His son, Dr. August Kinney, is living at Astoria.

Recollections of

Early Days at Geneva.

Published in the Muscatine Saturday Mail, September 11, 1897; written by J. P. Walton.

No. 35.

We came to Iowa on the 10th day of June 1838, twenty-four days before Iowa was made a territory. We disembarked from the good steamer Brazil, Orin Smith master, at the then promising town of Geneva, three miles up the river from Muscatine. The town consisted of a group of five or six cabins and a steam saw mill. Everything was lovely until August when the ague took us. There were five in the family and all took it within two weeks. We had it every day, or every other day—sometimes every third day—until the following April. At times we were all so sick that there was no one to help the others to a drink of water.

By the assistance of neighbors we were enabled to keep a supply of wood. It was very necessary that we should, for we kept the postoffice, my father being postmaster. We had four mails a week that had to be looked over. For the process seven minutes was allowed. The passengers got out and warmed while the mail carrier helped us overhaul the pouches. There were two pouches, one for papers and one for letters. The postmaster had orders to take out any loose papers that were without the proper direction. In this way we were supplied with papers. The only profit in the office was that the P. M. got his mail free; otherwise we would have had to pay 25 cents for each of our eastern letters.

The post office brought the neighbors in and helped us get through the first winter alive. It was more than many of the early settlers did. The first winter was spent in a small log cabin not more than 16 feet square. It stood within one hundred yards of where the Hare school house is now located, nearly south, or towards the river. There were five or six other families in the village; all got their water from the sulphur spring that is still running on the bank of the river. The water was cool but the taste was not desirable. I am inclined to think that the water helped to bring on the ague, for the reason that those in other places that got their water out of wells did not suffer so much.

The sheriff of the county, Jas. Davis, lived near us. He had originally kept a grocery store (a saloon), but when we arrived there was nothing left but a barrel of wine and it soon gave out.

One morning word came that a theft had been committed in Bloomington, and that the thief had been traced to our neighborhood. Davis was expected to look him up; it was a bitter cold day; Davis concluded it was not safe to follow in such extreme cold weather, so the thief took himself away much to Davis' satisfaction. Davis went deer hunting that afternoon.

The fact was that the people were glad enough if the thief did get away. There was no jail in Iowa, and it cost too much to send him away for safe keeping.

We recollect a case when a man by the name of Elrod had broken into a house belonging to Harvey Gillett and stole some money. He then stole a canoe and started down the river. Gillett offered a reward for his arrest and the return of the money. Two mounted men started down the other side of the river, and headed the thief off at New Boston. He was brought back. Gillett got his money and the sheriff got Mr. Elrod. He had to be kept some six weeks before court convened. It required a man constantly with him, and the expense was likely to be quite heavy. So it was understood that on a certain Saturday, a party of regulators was to take him across the river and place him on trial. If the fellow got away alive he would have been lucky.

The prisoner became aware of his situation and wanted his trial averted. No solution but escape seemed to offer. His guard was Isaiah Davis, a brother of the sheriff, who kept watch over the prisoner night and day. At night he locked him to the bedsted with a log chain around his ankle. Isaiah became convinced that if he were once taken across the river he would not get away alive, and concluded the best thing for him was to escape. He informed the sheriff's wife of the situation of affairs, and advised her to have an extra amount of food cooked. On the night before the day set for the trial across the river the prisoner got hold of the key and released himself from his fastenings. He helped himself to a supply of cooked provisions and left for parts unknown. He was not followed, and it was years afterward before Isaiah told me the particulars of his escape.

Horse stealing was dealt with in a different manner. It was considered a capital offense and punished accordingly, generally without the interference of the legal fraternity.

James Davis, the sheriff, was a great hunter and a very successful one. He kept the post office well supplied with game. We recollect seeing him bring in two very large bucks with their horns locked so tightly that they were never separated. The larger one had killed the smaller, and he in turn fell a prey to Davis' rifle.

Our first purchase of stock was some chickens, and soon after we secured a cow. We raised a good crop of potatoes, but succeeded in digging only a few bushels between spells of ague. The puncheon floor of the cabin was taken up and a hole dug in the ground to store what we succeeded in saving. By this means we managed to have potatoes most of the time, although many of our neighbors did not.

In the spring of 1839 Davis moved to Bloomington, and we to the farm now owned by Mrs. John Anderson. There we took the post office and the ague, experiencing a shake every few days all summer. When I look back at our former life I wonder we lived through its privations. It is frequently a question, is life worth living under such adverse circumstances? If viewed from the modern atheistic stand point it would not be, and suicide would have followed. Our uncle who came with us in June got disgusted and left in the following October to go back to New England. He started down the river expecting to go up the Ohio. But the water was so low that navigation on the Ohio was suspended, so he went by New Orleans. There were no coasting steamers, so he had to take a sailing vessel. On Christmas day, more than two months later he stood on the dock at New York city waiting for his trunk to be unloaded. His retreat from the Mississippi did not save him from the effects of the ague. It accompanied him to New England and stayed with him several years.

By the time winter set in we were in a better condition to meet it. Our money was all gone but we had raised some crops to live on. During this winter of 1839-40 there were many things to excite the early settler, none more so than the Missouri war. Of this we may speak in some other paper.

The location of the capital at Iowa City was considered that winter at the session of the legislature. Of course Iowa City was much nearer to us than Burlington and right behind us so that we had to furnish supplies for their citizens. No railroads were considered possible. The Moscow canal was surveyed that year for its possibility as a water way to supply Iowa City at cheaper freight rates. We were all in favor of moving the capital from Burlington to Iowa City.

In the spring of 1840 we moved back to Geneva and took the post office with us. My father was a carpenter and spent most of his time working in Bloomington while we run the post office, raised garden vegetables, kept a few cows and peddled vegetables and milk in Bloomington. We had a small field of corn, and I remember one occasion when the hogs got in we were in the act of running them out when we experienced one of the worst attacks of ague we ever had. I have not had an attack for many years but will attempt to describe one. It generally comes on about 10 or 11 a. m. The first sensation is a disposition to stretch ones arms, which is soon followed by a pain in the back and a weakness in the legs. Very shortly one finds himself involuntarily shaking and his teeth chattering with the most excrutiating pain in the back and limbs, accompanied by a thirst that seems to know no quenching. This shaking will generally last half an hour or more followed by an intense fever for two or three hours. After the fever subsides the subject is too tired to do anything that day. At night the night-sweats follow. If the person has strength enough the bed will be wet with perspiration. In the morning he will get up feeling quite well until 10 or 11 o'clock when the same symptoms will be repeated, and the same agonies endured. If the shake was hard the fever was light; if the shake was light—a mere chill as it frequently was—the fever was more intense. The ague itself was not considered very fatal.

In the spring of 1841 my father died. This left a vacancy in the post office. In place of having the vacancy filled we had the office discontinued. With it Geneva lost its legal existence.

BLOOMINGTON'S PART IN THE MISSOURI WAR,

IN THE WINTER OF 1839 AND '40.

Published in the Muscatine Saturday Mail, September 18, 1897; written by J. P. Walton.

No. 36.

When the treaty with the Indians was made ceding this part of Iowa, called the "Black Hawk purchase," to the United States, a portion of the southern part was reserved for a number of half-breed Indians, who were to occupy or sell as they chose. They chose the latter. There were originally about forty of them and their reservation amounted to some 30,000 acres. This land was sold to different parties, the largest portion to the Half-Breed Land Company, composed of Col. George Davenport, Antoine LeClaire, the Phelpeses and others. The New York Land Company were also heavy purchasers. One trouble was that the Indians would sell and keep selling as long as they could find purchasers. Some of the land was probably sold several times—Watered their stock.

We are indebted to the late Suel Foster for the following:

"These multipled titles found they had too small a tract of land for their 'watered stock,' and they found that their western boundary was at the head of the Des Moines river rapids which was previously known to be the name of the lower rapids of the Mississippi river, just above the mouth of the Des Moines river. To change this boundary from the Mississippi to the Des Moines river rapids, would increase the quantity of the half-breed lands from 30,000 to nearly 100,000 acres.

"This change of boundary carried with it also a change of the northern boundary line of the state of Missouri, from the Des Moines river westward to the northwest corner of the state. The Missourians gladly accepted the change. Thus was laid the nest-egg of the Iowa and Missouri war, which occurred in December, 1839.

"I have thought proper to be somewhat particular in describing the causes which led to the difficulty with Missouri, because I suppose there are but few who understand it, and because of the very conspicuous part the people of Muscatine county took in the fight.

"The change of this line threw a portion of Van Buren and Davis counties of this territory into Missouri. The tax collector of that county in Missouri came into the disputed territory, collecting taxes, and levied on some cattle and sent them off to sell for taxes. The owners of the cattle rallied among their neighbors, and raised a sheriff's posse and retook the cattle and their sheriff with them. The prisoners were sent to Burlington, the capital of the territory, where the legislature was in session; and from there the prisoner was forwarded to Muscatine, so that he might be out of reach of the enemy.

"Governor Boggs, of Missouri, found that one of the sheriffs of the state had been kidnapped by a strong armed force from Iowa, issued a proclamation, calling the militia of his state to arms. Gov. Robert Lucas, of Iowa, finding that our territory had been invaded by the Missourians, issued his proclamation, calling on the militia of our territory. Orders were sent to Gen. J. E. Fletcher to call out the Second Brigade. John Vanatter was commissioned colonel, and S. C. Hastings was appointed captain of a horse company. Two companies of infantry were also formed; a few from Cedar and Johnson counties were in the companies. But the cavalry was looked upon as the flower of the army.

"After all the volunteers had been rallied that could be enlisted the draft was resorted to fill up the army. [Our Father, Amos Walton, was notified "to appear armed and equipped as the law directs;" he was postmaster at Geneva at that time; he armed himself with his commission, together with paper, pen and ink, and reported for duty. Of course, he was excused and did not go.] J. W. Brady and Barton Lee were chosen lieutenants of the cavalry. Captain Hastings, knowing the importance of having an experienced orderly seargent, appointed a bright, active young man by the name of Suel Foster, for his orderly, who had had some military experience in the New Hampshire militia. The drafted men gave the captain and his orderly a great deal of trouble; we could not keep them anymore than we could water in a sieve.

"The baggage wagons were loaded with a month's rations of flour, pork and vinegar, and they, with the infantry, were ordered to march about 10 a. m. one cold winter day, about the 20th of December, 1839, with snow six inches deep. Captain Hastings' cavalry was some two hours later in starting, and then a halt was twice called, and squads sent back to town to bring in deserters. One of the most troublesome of these deserters was Dr. Lewis McKee. After McKee had given us much trouble in getting him along about six miles down the slough road, he suddenly became very cold and must stop at a farm house to warm. Captain Hastings sent Orderly Foster to bring up McKee; but Mc. plead for mercey, for he would die if he rode two miles further without warming. The orderly listened to his vehement pleadings. Lieutenant Brady and Seargent Howard were sent for the orderly. Mac swore he wouldn't go another step until the whole company came after him. Captain Hastings with Lieutenant Lee, rode back to the scenes of disorder. At this most extraordinary condition of demoralization of the flower of the army, the commander in chief, Gen. J. E. Fletcher, who was not far in advance, rode hastily back in somewhat of an excitement, as such a state of things must naturally make any officer of true military pride feel, and ordered Captain Hastings to the front of his company. The captain repeated the order to his orderly, the orderly repeated it to Dr. McKee. The general, drawing his sword, exclaimed: 'I say, Captain Hastings, to the front of your company, or I will have you arrested and courtmartialed.' The captain had an Indian spear, with an iron point on a long pole and that trimmed and ornamented with red flannel and feathers. The orderly had a long crooked sword in the shape of a sickle, only the edge was on the outside instead of the inside. These orders were repeated by the general's subordinates down to private McKee, as fast as delivered, and many times over with higher threats and louder voice. The two lieutenants stood back and laughed heartily without fear at the brandishing of these deadly weapons. By this time about half the company rode back to the scene to see what military items they could learn, for the most of them were quite raw in the service. McKee said, 'Gentlemen, as most of the company are here, I'll go now.' It seems that I could hear that beautiful, eloquent voice, as the doctor surrendered, as gentle and docile as a lamb. The doctor was a case and a character. Not so with Fletcher and Hastings. The general ordered Lieutenant Lee and Orderly Foster to arrest Captain Hastings, and then the general rode hastily away to save bloodshed and to organize the company. Captain Hastings swore he would not be arrested—that he would not be disgraced in that way, and sent General Fletcher a challenge. Fletcher replied that he would not compromise the dignity of his office, to fight an officer of so low a rank.

"Colonel Vanatter had proceeded that day with the infantry as far as the timber bottom of the Iowa river, opposite Wapello, and was preparing to camp when the cavalry came up. We dismounted, scraped away the snow, and pitched our tents, while some were building fires and getting supper. My messmate was Major D. R. Warfield who had a splendid coon robe and a blanket, and I had two blankets. Our tent fronted a big log fire and we slept comfortably, although the next morning the thermometer was 12 degrees below zero by an instrument across the river at Wapello. Fortunately for us that it was cold, for the river was not frozen sufficiently to bear teams the day we arrived; but next morning at 10 o'clock we crossed in safety on the ice. That first evening our surgeon, Dr. Eli Reynolds, broke through and went in, crossing on foot.

"Our drummer, Major W. T. DeWebster, who at home was styled the Duke of Bloomington, was a very small man, a very active and energetic man, of great military pride; he was elegantly uniformed with a cap and cockade, and a red silk sash. The drum, fife and horn composed our band. [That horn is now in the possession of the Walton brothers on Muscatine Island.] Colonel Vanatter thought the duke's appearance and pride too much for his achievements in time of action, and the colonel zealously hated the sound of that beautiful drum. In the dead of night the head of the drum was broken in, and the drum was used as a vessel of dishonor. Inquiry was made, and it is supposed that whilst the pickets slept an enemy came in and did it."

The army went as far as Burlington, when orders were received to return, which was accomplished in two or three days. The mustering out time was celebrated by the use of an immense amount of army vinegar.

I don't know of but two survivors at this time, William Gordon and Abijah Winn; but strange to say, neither has any recollection of the other being there. It is possible that they could get a pension if they could agree about their claims.

RECOLLECTIONS OF

The First County Jail.

Published in the Muscatine Saturday Mail, September 25, 1897; written by J. P. Walton.

No. 37.

There was one public building that seems to have been neglected. No one has written its history, while no other one of the county buildings has done more or better service than the old jail. Its most beneficial service was its terror to evil doers. It stood from the time of its construction in 1839 or '40 until its abandonment in 1856 as a place of punishment and safe-keeping for the law-breakers, thus being a protection for the law-abiders.

It would seem as though a building that had served its purpose so well for fifteen years should not go down to oblivion undescribed. It was erected on the northwest corner of the court house square; its location is yet observable by a hollow or low place at the top of the terrace a little back from the corner. It was erected in 1839 or '40 being the first public building in the county, and was probably paid for out of the proceeds of sales of the commissioner's quarter, as it was called. It was about 20x30 feet, two-stories high and was constructed with 12x12 hewed oak timber halved down at the corner so the timbers were tight together. The outside was stripped up and sided like other buildings; the floors were made of the same 12x12 timber laid crosswise to one other; the sides of the lower story were lined with the same 12x12 timber with a space of ten inches between the outside and inside courses of timber that was filled with broken stone. The floor, ceiling and walls of the lower story were lined with two-inch plank with a 20-penny nail driven in every inch over the entire surface. The lower story was divided into two rooms with a two-inch partition. It may have been the plan to have one room for the women and the other for the men. Each room had two holes not to exceed twelve inches square running straight through the three-foot wall for light and ventilation. It was little better than the "black-hole of Calcutta."

The lower story was used for the prisoners and the second story for the jailor to live in, the door being in the second story approachable with stairs from the outside. The prison rooms were reached through a trap door in the second story floor, a ladder being used for descent. When the prisoner was landed on the floor below it was drawn up and the door closed, food and drink were let down with a cord and basket.

Old Dan Smith was the jailor for some time. He lived in the second story and had his blacksmith shop on the lot where Judge Brannan now lives. On one occasion he had two prisoners in for some offence, who conceived the idea of escape by setting fire to their bedding, which they did one morning after Dan had gone to his work. They started the fire and raised the alarm. They wanted the woman to let the ladder down to keep them from smothering. She opened the trap door and let the smoke come up, and went for Smith, he came and commenced letting down water to put out the fire which they were compelled to do.

After the present jail was built the old one had to be removed. I went to the county judge and asked him what he would take for it. He said he had been offered $50 for it but wanted $60. I told him I would take it and gave him a check for it on Saturday after banking hours. I was quite impatient about it until Monday morning when he could get his money for fear he would back out.

The following week I commenced to take out the oak timbers. I had all the west side of the square covered with them, when the people began to find fault with the judge for selling so cheap. He had kept it nearly a year looking for a purchaser before I got it. I had contracted with the M. & M. R. R. Co. for bridges and tank frames so I had use for considerable of it, I also exchanged some $200 worth of the timber with Chambers for other lumber, and sold the city one bill of $300 for piling. On the whole I cleared about $1000 out of the old jail which I think was about the first cost of the building.

While the old jail was occupied the county had considerable difficulty to get a man to live in the second story and take care of the prisoners, so a new jail was built. As soon the new jail was completed and better accommodations were furnished for the prisoners, we had more of them. The dread of the old prison no longer existed so they increased in numbers.

This old jail was used for an insane asylum when the patients had to be confined. The state had no asylum at that time, so they were kept in the lower prison for the want of a better place. I think that they had a cage built in the upper story for the milder ones. It was no uncommon occurance for the passer-by to be saluted by their unearthly yells.

A word about the safety of the old jail. Shortly after it was built a couple of hard cases dug out through the drain and left without being captured. The drain was then securely repaired so no further escapes occurred without help from the outside. When a keeper did not live in the upper part watchmen were hired to guard the prison, then occasionally a prisoner would escape as they have many times from the present jail.

Recollections of

THE PHOTOGRAPHERS OF MUSCATINE.

Published in the Muscatine Saturday Mail, October 2, 1897; written by J. P. Walton.

No. 38

"Like a snow flake on a river
A moment white, then gone for ever."

As a rule the photograph business has been in the hands of a very transient class of operators. They would be here to-day and fill our houses with "choice gems," and gone to-morrow, the place to be filled by another of the same occupation. They would frequently lap on to each other, then the price was down. The rooms in the Burnett building have been occupied by an artist for more than 40 years. We don't know who was the first one there. We are satisfied it has been occupied by more than a half a dozen different operators, we can't name them all, neither do we expect to give the names of any but the prominent ones that have visited our city.

THE FIRST DAGUERREOTYPIST IN IOWA.

In August, 1839, Daguerre announced that he had discovered the art of making pictures by sun light. In the fall of 1840 a live young man from Connecticut, by the name of Chester Weed, brought a camera obscura and astonished the citizens of Bloomington by making a picture of his father. The old picture is yet in existence, and was quite a respectable picture. I have often seen it. This was probably the first daguerreotpye taken in the western states.

It is somewhat wonderful to think that the art would reach here so soon. At that time there were no steamships crossing the Atlantic, and not much railroad travel in America. It would take nearly two months for a man to start at Paris and reach Bloomington, and then to think that within two years a man had gone to Boston and learned the art and traveled clear to Iowa and made pictures. One will have to conclude that we had fast times then as well as now.

Chester Weed opened a studio in Muscatine and Iowa City. I think that he did not make much money at it, for he sold out his outfit and went to clerking for Jos. Bennett.

The daguerreotype art in America was taught in Boston and New York. After Chester Weed had completed his studies in Boston he started west, but stopped in New York and called on Professor Morse, the inventor of the telegraph, who was in a dark room connected with an old school house developing a picture. He afterwards became famous with his telegraph.

The process of making pictures by sun light was by rendering a polished silver plate sensitive by the use of chemicals; it took some six minutes to sit for a picture.

There was one singular occurrence. After Chester Weed came here he worked all the first winter with no success. He afterwards found that other artists were troubled in the same way. With the same chemicals in the spring of 1841 he produced good pictures. Mr. Weed sold his outfit to Arthur Washburn, who never made an effort to do anything with it. His children destroyed the old camera.

After Chester Weed went out of the business a number of tramp daguerreotypists came along; frequently a traveling gallery on wheels would give us a call; sometimes a floating boat on the river. I recollect the first time I ever sat for a picture was in the spring of 1854. I pulled out a studio boat for a man by the name of White, and had my picture taken as part pay. I have it yet. It is a good illustration of Burns' poem:

"Oh, would some one the giftie gie us
To see ourselves as others see us,
It would from many a failing free us."

In 1856 we had two operators, one by the name of M. D. Cook the other John Hunter, who also practiced dentistry. When they came and how long they staid we cannot say; at all events, when the directory of 1859 was published their names did not appear, but the names of George P. Hall and W. H. Martin appeared as photographers.

Mr. Fred Phelps thinks the first successful photographer who came here was James Hart, whose name occurs in the directory of 1866. Mr. Phelps says that Hart had his gallery in the second story of the building on the east side of Iowa avenue between Second and Third streets. Mr. Phelps says he paid $300 for one-half of Hart's outfit for his nephew "Bunk" (J. P. Phelps) who was also to receive instruction in the profession.

Early in the sixties James G. Evans appeared and opened a gallery on the west side of Iowa avenue, north of Second street. Mr. Evans was assisted by his wife, who spent the most of her time at the gallery. According to our recollections he was the leading photographer of our city. He was not satisfied with his quarters and when Mr. S. G. Stein erected the building that is now occupied by Batterson, on Second street, he asked Stein to fit up the third story for him which he did under Evan's direction, but when the room was finished Stein rented it to someone else greatly to the disgust of Evans, who commenced a suit for service as an architect. Stein settled it by paying Evans something like $75 or $100. Evans bought the building on the west side of Iowa avenue and fitted it up for business in the first story and a gallery in the second story. Many of our citizens recollect his keeping the avenue full of earth and brick nearly all one winter. Evans eventually left Muscatine. I have been informed that he is in Los Angeles, Cal.

In 1866 there were four photographers—J. G. Evans, J. Hart, T. J. Van Buren, and S. L. Long.

In 1869 we had J. G. Evans, H. B. Hagan, J. P. and C. F. Phelps. "Bunk" Phelps bought Hagan out and he left. His gallery was over Graham's drug store, north corner Second and Cedar street. Van Buren and Long had disappeared.

In 1879 we had J. G. Evans on the west side of Iowa avenue, L. A. Phelps on the east side of the avenue, J. A. Allen in the Burnett building, and J. P. Phelps over the postoffice in Stein's building where Batterson is now located.

In 1883 we had E. B. Edwards,

C. F. Phelps, and J. P. Phelps.

In 1886 we had E. B. Edwards, 210 Iowa avenue; W. W. Owens, over post office in Stein's building; Fred S. Phelps, in Burnett's building; Joseph P. Phelps, 309 east Second street.

In 1891 we had Clifford & Son, 309 east Second street; Grosheim Brothers, in Burnett's building; Joseph P. Phelps, 211 Iowa avenue, and L. M. Townsend at 117 and 118 west Second street.

In 1895 we had Clifford & Son in their new and present quarters, 210 and 211 Cedar street; John A. Groveslund, 117-119 west Second street; Alex and Oscar Grosheim, 117-119 east Second street, and J. O. Hole, 418 Mulberry street.

There was one tragedy that occurred in the Burnett building, the date of which we do not remember. A young man by the name of John Hall dressed himself in his best clothes and took a dose of cyanide of potassium which produced instant death. This, if we recollect aright, was the only death of a photographer in our city. The two Phelps boys who if not born were raised here, are still in the business, P. L. Phelps in Carbondale, Ills., and J. P. Phelps (Bunk Phelps) in Sheffield, Alabama.

Recollections of

CORNELIUS CADLE.

Published in the Muscatine Saturday Mail, October 9, 1897; written by J. P. Walton.

No. 39.

During the past week we have received the following letter:

Cincinnati, Ohio, Sept. 28, 1897. P. O. box 35. My dear Mr. Walton:—I have the copy of the last MUSCATINE SATURDAY MAIL, and have read Clay Richman's letter.

I watch with interest the career of all our Muscatine boys who are yet in the service, Will Reeder, Clay Richman, Rowland Hill and all others.

In reading Lieutenant Richman's letter I am strongly reminded of all of those in New York city whom he mentions. Wallace—In 1876 my father and I were in New York city, our birth place, together. We were in St. Paul's church yard, lower Broadway, looking at the tombstones of the Cadle's when, just across the street from an office window some one called "Cadle." We went over and had a pleasant hour with Wallace.

Will Ziegler. He was a pupil of mine when I had my experience as a school teacher near Sweetland Center in 1856. Then the teachers "boarded round." There are but few of that experience left. I am sure that my friend Mr. Witter has had no such experience in his work as a teacher.

Mr. Underwood was in a bank in Muscatine soon after I was a teller in Isett & Brewster's bank, and from their counter I enlisted as a private in Captain Ben. Beach's company "H," of the Eleventh Iowa,—a company of Muscatine boys from which twenty-six were made commissioned officers. They were instructed by Ben Beach, George Magoon and George R. White, and I think that I may say that all of us of company "H" did our duty.

John Lemp and his daughter, Ella, lived close to the Cadle house on Front street.

Dr. Reeder, the father of Lieutenant Commander Will Reeder, U S N., and Dr. Olds, took care of me in 1845, when I had typhus fever. I remember this the more distinctly because I have yet the scars of the "Spanish Fly" blisters that the doctors, in those days, administered. The scar of the wound that I received in the Vicksburg campaign is as plain as the scars that Doctors Reeder and Olds left in those of years ago.

Later, in 1832, when we were in "front of the enemy" I, not feeling well, went to Dr. George Reeder, surgeon of the Second Iowa cavalry, and he gave me medicine of a milder nature with satisfactory results.

I realize that I am an old man, though a Muscatine "boy," and find that I am exercising that prerogative of old people, prolixity. So, notwithstanding I have many other memories of olden Muscatine I will end this.

Yours very truly,
CORNELIUS CADLE.
To Mr. J. P. Walton, Muscatine, Iowa

This letter reminds us that our old friend, Cornelius Cadle, sr., has had little more than a passing mention, in our series of recollections, as a member of the firm of Chambers, Cadle & Co.

In October, 1843, Cornelius Cadle, sr., came to Bloomington with his father, his step-mother, his brother Richard and his wife and three sons. On the day of his arrival his father died, and on the following day his mother, both were buried the same day.

He soon commenced to build a saw mill on the ground where now stands the mill recently used by the Kaiser Box Company. This was the first saw-mill erected within our city. After getting the mill to running he sold one half to a man by the name of Riley. After the Chambers commenced to operate here Riley sold his half to the Chambers Brothers, hence the name of Chambers, Cadle & Co. When the firm was dissolved Cornelius was about down to first principals in the financial way of looking. He had a good name and managed to keep on in the lumber business for five or six years. I think Kessinger was in company with him and perhaps he may have sold lumber for Kessinger for a while.

After giving up the lumber business he kept the old office that stood on the north side of Second street, east of Mulberry, for a shop to work in. Here he made ornamental furniture and brick-a-brack of rare and choice woods, of which he made quite a collection. In his little shop he could be found most of the time, and we rarely passed that part of the city without calling on him to exchange a few stories or crack a few jokes. Cadle was one of the sharpest jokers in our city, a natural punster; for instance, on the first of January, 1876, he had charge of the Congregational church, and a proposition was made to have all the bells in the city rung at 12 o'clock p. m., to ring in the Centennial year; Cadle's bell was rung. On the following day he claimed to be out of sorts about staying up all night to ring the bell and declared he would not ring it again (meaning the second centennial.) The declaration went the rounds with all but a few seeing the point.

He was one the principal working members of the Congregational church, was senior deacon and sexton, and attended to the seating of the visitors. He was an active member of the old Scientific Club which was the beginning of the present Academy of Science. As a social, genial family Cornelius Cadle's had no superior At one of the Club meetings, held at Peter Musser's within a short distance of Cadle's, it was suggested we have a "pillow case party" and call on the deacon. (Of course Mrs. Cadle was let into the secret.) Mrs. Musser's bureau drawers and beds were levied on for sheets and pillow cases to the number of twenty-five or thirty. When properly clad we started out in single file and marched to the Cadle residence. At the front door we were met by the deacon, who welcomed us, although we claimed to be ku kluks. We are not going to recount the fun that followed.

As a public man Cornelius Cadle had more than the ordinary share of duties to perform. For a series of years he was deputy county treasurer. In the years 1855 and in 1856, and in 1868 he was on the city council as alderman; in 1862 he was city measurer and again in 1867 and 1869. At that time the office of city measurer was quite an office, most of the lumber sold here had to be measured when taken out of the river and most of the logs sawed at the mills were measured before sawing. Cadle did most of this work. It made little difference whether he was measurer or not, he gave good satisfaction and was selected to do it. In 1882 he was city treasurer and at the expiration of his term turned his papers and funds over to Will Block, his successor.

Mr. Cadle was a native of the city of New York, where his father was born and three of his children, Cornelius, Edward F. and William L; the three younger, Charles F., Henry and Abbie (now Mrs. F. Mahin) were born in Muscatine. Mr. Cadle was born March 11, 1809, was married to Miss Abigail Larrabee in May, 1836, had four children; after her death he married, on March 4, 1848, Miss Ruth Lamprey. They had two children, Henry now of Bethany, Mo., and Abbie the wife of Frank W. Mahin, of Clinton, Iowa.

If our space would permit we would be glad to mention something about Mrs. Ruth Lamprey Cadle, who died April 5, 1885, but will have to forego it until we write about the noble women of our city.

In December, 1885, Mr. Cadle went to Alabama to spend the winter with his son Cornelius, and on the 11th day of March, 1886, he died there, on the seventy-seventh anniversary of his birth. His remains were brought to Muscatine for burial.

Recollections of

HENRY CLAY DEAN.

Published in the Muscatine Saturday Mail October 16, 1897; written by J. P. Walton.

No. 40.

One day in the summer of 1851 old Squire Crandal, as he was called (Thomas Crandal) wanted a little job of work done—cleaning out his back yard or something similar—so he went out on the street to look for some one to do it. He observed a heavy-set man with very plain clothes, likely Kentucky jeans, with course shoes, and perhaps a white shirt, unbuttoned, with a common straw hat that had seen better days, and in all appearing much like a farmer with his working suit on. Crandal concluded that the man could do his work, so he accosted him, saying, "I want a man to do a couple of hour's work, to clean out my back yard, will you do it for me?" The man said he would do it, and went to work. He worked faithfully for two hours and got the yard cleaned. Crandal paid him 25 cents and complimented him on the dispatch of the work, and stated that when he had another job of work he would look him up. The man thanked Crandal and told him if he needed more help to call on Rev. Henry Clay Dean, the minister in charge of the Methodist church of Bloomington. It was then Crandal's turn to apologize, which he did in the best way he knew how.

I think that was Dean's first work in our city. During the term of one year he spent here no man attained a greater notoriety; not only in our city, but in the state at large. He became so famous as a preacher and towered so much above the other members of the conference that they got afraid or envious of him, so they "polled their interests together" and got him sent to the smallest circuit in the conference, believing that he would resign, which he did.

From a paper read to the Academy of Science, on March 29, 1883, by Hon. John Mahin, we make the following extracts:

"The most remarkable man in the history of the Methodist pulpit of Muscatine was Henry Clay Dean. He was a strange mixture of erudition and simplicity, and of earnestness and frivolity.— Capable, yet capricious, coarse, yet at times sublime, he was always entertaining, if not at all times edifying. He could preach a profound sermon with the same ease that he could lead a refractory boy out of the church by his ear, thus performing the duties of preacher and policeman. He was always most omnipresent— visited his parishioners at all hours, even in the night, and no matter how late the call, would request the sisters to furnish him a lunch from their cupboards. He knew almost everybody, and nearly everything about them. When he took time to study so as to become the walking library he was, nobody knew, for he was too restless to sit down and read. Although he did not complete his year at this charge, and although he was eccentric beyond measure, he was not a bad man. Indeed I do not remember any one I ever knew who seemed more conscientious in his way. He had no vices—nothing disagreeable except uncouthness of manner and dress. He severed his connection with the Methodist ministry soon after leaving Muscatine and turned his attention to politics and the law, developing as the war or the rebellion opened into a sympathizer with the south."

I think Dean was a native of Virginia or Kentucky, and educated as a lawyer, and practiced law before entering the ministry. He had the southern notion that the women should sit on different sides of the aisle from the men. I think this was the custom of the early Methodist church. They had commenced to change the custom here; some of the heads of the older families occupied the same seats. When Dean came here he at once disapproved of it; he announced that the men should sit on one side and the women on the other. There was a prominent brother, Thomas Morford, who declined to sit among the "goats." He attended church with his family and they took their accustomed seat. Brother Dean did not mince matters; he at once struck the names of brother Morford and wife from the church roll, and so announced it. I don't think he had any further trouble. Brothers Jacob Mahin and George Porter of course had to sit among the "goats." As soon as Dean left, the men got to sitting with the women. This arrangement was well enough on the part of Dean, for up to his time and since, there has been two women to one man attending church services, but during Dean's time the men attended, and it required as much room for them as it did for the women—the church was always full.

Previous to coming here, Dean served a term as chaplain of the United States senate; this made him acquainted with the noted men in congress, and other statesmen. When Henry Clay died, Dean was called on to prepare an address at the memorial excercises held by the Masonic fraternity of this city in the Methodist Church. It was a fine address.

Dean was a very social man; he always led in conversation, although always willing to learn anything from another he could. During his stay with us, on almost every evening, except Sunday, after meeting time, when it was possible he could be found at McKibben's office as late as 9:30 or 10 o'clock. In those days a number of our best informed citizens met at McKibben's place to compare notes and discuss different questions. This was congenial to Dean. I recollect one of his remarks: he said "that his enemies always told him his faults, his friends never did." We find that is generally the case in almost every man's experience.

Dean had a good law education and wanted to let the Bloomington people know it, and he had a chance. A couple of men got into a row and one killed the other. Dean defended the murderer and got him cleared; he made the jury believe that the deed was done in self-defense, but the people never respected Dean half as much after that—they could not think well of a preacher turning himself out as a lawyer. We felt a little that way ourselves and did not go to hear his masterly address to the jury.

Recollections of
The Presidential Campaigns of 1840 to 1848.

Published in the Muscatine Saturday Mail, October 23, 1897.

Written by J. P. Walton.

No. 41.

In 1840 Iowa had no vote for president, but she heard the noise and felt the spray of that great political wave that swept over the states to the east of us, placing for a brief month a whig president in the chair of state.

We had two political parties at that time—the whigs and democrats. The whigs advocated a protective tariff, internal improvements by the government and a national bank, and were the aggressive party. In the eastern states a high tariff and the national bank were questions of most importance; while in the western and southern states the national bank, and above all, internal improvements by the nation, was the greatest hobby.— They wanted the Mississippi river improved; Louisiana and Mississippi wanted the river levied; Iowa and Illinois wanted the rapids improved.

The democrats were a little divided on the tariff question.— The southern states wanted free trade. In the eastern and central states they advocated a tariff for revenue only. They were all decidedly opposed to a national bank. President Andrew Jackson, their then great politicrl dictator, had once vetoed a United States bank, and of course they had to indorse his act for at least one generation. In regard to internal improvements they were great "state's right" men, and, of course, they wanted each state to make its own improvements. They could run the government on that line for a while, but since the war of the rebellion they are all getting bravely over that idea. While at the recent Western Water Way convention in Davenport, we met several southern gentlemen, all democrats, but all in favor of national improvements on the western rivers. We "bridged the bloody chasm" on that point at least, and did not differ materially with them in politics only in name. They were mostly, so far as I was able to draw them out, gold men—had voted for Bryan, but were glad McKinley was elected.

But to return to our Iowa politics. In 1840 we had a good log cabin and hard cider celebration; not much cider was drank for no apples were grown in this region at that time—whiskey answered the purpose. The speeches were made in a grove on Front street, south of Mulberry, about where Batterson's dwelling is now located. We don't recollect who the speakers were, but believe it to have been the first political meeting held in this part of the state. The election passed off and it took more than month to get the results so far out west. William Henry Harrison was elected, the democrats claiming he was sung into office. This was probably the case in a great measure. It was the first time that songs had ever been used to any extent in political campaigns. The songs were numberless and were of the doggerel type; anybody could sing or halloo them, but they all had points.

Iowa was democratic. It remained democratic for some time. A majority of the first settlers came from democratic states and they held on to their old political faith. It took a new generation to change it.

At this early day, fully fifty years ago, both political parties had a vulture preying on their livers," neither one could get clear of it—both made obeisance to slavery. The democrats seemed to take the lead and to keep it unless the whigs gave their aid to slavery, and as slavery did not want a protective tariff and the New England states did, there was quite hot times at the elections. If any territory was in dispute slavery did the dictating. In the early days of the Van Buren administration, If I am not wrong in my date, there was a dispute over a tract of land on our northeastern boundary of the state of Maine. Slavery had concluded that we did not want any more northern or free states, so our claim was relinquished to Great Britain.

In 1844 the candidates were Henry Clay, of Kentucky, and James K. Polk, of Tennessee. Clay was the whig and was by far the most eminent man. Polk lived farther south. The great question at that time was the northwestern boundary line. The whig war cry was "Fifty-four, forty, or fight." The discussion became hot and Polk, in order to check-mate the whigs, declared he would suffer his right hand to drop off before he would sign any treaty to shut off fifty-four forty. The slave states knew better and they supported and elected him. The result was that during his term of office Texas was annexed, California was acquired and the northwestern difficulty was settled by surrendering to England all it wanted.

The whigs carried the election of 1848 and elected Gen. Zachariah Taylor, and hoped to recover some of their lost prestige, but as Taylor died in about thirty days, as Gen. Harrison had done, the whigs charged the democrats with poisoning or killing him in some way. Millard Fillmore, the vice president, succeeded to his place and turned traitor to the whigs; whether it was fear, money or the hope of future promotion that caused him to pursue such a course none have been able to learn.

Recollections of

POLITICS IN IOWA.

Published in the Muscatine Saturday Mail October 30, 1897; written by J P. Walton.

No. 42.

In our last article we mentioned the election of Zachariah Taylor (old rough and ready) in 1848. This was the first time Iowa voted for a president. It was my first vote. The election was held in the court house in the room now occupied by the auditor. We were a part of Bloomington township, which comprised the present township with Fruitland, a part of Lake, and all of the city. All voted at one place, the court house. We did not have the Australian ballot then. The parties selected about four challengers on each side, and a dozen or so on both sides to stay at the polls to electioneer and pass tickets. The result was that it was one grand row all day long. A stranger or a man that the challengers had any doubt about his right to vote, or a timid man, was sure to get challenged and would have to swear his vote in.

It took a strong determined man to act as challenger as he took some risk to do it. In 1848 Jacob Butler was one of the challengers on the whig side: I have forgotten who the democrats had, at all events I had a chance to swear my vote in. I expected it and did not get mad, although I soon found out who reported me. They expected to scare me away, which was a game practiced on both sides. The polls closed at 6 p. m.; a terrible rush was made to force the challegers away by first one party then the other, and while the row "was on" a few illegal votes were likely to be run in.

After this election no other one occurred that had anything like excitement about it, until the next presidential election in 1852. Then the whigs made another desperate effort to elect Major General Winfield Scott. He had been very prominent in the Mexican war; was a very fine looking man, and commander-in-chief of the regular army. An effort was made to sing him in, as had been done in 1840 with Harrison. We had in our little city more excitement than ever occurred before. Both parties tried to out do each other. The whigs secured an old scenic artist by the name of Scinnottie, who painted a huge banner with the "Hero of Lundy's Lane" of heroic size; the banner was probably twenty-five feet square, and hung across Second street. They had big political gatherings, drank some ale and lots of whiskey. Lager beer was not here then.

The democrats had a candidate from New Hampshire by the name of Franklin Pierce; while not much could be said for him, not much could be said against him. Such was not the case with General Scott, he was frequently known by the name of "old fuss and feathers." He started out to make a series of speeches, which proved too much for him; his meetings were large, for to see General Scott was a treat not to be enjoyed every day. Talking to the common people was different from commanding an army; in order to please his hearers of foreign birth he used the expression "I always love to hear the rich German accent and sweet Irish brogue." This saying preceded and followed after him wherever he went, and it got to be a laughing stock.

In 1852 two more parties made a showing; the Native American or Know Nothing party, which held as its principles that all foreign born persons should be here twenty-one years before voting, and never be allowed to hold office; their "slogan" was "put nothing but Americans on guard." The other party was the Free Soil party, who claimed that no more slave territory should exist and no more slave states be admitted. The two new parties had their effect on the whig and democratic parties, but more especially on the whig party.

In 1852 the American slavery could be considered at its zenith; it controlled the two leading parties; had secured the balance of power; had annexed Texas with the declared purpose of making four more states of it; had acquired California and a large slice from Mexico, all to be converted into slave territory and slave states. Such acquisition of territory changed their condition from the acquisitive to the defensive, and here commenced their trouble to take care of it.

Up to 1852 most of the immigrants had been Irish, from "old down-trodden Ireland," who came for freedom in America, but strange as it may seem, they almost to a man joined the democratic party and became strongly pro-slavery in politics. There was an interest that interfered with their calculations, the German emigration began to set in, large numbers were coming, while some joined the domocratic party, but very few were pro-slavery in sentiment. The Germans commenced to settle in the northern and western territory so much so as to endanger "the balance of power" when looked at from a slavery standpoint. But to complete their misfortunes gold was discovered in California. This took such a swarm of northern men there that all hope of slavery was abandoned in that quarter. The slave interest then began to talk very seriously about dividing the Union. They found that freedom was hedging them in on all sides and if a division could not be had, there would soon be nothing to divide.

The society in the southern slave holding states was composed of three classes—the planter, who owned about all the land; the slaves, and the third class, the "poor white trash," as they were frequently called. The latter class were very primitive in their habits, they did not like to work at anything that a "nigger" could do; they lived in the towns and in small cabins on the plantations, raised a little corn and tobacco for their own consumption; kept dogs to hunt runaway negros, and did the voting. Of course, the planter always managed to control their votes. The soldiers in the Mexican war were largely composed of this class of people. If a division of the union was to be made, and any fighting had to be done, they would be the ones to do it.

In order to keep them in line it was necessary to have a northern republican in the presidential chair. So the leaders divided the democratic party. That division allowed Abraham Lincoln to be elected. The war of the rebellion followed in which Iowa took its part, and especially Muscatine county which was the banner county in number of volunteers sent to the war.

RECOLLECTIONS OF

The Early Coopers of Bloomington.

Published in the Muscatine Saturday Mail, November 6, 1897; written by J. P. Walton.

No. 43.

The first cooper I have any recollection of was the grandfather of John Berkshire, a former superintendent of the Hershey saw mills. Mr. Berkshire came here in 1837 with his son, Montgomery, took a claim and built a cabin up in the hills about a half mile north of the Anderson tile factory; here John Berkshire was born. While the old man followed coopering, neither son or grand-son did—one was a tailor, the other an engineer.

The old man made churns, buckets, tubs, and barrels. There was not much business for a cooper until the merchants and packers commenced to pack pork. Then Mr. Berkshire moved to Muscatine and worked at his trade

Early in the forties a man by the name of Sam Bamford came here and opened a shop. I think it was located in Mad creek flat.

For a period of some sixteen years, from 1844 to 1860, a great many hogs were raised in this vicinity; there were no railroads to haul them off, so they had to be killed and packed for shipping on boats in the spring. This made coopering a very good business. The brick-layers all learned the cooper trade, and worked at coopering in the winter and layed brick in the summer.

One of the first coopers to open a shop in the town was Watterman Benner. His shop stood on the south side of Third street, east of the Avenue; he was an industrious, hard working Yankee, and accumulated some property. He took a notion to get married to old Tommy Odell's daughter. Odell run the ferry across Cedar river near where the Saulsbury bridge now stands. The wedding was arranged, the guests and preacher summoned, and all were there in good time, A fearful rain storm set in, so severe that Benner declined to go out. He may have concluded he could not cross Cedar river if he went, so he went into his shop and went to work. It came night and no Benner arrived; a messenger was dispatched for him, who came to town and found him coopering away. Of course, Brenner returned with the messenger and the wedding passed off all right. The following day he brought his bride home with him, but not before the circumstances had become known— the result was one the biggest charivaries ever known in the city. Benner would not treat to the whiskey; he wasn't that kind. The boys did considerable damage for him. He soon found out who the perpetrators were; then it became his turn; he prosecuted them to such an extent that they were glad to settle. He became quite wealthy, and I think that in 1850 he died with the cholera. His widow married the "dutch doctor," as he was called, Dr. Grand, but did not remain here any length of time.

About 1840 or '45, a man by the name of William Bevard appeared in Bloomington with an immense wagon loaded with pork barrels; on the top of the barrels, stretched lengthwise of the wagon, was mounted a large banner with the inscription "Pittsburg at your door." He was mounted on a high barrel playing an accordian and singing a doggrell like this: "Pittsburg at your door, with barrels good as heretofore," etc., etc. The wagon was drawn by four yoke or pairs of oxen. Of course, such a cavalcade as that brought the town out. The question was, where did he come from; he had gotten the name of "Pittsburg" impromtu, but where he came from was a question he answered by saying: "From Mt. Arrarat and this is my ark." His Mt. Arrarat, or cooper shop, was located on a hill on the road between Grandview and Wapello, about west of Port Louisa, where he made his barrels and hauled them all the way to Muscatine with an ox-team, making about two trips a week. For several trips he was mounted on his ark, grinding away on his old accordian. He got tired of hauling barrels so far. When the Bennett mill was opened and required an additional number of barrels from three to five hundred a day, he concluded to leave his Mt. Arrarat and move to Muscatine. He came here and located near where the Huttig office now stands; purchased the old Kinney mill and, I think, took George Hunt in business with him, and started what he was pleased to call his "cotton-bumper," a machine to cut staves for slack work (flour barrels, etc.) He built a long shed or temporary building near where the Novelty works now stands, to work in. He used cotton wood and elm logs which were rafted here on the river. The oxen that he formerly used to move his ark, were set to hauling logs to the mill. I hardly know when or how he came to stop. The old mill, cotton-bumper and cooper shop went into the hands of Coe & Wells, of whom we will write at another time.

Recollections of

The Early Coopers of Bloomington.

Published in the Muscatine Saturday Mail, November 13, 1897; written by J. P. Walton.

No. 44.

In our article of last week we left the old mill and cooper shop in the hands of Coe & Wells. Now let me speak a few words of the character of these two men. Coe was a "tight fisted," close figuring, reliable man; he was the business man of the firm. If any money was wanted for any extensive opperation he would start down to Connecticut and would always bring it back with him. Wells was a cooper, he run the shop. I think he is now living in Moline, Ills. They run the shop and stave factory for a while in Mad creek flat, near where the Huttig office is now located; but concluded they had not room enough to do the business they wished to, so they purchased ten acres of land, I think, where the Kaiser mill is now located. They built a shop about 24 x 200, two stories high, with a cellar under the whole of it. In the cellar they kept their hoop poles in the dark to keep them from getting wormy. They calculated to work a hundred coopers. When the war broke out the coopering business slacked up. Wells went into the army as captain of a company, in the 37th regiment of Iowa volunteers. Coe retained the shop but never run it very extensively. The shop was eventually taken down.

The coopers had another rallying point at James Bunker's shop which was built in 1849, it stood on the alley west of court house square. The building was underbuilt with brick and was afterwards converted into a dwelling house. It is now owned by Mrs. Schaffer. I worked on this building with J. J. Hoopes; I got 50c per day, worked from 12 to 15 hours a day. I was then a new beginner at the carpenter trade; it was about the time the ten hour a day rule came in, and it was very trying to have other mechanics do their day's work, go home, dress up, have their suppers and come around and talk to us until 7:30 or 8 o'clock, but I had to stand it—J. J. Hoopes was that kind of a man. Hoopes had one hobby which I used to take the advantage of; he liked to discuss politics; whenever a man like Alfred Purcell or John A. Parvin came around we always managed to start a discussion, it relieved our hours of toil very much. In building this cooper shop we used pine shingles made on the ground. We went to the river, bought large clear logs, hauled them to the lot and worked them up; the cooper split and shaved them. It was no trouble to get clear pine logs at that time as there were nothing but the clear part of the best trees cut and rafted. The sawed lumber that was rafted here was warranted to run one-third clear.

But to return to the coopers, their business was the best mechanical business here. While the best carpenters could get but $1.25 per day the coopers could get $2.00 to $2.25 per day. As a class of men they got the largest pay and, with a few exceptions, stood the lowest in character or in public opinion of any class of mechanics. There were exceptions. For instance, Barney Kemper, now following gardening on the Island, He quit coopering before his boys got old enough to learn the trade. Among the prominent names of coopers in the fifties that we recollect are Henry Dougherty who did the heading at S. O. Butler's pork house, James Brisband, Henry Martin, James Moore, John Richardson, Thomas Sween.

ey and Peter Vollberg.

The coopers made their money easily and spent it as freely. Most of them used plenty of whiskey, some of them dressed extravagantly; we recollect one in particular, John Reed, later Captain John Reed, he made big wages and dressed fopishley, went to dances and other amusements. At the end of the year if he came out square he was lucky. There was one of the craft that saved some money, Jacob Israel, he had a mother or an invalid sister to support, but in spite of all that he was ahead at the end of the year. When I saw him last he was running a small shop of his own in Burlington. I think James Bunker, the principal man, died with the consumption not long after his shop was built.

As we have before stated coopering was the best mechanical business we had here, especially in the winter. For instance in the year 1855 125,000 barrels of flour were shipped from Muscatine. This was all barreled, it being before sacks came in use. In the winter of 1854-55, 17,000 hogs were packed here, the products of these hogs being all packed in barrels, tierces or hogsheads, and they were all made here; the material for doing this coopering all came from this vicinity, the timber in the bottoms and on the islands had a great many large Burr oak trees, measuring from 3 to 6 feet in diameter that fell a prey to the business. I recollect buying 40 acres of land and cutting and selling hoop poles enough to pay for the land. The large white and red oak on the bluffs also contributed to the supply. All this was done when Muscatine was not half the present size.

Recollections of

Early Lumber Business of Muscatine.

Published in the Muscatine Saturday Mail, November 20, 1897; written by J. P. Walton.

No. 45.

As lumber is and has been one of the leading industries of our city we will venture a few articles on its history. The first saw mill built in Bloomington was erected by A. O. and D. R. Warfield, on Mad creek, near where Ninth street bridge is now located. Some 30 or 40 yards north of the west end of the bridge is a ditch 10 or 15 feet wide and 2 or 3 feet deep, running paralell to the creek. This ditch was the head race to the mill; the dam was some two or three hundred feet farther up the creek, both ends of which can be seen at this time. Asbury Warfield, one of the proprietors, told me that they lost $7.000 in this mill. They commenced in the autumn of 1837, and were building and having it wash out all the season of 1838 The creek was mad in name and deed, when the water got high. 1838 was a very wet season, and the creek got on "a high" several times.

In 1839 and 1840 the Warfields sawed some lumber, when there was water enough. It was a very serious drawback to the mill, the want of water, when it did not rain. If they could accumulate enough water in the pond above the dam during the night to run through a part of the day they were fortunate.

The mill would be considered a quaint affair at the present time. It was about 16x40 feet, two stories high. The logs were rolled in on the west side into the second story; after sawing they were carried back by hand. The mill had one saw about six inches wide and seven feet long; it had teeth half as large as a man's hand and was hung in a square frame which moved up and down in slides. The log was fastened to a carriage by dogs in the end of the log; they were fed with a ratchet that worked by a pall, and the sawing was very slow work, I don't think it was faster than a foot a minute. The saw was run by a flutter wheel.

This mill nearly broke-up the Warfields, and it next went into the hands of the Brooks Bros.—Sherman and Hiram. They were mechanics and did better with it. The joists in the main part of my present dwelling was about the last work they did. In August 1851, there came the heaviest rain on record (before or since). Of course the dam washed out and it was never repaired. This mill sawed hard wood lumber as a rule, occasionally a pine log was hauled up from the river and sawed. The mill worked mostly on dimension lumber. The rule then was to saw the inch lumber a little more than an inch thick, so when it was planed by hand it would be a plump inch. The saw-karf was near three-eighths of an inch thick, requiring near an inch and one-half of timber for an inch board. Now the saws cut less than an eighth of an inch and that is taken from the inch board.

There were other mills that contributed lumber to the town, such as the steam mill at Geneva, the water mill of the Longs on Sweetland creek, Nye's mill on Pine creek, and Drury's mill on Copperas creek. The river supplied most of the lumber; pine lumber was cut and rafted after about 1840. The merchants would buy a crib or two of lumber paying for it in trade (goods) and sell it out for grain to ship off and get goods. After 1844 or '45 the lumber trade settled down into the dealer's hands. J G. Deshler and T. M. Isett both kept lumber yards.

In 1843-'44 J. G. Deshler went in company with Col. John Vannata and brought the old steam saw mill from Geneva and put it up near where the Huttig office now stands, and run it for some time. On one occasion they disagreed. At that time the people had a way of settling their disputes without appealing to the magistry of the law. They fought it out; hence to be strong and skilled in the pugalistic art was an advantage, as it so proved with them. Deshler was skilled and Vannata was strong, and he concluded to punish Deshler for some misunderstanding and started for him. Deshler fell back on his skill, and as a result Vannatta was knocked out so badly that it dissolved the partnership. The Kinney Bros., Robert and Samuel, bought the mill, but as neither of them were suited for the business it closed up. The mill was afterwards used for a stave factory and shingle machine.

In 1843 Cornelius Cadle erected his saw mill, the first steam saw mill in the city, on Front street above Oak. This mill was built by Cadle, but being short of funds he took in a partner by the name of Riley (if I recollect aright) who afterwards sold out to the Chambers Brothers. The firm was then known as Chambers, Cadle & Co. Having recently written up the Chambers Brothers and Cornelius Cadle, I will not follow the fate of this mill.

In 1837 Ware Long with three or four sons, nearly all grown came here and erected a water mill on Sweetland creek about a mile from the river. They used an under-shot or flutter wheel, and did some sawing in 1846. As near as I can recollect this mill passed into the hands of a man by the name of Bruce, who fitted it up. I recollect helping him to build a turbine wheel of wood for use in the mill. It worked much better than the old one, but the same difficulty existed with this mill, when it rained hard there was too much water, when it did not rain there was not enough to run it. This man Bruce was an excellent mechanic; he had been farming over in the Illinois bottom on the farm now occupied by Henry Smull. Bruce had some cattle to sell. (I took a cow or perhaps two for my pay.) He also had a large family. He left the bottom and moved up to the mill, and what became of him I don't recollect. Before leaving he lost one of his children, a little girl some 5 or 6 years of age; she got lost in the high grass in the bottom; the town turned out to help hunt, and the child was found by the assistance of Jake Isrial's big dog after being lost some two days. It was in the summer and the little one had not suffered any permanent injury.

[TO BE CONTINUED]

Recollections of

Early Lumber Business of Muscatine.

Published in the Muscatine Saturday Mail November 17, 1897; written by
J. P. Walton.

No. 46.

In the spring of 1851 a man by the name of Samuel McKibben came here and went into the lumber business with T. M. Isett under the name of S. M. McKibben & Co. They occupied the lot north of the switch of the street car line on Second street, west of Walnut, where Isett had handled or piled his lumber on former occasions. I recollect building an office for them in 1851. They continued in business together some seven or eight years. After the panic of 1857 the firm closed up with quite a pile of over dry lumber on Isett's hands. This lumber would now be called high grade. Isett tried to close it out at ten and eleven dollars a thousand, but could not sell it. He was forced to hold it until the war broke out, when the price of lumber went kiting and Isett did well with it.

In 1847 a Mr. Brannum came here and went into the lumber business; he piled his lumber on the lots since used by S. G. Stein, on the northwest corner of Pine and Second streets. Brannum run the yard for about two years and sold out to S. G. Stein in 1849, and went to California.

Mr. S. G. Stein came here in 1849 without much money. I have been informed he borrowed a small amount from his brother, John G. Steine the hotel keeper, and bought out Brannum, and continued the business until his death. The biographies have dealt liberally with his official career, which was quite extensive. If something of the man as a citizen can be mentioned we consider it proper. S. G. Stein was a very generous man to the needy if worthy, but had no money for the unworthy if he knew it. He was willing to sell lumber on time if the sale was secure; this of course sent a great many doubtful customers to him, whom he managed to keep up with, on his part. His prices were usually a little higher than those of other yards, but to a cash customer he could b extremely low. We never thought he made much money in his lumber yard in later years. We thought he run it more for a business or a headquarters than he did for a profit. He was never so busy that he would not talk to a friend, on the contrary he was always glad to meet them. We have always thought his congeniality had much to do with his success. He had an assistant who was one of the most trusty men in our city, Jacob Erb. Mr. Erb came here about as early as Mr. Stein, remained awhile, went to California, came back and entered Mr. Stein's employ. In later years he managed the lumber yard. I have often seen customers who went there for lumber or prices who had to wait until "Jake" came in. Stein did not know anything about the price of lumber or what he had. Erb was the lumberman of that yard. I am well satisfied that Mr. Stein would have quit the lumber business long ago if he had not had Jacob Erb to manage it for him.

For many years Stein's office was the voting place for the first ward; it was about the only public place in that part of the ward for many years.

Mr. S. G. Stein and S G. Hill started a sash and door manufactory. It stood on Front street west of Pine. This factory had the first planing mill in the city. They run it very successfully until the war broke out, when Hill was appointed colonel of the 35th regiment, Iowa volunteers. He was killed at the battle of Nashville. The factory was then sold to Cadle & Mulford.

When the Oat Meal factory was started Mr. Stein was one of the principal owners; he was associated with F. D. Holcomb and others. Holcomb and most of the others withdrew leaving Mr. Stein the principal owner at one time. Here his early knowledge of milling came in good play, but as before in the lumber business, he was fortunate in getting managers in Mr. Frank P. Sawyer, a joint owner, and J. Risley Reuling assistant manager.

In 1851 Brinton Darlington and John Irwin opened a lumber yard on Front street, east of Sycamore street. Pappoose creek our old land mark is gone, we lost sight of it in 1896, so we have to name the street. Darlington & Irvin kept quite a stock of hard lumber. In the great freshet of August 10, 1851, the whole yard was flooded and most of the lumber washed away, some of it lodged on Muscatine Island and was recovered. This lumber yard did not last long after the wash-out. Irvin went to work at carpentering and Darlington into some other business.

Recollections of

Early Lumber Business of Muscatine.

Published in the Muscatine Saturday Mail, December 4, 1897; written by
J. P. Walton.

No. 47.

In talking with a prominent man, of a neighboring city, that had been quite successful in its manufacturing operations, I learned that the largest part of their trials was failures; in other words not one-half were successful. Such has hardly been the case with Muscatine, although we have had several disappointments and are liable to have more.

One of the most complete failures—so far, in not coming up to expectations—was the Union Lumber Co., with Hon. Thad. C. Pound as president, and William Van Name as manager. They were first located on the corner of Second and Orange streets, in 1873 or 1874. Their headquarters and mill were at Chippewa Falls. They first organized as Pound, Halbert & Co. when Van Name and a few others came along with some money to invest. The company was reorganized and started a yard in Muscatine, sawing the lumber at Chippewa Falls, Minn. They owned their own steamboat for towing rafts. Previous to this time most of the lumber had been floated down the river by hand, in the shape of large rafts with sweeps or oars, each oar being frequently worked by four men. The steam tow-boats came along and did away with that kind of rafting.

The Union Lumber Co.'s boat, the St. Clair Belle, was kept running, bringing down lumber. Their sales were good, but, like many others, they were not satisfied with letting well enough alone; they concluded they must do more, so they bought some thirty acres of land (the old cooper shop plant of Coe & Wells was a part of it) down on the Island, where the Kaiser mill now stands. They constructed a dry house, some 75 feet wide and 150 feet long, surrounded it with platforms and tracks, and run it a part of the time. They cut the old cooper shop in two and converted a part of it into a planing mill. The Union Lumber Co. purchased the right of way and constructed the railroad switch now used by the South Muscatine Lumber Co.

I built the office for the Union Lumber Co., furnishing all the material except the lumber. The result was, we had to use about all the crooked culls that had been through the dry house. This office, now occupied by the Kaiser Brothers, and the switch are about the only things left of the Union Lumber Co. By the time the office was constructed the money gave out, and we had to wait for more than a year for our pay. The company had piled up a large amount of high grade lumber during the season of 1876. Thad. Pound wanted money very badly to use in cutting more logs, so he sold the entire stock of lumber out to the Musser Lumber Co. By sticking tight to them I got the Mussers to assume the debt, and after waiting three months I received my pay.

The following season of 1877, if I am correct, the Union Lumber Co. bought more lumber and filled the dry house (report said culled lumber) and heated it up. All at once it broke out into a blaze and the dry house and three hundred thousand feet of lumber burned up. It turned out to be insured. This was so heavy a blow to the company that it never rebuilt at Muscatine. Thad. Pound and Van Name were not interested in Muscatine any more. The planing mill and cooper shop did not burn. It with the land and the office was sold to U. N. Roberts & Co., who were in the sash and door business in Davenport with a branch house at Muscatine. They built a saw mill in front of and used a part of the old cooper shop. If I am correct they had a saw mill man in company with them by the name of Burdick who afterwards bought their share of the mill and run it quite successfully, and finally sold it to Ben. Hershey. The report put the figures about this way: Burdick had paid the Roberts Co. $20,000 for their half interest and sold the whole to Hersney for $100,000, clearing $60,000. Hershey kept improving the mill until he had some $250,000 invested. It was afterwards sold to the Kaisers for something like $35,000. It was reported that Hershey cleared the cost of the mill the first year he run it. The mill is now being run by the Kaiser Brothers, who manage the affairs of the South Muscatine Lumber Co.

Recollections of

Early Tavern-Keepers of Bloomington.

A Letter writen by S. W. Stewart, of Wilton, to

J. P. WALTON.

Published in the Muscatine Saturday Mail December 11, 1897.

No. 48.

At our annual Old Settlers' reunion on August 27, 1897, we spoke about the early taverns and their keepers. Mr. S. W. Stewart, of Wilton, one of the vice-president's of the society, was present and volunteered to write up some of his recollections. He has selected four of the leading characters of the early times—John G. Steine, Capt. Jim Parmer, Josiah Parvin and Frederick Miller. John G. Steine occupied the "Bob Kinney" hotel on the west corner of Chestnut and Front streets. Captain Jim Parmer was located on the north side of Second street, between Chestnut and Iowa Anenue. The buildings were both frame and have been removed for many years. Josiah Parvin occupied the brick building on the west corner of Second and Walnut streets. Frederick Miller's tavern was a brick building on the west corner of Fourth and Mulberry streets. Both of the latter buildings have been enlarged and are yet standing.

MR. STEWART'S LETTER.

Wilton, Iowa, Dec. 1, 1897.— We want to draw on the patience of the readers of the SATURDAY MAIL to make an addition to President Walton's old settlers' day address; not to improve or criticise but to note some things his space would not allow. J. G. Steine, kept tavern in Muscatine when it was the supply center of the garden spot of Iowa, reaching as far west as Fort Dodge, and to west of the Wasapinican river as far up as Waverly in Bremer county.

Men left home to market wheat or pork, without money, taking their lunch with them, camping by the roadside, sleeping in their wagons, and when there was grass, turned their horses loose to get their supper on the prairie. Some times they would get 40 cents a bushel for wheat or $1.25 per hundred for dressed pork that had been hauled more than a hundred miles. They went to Steine's and exchanged something they had for lodging and food, if he needed anything they had. They were lodged and fed all the same, none were turned away; he had one of the best women for a wife that ever lived in Muscatine,

When John was sober he was a whig, when he had a full meal of liquid democratic enthusiasm he was a liberal. We understand a "liberal" in religion or politics to be one who has a little of this, less of that and not much of any thing. He was always a kind hearted man. In religion he leaned toward the Presbyterian church, at least he was a Calvinist. He kept an orderly house, was kind and courteous to all, no gambling, profanity or smutty talk; decency and order was the rule. [At that time smutty talk was quite common among the men and was considered quite an accomplishment. J. P. W.]

Captain Jim Parmer was kind and courteous like Steine. His house was not so quiet, he kept a bar. At that time Iowa had many fairly good men who were only partly civilized. When they got outside of their township they wanted to have a good time. They went to Captain Jim's place and filled up with liquid enthusiasm, and it often broke out at the mouth, then there was music in the air. Captain Jim knew his business and usually kept his customers in hand. It was a good place to stop; when a men had no money he was treated as well as the man who had plenty. He had a sign hung on the homeliest stick of timber we ever saw; it was about twelve feet above the ground, about eight inches in diameter, it run in one direction not more than twelve inches at a heat, at every other turn it sent out a limb as crooked as the main stock. These limbs had been cut about twenty inches in length and left on to embellish the main stock. From that post his sign swung, it was the most prominent object on Second street from where the Kemble house now stands to where Dr. Reeder lived on the hill. We think Captain Jim was a whig in politics, in religion he leaned toward the Episcopalians. He was a good man and filled his place well.

Josiah Parvin was a man after his own heart; he was ever loose on the handle, and would fly off if things did not go to suit him. Isett, Blades and Hastings had all the leisure needed to play practical jokes on him. They would find a stranger, fill him with whisky and send him to Parvin to employ him to pass counterfeit money on his customers at a big per cent. The man would get him out of hearing of others and tell him his business. If the old man hated anything on earth it was a counterfeiter or a horse thief. By the time the proposition was delivered, the old man would have his bottle of wrath ready for business. The adjectives and anthemas would roll out red hot and as thick as a coiled rope. When he got his vocabulary warmed up all creation stopped to listen. The idle "boys" who set the trap were sure to be in ear shot to enjoy the seance. Mr. Parvin was a good citizen and kept a good orderly house; he was a democrat without knot or limb or woodpecker hole. If you wanted to hear chin music hint that Jackson was not what he ought to be. He was a nothingarian with a leaning toward the Methodists.

Frederick Miller was a blacksmith with a shop on the back end of his lot; a rough workman, shod horses, made harrow-teeth, sharpened plows, mended trace and log chains and sich. Soon just south of his shop a sign was seen "wagon yard" that was for teams to drive in and feed at noon. A picayune if they found their own feed, a bit if he found hay, two bits if he found hay and corn. Soon he put up a stable along the alley west of the shop. Soon that was too small for his customers, and he extended his stable across his two lots to Mrs. Marks, his neighbor on the west; soon he was again crowded, then he built a shed on the south side of his stable. By this time he had stacked his tools and used his shop for a stable. His stable was a primitive structure, the frame was oar-poles set in the ground with girts nailed on the outside to attach the upright siding to the building; joists were nailed to the post for the upper floor that was laid with oar-blades. That floor was the old man's downfall. The oar-blades were laid a few inches apart, the horses would reach for a bite of hay and leave a wisp hanging, reaching down about to the horses' back. Miller had a lantern, it was square, its posts were made of tin in which were grooves to hold a pane of glass, in that a candle was used to furnish light, on one side about one-half the pane of glass was gone, leaving the candle exposed. My wife and myself had been out, when we came home about nine o'clock at night. We went to the edge of the platform to scrape some mud from our shoes, while there we saw the beginning of the calamity. Three men were in the stable about the middle, looking over their horses, one of them took the broken lantern, held it high as if he wanted to see the horse's back, the candle came in contact with one of the wisps of hay and in instant the blaze flashed over the hay as if it was in tow. At the back end of our lot within thirty feet of the tinder box we had a stable, in which was a cow, some hay and corn. We lost no time in getting to them; we turned the cow loose, by that time the west end of the tinder box was on fire. It was said that there was one hundred horses in the stable that night; seventeen I think perished in the fire.

Miller was a hustler, he was a preacher in one those little societies that flourished in such amazing quantities on the genial soil of Pensylvania, whose all embracing titles are often larger than the society, such as "the sons of God," "The true Christians." It was said of Miller that he often preached funeral sermons at three dollars a preach. He kept a good quiet house, was a kind hearted, pleasant man, and had a good kind motherly woman for a wife, who included all the world in her kindness of heart.

These men here spoken of were not saints of the popular pattern that so fitted that class of men called blessed in Mathew xxv, 34-40. We expect to meet them on the Elisian fields, enjoying the pictures of their hard work and poor pay in helping to blaze the way to better times in glorious Iowa. Few men could have succeeded with their opportunities. S. W. S.

We are much obliged to Mr. Stewart for the foregoing and are willing to admit that there were some things about those taverns that he can describe better than we did. We attribute that to the likelihood of his having patronised them the most.

Recollections of

The Early Lumber Business of Muscatine.

Published in the Muscatine Saturday Mail, December 25, 1897; written by J. P. Walton.

No. 49.

In 1850 Jacob Hershey, a cousin of the late Benjamin Hershey, came here, and in 1852 he built quite a good sized saw mill for the times. It stood on the site where the present Hershey mill now stands in South Muscatine. I think the mill had two rotary saws, a large one for canting and a small one for sawing the cants; with a lath saw, and I think a shingle machine. He run this mill until 1853, when Benjamin Hershey come along and rented it, and in 1855 he purchased it. Benjamin Hershey ran the mill for a year or more with good success. In 1856 or '57 he anounced that he was going to build a new mill and commenced to saw the timbers. It took about a year to build the new mill which he finished in due time. He introduced gang saws—a novelty on the Mississippi river at that time. He claimed he could save a fortune in saw dust, or by not making the saw dust, which proved true. The lumber sawed was very smooth but it was all full of short crooks, so much so that in anything but clear lumber it was hardly safe to plane it. We presume it was some defect in the machinery which has since been overcome.

Mr. Hershey got his new mill in running order just as the panic of 1857 struck him. He saw he would have to resort to some means to retain the mill; what they were I don't know but for quite awhile he signed his name as B. Hershey, agent. In the course of time the agent was dropped from the name. In this community where he lived no discredit was ever attached to his good name for the course he pursued.

This mill proved a "bonanza" to Benjamin Hershey; he soon found he had more money than he wanted to use in the saw mill business; so he purchased some eight or nine hundred acres of land only two miles west of his mill for which he paid what was then considered a large price. Considerable of it was on the bluff and covered with timber; he at once cut the timber off and sold it to the railroad company, using the teams he had about the mill to haul it during the winter, what they were not able to do he hired done. This was before the railroads used coal for fuel, and they took all the wood they could get. Hershey made enough out of the wood to pay for the land. This farm made a place for him to spend his leasure hours and he commenced improving it. In the summer of 1872 I erected the large brick dwelling on his farm, now used for an orphans' home. This was likely the largest farm house in the state of Iowa.

At that time Mr. Hershey thought of retiring from business, having made an arrangement by which he calculated the Musser brothers would take the mill. The arrangement miscarried much to Hershey's disgust but likely to his advantage, for this deal was not more than "off" before the Rock Island railroad offered him a large contract of sawing timber for the extension west of Washington at his own price. He had to enlarge his mill at once and it run night and day all summer.

In the year 1875 Hershey concluded he saw a place where some more money could be used to the advantage of the lumber interest in the way of securing logs, etc., and thinking that it would be better to have others connected with him, so the mill would not stop if an accident occurred to him, he concluded to incorporate and take others in with him. Accordingly the Hershey Lumber Co. was incorporated with $200,000 capital, Hershey having three-fourths of the stock, and being president and treasurer of the company. S. G. Stein was vice-president, William Ewart secretary, and H. W. Moore, G. A. Garrettson and Thos. Irwin were the principal moneyed men. Hershey took several of the working force in with him to manage the mill, etc. One of his first operations was to purchase the Burdick mill, which he fitted up and run until his death. The mill is now owned by the South Muscatine Lumber and Box Co.

Believing it to be an advantage to saw the small rough logs in the upper river and raft the lumber to Muscatine, he acted accordingly and built a mill in Still Water, Minn., and ways at Muscatine for drawing out the lumber which was used quite extensively.

Mr. Hershey was very charitable to the needy, quite autocratic at times, then again quite the reverse. We have often noticed that the stories told about a prominant man in a community are a good index to his character, although they are quite frequently incorrect. As they are public property we see no reason why they should not follow the man. Mr. Hershey had his share; some of them had a mirthful turn. No one enjoyed a mirthful story any better than Mr. Hershey, and probably no prominent business man gave a better opportunity for them than he did.

It was said that Mr. Hershey never gave the other stockholders of the lumber company any information about the condition of the company, neither did he make any dividends. On one occasion G. A. Garrettson accosted Mr. Hershey to know why no dividends were made, Hershey replied that "the company was not organized to make dividends, it was formed to give poor laboring men work." Garrittson was very indignant. When Hershey got ready he made a dividend of 35 or 40 per cent. After that no more stocks were offered for sale.

Another story was that Hershey kept a flock of turkeys on his farm, and among them was a very fine gobbler that chose the fence for a roosting place. One night a dog came around and killed the gobbler. Hershey was so indignant that he had a pen made to keep other domestic animals away, and kept poision in this pen for a full year for stray dogs. We wish there was more of that kind of pens in use.

On another occasion the wild geese got to feeding in his field, someone had informed him that corn soaked in whiskey and fed to the geese would make them drunk. One day he informed his man of-all-work that he had brought some whiskey for him to soak corn in for the geese and says "Daniel soak some corn in this whiskey and put it out for those geese and see if it makes them drunk. Don't you drink it yourself for there is strychnine in it," all of which Daniel assented to. Now Daniel was an Irishman and could be trusted with anything better than a jug of whiskey. It was too much for him. He reasoned this way: Daniel had better have that whiskey, and that whiskey was not poisoned for Hershey wanted the geese to eat, of course he would not want them prisoned. Daniel gave the geese the corn without the soaking and set the whiskey away. On the following day when Hershey came to the farm he accosted Daniel. "Did you put out that corn?" "Yes sir." Did they eat it?" "Yes sir." "Did it make them drunk?" "No sir; you had better bring some more whiskey." Hershey did not bring more. When Daniel got leasure he took a big spree on that whiskey.

On another occasion a neighbor of Heshey had a lot of hogs

he did not take care of, they kept trespassing on Hersney's place. After several offenses Hershey got out of patience and got his men and drove them up, then he says "Boys, I will sell these hogs to you, what will you give? I will guarantee the title." The boys bid them off and paid for them. When the neighbor came around to look for the hogs Mr. Hershey said "I sold those hogs of yours and here is the money I got for them; if you want any more than that you may get it if you can."

At one time Mr. Hershey got in a habit of lawing or at least got into several law suits. He was not successful, he disposed of his lawyer and quit the law business. One of the stories about Mr. Hershey's law experience was about this way: When he settled up his old indebtedness that he incurred in building the new mill there remained an old claim for interest which he did not want to pay at that time, and for which he gave his note "payable at my convenience on or before the judgement day." The parties holding the note waited until it nearly run out by limitation and commenced suit to collect it. The trial was before the court who decided against Mr. Hershey, saying "Mr. Hershey you had better pay that note now, as on the judgement day you will have plenty of other matters to attend to." The note was paid.

Mr. Hershey's death was the result of of an accident, leaving the largest estate of any former citizen, all of which he accumulated while here. We will say that no man of our city was more respected by both rich and poor. That was demonstrated by the largest attendance at his funeral obseques that the city ever witnessed.

Recollections of

The Early Lumber Business of Muscatine.

Published in the Muscatine Saturday Mail, January 1, 1898; written by J. P. Walton.

No. 50.

When the present Hershey mill was built it was not more than one-half the size that it is now. It stood close to the east side of the old one. After it got to running, I think in the fall of 1857, I moved the old one around to the east of the new one to be converted into a plaining mill. I am not certain that it was ever used for that purpose. For several years Hershey's land did not extend more than one-half the way west to the present plaining mill. This mill was first built and used by S. O. Butler as a pork house. On the bank of the slough to the south stood the old frame slaughter house that was first built by Green & Stone; used by them, then by S. O. Butler, later by James Hagan, and others. The upper end of the slough above the present road was used for a log harbor. The bark and other litter from the mill kept filling up the slough and damaging the drainage of the slaughter houses. Of course the slaughter house men and Hershey disagreed. One fall, just as the slaughter house was about to start, it took fire in the night. Hershey was on hand. The boys wanted to turn on the water from his mill and put it out, but Hershey would not permit it. The slaughter house burned. An interest in the property belonged to a man in Philadelphia. Hershey bought his interest and then dictated terms to the Muscatine men. He converted the pork house into the present plaining mill.

One of Mr. Hershey's good traits was his ability to measure the capacity of his employes. He succeeded in getting men of ability for the different places they had to fill, although getting them, in many cases, from almost obscurity. In the office he had Thomas Irving, a native of Canada. He managed the business whether Hershey was here or away. When Hershey was here he ordered him; when Hershey was absent he ordered himself. On one occasion he hired a man by the name of ———— Ellis, who was a very expert accountant, a splendid man for the place. After he became acquainted with the business, Mr. Hershey told Mr. Irving that he had found another man to take his place in the office. Mr. Irving was much disappointed. Hershey told him that he wanted him to go north and look after the log interest, stating that if he let him stay in that office a year or so longer that he would be dead. Irving had no choice about it and had to go, which was fortunate for Irving. He is now president of the Hershey Lumber Co. He lives in St. Paul and is frequently seen on our streets, here on business for the company.

Mr. Ellis did not live long after coming here. He was followed by a Mr. Brown. I was not acquainted with him. His place was soon filled by a nephew of Mr. Irving, Will Ewart, who was certainly a good manager while here. He went in with Mr. Hershey and bought a mill at Sargent, Mo., which, I have understood, was not a success.

Mr. Ewart's place in the office here was filled by Mr. Francis, another native of Canada, who is the present big man of the company.

As a salesman and manager of the yard the present incumbent, John Hahn, outranks most of them. He has been here fully forty years. At one time his business was loading cars. On one occasion Mr. Hershey went to Europe to purchase cattle. On his return he found John piling lumber. John said he was dissatisfied and was going to quit. Hershey asked what the matter was. John told him what it was. Hershey told him to take his old place in the morning. Hershey shortly met the manager, Mr. Ewart, who said to him, "John Hahn is going to quit, who will you put in his place?" Hershey's response was: "I guess we will put you there; have you seen Mr. Hahn?" He said he had not. Hershey then gave Ewart a lecture about interfering with the men.

When the company was incorporated Mr. Hahn took some stock. He kept it for some time and got no dividends. He built a new house and wanted money. He went to Hershey and told him that he wanted to sell his stock and must; if he could not keep his place without he would have to leave it. Mr. Hershey said: "Pay John for his stock; we can't afford to lose a good man be cause he can't hold stock." We rather think that when that 35 or 40 per cent dividend was made he wished he had kept his stock. John has been a very faithful man to the company.

Hershey took "Billy" Richards when a mere boy to take care of his horse, and kept him until the war broke out, when Billy went into the army, saved his little money, came back and went to work for Hershey in the lumber yard. He was soon entrusted with selling, and became the most popular salesman in the city. The other lumber men claimed his popularity was obtained at Hershey's expense by selling lumber too cheap; but as Hershey appeared to get rich much faster than the other dealers, we conclude that he was not made any poorer by Billy's accommodation. Billy, as usual, saved his money, and when the company was incorporated he was able to take a small block of stock, which increased in value all the while. Billy recently sold out to the Hershey Co. and is not now engaged in any business

During the year the mill was being constructed Hershey had a number of engineers and mill superintendents; none seemed to stick until John Berkshire came. Of him we can only say that John learned the engineer's trade under the venerable Charles Chaplin, of our city, and run on a steam boat on the Missouri river. It is enough to say that when John fetched up at the Hershey mill he was where he was wanted. He staid here and run the engine, and soon took charge of all the machinery. John, like others of Hershey's boys, saved his money and took stock in the company, sold it and went into the Barry Manufacturing Company, and later in a hard pine saw mill in Arkansas. John is now managing the mill and said to be owner.

When Mr. Hershey first came here he brought with him a young man, Andrew Cracker, who was possessed of a wonderful mechanical knowledge, that he kept for a general man. If a sawyer was hurt Cracker took his place. Hershey once told me that Cracker could do anything about the mill, from running the engine to running the saws. Andrew is there now as general manager of the machinery. The place was filled awhile by Michael Appel while Crocker was at the lower mill.

Here let me say a word about Michael Appel. He was one of nature's noblemen. He came here fresh from Germany; I think he could not speak the English language; he stayed right by his work. At the time of his death he had the charge of all the laborers around and in the mill; there was no man more popular.

To do their hauling it took some fifty teams. These were

under the general management, first, of George Funk; next James Paine, who remained for some years, and finally went west and took an interest in some way in Mr. Hershey's horse farm. The place is now filled by Michael Bryon, a young man who almost grew up in the company's employ.

When additions were made to the mill it was necessary to enlarge the power. A new cylinder and flywheel were put on to the engine and new boilers and a new engineer by the name of August Bierman. He commenced twenty-six years ago to run the big engine and has grown big at the job. We don't mean big headed, but big-hearted and big all over, a real whole-souled big fellow. There is nothing small about him—he weighs more than 300 pounds. We are satisfied that he is a big mechanic or Hershey would not have tolerated him so long. May August and his engine be companions for another twenty-six years is our vote.

There is another of the old stand-bys still there, Thomas Neitzel; I think he has control of the lumber hauling to the cars. We don't know how long he has been there, we will say twenty-five or thirty years or more; he is always moving at his business, don't seem to ever get tired.

And another, William Schaefer, who could be seen on the runway sorting lumber; he has been there as long as we can recollect.

In the mill we have seen James Parmelee as foreman saw filer for at least twenty-five years. When he first went there he was able to do most of the work himself; now it takes quite a detachment to do it. On the shingle machine we have noticed the energetic countenance of Irvin Earl for a long time.

In the old style printing office they had a "devil" to do the work that the regulars would not do. It is the same way with this lumber yard; they have a man of the same kind; they call him Denis for short; his quarters are down in the south corner of the yard. We don't know any other name for him but Denis; his business is to trim up and sort damaged lumber and make it saleable, which he does with success.

There are doubtless many other worthies whose names should be enrolled as helpers in building up this great interest, but we are unable to do it. Next week we will consider B. Hershey as a farmer.

Recollections of

B. Hershey as a Farmer.

Published in the Muscatine Saturday Mail, January 8, 1898; written by J. P. Walton.

No. 51.

It is said of General Grant that his greatness consisted in a measure of the greatness of the officers that he had surrounding him. This could be said of Mr. Hershey. After he secured the proper men to run and attend to the mill he turned his attention to developing his big farm. This farm was one of the oldest farms in the bottom. It had been in cultivation since 1836, over thirty of these years without any attention to the preservation of its fertility. I think Mr. Hershey was the first one to put any fertilizer on the land. After the timber was cut off from the bluff land, as mentioned in our last paper, he commenced to stock it with cattle. When we commenced building the large house in 1870 he had quite a herd of Jerseys and manufactured some very fine butter. In the spring of 1872 or '73 he brought his first stock of ponies from Canada; they have been considered the finest in the west. His noted stallion, Huckleberry, was known by all pony breeders. Soon after he brought them here I asked him what he did it for; he replied, "to make money;" that he could keep a pony as cheap as a sheep and it would bring as much money as a large horse. I think he came nearer realizing his expectations on the ponies than on any of his other stock experiments, unless it was the Herefords. His trotting horse experiments, and he had at times some 100 head of horses, were not a success to any great extent; he built large barns, had his own mile track, and spared no pains to make it successful; he raised some fine, elegant horses, but few trotters; his aim was to get a stock of horses that would rival the Bashaws without crossing them with the Bashaws —an aim he never attained. His biggest move in the stock line was when he imported his herd of 81 Herefords in 1881. They required more barn room, and building more was the order.

In one of his trips east he fell in with an old stray architect by the name of Wilkinson, who was endowed with an immense amount of pronouns He captivated Mr. Hershey and persuaded him to build the big creamery barn that, when compl ted, cost $38,000.

This Mr. Wilkinson had a scheme of sub-air ventilation. The scheme was to cool the air before letting it into the barn, then making the barn very tight so as to keep it cool during the warm weather, and warm during the cold weather. He claimed cattle would do much better under those conditions than in the ordinary ones. His fattening cattle he never let out The scheme looked well to Hershey, so he started to carry it out; built the barn, and put a tunnel through the hill back into a ravine several hundred feet away. They expected to cool the air while passing through this tunnel. In connection with the barn they expected to run a creamery. Hershey had quite a herd of Jersey cattle, but he expected to depend on the country for his milk. He fitted up a nice lot of creamery wagons and got the creamery in good running order.

During the time that the creamery was running in full force, Mr. Hershey told Mr. Fisher, his head manager, to put up a nice package of butter for the Chicago fall exhibit. Hershey took the butter to Chicago and exhibited it. It did not take the premium, which was given to a package of oleomargerine. Hershey bought the premium oleomargerine and had it sent home to Fisher. He came back and met Fisher, who inquired: "Did we get the premium?" Hershey replied: "No. I bought the butter that did get it and it will be down there at your house; try it." The butter came all right; Fisher tasted it, and the next time they met, Hershey said: "Did you try the butter?" Fisher replied: "I did." "Was it as good as ours?" Fisher said: "It was a little better than ours." Hershey said: "That is enough, we will dry up this butter factory at once, if we can't make butter that will beat oleomargerine," and it was done.

The barn proved a good place to keep cattle. He seeded down most of his bottom land to grass, cut it and put it in the barns. It was said that this one barn would hold 300 tons of hay.

When he built this big barn he got beat. The architect, Wilkinson, did not suit him. He kept him as long as it was profitable.

When he wanted him to leave, much to his disappointment, he would not go. Hershey gave him a room in the old office, and he went to the house for his meals. He claimed quite a large sum of money from Hershey, who refused to give him anything. He had no money, not enough to buy a drink of whisky that he had been used to for a long time. One of the hired men took pity on him and supplied him with a quart a week, which he managed to get along with.

Hershey hired J. J. Hoopes to superintend the work and told him to arrange to get the old fellow away as cheaply as he could. Hoopes got the two to agree to have the matter referred to mechanics, Hershey to pay the referees. Some four or five of the builders of the city went down to the farm; the old man was there and explained the particulars to them. They looked the matter over and decided that Hershey should pay the old man some $250, and each of the referees $3 each. The old man got his pay but the referees did not.

He had barn and stable room enough for two or three hundred head of cattle and at least 150 head of horses. Hershey's greatest trouble in raising cattle for profit was that he became attached to his stock—both horses and cattle —and would not sell them when they were ready for sale. He had as high as 120 head of horses at one time, and 100 head were driving horses. For many of these he was offered big prices; apparently the higher the price the less he was disposed to sell. For instance, he was offered $10,000 for Fleta; she got crippled up and had to be killed. For Whitefoot he was offered $3,500, he eventually sold him for $150. For Connor and Nigger he was offered $6,000; he finally sold them for $300; he had two others that he was offered $1,000 each that he sold for $100 each.

His cattle he treated in much the same way. He imported 81 head which he picked up at different places; some of them were very fine, many were not, but all had the white faces, and to the uninitiated they appeared all right, but they would all sell well. Those that he sold young, yearlings or two years old, that were shipped west, sold well; those he kept were sold at a great loss. Many of the cattle that he had refused eight hundred to one thousand dollars, sold at from forty to fifty dollars. There were two heifers that Hershey was offered $1,200 cash, sold for $50 each.

On one occasion he put up twelve head of white-faces; he fed them until they would not take on any more fat; his foreman wanted him to sell them, the market was good and they were out of corn. Hershey would not consent to have them sold, so they were fed a year longer and sold for some $500 less than they would have sold for one year earlier. The market had dropped.

While Mr. Hershey devoted much of his time to the farm, he had to have a superintendent of great executive ability. It required two kinds of ability, one to manage the farm, the other to manage Mr. Hershey while on the farm. The latter was frequently the greater one. After making several trials he found in Mr. A. H. Fisher the man he wanted. Mr. Fisher came here in 1870, not expecting to stay more than a season or so, but staid for eighteen years, and then left to go on his own farm on Muscatine Island. Mr. Hershey found in him an active, reliable, straight forward man, one that he could rely on every time.

This is the third paper we have devoted to Mr. Hershey. There are many who have helped Mr. Hershey in building up these large industries whose names are omitted from the want of acquaintance and space, and some errors have occurred. For instance, Michael Appel in place of Martin Appel, whose name should have been used in connection with the mill. There were two old Germans that worked early and late, rain or shine, wet or dry—John Neibert Sr. and John Benson—and likely dozens of others that I can't mention which we will have to leave for the present.

Recollections of

MUSSERVILLE.

Published in the Muscatine Saturday Mail, January 15, 1898; written by J. P. Walton.

No. 52.

If we look back forty years say January 1, 1858, we will find but few buildings in South Muscatine—Musserville as it is frequently called. At a very early day, in 1837, Josh Stearns and a brother built a cabin on the upper end of the Island and lived there a few years. The second house built within the city limits on the Island was where Mr. M. D. Manlove's house, that was recently destroyed by fire, stood. We are not sure but the house just destroyed was the old one, I think it was built by Ed. Browning on what we call the Day land. The third house built was the residence of S. P. Hopson. It stood where the Musserville plaining mill now stands. I think it was built in 1850.

Soon after the dam was put across the slough in 1845, a levee was built by subscriptions down as far as the high ground of the Day place. In building this levee a great many drift logs were used. When the high water came this log-levee washed out, of course it was repaired in a very temporary manner. When the high water of 1851 came the whole of the upper end of the Island, above Mr. Manlove's, was overflowed, in some places the water was deep enough to swim a horse. I lived in town then; on Sundays we went down on the Island; on one occasion when the river was about the highest, three or four of us boys including my brother—who went along to see his girl—went down in a skiff. He got off at the Day place; we went down farther, and it was agreed that we all meet at the Day place at 3 p. m. We were late in getting back and did not find our brother there; we waited until near night and concluded that he must have gone ahead of us in some other boat, so we started for town. About the time we got up to the Hopson house he came and started to follow us, he waided out to the Hopson house waist deep, got on the roof, shouted himself hoarse, and nearly swung his arms off, without our seeing him. He staid on the top of the house until nearly dark when some one saw him and went to his relief. To say he was in good humor would not be telling the truth.

During the high water of 1851, a lumber raft got away and went down over the Island some two miles and staid until the water subsided when it was hauled off with teams. After the flood subsided a levee was built that stood the high water very well. After the levee was rebuilt confidence was restored and one improvement after another began to be made on the Island.

Near where Mr. Manlove's house stood, a brewery was built by Binz & Stengele. They run this brewery with profit for awhile. It was before ice was used in storing beer, so they went up on the bluff near the cemetery and built a large cave for storing purposes. While everything seemed to be prosperous the brewery stopped running. The building was later used for a canning factory, the portion that was used for a dwelling was moved away.

On the upper end of the Island the railroad company built a brick engine house and turning table, together with one or two more buildings that were to be used for repairing, etc. The engine house stood for some time in use. During one of the high waters a portion of the building fell down; it was repaired, but in the high water of 1870 it became unusable and was taken down.

There was an agricultural warehouse and factory started near where the school house now stands. They had a great many threshing machines stored there and possibly other agricultural implements. When the hard times of 1857 struck us, it stopped this industry.

In this part of the city Hatch & Fullerton had a wholesale lumber yard, later Ed. Hoch.

The upper end of the Island where the lath piles are now, was used by the railroad company to pile wood for locomotive fuel. After Hershey got posession of the Butler pork house he filled up the slough and got posession of the railroad grounds by purchase or some way, and filled it up to use it for its present purposes, much to the annoyance of Mr. Smalley who claimed the property should revert to him when abandoned by the railroad.

A little later Leindecker & Zeigler built the old Kleinfelder foundry, which they run without any profit to themselves. In fact I have an idea that it came very near breaking Mr. Zeigler up.

This building has since been used for various purposes. At one time a file manufactory was running there, later a saw factory, then a wind mill factory by Greeley & Rockafellow. They expected to manufacture reapers but could not reach it. When the Kleinfelder foundry up in the city burned, Mr. Kleinfelder bought this building and used it for foundry purposes for quite awhile, after he closed it up it was used for a ventilated barrel factory, and lastly for a button factory.

When Coe & Wells put up their big cooper shop where the Kaiser mill now stands, it brought a few other buildings. Barney Kemper built a cooper shop and dwelling house near where the lower end of the street car track stops; out on the ridge west of the ponds Geo. Connor lived in the old fair ground office, near him — Washburn, Norman Oakes and one or two others. Near where the lower school house stands, the brick house now standing, owned by Lewis Coe, was built quite early. Alexander Clark had a house near by. About all the dwelling houses that were built in that locality previous to 1870 were built on high ground. But few if any dwellings stood on the space (nearly three-fourths of a mile) between the two school houses. When the high water of 1870 broke through the levee it was very fortunate that none were there. The break occurred where the Musser saw mill now stands. For a description of this break we will copy from O. G. Jack's History of Muscatine, page 51 and 52:

"1870. During the spring of this year the water in the Mississippi was higher than ever before known by the oldest inhabitant— seventeen feet above low water mark. On the morning of the 25th of April the Island levee broke, near Binz's brewery and the lower part of the Island was soon covered with water. Many skiffs were employed for several days in bringing parties from their submerged homes to places of safety, driven from their crops and much other valuable property, and glad to escape with their lives. The sight, which was witnessed by thousands of our citizens, beggars description. Large fields, whose rich and fertile soil promised an abundant yield, and handsome gardens, whose vegetables were so enticingly springing from mother earth, were in a few moments changed to a great river bed and became a worthless waste."

After the water subsided, Musser's built their mill, which commenced running in 1872. This gave South Muscatine a boom; settlers came in and building lots advanced in value. I know one man who gave Mr. Smalley, who laid out an addition, $100 for one of the choice lots and soon sold it for $350. I don't think it is worth more than that now.

Bartlett & Hoopes put up a pork packing house, built a big ice house, and fitted up and did summer packing for two seasons. I recollect seeing them put up ice three feet thick, cut in the channel of the river.

On the upper part of the Island the Brent Bros. started a window shade and wash-board factory. Their kind of shades seem to have gone out of use, they were much like a Rush-matting, using pine sticks a little longer than matches for filling, they would color these sticks green or any color they wanted; they were woven in a hand loom. The firm also manufactured wash-boards and other commodities. They were burned out two or three times, but every time they rebuilt larger. This factory was the beginning of the Muscatine Sash & Door Co., of which W. L. Roach is manager. After this factory was started the dread of an overflow seemed to have disappeared.

Among the early settlers I recollect the names of William Plocke, George Kinsley, William Hoover, George Jones, William Dungan, Gill Washburn, Barney Kemper, Gates Washburn, H. V. Howard.

About 1875 the Union Lumber Company commenced operations on a large scale. After a year or two they got tired. About that time the Musserville Methodist church was erected, a year or so later a school house. The saloon has been there in a kind of a transient manner, sometimes there and sometimes not.

Recollections of Muscatine's Early Lumber Deales.

Published in the Muscatine Saturday Mail, January 22, 1898; written by J. P. Walton.

No. 53.

In looking over the list of lumber dealers that have done business in Muscatine from time to time we find the following names: In 1856 we had Dunsmore & Chambers, Hoch & Musser, S. M. McKibben & Co., S. G. Stein, and B. Hershey. Three years later, 1859, we had added or changed the list to Hatch & Fullerton, Hoch & Whitehouse, R. Musser & Co., and C. C. Washburn.

After the war was over in 1866, and business began to boom, the list stood John Chambers & Co., Front street northwest corner of Spring; B. Hershey, Burlington road, C. Cadle, corner Second and Mulberry; S. G. Stein, Pine and Second streets; J. S. Garlock, Second street west of Walnut.

In 1869 Muscatine had twelve lumber dealers as follows: Cornelious Cadle, corner Second and Mulberry; Chambers Brothers; Charles Drury, northwest corner Second and Mulberry; W. H. Delaney, corner Fourth and Orange streets; Levi Eckle, south side Second street between Walnut and Mulberry; O. W. Eckle & Bro., corner Second and Orange; John S. Garlock, Second street between Walnut and Cedar; Edward Hoch, Front street above Sycamore; R. Musser & Co., corner Second and Walnut; S. G. Stein, Pine and Second; B. Hershey, on Burlington road at mill, and Huttig Bros.

Five years later in 1874, the list stood: Eckle & Patten, R. S. Hawley, B. Hershey & Co., P. M. Musser & Co., Ed. Hoch, S. G. Stein, Union Lumber Co.

In 1879 we had E. E. Burdick, South Muscatine; Musser & Co., South Muscatine; Hershey Lumber Co., South Muscatine; Levi Eckle; J. S. Garlock, and J. S. Patten & Co.

It will be seen that in 1869, some thirty years ago, we had twelve lumber dealers or twelve lumber yards. Among these twelve two saw mills were included; in the whole number I don't think that as much lumber was carried at any one time as one of our largest mills have had at one time in recent years. These lumber men were young men, in many cases just starting on the road to wealth—where few arrive. Of these twelve 25 per cent became wealthy which is a better showing than almost any other branch of business ever carried on in this city.

A review of the character of these men will be in order; in doing so we will confine ourselves at this time to those who are not now in business here. Among those not mentioned in any former paper was Hatch & Fulerton; they handled considerable lumber from 1858 to 1860 they had a wholesale yard down on the head of the Island in South Muscatine and a retail yard at the corner of Mulberry and Sixth streets, where the United Brethren church now stands. At this time it would be considered an out of the way place for a lumber yard, but then it was not, as most of the lumber used north and west of the city many miles was hauled out of the city on Mulberry and Sixth streets. Farmers would bring in their produce and sell down in the city and load up their wagons there as they went home. When the railroad to Iowa City was completed it soon made the Sixth street locality undesirable for a yard and it was closed. The principal or head man was Edward Hatch, he was a native of Maine; I think raised in the pine timber district, came west and stopped awhile in the pine regions of Pennsylvania, and later he turned up in Muscatine; he had charge of Mr. Hershey's interests here for a year or so, about 1856; he then went in company with W. H. Fullerton and opened lumber yards for wholesale and retail. William H. Fullerton was a native of Windsor, Vt.; he appeared to have been inspired with the idea of "go west young man, go west;" for he with three other young men of that place located here about the same time and all removed together. They occupied the rooms now used by F. H. Little, then over Green & Stone's bank. The quartette consisted of W. H. Fullerton, George R. White, W. H. Hubbard and M. Holden. I am not certain about Mr. Holden coming from Vermont, if he did he certainly did not belong to their tribe; he was not endowed with that generous impulse that the other three had. White and Holden were clerks in Green & Stone's bank, Hubbard was a bookkeeper in Charles & W. R. Stone's hardware store, and Fullerton, bookkeeper and general manager for Joseph Bennett, who was at that time running the big brick flouring mill (the present oat meal mill) and packing large quantities of pork. Fullerton got tired of working for others and went in the lumber business with Hatch. I think they did not work together more than a couple of years; If I recollect aright he sold out to Hatch, who got his brother Robert here to help him. When the war broke, out Edward Hatch got up a cavalry company and was elected captain, which was his first military position. Fullerton went back to Windsor, Vt., where he still resides, in independent circumstances, but in poor health; he is much respected by his associates.

The history of General Hatch (Ed. Hatch) should be written up by some of the veterans, as I do not like to take the honor from those to whom it belongs. It is enough for me to say that Hatch was soon promoted to major, then to colonel and later to brigadier general; he was wounded once or twice, and at the close of the war he was appointed colonel in the regular army. He died quite recently while out on the frontier. General Hatch's early education in the pineries and with working men proved very valuable to the government in erecting frontier forts, of which he informed me that he had constructed more than any other officer in the army. When Gen. Hatch went into the army his brother Robert staid here and sold out the lumber and closed up the business.

There was another lumber man that kept bobbing up all the time, Edward Hoch. He was a jolly good fellow, quite witty and affable, pleasant and winning in his address. We hardly know where he came from, the first we heard of him was in 1849, he was then working with a threshing machine party, traveling from one location to another threshing. We next heard of him as a lumber man with Richard Musser, along in or about 1854 or '55; how he came in with him we can't tell. He next appears as the head of the firm of Hoch & Musser. I have always thought that Musser furnished the money and went in with Hoch on account of his knowledge of the lumber business. We next heard of him as being associated in business with a man named Whitehouse. I think this Whitehouse was a raftman or a man who followed running lumber down the river, finding this to be a good point to sell lumber he likely concluded to start a yard with Hoch at its head—a year or two was sufficent for that firm. Ed. Hoch next located a lumber yard on the head of the Island, later on Front street above Sycamore. I think his office was brought from the Island to this locality, later it was taken up to the north side of Second street, east of Mulberry.

Mr. Hoch had all the qualifications to make a valuable cetizen; he had gotten the idea that to be popular he must be convivial and he practiced that habit. Whatever his shortcomings were he was a good fellow socially all the same. As a lumber seller there was none better known or more popular in our city.

RECOLLECTIONS OF

Sash and Door Manufactory of Huttig Bros.

Published in the Muscatine Saturday Mail January 29, 1898; written by J. P. Walton.

No. 54.

In the year 1869 Fred and William Huttig started two lumber yards, one in Kellog, the other at Muscatine. The yard in this city was located on Front street west of Linn street. Fred Huttig managed the lumber yard in Kellog and William the one in Muscatine. They also kept sash and doors, buying them in Davenport. One day Mr. Falter, the Davenport traveling man, came along and stated that he would soon be out of a job, and wanted the Huttigs to go into the manufacturing of sash and doors; he showed them that there was money in the business. William wrote to Fred. stating the Falter proposition and asked what he thought about a deal of that kind. It so happened that Fred had just received an offer for the yard at Kellog, at a good fair price, and they sold it. They took Falter in with them and opened a shop in the rooms now occupied by the Commercial Club, but not liking the quarters they purchased the present oat meal mill of the estate of Chester Weed for the sum of $11,000, and used it for a warehouse and shop.

After leaving this location the building was sold to the Oat Meal Co. that was organially composed of William Huttig, F. P. Sawyer, S. G. Stein, H. W. Moore and F. D. Holcomb. The stock has recently been owned by F. P. Sawyer and S. G Stein, jr.

Huttig Bros. & Falter received the sash in the knock-down; they set Dick Flint at work putting the sash together. Dick Flint commenced work by the piece at the price paid at other places for such work; for the first week or two he could earn but $1.50 a day; he kept on at it till he becam used to it and got it systematized. At the end of a couple of months he could earn $5 a day; at the end of the year the firm cut his wages down. Dick did not quit, but worked a little harder and made the $5 per day all the same; he had to stand a second cut down, which resulted in more hard work. In all he worked some four years for the firm.

The Huttigs soon found that running a lumber yard and a sash and door factory together did not go well, so they closed out the lumber yard and devoted their attention to the sash and door business. After running awhile, Mr. Falter withdrew, going into business in St. Louis. The Huttigs managed the business without his help.

Up to 1875 but very little polished plate glass had been used in this city. Harry Cannon had the monopoly of that business, he had a price list and had so mutilated it that no one could tell where it came from; he claimed he had an arrangement by which he could sell the glass at the list price delivered in Muscatine I had occasion to figure on a couple of store fronts, the glass listed near $700, which put the job so high it was not done. I went to the Centennial at Philadelphia in 1876, and while there I saw a very fine display of plate glass made by a house in New York. I took their address and when I got home I wrote them to send me a price list, they in answer sent me a price list, with an offer to sell at 60 per cent off. Taking advantage of that offer I got the job of putting in the two store fronts. I was not in the shipping business and I soon found that a man in that line could do better than I could. I took my price list and discount down to Huttigs and got them to order the glass for me. It was shipped to me. That was their first deal in plate glass. After that I sold most of the plate glass for some time, the Huttigs ordering it. I think they now handle most of the plate glass used in this city.

Cadle & Mulford got tired of the old plaining mill and shop, down near the present. freight depot, and concluded to build a new one. They got the two lots on Front street, east of Sycamore, and put up their new factory, the Huttig Bros. putting some $15,000 in with them. This factory run but a few weeks after the Huttigs were interested in it before it took fire and burned dowg. I think that George D. Magoon had some stock in it with the others but sold out before the fire.

After the fire the company gathered their resources together and re-organized with $200,000 capital, under the name of Huttig Bros. Manufacturing Co. The new company was composed of William Huttig, Fred Huttig, Joseph Mulford, Richard Cadle, Fred Lumpe, Allen Bowers and some others. When they came to reorganize they wanted to get some of the lumber men to take stock, to have their interest. They got some taken by P. M. Musser and went to B. Hershey and wanted him to take a little. Mr. Hershey said: "How much do you want me to take?" Huttig answered, "at least $5,000." Hershey's reply was. "Mr. Huttig you put me down for $45,000 of stock, I will take that, and if you want money come around and I will help you get that." Hershey got no stock and Huttig did not have to call on him for money.

When the Huttigs concluded to rebuild they wanted more room and located their plant where a place could be had at that time, on the south side of Second between Oak and Orange streets. After the mill was started and began to pay something, the race began to acquire more room. They only wanted the lot next to them until they got some 12 or 15 lots. They have enlarged their mill and built warehouses until they have covered floor room that can be counted by acres. They now buy their stock in large lots and have all the latest improved machinery, and a capacity to work 300 men.

The officers of the company are: William Huttig, president; Fred Lumpe, vice president; H. W. Huttig, secretary; D. S. McDermid, treasurer.

To go back to our first acquaintance with the Huttig Brothers. Early in the fifties a stone mason came here by the name of Fred Huttig and went to work at his trade. Shortly afterwards a younger brother, William, came and tried to earn a living by teaching music, which went very slow. He was compelled to go to work at something else. He started at tending stone mason, which soon proved too much for him; he had to give it up, but the lack of a better job forced him try to it again. The foreman, John Knopp, sr., saw the difficulty and set him to laying stone and showed him how to do it, and put a stronger man at tending mason. With the assistance of the tender to help him to lift the heavy stones, he got along fairly well. He worked quite a while at this business with the desire of accumulating a sufficient sum to take him back to the old country. By the time he began to reach that amount he had secured quite a number of music scholars and was doing very well. He had gotten over his home sickness and married and settled down, as most of the young Germans had done. When he gave up the stone mason trade he went into the grocery business with success. but wishing to do a larger amount of business he went in with his brother Fred in the lumber business, as before mentioned. Fred recently sold his stock in the manufacturing company to Willliam and moved to Kansas City.

While calling at William Huttig's house recently, we could scarcely realize what a change 40 years had made with him. We had frequently had occasion to visit his first house on the south side of Seventh street, one lot east of Cedar street. The house was about 16x24, one story frame. It stood several feet below the grade of the street, we raised it to grade. He now occupies a house on the northeast corner of Third and Pine streets, that is one of the finest in the city. It did not cost less than $10,000 to build it. When we called we found him at his early occupation, teaching his grandson music.

Recollections of

The Sash and Door Business.

Published in the Muscatine Saturday Mail February 5, 1898; written by J. P. Walton.

No. 55.

At an early day the carpenters and joiners made their sash by hand. It was the test of workmanship to be able to make a window sash. The carpenter that had a house to build, figured on making the sash, frames, doors and blinds in the winter before commencing the building.

The first man that made sash for a business was Abraham Smalley, in his wind-mill at the south corner of Third and Cherry streets. He had an old man named Jacob Pickel, who put in his entire time making sash. If he run short of orders he would get out the material and keep a small stock of 8x10 and 10x12 8 light sash on hand. They never glazed any; a builder usually had to leave his order and have the sash made. The sash in my house were made there in 1851. For machinery they had a circular saw and a common mortising machine run by foot power. The circular saw was run by wind, when it blew; if there came a still time and not wind enough to do the sawing orders for work had to wait. I have often taken orders there and had to wait on the wind.

In 1851 or '52 a man by the name of Worthington came here; he brought some sash machinery and started to manufacture sash in the frame building on the east corner of Second and Sycamore streets, owned by Jos. Freeman. Worthington started his machinery but lacked capital to run it and he took J. S. Patten in with him. Worthington afterwards sold out to Patten who run it awhile and sold to John Glover, who run it in 1856, and Patten followed carpenter work. I think E. M. Kessenger had something to do with the sash factory. Their machinery was quite limited. I believe the windows in the Ogilvie house was their largest contract. Their sash was not considered as good as those of Jacob Pickel's were, so he kept at work.

In 1852 S. G. Hill came here and brought a Nockcross planer, and went in with S. G. Stein. They erected the factory on Front street, west of Pine; they added sash machinery and manufactured sash and doors. The price was so high and the goods so inferior that Jacob Pickel could still manufacture. I find in the directory of 1856 that he was at the business in the old Smalley wind-mill; in 1859 he followed carpenter work and lived on the north side of Fourth street, between Linn and Spruce. I think it was probable that when Smalley sold the old wind-mill and went to farming, Pickel had to give up the business.

These early sash factories made few if any doors, the carpenters had to make them by hand. It used to be considered a good day's work to make a door, but frequently under favorable circumstances a man could make two.

My first job after I struck out for myself, was building a good sized two story house for Gamaliel Olds, out on Cedar river, in 1849. We bought the sash of Smalley. There were 40 two-pannel black walnut doors in the house; I made them all by hand, which took all winter.

Stein & Hill had a monopoly in the planing mill and sash and door business until the war broke out; they made the old planer clear them $30 or $40 per day, and kept it running most of the time. They saved enough to purchase the lot and erect the building where McColm's store is now, No. 122 and 125 east Second street, (Stein's Music hall). At the beaking out of the war S. G. Hill was appointed Col. of the 35th Iowa Infantry. He was killed at the battle of Nashville. His brother, S. B. Hill, tried running the planing mill but did not continue a great while until Cadle, Mulford & Co. bought it out. The company was composed of Richard Cadle, Joseph Mulford and William Albers. Cadle and Mulford were carpenters. Albers had run the planing machine for a long while; he soon got tired of the business and sold his share out to Cadle & Mulford. They hired George Magoon to make doors for them; the first contract was for 500 doors; Magoon went to work and cut out material for 100, this filled the shop so full of stuff they could not get around, and this first hundred was all he made for them. After running a while there, they concluded to build a new shop and erected one on Front above Sycamore street. After they got their new shop up they bought the old machinery from Patten & Co., in Freeman's building; they run a while but did not get along well, they did not have money enough to run successfully, so they sold out to George D. Magoon and C. U. Hatch. In the deal Magoon was to run the shop and Hatch the outside work. Magoon fitted up the old machinery and threw out some, one in particular was a rabiting machine, it had injured the hands of four men—Kessenger, Cadle, Rowland and Kincaid—before it went into the creek. Magoon and Hatch not agreeing they sold the planing mill back to Cadle & Mulford, who got help from Huttig Bros. to the extent of $15,000. They rented or bought the Fimple three story brick building, adjoining on the east, which was about 30x90 and converted that into a factory, a wooden connection was made between the two buildings, the sash and door machinery being placed in the brick building. With Huttigs as salesmen every thing promised favorable. In the spring of 1877 on a Sunday morning, about 9 a. m., a fire broke out in the factory and by noon the whole establishment, brick building and all, was a pile of ruins. This was shortly after the fire department was organized. It was the first big fire they had tackled and it proved too much for them. The firemen were quite downhearted, but they have since found it is no uncommon thing to have a fire too big for almost any fire department. This factory was never rebuilt, Cadle & Mulford put their mite in the Huttig Bros'. factory.

We wish to say that at the old wind-mill Mr. Smalley manufactured various articles, such as wind-mills, harrows, cultivators and other articles of a similar character. He also occasionally made sleighs; we saw one on the street the other day that he made long before the war.

Jacob Pickle was little known save among his German friends, he never made any considerable amount of money, but he saved what he made. At his death he bequeathed to the German Congregational church quite a large sum of money.

Joseph Mulford was an outspoken, honorable, square man, a prominent democrat; he was here during the time of the war but was no copperhead as several of the democrats were. When the war excitement got up quite high and many were joining the home guards and volunteers, one day Joe and I went up to the court house square together for the purpose of joining the home guards, when we saw in the ranks J. J. Hoopes, one of our own cronies, and Marx Block, two out-spoken southern sympathizers, marking time. We concluded the country was safe and did not go in.

Neither Mr. Mulford or myself

could go to war. We both paid our ward.
money, with others, as a bounty to keep our ward from having a draft. I think it cost us about $250 each. Joe was quite exciteable, and when a draft was talked about he would offer his house and lot to be kept clear of it. No one took him up. The war closed without any draft in our ward.

When the Huttig Brothers Manufacturing Co. started he had charge of the carpeter shop and the stair building, a branch in which he became very proficient. He remained here until his death.

Richard Cadle went to the war, but we will have to forego writing up Dick this time.

Recollections of

Some of the Early Items in the City Records.

Published in the Muscatine Saturday Mail February 12, 1898; written by J P. Walton.

No. 56.

We had occasion recently to read over the old city records for the year 1854. The first item that attracted our attention was that J. P. Walton was allowed one dollar in city orders for acting as clerk at an election. This counted one dollar on taxes. The cash value of city orders then was not more than 50 or 60 cents, just as one could find a purchaser. On that night, January 14, 1854. Hon. J. Carskadden resigned the office of Recorder; Dr. D. P. Johnson took the place. The same night $6.00 was claimed for printing forty-five railroad bonds, I don't know that the bill was ever paid.

On another occasion S. G. Stein was allowed $1 for the use of his office for election day. There seemed to have been two permanent voting places for many years, Stein's office and the court house. The voting place of the

Second ward has had four or more locations; the first one I recollect was in T. M. Isett's office in the second story of a two-story brick building on the south side of Second street, between the avenue and Sycamore street; another location was in the mayor's office, one block further west where J. S. Richman & Son have their office; later the voting was done in the front room of the second story of Stein's music hall, in the room now occupied by E. M. Warner. In 1876, when the city bought the old Methodist church, the voting place was moved there, where it still remains.

On March 14, 1854, stationery was ordered from R. M. Burnett, to be paid for at cash price, with city orders; no mention made what the discount was—likely about 50 cents on the dollar.

Up to 1854 we had paid but one cent tax for city expenses. In 1853 the city got it raised by an act of the legislature from one to three per cent, the limit now allowed by law; this includes the bonded indebetedness. The council commenced to increase the taxes, this gave them more funds, the city orders advanced to 65 cents at wholesale and 75 cents at retail. The marshal collected the taxes, from the non-resident he got the money, and he would go to the resident, ask him if he had any city orders, if he had not he could generally settle his tax at 75 or 80 cents on the dollar. The marshal dealt in orders. The marshal collected some money, but he never accounted to the city with anything but orders if he could help it. I think the cash deal with Burnett for stationery was an effort to squeeze some cash out of the marshal.

Under the new charter heavier taxes were levied and orders were raised to par. Hundreds of us never thought we gained by the raise; we had more tax to pay and had to get the money to do it with. The non-resident tramp would come and work a day get his money and go away, he thought it was a good scheme.

At the meeting, March 14, 1854, an application to sell beer and ale for one year was introduced, the license was to be $50.00. At the next meeting it was laid on the table. Those were temperance times in Muscatine. We had for mayor John A. Parvin and four out of the six aldermen were out-spoken temperance men. No permits were given that year to sell beer or ale. At that time there was more English ale sold than beer, the breweries had not got hold of Iowa, so people took to ale and whiskey. About all the business done in that line during that year was done in a clandestine manner.

On April 4, 1854, the council ordered the marshal to purchase three candlesticks and three pairs of snuffers to cost not to exceed

50 cents each, for the use the council. This may have been about the time that their headquarters were moved to the Green & Stone building on the south side of Second street, between the avenue and Chestnut streets. They appeared to have been fitting up with new furniture and used tallow dips.

On May 3, of the same year, Green & Stone were allowed $29.40 for filling clay between Second and Third streets on the avenue. At that time there was a ravine some twenty or more feet deep running from the west corner of the avenue and Third street to the east side of the avenue at the alley between Second and Third streets. This ravine was bridged on the avenue when that street was first opened. About 1853 the city took charge of the west branch of the creek and turned it along Third street, and commenced to fill up the avenue. The clay from Green & Stone was likely used for filling that hole.

In the same meeting, May 3, 1854, an order was passed to collect the unpaid subscription for the construction of the levee. We conclude they meant the first wharf which was probably built by subscriptions in 1847 and '48.

In the year 1853, M. M. Berkshire was allowed $66.00 for making the city assessment. The present assessment in 1897, cost the city $350.00 and the assessor made little or no canvas.

On September 5, 1854, M. Block reported "the necessity of having the dams on Sycamore, between First and Second streets, repaired."

When the town was first settled Pappoose creek crossed Second street near Sycamore in its course to the river. It wound backward and forward over about five lots, and west of Sycamore street, where it crossed Front street, there was four or five feet depth of water at low water mark on the river; one could row a boat almost up to Second street. Efforts were made to bridge it at First and Second streets, but without any success, especially on Front street. In order to make it passable the town or city had a lot of brush cut and the mouth of the creek filled up with it, and had it weighted down with soft stone obtained from the bluff. This answered the purpose as long as the stone and brush lasted. It had to be repaired every time a big rain occurred. When Romulus Hawley was street commissioner, probably in 1878, he drove some piling and covered them with plank in such a manner that it stood all attacks until removed for the big sewer in 1896.

On Oct. 6, 1854, $100 was voted to help make a railroad survey for a road to be called the Keokuk, Mt. Pleasant and Muscatine R. R. At this time an effort was made to establish a fire department, but it was not accomplished. On Dec. 5, 1854, a memorial was presented to the legislature to extend the city limits, and amended on the 30th. These memorials were made and presented without submitting the question to the voters. It was a cowardly act, but the courts said the legislature had a right to do it. But it is also said in the case of Morford vs. the City that nothing but road tax should be assessed on farming lands.

Recollections of

The Lost Creek.

Published in the Muscatine Saturday Mail February 19, 1898; written by J. P. Walton.

No. 57.

When Bloomington lost her identity by that name, and assumed a more appropriate one—Muscatine—it was considered a rough town. It had a beautiful little rivulet running in a circuitous route from Eighth and Sycamore streets to the river, at or near Sycamore street. It entered block 145 west of the middle, thence southeast across block 145 and to near Sixth street, in block 120. It thence sheered off northeast and crossed Cedar street up near Seventh street; thence southeast for three blocks nearly over to Walnut street at Fourth. It followed the street southwest until it crossed Cedar street and half way down the next block, 57, thence to the river. In doing this, it run over nine blocks to get the distance of seven.

At our first acquaintance with this little rivulet from Eighth street to the river, it was called Pappoose creek. Its banks were not high or abrupt in only two places, they were mostly grown up with willows and bushes, where they were not the banks and bottoms were covered with grass. At an early day this creek very nearly dried up in the summer time. The lots along its banks were not high priced, so the new comers frequently managed to get possession, of one and built a house on the high part of the lot, and a pig pen and goose house on the lower part. They soon got a cow and quarters for her were secured with the other stock; all stock was allowed to run at large. It was often remarked that an old German woman with a pair of geese would make as much money as anyone could with a cow. The exact number of geese raised along the creek was never ascertained. I am satisfied that the number run away up into the thousands. At times one could hardly drive along the street without being forced to turn out or drive over some of them.

The lots along the creek from Eighth street, the city limits, to the river, were about all taken sooner than more valuable lots. Little or no preparation was made for high water, none had been observed that had done any damage other than wash out some of the pole bridges. In the year 1851 the creek was quite high. We recollect coming home one night, early in August, and finding the water flooding a house belonging to a Mr. Hindlemeister. It was a story and a half house, about 16x20 feet, it stood on lot 8, block 145, where Henry Fuller's brick house now stands. We helped carry the goods out of the house to dry land When the water got over the chair bottoms on the main floor the rain ceased and the water subsided and we helped to carry the goods back again. In the course of two or three days, August 11, 1851, there came a rain and washed the building and all of its contents away, the occupants were fortunate in getting out. The water rose so fast they could not save anything.

On the block between Sixth and Seventh streets, near Cedar, stood a small house occupied by a Mrs. Laferty and three children. The house stood in the creek bottom, and the water rose upon the house likely four feet deep. She took the children in her arms and tried to wade ashore, the current was too strong, they were overthrown and drowned.

At that time Hon. T. S. Parvin was taking the weather records here, he reported a rain fall of 11 inches in this one rain. There have been many hard rains since but not one-half that amount has fallen at any one time.

At that time the town was cut in two. We had no bridges back of Second street, and that one washed out. Up to that time we depended on fords for crossing.

This big flood washed them out so much that it made the crossings very bad for awhile. The channel commenced to cut out, and the banks to fall in, until it was lowered from 10 to 15 feet in many places making a creek bed of 20 to 30 feet wide. The residents along the banks began protecting their lots mostly by planting willows. Some put in posts and planked up. It soon appeared that the cheap lots along the creek were costing all they were worth to take care of them.

This creek gave some trouble at times to the bridges. In the early days of our village, 1838 or '39, the road supervisor, John Marble, called out the road work to put in a bridge on Second street. It was made with round stringers long enough to reach across the creek. These were covered with poles (some of them may have been split) and these covered with straw and earth. One of the men summoned to work, was one of our prominent lawyers, S. Clinton Hastings, afterwards Judge Hastings. He appeared with a hatchet and claimed he had complied with the law, as this was all the tool he had and all he could use. Hastings was quite a talker and considerably in the way, so it was suggested that he get a couple of gallons of whiskey in place of the two days road work he owed the road district. He got the whiskey and his road work was settled.

This old pole bridge very frequently got out of repair, and the creek had to be forded near Third street. In 1840 a permanent improvement was undertaken in the way of putting in a stone gothic arch, six feet in the clear. This was built and some of the earth may have been put on it, but it washed away as soon as the water was turned through it. We had to use the old pole bridge for awhile longer. In the summer or autumn of 1842 the village put in two stone abutments, I think about 12 feet apart and some 12 feet high, the top was covered with stringers and floor. It did not last long. This bridge stood open before covering for quite a while. It was looked upon as a banter to the gymnasts, of whom we had quite a number, to jump across, but none of them attempted it. One day while the boys were jumping in front of Tiley Smalley's blacksmith shop, within a hundred and fifty feet of the open bridge, old Michael Green walked down and jumped across, a hand spring without any run, likely 12 feet. It astonished all who heard of it.

At the end of two more years in 1844 we were in need of another bridge. Bub Cullen, and I think, Jack Reese, drove the piling and put in one with an opening 24 ft. wide, 16 feet high.

The old stone pile driver now lying in the court square was used for driving those piles. In the the summer of 1858 the grade of the street was raised at the bridge and a second story was put on, making the bridge some six or seven feet higher. About this time a system of daming the creek at Front street had been adopted, it caused the bed of the creek to fill up some four or five feet deep.

At the noted flood of August 11, 1851, this bridge went out. It then dawned on the citizens in general that our bridges were not large enough. William St. John and Henry Reese put in a pile bridge 36 feet wide, 18 feet high and 60 feet long up and down the stream. This stood with little repairs until November, 1872, when J. P. Walton rebuilt it an expense of about $1,000, paid by the county. At this time there was a law or a rule that no appropriation should be made by the county for a bridge less than 60 feet long. In order to get the appropriation the bridge had to be measured up and down stream. This wooden bridge stood until the Mathewson arch bridge was put in some ten or twelve years ago.

At an early day, way back in 1842 or '43, an effort was made to put in a bridge on Front street by building up two wooden abutments and filling them with earth and putting stringers across with floor on the top. It did not succeed. The dam with ford on top was used until quite recently when the stone and iron bridge was built which was removed for the sewer.

The first bridge of any note on Third street was erected in 1851 or '52 with county funds under the supervision of Amos Lillibridge, the county commissioner, and Sherman Brooks, the road supervisor. It stood near where the present invisable stone arch is. I think it was rebuilt twice before the arch was put in. The bridge which spanned the creek at Fourth and Cedar streets was put in quite early, sometime between 1857 and 1860. It had to be rebuilt once or twice before it was removed. At Fifth street we had a long foot bridge, put in about 1870. The creek was fordable there. The road bridge was put in under the direction of Hon. G. W. Jones, while a member of the city council.

The citizens chipped in and got some oar stems and got them put across the creek on Cedar street near Seventh for a foot bridge, about 1870. In 1872 or '73 a paper was circulated to get a bridge for wagon purposes put in, and some $250 was raised. The bridge was built and with the usual rebuilding and raising, it lasted until the sewer was put in.

There was a wooden bridge at Eighth street, I think built about

1855. It, like others, had to be rebuilt several times, but for years this was the only bridge that one could cross the creek on, going east or west, back of Third street.

There was a high bridge on Linn street that cost the city a large amount of trouble, it had to be bebuilt quite frequently and was often unsafe. There was general rejoicing when this bridge was removed.

The last bridge erected by the city was the most comical one. It was on Seventh street east of Sycamore; it was some 25 or 30 feet high, was braced and re-braced from within and without, and by the time the earth was filled against it, it resembled a huge collapsed corn shock more than anything else I can compare it to. It certainly added more to the picturesque appearance of our enchanting little creek than any other improvement it ever had, and strange to say it appeared to have been of spontaneous growth. His Honor, the mayor, Gus Schmidt, would not father it, neither would the city engineer, J. J. Ryan. When the big sewer was completed it with all the other charms of Pappoose were buried in oblivion.

Recollections of

The Lost Creek.

Published in the Muscatine Saturday Mail February 26, 1898; written by
J. P. Walton.

No. 58.

In our last, we told about the lost creek, old Pappoose creek. Although it was a very conservative stream ordinarily it was a terror when it "got on a high," as it did once in a great while. The first noted flood occured on Aug. 11, 1851, at which time a woman and her three children were drowned, and one house and several barns washed away. A quite extensive hardwood lumber yard, situated on Front street, above Sycamore, went down the river and but little was ever recovered. This big rain was not confined to Muscatine, it extended up the river. On the following day this side of the river was covered with all sorts of floating debris which came from above. This creek caused the city and the citizens immediately connected with it much trouble for the sixty years it was with us.

One cold winter in the early fifties L. D. Palmer occupied a store room on Second street, just east of Sycamore, for a general store. I think G. Schmidt & Bro. occupy the building now. Parmer took wheat in exchange for goods and stored it in the cellar. It was supposed to be safe, but the water of the creek kept running and freezing until it had filled the creek with six or eight feet of solid ice. Just at the breaking up of the winter, there came a big rain and raised the creek on top of the frozen ice quite high. It got into Parmer's cellar and wet some 3,000 bushels of wheat. This was a serious loss as little could be done with it but to feed it to stock. Steamboats were not running and we had no railroads here to carry the wheat to where it could be used.

Along in the fifties the city put in a wooden drain or sewer, some three feet square, from the avenue to the creek on Third street, expecting to care for the water of the west branch of the creek by turning it through the sewer to Pappoose creek. During the first heavy rain it became choked, the water turned down the avenue and filled up all the cellars on the north side of Second street from the avenue to Sycamore street. Of course the city had to pay the damage. It was wonderful the amount of old boxes and barrels that were damaged. The damage did not stop here; the wooden sewer was repaired and got choked a second time, and another lot of suits were commenced. The city paid over $60,000 for damages for the west branch before they got through. The trouble did not cease until the property holders along the avenue fixed their property so the water could not get in.

On another occasion there came a heavy rain about day light; the water of the west branch choked up the sewer and flooded the avenue some two feet deep. A large portion of the water started down Second street, it overflowed the walks and filled a cellar under a store room next to John B. Dougherty's. It broke the division wall between the two buildings and they both fell down.

When property along Second street became more valuable the property owners began to crowd the creek onto Sycamore street. The city drove a row of piling along the west side, Johnnie Hoehl drove some on the east side above Second steet, and put up a building. In 1876 the creek took a notion to clear itself out, it took off the rear part of Dr. G. W. Fulliam's building and done the same with the Hoehl building. Of course the city had a law suit with both of them, but strange to say, it did not come out second best in either of these cases.

We nave bid good-by to the creek but have we bid good-by to the danger from future floods. We hope so, but have some misgivings. We have a sewer at Eighth street that will carry 200 feet. We have seen a great many more than 200 feet running in the creek at Eighth street. On the 20th day of August, 1878, a rain of 4.68 inches fell making a run of 500 feet of water. We have our doubts about 500 or even 400 feet of water being crowded into the 200 feet sewer. Well if it don't get in there we presume it will start for the river down the streets and low lots, but we will bid the old creek good-by for the present hoping we will not hear from it again.

There are but two or three of the very early built houses standing along the channel of the old creek. The oldest one is the large square frame on the alley between Fourth and Fifth streets west of walnut. It was built by old Mr. Grossman for nis dwelling house, in 1841 or '42.

Mr. Grossman and wife were grossmen in every sense of the word. They were not more than 5 feet 8 inches in height but they would weigh 250 to 300 pounds. they were immensely strong. One day we noticed Mrs. Grossman carrying a full barrel of flour on her head, her husband was walking by her side and carrying her hat. Going down town we learned that some one of the boys had offered her the barrel of flour if she would carry it home without dropping it, which she did. She must have had a full quarter of a mile to carry it. I never heard of her suffering any harm from doing this.

There is a brick house standing on the north side of Third street, the third house from Cedar street, that was built there very early, likely in 1841 or '42. by Robert Tillard, a tailor. He worked at his trade here until he moved over the river, near Illinois City, where he since died. The brick house on the west corner of the alley and Sycamore, between Second and Third streets, was built by Jos. Freeman early in the forties. I think that most of the very early built houses have disappeared.

Recollections of

A Crockery House Since 1854.

Published in the Muscatine Saturday Mail March 5, 1898; written by J P. Walton.

No. 59.

Over a year ago we started to write a brief history of our business men. We have confined ourselves mostly to those who have retired. We have found but few, if any, that have passed forty years uninterruptedly in the same business. The crockery business in our town merits our attention.

In 1854 John H. Turner came here, bringing a stock of queensware and did a wholesale business. Situated as we were here, on the bend in the river, without any railroads, a good business was done in selling to the country stores. Turner lacked capital enough to carry the goods, the customers, and the grain or other products used as money, and he had to sell out.

In 1857 a thin faced, dark eyed Yankee came here, named George W. Dillaway. He had been born and raised under the shadow of the old North church of Boston, and had acquired all the peculiar traits of a Yankee. He lived a near neighbor to Paul Revere, and was the eleventh child out of the dozen—a common family number in New England. He learned a mechanical trade, a ship carver. In his younger days he had lost his health, and crossed the ocean, visited the Czar of all Russia, and finally came west to look for that common boon that most of us enjoy—good health. He concluded it could be found in our town, and in 1857 he bought out J. H. Turner and has been in that business ever since. We can't understand it, for the kind of goods he handles are more subject to breakage than any others we know of; still he has not broken up, but kept right along in the same breaking business for more than forty years and is still at it. Well there is no telling what a man from Boston can do. In 1859 his brother, Joseph, came here and staid some ten years, he then went back to Boston.

Among his present employes is W. R. Durkee, who has been with him thirty-four years; he has been most of the time on the road, and is one of the oldest traveling men on the road. He is a good fellow and when he gets away from the Baptist influence in Muscatine he can enjoy as good a story as any other knight of the grip. J. Fahey has also been on the road for Mr. Dillaway for some eighteen or more years.

Mr. Dillaway usually employs from twelve to fifteen persons about the premises. But the most unique character of the concern is Charlie Narvis; he appears to have charge of the buying and shipping, and a general supervision over every thing. He has been with Mr. Dillaway near a quarter of a century; he went there when a small boy and one would suppose he knew nothing else, but such is not the fact, he is well informed on almost any subject. An acquaintance of ours told us that Charley at one time took a lay off for a week or so and nearly went crazy before his vacation was over.

Mr. Dillaway has adopted the old Yankee rule of letting the children work as soon as they are large enough to "pick up chips." His wife, son and daughter-in-law are on hand when needed. If any one expects to beat any of them in a deal in the store they are liable to be mistaken. We never heard of anyone getting beat at Dillaway's counters.

Such men as G. W. Dillaway are poor material to make commercial history. They don't change enough. He is about the only one of the kind in our city. We don't recollect but one other man in business for the same length of time.

Mr. Dillaway served on the city council for five years. In 1876 and 1877 he represented the Frst ward as alderman, and the three succeeding years of 1879, 1880 and 1881 he filled the office of mayor. He has been a liberal contributor to the general welfare of the city. He has been a staunch member of the Baptist church and one of its most active workers.

When Mr. Dillaway bought out Mr. Turner he was located on the south side of Second street west of Chestnut. This was a good place for a wholesale business. After he had been there a while Bill Stone, or some one else, told him the story of the "Dutchman's one per cent" and Yankee like he concluded to try it. so he added retailing. He was successful at it. He bought a fine stock of goods and sold them, but he was hampered with two difficulties, one was the building did not suit him, the other was the location did not suit. We don't think there was much in the location, for Dillaway would do well in any place. He did not think so, however, and he erected the present building, which is undoubtedly the finest store building in our city. There are several that are larger but none so well built and finely fitted. In the new building he added silver ware and notions—dry goods, hardware and groceries were not included, although we noticed that lamps, oil and eggs by the bushel were among his goods.

To thoroughly enjoy Dillaway's store you want to go there when he has his Easter or Christmas goods on exhibition.

Recollections of

The Doctors of our County and their Practice.

Published in the Muscatine Saturday Mail, March 12, 1898; written by J. P. Walton.

No. 60

When we came here in the spring of 1838. we found but one leading physician, Dr. Eli Reynolds. He resided at Geneva, three miles up the river from Bloomington, now Muscatine. He was rather tall and slim, a native of Indiana, and likely came to Iowa, then "Black Hawk purchase," in 1835; he could read and write, and had studied medicine with some pioneer doctor in Indiana; he liked to drink whiskey, although he rarely if ever got very drunk. He always had a good horse, his practice required it; he was kind hearted and reliable, although he rarely accumulated enough to meet his obligations, but he liked to have a spree, as he was pleased to call his frequent hilarities. He could be found at all the horse races or other sporting places. He represented the county in the early legislature of our state and got an act passed to move the county seat of this county from Bloomington to Geneva, but the bill was vetoed by Governor Dodge. Dr. Reynolds lived in a double round log cabin that stood on the bank of the river near the sulpher spring south of the Hare school house; his family consisted of wife and one son, Loring, one of the smartest and most worthless boys or young men that we had ever seen. I don't know what ever became of him. Dr. Reynolds lost his wife and married a widow with a little girl; they raised the girl and gave her the advantage of a good education. She is now one of the prominent ladies of our city. The doctor lived to an old age, having practiced medicine for fifty-six years, which was not common among the physicians of those times.

Dr. McKee was another prominent physician of the early times, he lived in Bloomington (now Muscatine) in a small cabin on the top of a hill since graded down on the northwest corner of Third and Chestnut streets. He kept bach when he could not get board on credit or for doctoring. He was a young man and was educated in Philadelphia, from which city he started west with little or no money. He stopped at a house on the road to stay all night, it so happened they mistook him for a preacher and invited him to preach for them, which he did and they took up a contribution for the preacher; it proved to be quite a liberal one so he followed preaching all the way out to Iowa. After he got here and hung out his "shingle" as a doctor he quit preaching; he built his cabin on the brow of the hill, which proved to be a healthy place, hence he was not sick to any extent—that left him time to practice on others, which he did to their sorrow. There was probably more stories told about Dr. McKee than any other doctor here, without it was Dr. Blaydes; they occasionally practiced medicene in partnership.

Dr. McKee believed in a practical application of King James' translation of the Lord's prayer, "forgive us our debts as we forgive our debtors." He was compelled to forgive a great many that were in debt to him, so he concluded it would be the same with those he owed. He was mistaken on one occasion, he got his saddlebags packed and mounted his horse and started across the river on the ferry boat. He happened to owe the ferry man, Bub Cullen, a small sum. Bub took a look at him and concluded that he was going to leave, so he asked him for his pay. The doctor declared he had not the money to pay with, but would pay on his return in a few days. Bub would not be put off in that manner so he turned his boat back toward the Iowa shore. McKee concluded he had better pay and did so, and went his way to the east, turning up in Philadelphia where he was followed by one of his western creditors and put in jail for a season.

Dr. Blaydes was another pioneer doctor, he came from Kentucky and brought a beautiful young wife here with him. They lived in a small building on the east side of Chestnut street north of Second street. I don't think she lived more than a year after she came. The doctor then married one of the Dibble girls and went to live with the family on the top of the hill. The old house was removed some three years ago. It stood on the corner of Fourth and Pine streets. Dr. Blaydes was engaged with T. M. Isett in the pork packing business for a while, he claimed to be an expert in making bacon for the southern market. I think he knew more about that than he did about doctoring. He drank his share of whiskey and frequently more; when he got hilarious he would start home and would commence calling the roll. He would mix some of the most outlandish names with those of our citizens, and go through the streets and over the hill hallooing them as loud as he could, most of the people listening to him could but laugh at his roll.

There was a Dr. Coval at Salem, now Fairport, who was one of the same kind of doctors: I don't know what became of him.

Most of the diseases those early doctors had to treat were billious fevers and the ague. Their system of treatment was first a heroic dose of calomel to be followed with Epsom salts or oil, then a heroic treatment of quinine if the fever was not disposed to yield. Dover's powders and bleeding was resorted to, excessive pain was allayed with a pill of opium. Morphine was not in use at that time. The doctors pulled teeth as a part of their practice, dentistry had not reached here as yet. In the year 1838 there was but one turn-key for pulling teeth in the county, it belonged to Dr. Reynolds. During the winter of 1838-'39 we suffered all winter with the toothache for the want of something to pull it with. The doctor had loaned his instruments and could not get them back.

Doctoring in those early days was simply a "survival of the fittest"—if the patient was able to survive the treatment he got well. It mattered little what the disease was.

In 1839 and '40 a different class of doctors came here, such as Dr. B. S. Olds and Dr. Weed from the New England states, and Dr. George Reeder from Maryland, all educated men and men that were fitted for a higher social station.

Recollections of

The First Settlers.

Published in the Muscatine Saturday Mail, March 19, 1898; written by J. P. Walton.

No. 61

In the fall of 1835 James W. Casey and Thomas Burdett came here. They stopped at the Grind Stone Bluff, the name Muscatine was known by then. There was a trading house situated near the present railroad depot, owned by Col. George Davenport and superintended by a Mr. Farnum.

Under the old claim rule a man could measure off a half square of land, set his stakes, blaze his line and hold it against other claimants. Davenport claimed a quarter of a mile each way up and down the river and a half mile back from his house; the claim extended from Spruce street to Oak street and from the river to the north side of Eighth street. James W. Casey took the next half a mile south and built his cabin. The place was soon known by river men as Casey's landing.

Davenport sold out his claim to Col. John Vannatta, who commenced to lay out a town to be called Bloomington. About the same time Casey commenced to lay out a town which he called Newburg. Thomas Burdett, who came here with Casey, took his claim in the bottom above the city where the elder Giesenhaus and John Berry now reside. The following year Samuel Gilbert came west and took his claim on the north of Burdett's. Thomas Burdett married a sister of Mr. Samuel Gilbert's.

When we came here in June 1838 there were three Burdetts—Thomas, Humphreys and Lewis—living along the road under the bluff above the town. The next farm belonged to W. H. Sams, a crazy man; it was where the recent tile factory was located. Addison Reynolds had the next farm, then came the town of Geneva which had five or six houses and a steam saw-mill within its limits, the Walton family occupying the smallest house in the village, and keeping the post office. The census of the town would include Dr. Eli Reynolds, wife and son, Loring, and a boarder, Mr. Smith who was the engineer at the steam saw-mill; Harvey Gillett, wife and six or seven daughters; Addison Gillett and wife; James Davis, the sheriff of the county, and wife. Davis had a small building standing near his dwelling that he had kept a store in, and all the stock that was left when we arrived was a part of a barrel of wine. It did not last a great while, for the early settlers were quite thirsty at times—if whisky could not be had they would take wine.

The first resident above Geneva was Samuel C. Comstock, the next was Chris. Burns. The latter claim was taken by some squatter and sold to a Mr. Newcome, who was the rightful owner, but Chris Burns was a kind of an outlaw who came along and found the claim in the possession of an easy going man with a large family by the name of Alonzo Standard. He was there to hold the claim for Newcome. Burns jumped a portion of the claim and put up a little cabin, and undertook to drive Standard away by all means of persecution he could think of. On one occasion Burns took the stay-chains and clevises from his wagon and hid them under Standard's house and went and got a warrant and had Standard's house searched; of course he found them. The neighbors came to Standard's relief so far as they dared to, as Burns was a terror to all of them. My father being among the best educated and one of the most fearless of the number was selected to act as an attorney for Standard. He so managed the case that his client was cleared. Burns then swore vengeance on my father, and swore he would thrash the life out of him. My father was a heavy set man, he weighed 200 pounds, and was always cool, having been schooled from childhood to never commence a fight or never to back out for fear of a fight. Burns was a little afraid to tackle him. Burns finally scared Standard away. I think Burns never got a title to the land. When it came into the market the neighbors did not stand by Burns as they did by many others. They allowed Newcome to bid against him, the result was the land was run up beyond its value and forfeited. It was just at the close of the land sales and was not put up again at that sale. Before it was offered a second time Burns concluded to move to Missouri, where he was afterwards shot by some one he was imposing on.

When we came here in 1838 Mr. Barclow occupied a cabin which he probably built in the spring of 1836. The history says he had a child born in 1837. I cannot say that it was the first birth in the county or not. This cabin is now standing on the south side of Dr. Weed s farm and has been occupied ever since it was built 62 years ago. I think it is the oldest inhabited building in the county. It is worth a trip for our sight seers to see so old a log cabin. It is situated 300 or 400 feet east of Park avenue church on the north side of Washington street.

In going up the river we had to cross Mad creek where Ninth street bridge is now located. The Warfield brothers, Asbury O. and David R., had a saw-mill there. Here the roads forked, the one to the left led up through what is now known as Park Place out by the Gilberts, Samuel and Hiram, and their father, Mordecai, there with their mother made the Gilbert settlement. Near flat iron point a man by the name of Harger lived; a mile or so north on the edge of a hickery grove Stephen Headly resided, his son, John, is yet living in our city. To the east of Harger's, on or near the farm now occupied by James Featherston, Robert Bamford lived, he had several children some of them yet living although I think none are here. The next place was the Sherfey farm; near that was the farms of Azel Farnsworth and Amos Lillibridge, father of Chester Lillibridge and Mrs. Emma Mahin. To the south of the Sherfey farm between the two roads a family by the name of Combs lived. South of the Gilberts a Mr. Berkshire lived with his son Montgomery; Montgomery was the father of John Berkshire, formerly one of the managers of the Hershey Lumber Co's. big saw mill. Berkshire had a 40 acre farm on which he managed to raise what corn he wanted. He followed light coopering, making churns, well buckets, etc. His son, Mongomery, was a tailor by trade and had to move to Bloomington, now Muscatine, to make a living.

Recollections of
The Muscatine Sash & Door Company.

Published in the Muscatine Saturday Mail April 2, 1898; written by J. P. Walton.

No. 62

It is said that small beginnings frequently assume large proportions. Such is the case with the Muscatine Sash & Door Co. Away back in 1851 Rev. R. W. H. Brent came to our city and opened a hardware store under the name of Brent & Miller. The firm disolved, Miller taking the goods and moved away. The directory of 1856 states that Rev. R. W. H. Brent lived on north side Seventh street, east of Cedar; he is put down as a farmer; he was well fitted for farming having a daughter and four boys, but unfortunate for him, the boys did not like farming; they were industrious but preferred to live in town and go to school. These boys soon grew to be men and had to look out for themselves. Rev. Brent moved to a farm on the Island. In 1866 he had sold his farm and built a house on the southeast side of Fourth street, west side of Linn. Two of his sons, Theodore and William, lived with him.

In 1876 Rev. R. W. H. Brent was in the insurance business, but his sons, Edward, William, Theodore and Richard, were all connected with the Brent Manufacturing Co. In 1879 we find that William had left the company and gone on the road for G. W. Dillaway, and that Richard was president of the company and lived in South Muscatine. In 1883 the Rev. Brent and all his sons were engaged in the manufacturing business, they advertised as "manufacturing packing boxes, etc., with planing mill." Up to this time they seem to have run without calling in any additional capital. They first started to manufacture window shades; they were made of small pine wood sticks about an eighth of an inch in diameter, woven together like a Rush carpet or mat, and were colored to suit orders. The shades were hung and rolled up from the bottom. The Brents added washboards, using the trimmings from the saw mills for lumber. They also made door screens and various other things, one in particular which they called a "jumping rabbit." I have been informed that they made as high as 60,000 screen doors in a season. They had a grocery store in connection with the factory, run by Edward Brent, that contained quite a stock of goods.

There was one thing very remarkable about this factory, it burned down, or partly burned down, at least three times, with little or no insurance, and was rebuilt larger with double the capacity every time. It is probable that assistance was given them from sympathising friends.

In 1885 a company was organized with a capital of $90,000 and outside stock was taken. William Hoffman represented some $12,000 or $15,000 worth, and A. F. Demorest had some stock and served as secretary in 1885 and '86. It was run under the name of the Muscatine Manufacturing Company, with five of the Brents connected with it. Richard Musser, Charles R. Fox and S. B. Cook were among the number of stockholders. The factory was improved and sash, doors and blinds were added to its products.

In June 1889, the present company was organized, some of the old stocholders selling out their interest and withdrawing, and others coming in. The present president, Wm. L. Roach, who was in business in Kansas City was induced to sell out there and take stock here in the present Muscatine Sash and Door Co.

The present officers are: Wm. L. Roach, president; C. R. Fox, vice president; S. B. Cook, treasurer, and Clifford R. Musser, secretaly. Among the other stockholders are P. M. Musser, A. A. Bowers, Marx Block and the estate of Richard Musser. During the last season they have employed from 180 to 200 men. In brisk times their pay roll included 250. Of the working force about the mill we find D. B. McKenzie superintendent; A. A. Bowers, superintendent sash and doors; Joseph Fuller, engineer, and John Reay, shipping clerk. Mr. Reay has been employed in the factory for thirteen years.

The capital stock of the present company is $200,000. One of the first things after the new company took control was to enlarge the plant. A brick smoke stack was erected and a new boiler and engine house was put up. New boilers and engines were put in, and in fact new machinery all the way through the factory. There is hardly a piece of the old machinery left. There has been three or four large two-story brick buildings erected, and the plant occupies some fourteen ordinary city lots, which are all covered with buildings and lumber piles. An inventory of the different plants in the northwest along and near the river was recently made with a view of forming a trust, the Muscatine Sash & Door Co. was found to be one of the best equipped, there was none better.

They have connected their force pump with the main water pipe that connects the Hershey mill, the Muscatine Sash & Door Co., the Musser and the Kaiser mills. The union of the four make a fine fire protection. They have an excellent fire company of some thirty men ready to turn out on short notice.

They have a branch house at Kansas City known as the Roach & Musser Co. that is doing a large business for these dull times.

The sash and door manufacurers of the Northwest were well organized at one time. They got out a price list that set big prices on their goods; they met regularly and fixed the discount to be made to the dealers. The dealer had the price list to show the customer what the goods were rated at, and had no trouble in getting a good price. When the recent hard times came on the demand slacked up so much that the mills did not have near enough to keep them employed. One manufacturer would cut a little; so would another, to get the orders. To keep their mills running, they would cut down on their labor to make up on the loss. As soon as one cut on the prices another had to or do no work. In places where there was no labor organizations they could do that.

We are told that during the year 1897 there was a fair amount of sash and doors sold by the retailer at fair prices. But for the want of the former organization of the manufacturers many of them made little or no money. It any has been made it was by those who employ men at low wages. Such conditions are not uncommon in our land. They are sure to be corrected by the great law of supply and demand.

While Muscatine sash and door companies have slacked up during the past three or four years they are now running up to the normal condition for this season of the year, but it has required close figuring, low prices, and the untiring efforts of its managers.

Recollections of

The Early Cemeteries.

Published in the Muscatine Saturday Mail, March 9, 1898; written by J. P. Walton.

No 63.

In article No 61 we stated that Col. John Vannatta took the first claim of a half a mile square, and that James W. Casey took the one to the southwest of half a mile and Charles H. Fish the one to the northeast of a half of a mile. Mr. Casey was really the first settler of the lot; he came here in the fall of 1835, he lived about one year, died and was buried near where the Third ward school house now stands. The grave was on Charles Fish's claim. When Fish plotted his town, or laid out an addition to the town, he marked three lots on the plot for a cemetery. This ground was used for a burial place until the city laid out the eastern part of the present cemetery In burying in this old burial place not much regularity was preserved, the graves were dug where the friends thought proper, there was no one to take charge of anything, and they were not confined to the proper lots, but extended along the top of the hill clear to Eighth street. If a grave was marked at all it was with a stake. I don't think any monuments or stones of any kind were placed on the graves or any record kept of the interments. I presume that fifty persons were buried there.

On the 18th of August, 1837, the steamer Dubuque exploded her boilers some seven miles down the river, killing 22 persons. Seventeen of these were buried in one grave where the Third ward school house now stands, the grave was fenced with a picket fence and some one planted a tree in the inclosure or near it. After the establishment of the new or present cemetery many of the remains were removed from the old burial place.

When old No. 1 school house was built in 1849 and '50, it was set on top of the graves, on the top of those that had not been removed during the six years the lots had not been used as a cemetery. The old house covered the seventeen as no one had disturbed them. In 1868 the school house burned down and was replaced with another in 1869-'70. At that time some twelve feet of of earth was graded from the top the school lot on the hill; this of course removed all the remains left, which were taken to the cemetery and interred.

During the early days there were several persons who declined to bury their dead in the common grounds. The first, I think, was Mathew Matthews, who was buried on Trinity church lot, When the principal part of the present church was built in 1854, his remains were taken to the city cemetery. On the corner of Sixth and Mulberry, where the U. B. church now stands, the Van Antwerp family had two children buried; they were removed. On the lot at the southeast corner of Cedar and Second streets Dr. and Mrs. Fitch had one or two children buried, after the death of the doctor they were removed to the cemetery.

In the country outside of the city the custom of having private burial places on the farm in some secluded spot was quite common. I think it was quite likely a relic of tne old Virginia custom that had followed their descendants to Iowa. For instance, the oldest Burdett boy married the oldest Gilbert girl and the families were on the best of terms; they had both come from the same place in Kentucky and at about the same time, nevertheless they both had burial grounds. The Burdette ground was on a beautiful round knoll some tnree hundred feet to the north of the house where John W. Berry now lives, a mile or so east of the city. This knoll is in fair sight of the road. There my father was buried in 1841. There are probably twenty graves in that knoll. The Gilbert burial ground is near the south side of the old Gilbert farm.

On top of the hill on the old Sams farm west of where the recent tile and paving brick factory stood, are the graves of two men who were victims of the Dubuque explosion; they were acquaintances of Mr. Sams and he had them buried there.

Some two or three hundred yards north and east of the Hare school house, was the burial place for the town of Geneva. The first two persons buried there were two gentlemen from Connecticut or New York, friends of Mr. Harvey Gilbert. They had come here with a view of purchasing land but sickened and died as many others did in 1837. I think two or three of the Combs family were buried there.

Along the river there was quite a number of graves. When a man died on a steamboat, they usually left the body at some town and got some one to attend to burying it. When the cholera broke out they were not allowed to do that, so the carpenter of the boat would nail up a box (boats carried lumber for that purpose) and the boat would land more frequently along Muscatine island and dig a shallow grave and bury the body. After the first scare got a little over the boatmen frequently could get Seiler, the city sexton, to have the box taken out to the cemetery where it was buried and the man's friends notified. On one occasion a couple of strangers came along and get Seiler to exhume the body which they could identify and took from it a belt containing $2500 in gold. It was a common way of carrying money in a belt around the body at that time. The boatmen had such a dislike to handle a cholera subject that they put the body in the box without any examination other than his pockets.

Previous to 1852 the Catholics had used our city cemetery for a burial place. At that time an effort was made by their priest, Rev. Father Laurant and the leading members, to secure a place of their own. An option was secured on four acres in the forks of the roads, opposite Mr. Sinnett's residence, for $25 per acre. The owner of the land backed out. An acre or so was then secured out on the north side of the Iowa City road some two miles out of the city, at $50 per acre, and was used for burial purposes until 1876 when the present Catholic cemetery was started.

Early in the seventies the Hebrews concluded to have a burial place of their own and secured a small tract of ground to the south and adjoining the city cemetery. Previous to this time they had buried elsewhere not in our cemetery.

Recollections of

The Musser Lumber Company.

Published in the Muscatine Saturday Mail April 16, 1898; written by
J. P. Walton.

No. 64

In the old Mahin directory, the first one published in Muscatine in the year 1856, Richard and Peter Musser are put down as "lumber merchants (Hoch & M.) 249 Second street; board at the Clover house." Hoch & Musser's yard was on the east corner of Second and Walnut streets. The Clover house, where they boarded, is now the Kemble house, on the opposite or west corner of Second and Walnut street.

The two Musser brothers, Richard and Peter, had followed the tanning business in Schuylkill county, Pennsylvania, some six years, but like many of the younger men of the old Keystone state they concluded to go west, and in 1854 they came to Iowa City, and spent a year there. In 1855 they formed a three years partnership with Mr. Edward Hoch here in Muscatine, and carried on the business together. They of course furnishing the money and Hoch the experience. Hoch had been in the lumber business some five or six years, being a stirring man he was well known as a lumber man. He resided on the south side of Fourth street, east of Linn, where Robert Thompson now lives.

How the Mussers came to be boarding at the Clover house I cannot say, they were both married men and had been here near a year. Mr. Peter Musser explains it in this way: During the year they lived in Iowa City before coming to Muscatine they bought a double house and when they came here they left their families there. They took turns or changed off every two weeks in staying in Muscatine, so both boarded at the Clover house, but only one at a time. Richard Musser soon built himself a small house on Front street east of Mulberry.

In 1856 the firm established a branch yard in Iowa City. Peter

Musser took charge of this branch until 1864. In 1858 the firm dissolved by limitation, Mr. Hoch retiring. The title of the new firm was R. Musser & Co. In 1850 another Pennsylvanian, a native of Berks county, by the name of Charles R. Fox, came and went to work in the lumber yard at Iowa City, where he remained as a clerk or salesman until 1864, when he came to Muscatine. When Charlie Fox commenched to "shove lumber" he was only 20 years old; he has staid right along with the lumber firm for almost 40 years. We don't know of his taking a vacation of more than four weeks in the entire time.

In 1863 a nephew of the two elder Mussers, by the name of Peter M. Musser, came here and went to work in the lumber yard. Peter M. was quite a dasher for a Musser; he bought a fine horse, took extra care of him and tried to make a "goer" of him but the horse was not that kind. There were several "plugs" on the street that would go by him so Peter M. had to give it up on the fast horse business. He staid in Muscatine about a year and then went Iowa City where he bought an interest in the firm of R. Musser & Co., and took charge of that yard, his uncle, Peter Musser, going to California. Peter M. Musser managed the Iowa City yard until 1873, when he formed a partnership with J. W. Porter and purchased the interest of the other Mussers, and continued in business with Mr. Porter until 1881, when he sold out to Porter.

In 1870 the lumber firm of Musser & Co. was organized, consisting of Richard Musser, Peter Musser, Peter M. Musser, Chas. R. Fox and John Musser, of Pennsylvania, father of Peter M. Musser. The company was formed for the purpose of building their present saw mill. which was completed in 1871, and commenced sawing lumber. In 1873 Richard Musser sold his interest in the business to P. M. Musser. The firm was then known as P M. Musser & Co. Three years later Richard Musser renewed his connection with the company and the firm name was again Musser & Co. In 1877 the company rebuilt the mill and enlarged it to near double its capacity. We recollect taking the old iron chimney down and having it spliced out to nearly 100 feet high, and putting it up again.

In 1881 the business had increased to such an extent both in the mill and lumber interest that it became necessary to incorporate under the name of Musser Lumber Co. Their mill was again enlarged, the old iron smoke stack taken down and the present brick chimney put up. In 1882 they put up a planing mill and moved the planing machinery from the saw mill. At this planing mill they built a tall brick chimney on a large stone foundation. In order to get the chimney where they wanted it they put it on the corner of the stone foundation. The result was it soon began to settle unevenly and the chimney soon got some three feet out of plumb, it looked like the "leaning tower of Pisa." Of course we were called on to straighten it up, which we did with good success.

When the mill was first built its capacity was about 11,000,000 feet annually; after its improvements and enlargements it could cut 50,000,000 feet. The mill stands on the upper end of Muscatine Island where the ground originally overflowed fully four feet deep, it was protected by a levee. In the spring of 1870 a break occurred where the mill now stands; it was filled up and the mill built over the break. There was not more than two or three houses within a half mile of the mill at that time. Now the land is laid out in city lots and is quite well settled all around largely by mill operators or hands working in the mills. This low ground has been largely filled by offal from the mill. It become so expensive to get this offal hauled away from the mill that a consumer was built at cost of $7,000, to burn it in, which paid for itself in two years. This consumer is a high iron cylinder or cone, lined with fire-brick. The spare saw dust, bark and planing mill shavings are conveyed or blown into it and burned with a fire that does not go out from spring to fall. This consumer is often called Musser's hades.

The Mussers in the start put in a system of water works with mains and hydrants, reaching all over their thirty-five acres of ground. Later they have connected their mains with the Kaiser mill water mains on the south, and on the north with the Muscatine Sash and Door Co., and the Hershey saw mill water mains. The four mills each being well equipped with pumps, makes the best system of fire protection in the city.

The Mussers were the first to introduce the electric light in place of the old head-light used when working during the short days in the autumn. They have their yards and mill well supplied with "Dutch clocks" for the benefit of their watchmen. Their yard is well supplied with railroad tracks and overhead truckways for hauling out lumber. They have no dry house, they believe in carrying a larger stock of lumber and drying it by air. Muscatine Island is a superior place for drying. They saw nothing but pine lumber from logs cut in the northern pineries.

The Mussers are interested in the Chippewa Logging & Boom Co., and in the Mississippi River

Logging Co. They were among its incorporators and are heavy stockholders, hence their ability to secure logs when the outside mills are short. The logs are towed down the river from booms at the mouth of Chippewa river by steam tow boats. The Mussers for several years owned their own boats. Recently they have sold to Capt. S. R. Van Zant and and he does the towing for them.

When the Mussers first started in the lumber business with Mr. Hoch the amount of money handled in a year for the purchase of lumber, for work and expenses amounted to some $100,-000. The present annual business of the company amounts to over $750,000.

When Hoch & Musser first started the lumber was sawed in the pineries and floated down in rafts on the river. Lumber sold at from seven to nine dollars a thousand feet; it was all sawed plump one inch thick and was usually warranted one-third clear, one third second clear and the remainder was common with little sheathing. The retail price for clear was from $20 to $25 per M, with common about $10 to $15.

The Mussers saw it was a good business and kept at it. Members of the company are interested in Pine Tree Lumber Co. at Little Falls, Minn.; that mill has a capacity of 92,000,000 per year.

They are also interested in the Musser Sundry Land Logging & Manufacturing Co. This company is large owners of pine timber lands.

Recollections of

The Musser Lumber Company.

Published in the Muscatine Saturday Mail April 23, 1898; written by J. P. Walton.

No. 65

The two elder Mussers, Richard and Peter, were born in Adamstown, Lancaster county, Pennsylvania, on November 15, 1819, and on February 22, 1825. Before coming to Muscatine they were both engaged in the tanning business. Tanning under the old style was quite slow when it took a year to tan a side of leather—nevertheless some noted men have been tanners. In 1854 they sold out and came west locating in Iowa City, as we stated before. They went into the land business, bought government land at $1.25 and soon sold at it at $2.50. For some reason this business did not hold out and they were looking for something else when the lumber business showed an opening. In 1855 they came to Muscatine and for a year or more boarded at the Clover house.

Richard Musser having lost his first wife some five years previous. About the time he became permanetly located in Muscatine, he journed back to his former home in Pine Grove, Pa., where he married Miss Sarah Borger, in March, 1855. He died in Muscatine October —, 1897. His widow, son William of Iowa City, and daughters Mrs. Sue Zimmerman, Mrs. Kate Huttig (wife of Col. H. W. Huttig) and Misses Grace and Gertie Musser survive. Two sons and two daughters died in childhood. Mr. Musser was a kind and indulgent parent; having but a common school education, he was remarkably well informed and of a very marked character; always pleasant, he could say "no" without giving offense to the most sensitive. In his social standing he was very popular. We recollect helping to get him to run for mayor as a republican candidate. He was elected by a handsome majority when the democrats had a strong ascendancy. Sometime in the sixties he secured the Musser mansion on the corner of Third and Locust streets, where the family now reside. The son, William Musser, is in the lumber business at Iowa City, occupying the same yard that his father helped to start in 1856.

As we stated before, the owners of the Musser Lumber Co. were Richard Musser, Peter Musser, Peter M. Musser, Charles R. Fox and John Musser, of Pennsylvania, and in order to perfect their system each one had his part alloted. Richard Musser attended to the rafts and getting the logs into the mill. Peter Musser traveled in the pineries and had the supervision of the machinery and the mill, when at home. Peter M. Musser managed the cash and office department, while Charles R. Fox attended to the lumber as it came from the mill until it was shipped on the cars. Each one invariably attended to his department and did not interfere with the others. Since the death of Richard Musser the log department has been managed by the log men of the mill.

Ricnard Musser could be called a public man, he served two years as mayor and two or more years as alderman; was on the school board for three or more years. When any public enterprise was started such as building the Muscatine Western railroad, the bridge, or the water works he contributed his share. By his death Muscatine lost one of its best citizens.

Peter Musser came here in 1855, staid a year or so then went to Iowa City and took charge of the branch lumber yard there; in 1864 he went to California; he liked the outlook so well that he retured the same season, organized a mining company and went again with his wife and child in 1865 by way of Panama. In 1869 he returned to Muscatine and in 1870 he joined with his brother Richard Musser and Chas. R. Fox and organized the firm of Musser & Co.; Peter Musser was chosen president and yet remains in that position. While in California he secured the Eagle gold mine and worked it to the extent of his ability, but it not paying to the satisfaction of the stockholders of the company, he was compelled to close down the mine and finally bought the other stockholders out. He had faith in the mine and made several efforts to sell it, finally in 1895, after 26 years of waiting, he gave an option on the mine to a company who developed it. They kept the mine and it is now paying untold amounts of gold Mr. Musser's option was large enough to pay him for his trouble and expense, but nothing to what it would have done if he had developed it himself. Our intimate acquaintance with Mr. Musser commenced in the autum of 1870.

He had recently returned from California and had a very fine collection of minerals. He and his wife were among the first members of the old Scientific Club, which afterwards became the Academy of Science. The second meeting was held at their house. For years they were leading factors in the club and academy.

Mr. Peter Musser never allowed his name to appear as a candidate for a public office, but, like his brother, when anything was wanted for the public good, such as taking horse car stock, or building churches he responded with more than his share. His connection with the log department necessarily made a traveler of him; he traveled all over the northern pineries, locating timber land and made several trips to California, Oregon and Washington, and a trip to Alaska but not to the Klondike, he had fun enough of that kind in California. During the summer and autumn of 1897 he and his daughter, Laura, traveled over Europe, and came home and enriched our city with some of the finest paintings extant. Peter Musser's family in Muscatine consisted of a wife who recently died, a son and two daughters. The son, Drew Musser, is the successful treasurer of the Pine Tree Lumber Co., of Little Falls, Minn.; the oldest daughter, Anna, married Chas. H. Huttig, of St. Louis; the youngest daughter, Laura, is at home with her father.

Charles R. Fox, one of the older members of the Musser Lumber Co., was born in Berks county, Pa., November 26, 1839. He commenced working at the lumber business with the Mussers in 1859; he is one of a few men who commenced as a hired hand without any capital and became a prominent member of a great company, but Charley has done it. He has stuck tight to his work, and has hardly been absent a month in ten years. We used to think that Charlie had the idea that the old mill would stop or the concern become bankrupt if he did not stay there. One might suppose that the expense had something to do with Charlie's want of vacations, many have thought he could not afford the time, but Charlie is not stingy, on the contrary what he wants he is willing to pay well for. He is seen but little on the streets and usually attends church about once a year then he makes a liberal contribution. He leaves the church going to his family. Perhaps we have taken too much liberty with Charlie's peculiarities; we are quite intimate with him and will vouch for his being a first rate man. He is a little gregarious, he likes to spend his evenings with a few chums in a private club room where nothing hilarious is indulged in. Mr. Fox was married to Miss Sarah E Eckel, of this city, on February 4, 1872. They have had six children, four boys and two daughters. Charlie joined the Masons in 1867 and is a member of the Chapter and Commandery; having been master of Hawkeye Lodge and commander of DeMolay Commandery No. 1, and has devoted much of his spare time—that is evenings—to masonic work. Well, we think that in the thirty-nine years of continuous work Charlie Fox has earned a rest, if one can be had for him away from a lumber pile.

Recollections of

The Musser Lumber Company.

Concluded.

Published in the Muscatine Saturday Mail April 30, 1898; written by J P. Walton.

No. 66

John Musser, of Pennsylvania, one of the stockholders in the Musser Lumber Co., was but little known here. He was a brother of Richard and Peter Musser and the father of Peter M. Musser. He appears to have been a man of considerable means and invested some of it in this city for his son and brothers to look after. He has recently died. Peter M. Musser, his son, was the youngest member of the firm; he was born in Lancaster county, Pa,, April 3, 1841. In March 1863, he came to Muscatine, staid about a year working for the firm, and then went to Iowa City and bought an interest in the R. Musser & Co's. two yards, one in Iowa City the other in Muscatine. In 1864 he took charge of the Iowa City yard; in 1870 he came to Muscatine and has since remained here.

While at Iowa City Peter M.

Musser became captive to a small Yankee girl by the name of Miss Elizabeth Hutchinson, a descendent of the Hutchinson family that governed Massachusetts in Colonial days. They have lost several children, the only remaining one, Cliff R. Musser, is connected with the Muscatine Sash and Door Co.

During P. M. Musser's stay at Iowa City he formed a partnership with John W. Porter, who was a prince of good fellows, and one that liked to enjoy himself as much as Peter M. did. In 1876 they and their wives went to the Centennial at Philadelphia and were gone some four weeks. Before starting they drew $1,000 from the bank and at the end of the trip they divided the cash remaining, which was less than $2; there was no account kept of that money, they calculated that the fun paid for that thousand dollars.

Peter M. Musser appears to have accumulated more money than was needed in the lumber business, so he went in with S. B. Cook and Henry Funck in the banking house of Cook, Musser & Co., now a State bank. He, with S. B. Cook and perhaps others, invested in a Texas cattle ranch, which now appears to have been a good investment. But when the What Cheer coal mine excitement was on he put $40,000 in the coal mining interest and took nothing out. He was not always so unfortunate in outside investments. He has been known to be a stockholder in the Huttig Bro's. Manufacturing Co. I was recently told how he came to invest. The company had a foreman that had an eye for business and possibly knew J. W. Porter, of Iowa City, Musser's former partner, and wrote him to come to Muscatine and start a factory, telling him the profit that was in it, etc., etc. In place of coming down to look it up Porter sent the letter to Peter M. Musser, who at once concluded he wanted stock in the Huttig company; so he took the letter and a check for $10,000 and went to the Huttigs and wanted stock for that amount; he got the stock; they took the money put it into glass—that proved to be a big investment. The foreman lost his place all the same.

While P. M. Musser has been very fortunate in acquiring property he has also shown a liberal public spirit. He purchased the building the Old Ladies' Home occupies and gave it to the society—a very valuable gift to any community. On another occasion he purchased a bed in the Presbyterian Hospital in Chicago at an expense of some $7,000, the use of which he has given to many a needy sufferer. He is a member of the official board of the First M. E. church and one its largest contributors. The large memorial window in the avenue front of the church was put in by him at an expense of $700 or $800. He is also on the official board of the Musserville M. E. church and one of the building committee.

When Peter M. Musser came here to commence working for his uncles he did work. I don't think he drew lumber or ever piled it, but nevertheless he was always on the go. I think the labor unions, if there had been any, would have admitted him. During the years of his sojourn at Iowa City, we were not so familiar with his opperations. We have heard the people of Iowa City tell some marvelous stories of his financial schemes. When he came back to Muscatine his opperations indicated a rich man. He bought two dwelling houses on Front street, just east of the bridge, where Jas. Wier lives, raised them up and then took down one of them a house good enough to bring $200 a year rent. He fitted up the remaining one in fine style for his own use. After occupying it for a short time he purchased the two corner lots he now occupies and took down the old Dr. Reeder house, a house that would have cost $3.000 to build, and erected the palace he now occupies. He is looked upon as a successful business man, opportunities of all kinds are offered him. We understand that he is one of the few who are going to build the North and South railroad for which the citizens of this city were called on to vote a tax last fall. Where and when the road will be built and what his share in the deal will be is a little problematical.

At an evening party at one of the suburban residences of our city, shortly after the completion of the high bridge, we recollect hearing Peter M. Musser do some very energetic talking to one of the directors of the high bridge. He presented it this way, the bridge company came to the Mussers and said we lack so much of having enough to secure its construction, you must advance the money and take stock for it. Peter M. said we will give you so much, $500 or more each, and take no stock for it. Of course when they could get no more from the Mussers they took all they could and went ahead and built the bridge. After their bonds were placed and the bridge built the company found they had quite a little money left. There were some very hungry stock holders in the high bridge company, so they concluded to make a dividend of the remaining funds amounting to 15 per cent. The Mussers who had not taken stock were not included in the divide. Peter M. claimed they had collected money of him and his uncle at his sugestion to make the dividend to the stock holders. The bridge man did not want to discuss the question but admitted that the thing did not look right. After they had seperated I asked Peter M. why he did not take stock; his reply was that he would have had to take twice that amount and he would have been just that much poorer; he got out of it just the cheapest way he could, but he did not relish the idea of donating money to make a dividend to the stock holders.

There is one very important member of the concern although not a stockholder, Mr. Z. W. Hutchinson. He is the chief office man, has been with the Mussers for many years, and is a brother of Mrs. P. M. Musser. He was educated at the State University in Iowa City and in early life was a practical civil engineer. During the preliminary survey of the Union Pacific railroad he was one of the corps under the supervision of S. P. Reed, the engineer that constructed the M. & M. road, now the C., R. I. & P. in our city. "Zell," as they call him, is a modest, unasuming man and well liked by every one. He was generous enough at the last school election to allow his name to appear as a school director and was elected without opposition. He is chief salesman for the company and can always be found at his post. We did once pursuade him to go a fishing; we had good success and concluded to go again, but we could never arrange a time to suit. He is one of the leading members of the Baptist church, sings in the choir, and can be relied on at all times.

We have an apology to offer the readers of the SATURDAY MAIL for using so much space in writing up the Musser Lumber Co. We will say that to write up a company that has been in existance more than forty years and do justice to its members requires time and space, although we try to be as brief as we can. We have a suggestion to make to the Mussers. The city needs a public building for an Academy of Science and a Library. If they would now in their life time devote a few thousand dollars and put up a "Musser Building" to be used for such purposes, it would place the Musser name on "perpetual record." I have no doubt but that the school board would appropriate the necessary land for it on the east end of the high school lots.

Recollections of

Bloomington in 1845.

Published in the Muscatine Saturday Mail May 7, 1898; written by
J. P. Walton.

No. 67.

There are a few copies of an old lithograph of the town of Bloomington in 1845 yet in existence. In the foreground is a steamboat, two sail boats, and a hand ferry boat. On the ferry are two horses and two or three passengers, two men rowing and one steering. Most of the ferrying across the river at Bloomington, now Muscatine, was then done in that way, it was hard work especially if the wind was a little adverse.

The most prominent building in the picture is the court house. It stood then in 1845 essentially as it does now; it was commenced in 1840 and completed in 1841, and is probably the oldest brick building in the city. The interior wood work was burned out in the winter of 1864 and replaced in 1865. The walls were so solid and thick with heavy brick partitions that they suffered but little by the fire. When refitted after the fire the transcept was put on across the north end This old court house was built by funds accumulated from the sales of town lots in the city on the commissioner's quarter, as it was called, and cost some $15,000. W. A. Brownell was the contractor when it was built. The foundation walls stood some four or more feet out of the ground; when graded it was filled up considerably, say two or three feet, there were four or five steps buried in front of the porch. I have probably described this old court house enough for the present time, but will say that it is the oldest public building in the state, has been longer in use than any other public building, and is in good condition, and should be kept as a historical monument to our territorial days, as there is very little else left in the state.

In the two blocks in front of the court house in 1845 there were but five houses. The most prominent one in the picture stands on the bank of the river. It was a brick dwelling built and owned by Hon. John A. Parvin, he was an uncle of Hon. T. S. Parvin, of Cedar Rapids. At that time John A. Parvin was probably in the mercantile business; he had been teaching school in our city some four or five years previous. I am not certain, but I think he taught the first school in our city in 1839; I don't know but George Bumgardner would dispute that point with him. This house was likely built in 1843, of brick, and it may be the oldest brick dwelling house in the city. It now stands on the rear end of the lot on which Mr. S. M. Batterson now lives. When S. L. Waide concluded to build himself a new house he got me to move the old house to the rear of the lot, and the Waide family lived in it during the construction of the new house. While Mr. Parvin occupied this house the cholera afflicted the town. Mr. Parvin lost his wife and several children. He was one of the three Parvin brothers, Josiah, William and John A., who came here in 1839. His first occupation was school teaching and surveying; he went into the mercantile business; I think he was a member of the first constitutional convention that framed the first constitution for the state of Iowa; he was in the legislature several terms; was one of the directors of the Reform school at Eldora, helped to locate it there, though using his influence to have it located in Muscatine, to no effect. In 1853 he was president of the board of township trustees, and in 1854 was mayor of the city. He came here a strong pro-slavery democrat, but during the exciting times of the Kansas and Nebraska bill he found himself a free soil democrat along with R. M. Burnett and others of that kind. When the republican party started he joined that and remained there. He was one of the leading members of the Methodist church, although not an exhorter he always responded when called upon at prayer meetings or love feasts. In his dealings he was strictly honest but very close and by frugal management he always kept his wants within his income. He was an out and out prohibitionist and was always willing to be classed as such.

On the northeast corner of Walnut and Second streets stood a two-story frame dwelling, the residence of John G. Deshler, a prominent man of our town. He was a lawyer, belonged to the firm of Lowe & Deshler. Lowe at that time lived out on the Fletcher place where John M. Kemble now lives. Lowe was afterwards governor of Iowa. Mr. J. G. Deshler had means, bought many of our best corner lots and much of our best lands. He came from Columbus, Ohio, and after staying here some ten or twelve years he returned. He practiced law with good success, but was not considered quite as profound a jurist as Stephen Whicher, although superior to most of the other members of the bar. He bought pine lumber and sold it, was one of the first lumber dealers. While he was a rough and tumble kind of a man his wife was the most toney woman of the village, she had the means to and did dress the most extravagantly of any in the place; full skirts were the fashion and the boys used to say that she would knock the glass out of the windows on both sides of the street with the swing of her skirts. They had no children. After they went away Deshler occasionally came back here to look after his property. John B. Dougherty, sr., was his agent for many years.

A frame cottage stood on the southeast corner of Walnut and Third streets, it was owned by Peter Petrican. Peter was was an old bachelor, had one room for his own use and rented the house and boarded out the rent. Old Dan Smith, the village blacksmith, lived in the house quite awhile. Petrican was a stone cutter from old Scotland; he was in company with Chas. Ogilvie in several deals, they owned the stone quarries at Wyoming Hill and tried to use the stone but it did not give satisfaction and the quarry was abandoned. The old stone pile driver that now lies in front of the court house was a piece of his handiwork. It was cut to drive the piling of one of the bridges across the creek on Second and Sycamore streets, probably in 1843. The stone hammer did not give satisfaction, so it was left in the creek for years. During one of the floods some twenty years or so ago the old hammer became visible. A number of us threw in a quarter each and got O P. Connor to get it hauled out and placed in court square by consent of the board of supervisors and the auditor. It was the first pile driver used within the county. it answered in a way the purpose it was made for.

On the rear of the lot now occupied by W. S. Richie, in front of the court house, stood a small cottage, with say three rooms, it belonged or was occupied by Ahimaaz Blanchard, he was a native of the northern part of New York, came here in 1836 or '37, bought a large farm on Muscatine Island—M. A. Smith occupies a part the land now. Blanchard got tired of farming, came to town and went into the livery stable business, got tired of that, traded his farm for town property. He then went to the pineries and undertook to cut pine timber and get it out, at which he was not successful. When the California fever broke out he went there, I think he never came back. Mr. Blanchard was too visionary, he would rush into schemes, many of which he never realized on. He left a widow and one son, Frank Blanchard, of Summit, who has recently died. His widow, now dead, was a sister of William and Hamilton St. John and of Mrs. Piiney Fay.

The four persons that occupied the four houses above mentioned were prominent citizens of our town in their time and as such we are willing to so record them.

There was but one other building, the Episcopal church and Masonic hall, standing on the two squares. We will promise to mention it in our next paper.

On the east corner of Mulberry and First streets stood a double log cabin built by Chares H. Fish, one of the earliest settlers of our town. He was connected with its survey into lots; when Charles L. Warfield was deputized to purchase the land of the government and deed it to the claimants Charles H. Fish was one of the witnesses.

This cabin was the "Mecca" of the town society. "Mother Fish" presided with her two fascinating daughters, Cad and Emmiline. Emmiline soon married Ben Howland—I think he was an uncle of our Ben E. Lilly.

"Mother Fish" was one of those whole souled women that was known by every body; she went all over the town and carried sunshine wherever she went. She was the leader among the women. The Fish family consisting of Jerry, Charles H. and son William B., came from Camden, N. J., staid awhile at Cincinnati, where one of Charlie's daughter married a Mr. Gould, and came here in 1836 or '37. Charles H. and Jerry followed butchering and fishing and kept a boat store. The son, William B. Fish, lived on his farm (it was where the latest additions to the cemetery are located). His house stood some sixty feet west of where the Huttig tomb now stands. In the spring of 1842 Charles H. Fish moved to St. Louis and Wm. B. Fish moved into the house in town. He planted boom corn on his farm. In the autumn of 1842 I went to work with Wm. B. Fish to help harvest the crop at $6.25 per month. We gathered the broom corn and filled the house on the farm. During the long cold winter of 1842 and '43 I worked for W. B. Fish for my board. I hauled wood, scraped corn and did anything that occurred to do. I said long, cold winter. On the 2d of April I hauled wood on the ice on the river, it was some three feet thick on the channel. The river did not get clear of ice until the 16th of April.

Willam B. Fish left sometime about 1844 or '45 and went to St. Louis, where he staid awhile, but came back and bought a farm on the head of the Island. He went into the fishing business with Wm. Middleton and was killed by the explosion of their small steamboat on August 16, 1863. I think some of his children yet live on Muscatine Island.

Recollections of

Bloomington in 1845.

Continued.

Published in the Muscatine Saturday Mail May 14, 1898; written by J P. Walton.

No. 68.

In 1845 in the square in front of the court house on the north side of Second street where the Episcopal church now stands, stood the first Episcopal church and masonic hall. (See cut.) It was commenced by Mathew Matthews in 1839 but not finished until the spring of 1841. Matthews started to build a one-story building for a church, but he being a mason and most of his helpers being masons, and the masons wanting a hall to meet in, the church and the masons united in the work of erecting the building. The masons using the second story and the church the first: It was said that Mathew Matthews donated the lot, which was probably the case, although the deed came directly from the county commissioners to Trinity church. This was probably the first Episcopal church and the first masonic building erected in the state. From 1841 to 1851 it was used by other denominations as a place of worship; for quite a while the Presbyterians held their meetings there, they had a church bell that was mounted on a frame on the top of the little vestry room or the side at the rear end of the building. The old building stood so far back on the lot that there was room to put up the new building without disturbing the old one. The new building was commenced in the autumn of 1851. In 1854 it became necessary to enlarge the new structure, then the old church had to be moved to the rear end of the church lot. It was rented to some kind of a German church whose members sang so loud as to greatly annoy the Episcopal society, so the old church was again moved out endwise to Walnut street and sold to J. P. Walton, who rented it to the Universalists under Rev. Woodhouse, later to the German Lutherans, and finally to the city school district for school purposes. During the war of the rebellion a furloughed soldier was taken down with the small-pox in the hotel on the corner. The first thing the owner of the old church knew they had broken open the upper story of the house and converted it into a pest house by taking the sick soldier in there thus spoiling the building as a school house. The lease on the ground ran out and could not be renewed so the building had to be taken down. Mr. Walton lost his house that he got a rent of $150 a year for. That was not the only bad part of it, the sick soldier belonged to Captain Anderson's company, Mrs. Anderson took care of him and caught the small-pox and died while the sick soldier got well and never thanked any one for the house or the treatment he received.

THE OLD EPISCOPAL CHURCH AND MASONIC HALL.

Sometime about 1845 the double log cabin belonging to Charles H. Fish which stood on Front street west of Mulberry was removed to give place to a good brick structure belonging to Hon. W. G. Woodward. Later it went into the hands of Peter Musser who enhanced its value by adding a second-story and otherwise improving it. Hon. W. G. Woodward and wife came here in 1840 or '41 from Massachusetts. They were two of the most accomplished people I ever met; both were fine singers, and when Rev. Dr. Robbins, the long-time Congregational minister came here, they joined his church. I think they had attended Rev. John Stocker's Presbyterian church that met in the old Episcopal church previous to Dr. Robbins coming here. Mr. Woodward was a lawyer by profession and practiced law quite successfully. I see in the directory of 1856 he was put down as associate chief justice of Iowa. He occupied that position for quite awhile, having at one time a very fine law library but as he gave up his law practice and his term of office expiring he sold the books to any one that would give anything for them, and finally sold the balance at auction for a song. In our youthful days the Woodward house was one of the places we visited quite often; I have often wondered how it came about as there was nothing very attractive about us, but they were very pleasant and genial people, their home was a pleasant one and we were always warmly welcomed, and many a Sabbath afternoon found us there.

There was another house we frequented quite often, it stands on Front street west of the high bridge; it belonged to Hiram Matthews—Pap Matthews as he was usually called. He was quite a funny old fellow, very fat and corpulent. He came to Bloomington in 1839, was a brick layer, his first job was to build his brother a house which was the first brick house built in Bloomington. It stood on Front street west of Cedar. When Hiram Matthews came here he built himself a log cabin on the rear of his lot lived in it until he built his brick some five or six years later. He had a wife and two daughters by the name of Orrell and Orpha. One, I think Orrell, was the mascot of the family. married a merchant by the name of Robert McClelland the other married John B. Dougherty, sr. Mrs. Dougherty and two sons are the survivers of the Matthews family. Pap Matthews was a great story teller, he was a teamster, and had a small pair of mules and a shallow short sort of a dump board, and did considerable dirt hauling. If asked why he used so small a dirt bed he would reply that he made the load up to the standard when he got on it—most everybody admited that. He served as constable for several years and as marshal in 1840 and in 1844, and street commissioner in 1845, '46 and '47. His wife was a splendid woman, his daughters married and were gone before we became acquainted to any extent with the family. His gandson, Johnnie, He was a "brick," I assure you, and he had a very apt tutor in his grandfather. I wonder he turned out as well as he has. I think he would hardly have done so had it not have been for the instructions and admonitions he received at the Sunday School. Johnnie always went to Sunday School, he was frequently loaded with very knotty questions for the teacher; these questions frequently originated with his grand father without a doubt.

After serving three years as street commissioner Mr. Matthews commenced mercantile business in a limited way, he fitted up a small store in the front part of his house to sell supplies to the emigrants that crossed the river on the ferry boat and landed at the foot of Walnut street. We recollect seeing a sign with "Ginger Braid" on it. I don't think he accumulated much at that business. In towns the size of Bloomington at that time almost every one was a character of note, Pap Matthews was certainly one.

On the alley end of the lot west of the bridge stood a frame cottage. It was occupied by J. J. Hoopes, a man who soon became prominent and remained so until his death over fifty years later. He was a native of Pennsylvania, came to Cincinnati when a young man, where he married. When coming to Iowa he brought his young wife and likely a child, afterwards their family increased to four children, three are living yet. He brought some means with him and went into a store in Linn county which was not a good investment. In fact it was a little disastrous to Hoopes as one of the partners, while the other who had the experience and no money invested, fared better, Hoopes was a builder and confined himself to his business. In the course of time he recovered all he had lost in the Linn county store. I commenced to work for him in the spring of 1848 at carpenter work for 50 cents a day and board, and staid with him most of the time for two years. In those two years I don't think I received $10 in money; the first year I got the lot on which I now live, the price was $50. Hoopes was the hardest working man I ever saw and he would make his men work hard and long. At that time there was no circular saws or planing machines, all the wood work of a house had to be worked by hand. We worked all day from thirteen to fifteen hours, it was the time that an effort was being made to have ten hours a day's work, and Hoopes was the last fellow to give in. He was a strong "dyed in the wool" democrat and loved to argue politics, he would stop his work for that purpose if he got crowded a little. There was another man of about the same character, an out-and-out whig, by the name of Alfred Purcell, he was a plasterer and of course he and Hoopes were brought together on the same job quite frequently, and we never missed a chance to get up an argument between them as we got a rest then.

In the spring of 1848 J. J. Hoopes' brother Reece came here and worked with him, later another brother, Lindley, came and worked with the others, although the latter two soon went to farming. J. J. Hoopes staid in town most of the time and loaned out his money. When the war broke out he managed to have quite a lot of gold coin on hand, he kept it until it went up to $2.50, then he sold it or bought a farm at the premium price. In 1843 he was on the board of town directors, and it was during his term of office and largely through his exertions the grave yard was moved to the west side of the city. In 1875 he served a term on the city council; he was the hardest kicker the Water Works company had to contend with; how they managed him I never knew. Several modifications in their propositions were made at his request. During the term of two years that Mr. Hoopes represented the Second ward the First ward was represented with just as positive a man in the person of Alex. Jackson. These two aldermen did not always agree, for when one got to spouting Shakespeare and the other Burns that meeting of the council was about through business for that session. We want to say for Mr. Hoopes that while he worked us unmurcifully hard he gave us good board and treated us kindly. We were unfortunate enough to be sick a short time while there and Mr. and Mrs. Hoopes gave us the best of attention. While living with them I always felt at home, and so did every one who visited them. I never saw any more hospitable people than they were.

Recollections of
Bloomington in 1845.
Continued.

Published in the Muscatine Saturday Mail May 21, 1898; written by J P. Walton.

No. 69.

In 1845 there stood on the west corner of Front and Cedar streets a very preposessing brick dwelling house, It was the first brick house built in the town, it was probably erected in 1839 or in 1840, I am not sure which; Hiram Matthews built it for his brother, Mathew Matthews, who lived in it until his death early in the forties. I don't know who lived there until 1849 when Dr. James S. Horton occupied it. In 1850 I commenced working for Horton, I occupied a room in the basement for a shop and lived with the family. Hon. Jacob Butler also lived with them.

Here let me say, I had had a an unusual streak of luck in my places for working after I had became old enough to do a man's work. I started in with J. J. Hoopes in the early spring of 1848, as mentioned in my last article; after living with him until the autumn of 1849 I commenced with Gamalial Olds and started a large house for him, of course I lived with the family, and between Olds and Horton I put in most of the time until 1852.

But to return to the Horton family, the doctor was an old school allopathic doctor and used plenty of calomel. He had left a large practice in Orange county, New York. When he came to Bloomington of course he found he had plenty of leisure time. The country was new, vegetation grew very luxuriantly, and the doctor for the want of something else to do commenced to make a botanical collection that took him all around over the country. The people saw him collecting plants and drying them and knew he was a doctor, and concluded he was a botanical doctor. We had one botanical doctor in G. W. Fulliam, and the people often spoke of the old botanical doctor meaning Dr. Horton, and of the young one, meaning Dr. Fulliam. Of course Horton did not hear of this. The first two years Dr. Horton was here there was a great deal of cholera. If a case of cholera occured the first doctor to be had was called; under those conditions Horton got his share. His medicine was calomel and opium, he never lost a case, and his reputation as a cholera doctor soon gained prominence as he cured some very bad cases. While the doctor practiced medicine when called, I don't think he ever hung out his "shingle." He had come west to go to farming, he happened to go down on the Muscatine island when the river was low, in the fall of 1849, shortly after he came here, and found some government land he could enter very cheap, so he entered it and started to build a gravel-house on the head of the sand mound. Getting out material and making the frame, doors and sash, furnished me with employment during the cold days of the winter. The house was built but before the doctor got ready to move there in 1851 he bought the Humphrey's place now the Horton farm and moved out there. After Horton left the house on Front street it passed into the hands of S. B. Crane who had it taken down and the present building now occupied by Dr. J. D. Fulliam erected out of the old material. The Horton family were strong Presbyterians. At the time I lived with them there were several strong factions in the church. The Hortons with their conections, the Cummings and the Waters families, made a strong party, while T. S. Parvin and his associates, the Ogilvies and others made another interest to be consulted. Mrs. Horton was an excellent woman to pacify the disaffected and she was realy the mordant of the whole church. The doctor had turned his attention to improving his land and worked very hard; he was excitable but would not use any profane language, he would manage to vent his indignation some other way, and while he worked hard he loved a little recreation. He would go hunting or fishing occasionally. I have had had many a hunt with him. When the war broke out two of his sons enlisted in the army, Col. C. C. and James Horton, the latter died in the service. During the war Mrs. Horton devoted much of her time to the relief of the sick and wounded soldiers. She was a prominent member of the Ladies' Soldiers Aid Society.

On the southwest corner of Cedar and Second street stood a two story brick house erected in 1842 and '43; there was a wooden building in the rear that was built some two years earlier. The brick house was built by Thomas Johnson while he was United States marshal for Iowa. It is probable that he borrowed some money of T. M. Isett to build the house, for as soon as he left Isett got it and lived in it. Johnson was a sporting man, would gamble or do almost anything that a good citizen would pronounce out of character. T. M. Isett who followed Johnson as an occupant of the house was a kind of a last man in many ways but kept his money all the same. I think I described him in one of my former articles. Later the house passed into the hands of Jacob Openheimer and afterward into the possesson of W. W. Webster, who got me to move it back to the alley. It was recently removed to give room for the improvements to Hotel Grand.

On the east corner of Cedar and Second street stood a very pretentious one-story frame cottage. It was the residence of Dr. Fitch, who was a wealthy man, he owned the big farm lately known as the Hershey farm. For one or two years he hired men and tried farming, it did not pay him to live in town and go out to the farm to work. He was said to be a very close man, so much so that he would pull off his shoes and go barefoot to save shoe leather. I cannot vouch for the correctness of the story. I think the doctor died about 1851 or '52 leaving a widow and one daughter. In the course of time the daughter grew to be a woman and like many other young women was willing to marry and did marry a young man by the name of Harry Campbel. I don't know whether the old lady consented or not, at all events she undertook to run their affairs in a manner that made lots of gossip and fun for the old settlers. She succeeded in separating and divorcing them before the birth of their child. The old lady packed up her daughter and grand-child and left for parts unknown, leaving her former son-in-law to look out for himself. Shortly after this Col. T. M. Isett and his wife Lucy were separated, a divorce was granted but not until a nice dower of $10,000 was arranged. Harry Campbel then married Lucy and they went to Florida to live. Col. Isett soon left and went to New York city, he did not return for many years and then only temporarily.

On the rear end of the lot on the northeast corner of Second and Cedar streets (back of Granam's drug store) stands an old frame building. It was the first Catholic church erected in our city. This building was first built in Prairie du Chien, Wis., and brought down to Bloomington on a raft and put up here in 1843 or '44. The Catholics had no regular pastor until 1848 when Rev. Father McCormick officiated perhaps for a year or more. I am not very familiar with the history of this church, I hope some one will write it up, if Father Laurent would do so he would confer a great favor on the city. There is so much of interest about the Catholic churches of our city that he knows better than any one else, it seems a pity to have him go away without it being written. We hope he may be induced to do it.

If I recollect aright the one story dwelling on the opposite side of Cedar street was built by old Mr. McCrow, likely in 1839 or '40. Mr. McCrow and family were probably the first Catholics here. Occasionally a traveling priest would come along and hold meetings in his house. Mr. McCrow went out on the north side of the road opposite the city cemetery and built himself a house, the first one along that road this side of the Fletcher house. I think he was a shoemaker and one of the first ones here; when he moved out to his new place he gave up shoemaking. I find in the directory of 1856 that Mrs. Elanor McCrow resided in the house on Cedar street, I presume she was his widow.

A little later the two Becke brothers, Theodore and Joseph, came here, both poor but honest laborers. They soon got to doing stone masonry and lived to a good age, leaving a nice little property for the younger Beckes. Jerry McMinnomy and Jimmy Dunn were also among the early members of the Catholic church.

This old building was undoubtedly the oldest building standing in the city that was built for church purposes. The street was originally up to the second story, the lower story was dug out and underbuilt when the street was graded; there was a wing added on the south side that was surmounted with a little bell, this bell was sold to the city school district and mounted on "old number one school house;" the bell was destroyed when the school house burned down. When Father Laurent came here he soon found that the church was too small and he started out to build St. Matthias church which was then out of the town. It used to be often remarked that no other denomination would go so far out of town to attend church. When St. Matthias was built the old church and its belongings went to the Chambers brothers, they did not keep it long, it is now used as a work shop.

Recollections of
Bloomington in 1845.
Continued.

Published in the Muscatine Saturday Mail May 28, 1898; written by J P. Walton.

No. 70.

For several of the early years there was a solitary building standing on East Hill. At that time East Hill stood a mile and a half away, or in other words, to get there one had to go to Ninth street to cross the creek and then another half mile or more to the hill. There was a foot log across the stream occasionally used when the water was not to high. The occupants of the building were Mr. Lockwood and wife. We have but little recollection of him; he lived but a short time after locating there. His widow was a sharp, broad minded, energetic woman; she staid here some time after the death of her husband. I think she got a position as a school teacher at some Indian agency through the influence of General Fletcher, an Indian agent from our county.

A good many laughable stories were told at her expense. It was said that on one occasion an old Indian chief came a wooing, she not understanding the Indian language would answer yes to all his propositions; all at once it dawned upon her what he wanted, she did not faint, but got terribly mad and made the old Indian get out. (Puckachee.)

On another occasion while living on East Hill, "Pars" Washburn, then a boy of 17 summers, had occasion to go after Mrs. Lookwood. He went in a canoe up above the mouth of Mad creek, hauled his canoe on shore and went up to the house for her. They returned together to the river, but to their disgust they found the canoe had got adrift and was fast floating away. She at once ejaculated "Can you swim?" "Yes!" "Well, then pull off your clothes and jump in and get it." She turned her back to him. This was a little embarrassing to the boy but, of course, he did as ordered and commenced to disrobe. It took apparently longer than usual, Mrs. Lockwood became impatient and turned around just as "Pars" was ready to take to the water, and she ejaculated "jump in, jump in!" which he did and saved the boat.

After Mrs. Lockwood's connection with the Indian school was closed, she went east and became Mrs. Fales of Washington, D. C., who with the noted Mrs. Wittenmeyer, both former citizens of Iowa, visited the hospitals in the south and as ministering angels relieved the sick, cheered the despondent and smoothed the bed of the dying. They took the first steps to organize the Sanitary Commission that rendered so much relief to the sick and wounded during the war of the rebellion. Shortly after Mrs. Lockwood left Bloomington there come a very wet season and the hill side got to sliding and her house stood at an angle of some 30 degrees for a long time before it was taken down.

Along in 1851 or '52, when the cholera was at its worst there were a great many cholera patients left on the wharf by steamboats, and frequently deaths occurred before shelter could be found for them; no one wanted to admit them to their houses. In order to accommodate such cases the city built a one-story frame house on East Hill for a hospital. I think there never was but one case taken there, but the building stood for several years without being occupied. I think it was the second building erected on East Hill. After Second street was graded and the bridge built across the creek in 1856 or '57 people began to settle on the hill.

In June 1052 or '53 a German— I think his name was Skinnottie or a similar name—built a huge dance house out on the brow of the hill, he called it the Trevoli. He rushed it along and got it enclosed and the floors down by the Fourth of July. The lower floor was for dancing, the second story was for card tables and drinking. The Germans held their first celebration there as Germans, that was ever held in this city. It did not go off very big, there were not enough Germans here at that time that were willing to throw down the gauntlet and say "we will celebrate your Fourth of July as we please," which has been done on a few occasions since. That celebration was to have dancing during the day and night. During the evening a clan of young men of the city went over there to dance with the "dutch" girls; there were only a few of them, and the fellow that could not waltz was not in it, but the beer was there in abundance. The young men had a hilarious old time and all agreed not to tell on one another, hence I can't, but perhaps Ben. Beach or George Magoon could tell if they chose. I think the Trevoli never had but one day's business, it was not popular. I have forgotten what became of it.

In the autumn of 1852, on Oct. 9th, our citizens organized an agricultural society with James Weed president, William Millar vice president, John H. Wallace secretary, and J. G. Gordon treasurer. They secured a piece of ground on the west side of the graded road, where Jos. Bennett now has his garden. The society cleared out the brush, using it for a fence, and made a track of a quarter or a third of a mile around and held a fair. It was a a new thing in Iowa and proved a success. It was patronized from Scott, Cedar, Johnson, Washington and Louisa counties. Three fairs of a similar kind were held here. The society had accumulated quite a little sum of money and went down on the Muscatine Island where they bought forty acres of land for fair purposes. This forty acres on the island is where the Musserville brick school house and where Mr. B. Kemper's dwelling are located. The fair ground association which owned the land was a joint stock company; the county agricultural society having stock agreed to pay rent to the association for use of grounds for holding fairs and with the privilege of buying the land as soon as they could accumulate sufficient funds. This was all right and would have worked all right, but the fair people over done the thing. A state agricultural society had sprung into existance and the association thought it would be a good thing to have the state fair held here; so they bent their energies to that purpose. They got J. G. Gordon elected treasurer and Hon. John H. Wallace secretary, and the state fair was held here in 1856 and in 1857. At the same seasons the county agricultural society tried running county fairs which proved a failure in both years, leaving the society badly encumbered with debts. The panic of 1857 and war that followed in 1861 so effectually used up the county agricultural society that it lost its claim on the fair grounds. The stock was sold at a very low rate and finally went into the hands of George W. Connor who converted the fair grounds into a farm, selling a portion of it to Barney Kemper for a garden patch.

At the state fair in 1857 a larger amount of perishable stuff was offered for exhibition than could be sheltered, so the society put up temporary frames and covered them with cotton sheeting and ducking. When the fair was over this was stored in one of the dry rooms (the office.) The association had contracted some debts and they turned out the sheeting, etc., to help pay the debts. I had the last chance and got some 500 or a 1000 yards at very low figures. The sheeting I could use but the lot was mostly heavy ducking which I kept until the war broke out and cotton got away up beyond any known price, when I disposed of it without any trouble. For a while anything that had cotton in it sold for fabulus prices; it got so scarce that in many cases mattresses were ripped up for the cotton filling to be wove into clothing. It was quite a God send to some of our old merchants who had their shelves encumbered with a lot of out of fashion dry goods. The high price of cotton sold them. Cotton was so scarce that paper was spun into twine for common wrapping purposes, it made a good substitute if it did not get wet.

The agricultural society held fairs during the war but it was a losing business and they had to give it up. After the war was over a ralley was made and ground secured of John Barnard and fitted up with an octagon hall; after holding two or three fairs out there it proved to far out of town, and the improvements were moved on the Smalley lands on the top of East Hill. The octagon hall at Barnard's was taken down and put up on the Smalley land; new stables and fences were built, a half-mile track made, and some good fairs were held there. By some means the octagon hall was burned down and temporary sheds were erected for a year or so; later some one started the scheme of buying new grounds where the fair grounds are now located.

Recollections of
The Baptist Church.

Published in the Muscatine Saturday Mail June 4, 1898; written by J. P. Walton.

No. 71.

All of our churches have had periods of prominence before the public, such as revivals, introductions of new ministers, or the building of a new church. As the Baptist brethren are about to enlarge their church we are going to venture on a brief history of its organization, etc. From a paper read by Rev. G. F. Linfield before the Academy of Science on January 29, 1883, we make the following extract:

"The first Baptist meeting in Bloomington, now Muscatine, was called October 2, 1841, and October 17, articles of faith were adopted, and the on 30th the church was duly organized with 9 members, at the hotel kept by Robert C. Kinney, corner of Chestnut and Front streets, known as the Iowa House, and Rev. E. Fisher was called at a salary of $100 a year, to preach one Sunday in each month. At the beginning of 1842 the society wanted half of Elder Fisher's time for $200, and the home mission was asked, in May, to lend a helping hand. Deacon Carpenter succeeded to the pastorship in June, 1843, and preached twice a month, and in 1844 Rev. Jesse N. Seelye was in charge and trying to raise funds to build a church. In 1848 Rev. S. B. Johnson was pastor, succeeded in 1852 by Rev. W. A. Wells. The records are silent upon the dedication of the new building, but they speak of a vestry January 25, 1851, which would indicate that the upper room was then occupied. This building is the litttle brick church back of the present edifice and is now (1883) owned by some German society. [It has lately been removed by Clifford & Son and a photograph building erected in its stead.] Rev. A. G. Eberhardt came in 1853 and remained three years, and in 1855 R. M. Burnett and

Willis Davis were elected deacons. In this latter year the final debt of $300 on the church was paid. Rev. Geo. I. Miles followed Mr. Eberhardt in April, 1856, at a salary of $800 and the society swung loose from the home mission and endeavored to meet its own expenses. In July thirty-four members withdrew to form the Holland Baptist church. The pastor died December 10, 1857, and was succeded by his brother, Edward Miles, and in November of the following year Rev. John Cummins became pastor. February 4, 1859, the German Baptist church was organized, and in June of the same year fifteen members were dismissed to form a church in Lake township. The following August Rev. C. H. Remington was installed pastor, resigning in 1862 to become chaplain of the Eleventh Iowa volunteers. In May, 1863, Rev. S. S. Burnham was called to the pastorate and was succeeded in 1866 by Rev. Edwin Eaton. George W. Dillaway started the Ninth street misson April 17, 1864, and the chapel was built a year later. This period also became memorable for the building of the present church edifice, the corner stone being laid in August, 1864, the basement occupied July, 1865, and the upper part finished and didicated on the first Sunday in November, 1868."

In May, 1863, when S. S. Burn-ham became pastor he soon commenced to raise money to build the new church that had been talked about for some time. It was during the war of the rebellion when a dollar in gold was worth $2.25 to $2.50 in greenbacks. The greenback was legal tender money; it had gotten to be quite abundant and every one felt flush and subscribed liberally. The church was started in 1864 and in Aug. the corner stone was laid, and then the fun began. At the commencemet of the ceremony the minister invited any one to deposit whatever they chose to be laid away there as a memorial of events of the times. There were several articles presented, among other things a copy of the Muscatine Journal, an intensely loyal republican paper. There was a strong democratic paper that was considered by many somewhat disloyal by the name of "The Democratic Enquirer" published in this city, but as no one offered a copy the box was closed up and placed in proper position and the ceremony ended, and every thing was supposed to be lovely. It soon became known, probably through the papers, what articles were deposited in the corner stone. In the church there was a very prominent family of out-spoken democrats and they were large subscribers to the new church funds. They claimed to be very much dissatisfied at the omission of the democratic paper and declared they would not pay a cent towards the construction of the church. They had influence and no one in the church wanted to lose their subscription, so efforts were made to pacify them, but to no purpose, as the more they were labored with apparently the madder they got. The dissatisfaction was mostly confined to the members of the church but they did a great deal of talking, and the controversy soon got outside among the town people who began talking it up. One of the deacons of the church made a laughable remark in connection with the names of the democrats which set the town off. If any one wants to know what that remark was they can ask G. W. Dillaway or R. W. Durkee. The deacon had to apologize; the democrats referred the matter to Deacon Burnett, he would not not say anything but laughed.

After the corner stone had been laid a few days it got noised around to the building committee that the stone was going to be removed, so brother Dillaway walked up to the church the threatened evening, and sure enough some one was there working away at the brick wall digging it out. Dillaway sung out and wanted to know what the person making the noise was doing, the man came out and his reply was "he wanted peace!" Dillaway was dumbfounded as the man who stood before him was one of the oldest citizens, a straight forward upright, honest Christian man, a prominent member of the Methodist church, and one that no one would suppose would be guilty of such an action. In performing the act he had no malice. It soon leaked out that several fun lovers had put him up to it and made him believe that if the corner stone was taken up and had to be re-laid that a copy of the democratic paper could be put in, thus making the disaffected parties all right. The stone was not taken up and the democratic paper did not get in. It was the opinion of some who were familiar with the financial standing of the disaffected ones that they "had bit off more than they could chew,"— had subscribed more than they could pay, and took that way to get out of it. I think their subscription was not paid at that time. But they remained with the church and were liberal contributors afterwards.

To be Continued.

Recollections of

The Baptist Church.

Concluded:

Published in the Muscatine Saturday Mail June 11, 1898; written by J. P. Walton.

No. 72.

(Correction: In my last letter I mentioned the name of the Democratic Enquirer, when it should have been the Courier.)

In the year 1844 Rev. Jesse N. Seeley commenced to raise funds for a church. Rev. Seeley was small in statue but large in works. He had but a small flock to labor with and no wealthy members. I recollect a few of the members; Deacon Plumber was a fat, heavy set old fellow, a little extra exertion would put him "out of wind" but he was always splurging around the church, he was a baker and confectioner by occupation, his shop stood on the south side of Second street between the avenue and Sycamore, it was in a low two-story building, he kept pop for sale which was probably about the first ever sold here, he also had ginger bread and ginger beer and a few candies and baked a fair loaf of bread. On one occasion a fire broke out on an adjoining lot although Plumber's house did not get on fire he removed his furniture, he threw his looking glass out of the window and lugged out a pair of andirons in his hands.

Rev. Seeley had another member of his flock who was quite a prominent man, Deacon Stephen Hadley; he came to Iowa in 1837 and secured a large farm out on the east side of Hickory Grove on the head waters of Mad creek, some four miles north and east of our town. After farming some three or four years he moved into town and went to making brick, probably in 184, he built and lived in the house on the southeast corner of Sixth and Orange he was something of a wag, a story got in circulation too ridiculous for any one to believe implicating him as one of the parties. The report had it that brother Plumber prefered charges against him and had him up and tried him before the church, and he was acquited much to Plumber's disgust.

In those early days all the orthodox churches tried to discipline their erring members. The Baptist church was no exception. The Episcopal church had a preacher that did not come up to the desired requirements, he was tried and suspended. The Methodist church had a more summary way of dealing with its delinquent members, the minister simply struck their names from the church roll, as in the case of Bro. Thomas Morford who was stricken from the membership roll by Rev. Henry Clay Dean for sitting with his wife in church. Dean did not allow the sheep and goats to sit together.

The Baptist church had another prominent member in the person of Myron Ward, he was a brick layer and stone mason, a stout, strong passionate man. On one occasion, while working on the roof of the church perhaps topping the chimney or he may have been shingling, when something was said that riled him, and he seized the little preacher and would have thrown him from the roof if he had been permitted to do so by the other men on the roof.

Rev. Seeley persevered in the good work, securing a day's work here or a load of hauling there, or in fact anything that could be used in the building of the church. He got but little money for little was to be had. A common laborer had to do two days work for a dollar, and such jobs as that were not to be had every day. Rev. Seeley probably got the roof on the building in the autumn of 1845 and had most of the window boarded. A room in the basement was plastered and used for meetings, and for a school. Miss Lamphrey, who afterwards became Mrs. Cornelius Cadle taught school there.

Among the different ministers the Baptist church has had we consider Rev. Seeley "the noblest Roman of them all." He was on hand to do his Master's bidding under almost any circumstances and in almost any circumstance. I recollect attending a meeting at Drury's Landing one Sabbath afternoon, there was a goodly turn out, the women went inside of the room together with a few of the more devote men, but most of the men staid outside and played cards and pitched dollars in hearing of the minister's voice. This was one of Rev. Seeley's regular appointments which he made but I think he wasted a good deal of Christian labor over there among the "suckers," perhaps not.

In the early part of the winter of 1847-'48 the carpenter work was commenced on the upper part of the church. I helped Fred Hoffmeyer get out and put down the floor. I think the main room was finised in 1848. This building was the one taken down by Clifford & Son to make room for their photograph building which they now occupy.

The early churches in Bloomington and Muscatine were truly pioneer churches, they had all the requisites, they admired a long sermon. I recollect attending a funeral, the church was crowded and I with others had to stay outside, the service lasted nearly two hours.

During the troublesome times previous to the war of the rebellion the democrats as well any one else could find a home here provided they had been immersed. Such was not the case in some of the other churches, but they must be immersed for the Baptist church. When that church received new converts they would furnish the town with a Sunday afternoon entertainment by resorting to the river bank for baptism. I have seen hundreds gather to witness the ceremony. After the completion of the present church building they no longer met on the river bank. These entertainments sometimes took a mirthful turn, especially to the by-stander On one occasion we noticed a party wending their way to the river bank and following were four or five candidates for immersion, among the number was a well built young lady, she was dressed in a fine white dress, but she had undoubtedly never visited Long Branch or any other sea side resort and did not know of the advantage of having woolen underclothes or weighted skirts. The bank of the river was quite shallow, they had to wade out a considerable distance to get into water deep enough. The minister had a great deal of trouble in keeping the young lady's dress down, it would float up like a balloon, but after becoming wet it stuck very close, thus making the young lady present one of the finest specimens of living statuary we ever saw. I think this party did not belong to the straight set, but they were Baptists all the same.

Rev. Edwin Eaton who was pastor of the Baptist church at the dedication of the present edifice on the first Sunday in November 1868, was a very popular minister. I am indebted to Rev. Linfield for the following extract taken from a paper read before the Academy of Science, February 1st 1888:

"Mr. Eaton's poor health compelling his retirement after five years labor. Rev. N. A. Reed became pastor in October, 1871, and was followed by Rev. A. G. Eberhardt in 1876.

"The winter of 1877 was made memorable by the labor of Elder Hunt and his death during the progress of protracted meetings. Rev. D. T. Richards became pastor in the fall of 1878, and was succeeded by the present pastor, Rev. G. F. Linfield, in 1881.

"During the existence of the church the whole number of admission is 759, of which 399 have been by baptism. The first baptism in Muscatine was of Mrs. Loret Headly, June 26, 1842. Mrs. Eliza Washburn has been a member longer than any one else now living, having been baptised Jan. 18, 1846.

"A vote of the church is recorded Nov. 30, 1844 that a Bible class be held which was the beginning of the present Sunday School believed to be the largest in the State, in respect to which Mr. Linfield mentions that Hon. R. M. Burnett, the present Superintendent, will have served in that office by next June, nineteen consecutive years."

While the Baptist church did not start quite as early in our town as the Episcopal, the Methodist or the Presbyterian, I have often thought and still think that they are the best fitted for a Pioneer church of them all. The Episcopals had the first church organization here, and built the first church building. The Baptists built their church long before the Presbyterians, who led the Methodists. The Methodists got control of a school house that they used for a meeting house. The Presbyterians used the Episcopal church. The Baptist built their own church.

PERSONAL
RECOLLECTIONS OF
Events for Sixty Years or More by J. P. Walton.

Written by himself and Read at a Family Reunion, held June 11, 1898. Published in the Muscatine Saturday Mail June 18, 1898.

No. 73

Sixty consecutive years in one community rarely occurs in this new state of Iowa. We don't think of but one person that will fill that role at this time in our city.

On Saturday, the 11th day of June, Josiah Proctor Walton celebrated the sixtieth anniversary of his landing in Iowa then Wisconsin territory, at Geneva, three miles east of Muscatine, by gathering his family of three daughters, their husbands and four grand children, at Evergreen Nook, his home in this city. There were present J. P. Walton, Mary Elizabeth (Barrows) Walton his wife, her sister Mrs. Carrie (Barrows) Fezler; the oldest daughter Mrs. Alice (Walton) Beatty and her husband James Q. Beatty; the second daughter, Mrs. Lillie (Walton) Hopkinson, with her husband Amos C. Hopkinson and their two children, Cora W. and J. Walton Hopkinson; and the third daughter, Mrs. May (Walton) Hoopes, with her husband Joseph E. Hoopes and their two children, Amy and Lindley Hoopes.

It was their intention to have the reunion at the landing place and drink water from the same sulphur spring that the subject of this sketch drank from sixty years ago, but the excessive rains prevented it, so Evergreen Nook had the honor of the reunion and well was it entitled to it, for in 1848 fifty years before Josiah Walton bought the lot, working one hundred days at carpenter work to pay for it. In 1851 he built the house and has made his home ever since in that house, being the longest continuous resident in one house in the ward if not in the city. The house when first built was 17x26 feet two stories, it has had seven different additions put on at seven different times. When this house was first built and for some years Eighth street from Mulberry to Cedar was impassable, a swamp existed near the corners of Walnut and Eighth streets, Josiah Walton cut off the ridge in front of his house and hauled the earth into the swamp, and cut a drain down the north side of Eighth street, turning the water toward the creek and thus made the street passable at his own expense, with the exception of his two days road work which the road supervisor credited him with.

At that time politics did not appear to figure much in city offices, any one could run for a city office if he chose and vote for himself and get others to vote for him if they would. The offices were largely controlled by a lot of men that were interested on Second street, any one that was offered as a candidate if not satisfactory to their views generally got left—thus no improvements were made that did not point to Second street. The residents along Eighth street wanted some improvements which they could not get so they concluded to offer J. P. Walton as a candidate for alderman. Of course, the Second street interest objected; they selected W. H. Stewart as a candidate, Henry Funck was also a candidate. On election day it turned out that Walton had but few votes but had secured enough to elect Funck and defeat the Second street ring. After that Eighth street was considered in the city, we got the street worked and made passable except in muddy times. We had no sidewalks only those laid by subscription which was one board wide from Cedar to Mulberry streets. On one occasion the Presbyterians had a social at the parsonage, where Fred Daut's house now stands, Philip Stein was on the council at the time, and he with a party of ladies undertook to travel over the one-plank walk along Eighth street to get to the parsonage on a dark night. How badly Stein and his party got stuck in the mud I never knew, but he got very mad and at the next meeting of the city council he had walks ordered for that locality. Of course, the residents all put down walks, but there were two vacant lots belonging to F. H. Stone who utterly refused to put a walk down. It was then a question whether the city could collect pay for putting down walks when the property owners refused, but Stein kept mad long enough to have the walk put down. J. P. Walton did the work and took city orders for his pay, the cost was taxed up to the lots and was paid.

For years J. P. Walton was a guardian to the interests of Eighth street, and other interests in his neighborhood. When it became necessary to open Cedar street, a bridge near Seventh was required, Walton built the bridge for $250 and donated $50 toward it. If I am right, the city, or county for the city, paid some $150, the remainder was raised by subscription, Walton circulating the paper. When the water from Broadway was turned down the north side of Eighth street, the grade of the street was changed; by permission of the city council, Walton fixed the grade on the east side of the creek so as to conform to the surface of the ground and the convenience of the property. Not a murmur has ever been heard about the grade since the change. The property has nearly all been improved, if the grade had not been changed it is doubtful if one-half would be improved at this time. When gas was extended out Mulberry street, Walton concluded that Eighth street wanted it and he interested Rev. Father Laurent in it, he wanted it in the church. This was a mistake on the part of Walton at that time for Hon. John Knopp was a member of the city council and he had just had a misunderstanding with Rev. Laurent about the stone gutters and worked against the introduction of gas on Eighth street. Walton had an eye to business and had the primaries attended to, and John Knopp was left out and the gas lights went in. Before the sanitary sewerage was put in the cellars along Eighth street were flooded with water, Walton found a drain tile could be put in from Mulberry to the creek for about $50; he drew up a contract with the city to put it in and maintain a drain for the amounts signed on the contract, which was about $60, Walton heading the list with $20. The city put in the drain at a cost of less than $60, and they have received $10 each from some four or five other parties making a profit of $40 or $50. Walton has kept a vigilant eye over the drain to keep the plumbers from cutting it off.

When the water works were put in it was the intention to put Eighth street in the district, but Walton fought it so hard it was left out, but when the proper time came to have a water main laid on Eighth street he had the tax on the property of that street to offer as an inducement. In this last water move he had the assistance of T. N. Brown who had then recently moved into the neighborhood.

Walton has about concluded that the old adage is very nearly correct "That a prophet is not without honor save in his own neighborhood or among his own people."

We have got away from our starting point, we undertook to tell about the events of J. P. Walton's coming to Iowa sixty years ago. He was born in the town of New Ipswish, N. H., on February 26, 1826; at an early age he moved to the town of Antrim N. H. Here memory first made an impression on his mind, the first thing he recollects was going fishing in the Contucook river. This was perhaps natural for while he is not a descendant of Izaak Walton, he is a descendant of Rev. William Walton, who was probably a member of the same family and who graduated at Emanuel college, Cambridge, England, taking his degrees in 1621 and 1625 and came to New England before 1634. J. P. Walton moved to Lowell, Mass., at the age of 4 or 5 years, where he obtained a grammar school education, and came to Iowa at the age of 12 in 1838; the next ten years to 1848, were the most trying days of his existence. It was the old story of the survival of the fittest. (So much has been written of trials and triumphs in our former recollections that we omit mentioning them now.) In 1857 he paid a visit to New Ipswich, N. H., and again in 1895, and while visiting the scenes of his birth place wrote the following description in his note book:

"Wilder Village, New Ipswich, N. H., August 31, 1895. I am standing and leaning against the house I was born in, on February 26, 1826. On my left in the rear rises Temple mountain, a little further in front is Barret's mountain; the place here is now known as Wilder's Village. The old mill and dam that my father owned when I was born, were washed away some twenty years ago, the mill pond is grown up with trees. A gentleman living in Boston owns the house and uses it as a summer resort, he left this morning for the city; the building is in charge of a neighbor lady who kindly opened it for our inspection. It commenced to rain and I was compelled to leave the enchanted spot."

Recollections of

The Muscatine Light Guards and the Davenport Fire Department.

Published in the Muscatine Saturday Mail June 25, 1898; written by
J. P. Walton.

No. 74

The recent firemens' tournament calls to mind the visit of the Davenport firemen to this city in by-gone days with other events somewhat connected with the occurence. In the year 1855 or '56, the young men of our city organized a military company. They called it the Muscatine Light Guards. I think there were some thirty or forty in the company; they had a beautiful uniform, with white horse tails for plumes on their helmets; on the whole it was a very nobby suit, it cost some $75. Their guns were furnished by the state. We can recollect but few of the members' names. John H. Wallace was captain, W. R. Stone, O. P. Waters, Ben Beach, and perhaps others were lieutenants; G. D. Magoon was orderly sergeant; Benjamin Neidig, Sam. Dunn, A Johns, George Satterley, in fact about all the young men in the city that could get any money were in the ranks. This company was the pet of the town, as many of the best society young men belonged to it. Any prominent event or celebration was not complete without them. When the railroad was opened to Washington they were offered a free ride with others of our citizens. Of course, the Light guards went. They were expected to furnish amusement and look after the social interests of the city.

Now, it so happened that Davport at that time was a city of about the size of Muscatine, say 7,000 or 8,000 inhabitants, and had a fire company that they petted about the same way we did our military company. I have been told that Bob. Littler was the chief. On one occasion this fire company took a boat ride and came as far as Muscatine, they landed and marched through our streets, in full uniform with red shirts, etc., but as they had neglected to notify Muscatine of their coming no one was on hand to receive them. They had only fairly gone when the papers began to pitch into the Light Guards for not treating them better. Of course, our Light Gaurds were a valiant organization and were not going to be out done by a lot of firemen, so they resolved to be courteous and invite the firemen to a banquet. Money being a needed article they started a subcription, the business men subscribed libereally and a sufficient amount of funds was thought to be in sight, so an invitation was sent to the Davenport "laddies" and ther sweethearts. A special train was secured on August 6, 1857, and free transportation was furnished which helped to swell the number of expected guests wonderfully, the cars were crowded and arrived on time. The Light Guards were on hand and escorted their visitors, or a part of them, to the old fair grounds, where an address from the captain tendered the freedom of the city to them, and was responded by Hon. John P. Cook, of Davenport. Dinner was then announced, it was a little on the picnic order but plenty was to be had. The freedom of the city was different from the freedom of the city of London tendered Gen. U. S. Grant, which can be seen in the Grant collection at Washington, it is a gold medal and was accepted by Grant, he paying for his own cigars, etc. The difference was the Light Guards gave no medal but promised to pay for the cigars, etc.—at all events the Davenporters paid for nothing, at least the saloon keepers said so. One firm in our city thought they knew the habits of the invited guests and accordingly donated two barrels of whisky, the heads of the barrels were knocked out and tin cups were hung around on the sides for all to help themselves. This whisky was all disposed of; I don't think for a minute that the Davenporters drank it all, neither do I think that this was all the Davenporters drank that day. Well, they took the town and some of them staid a week before they got away. Many of them left in the afternoon, some with their heads full of whisky and their hats full of cigars.

"After the ball was over" the bills began to come in, the company commenced to collect the subscriptions, considerable of which was repudiated; the boys had to make an assessment on themselves of $20 each, soon another $20 assessment and then a third one was paid when the city council came to their aid and donated $700. This reception proved too much for the company, it eventually broke them up with an unpaid debt of $1,400. This day's reception is supposed to have cost or at least bills were presented for over $3,000. The company could not survive the reception.

A year or two afterwards Capt. Teller made an effort to and did organize a military company; he wanted the guns the Light Guards had used and got an order from General Gordon or some one else for them but Captain Wallace had given a $200 bond for them and refused to let them go without his bond was cancelled. The guns were stored in Chester Weed's warehouse. Chester said he would open the warehouse and let the two factions settle who the guns belonged to. Wallace's friends were on hand and threatened to knock down the first man that touched a gun. Teller's friends believed they would and did not touch a gun, but got the bond cancelled and then took the guns. These guns changed hands again before they were sent to the war.

The other day we were standing on a corner talking with a couple of men who were formerly members of the old Light Guards when a squad of Davenport veteran firemen came along, one of our number ventured the remark that they were the fellows that drank our whisky. We commenced inquiring and several denied it at first, but recollected it afterwards.

Recollections of
Early Railroading in and About Muscatine.

Published in the Muscatine Saturday Mail July 2, 1898; written by
J. P. Walton.

No. 75

February 8, 1854, the first ground was broken on the M. & M. R. R., now the Chicago, Rock Island & Pacific, on the river bank near the freight depot. The earth was carried on a tramway and deposited along the river out side of Front street and the grading continued along up Mad creek toward Wilton, the big cut near the pickle factory was largely made during the winter of 1854-5. In the summer of 1855 railroad iron was landed from steamboats on our wharf and road building begun towards Wilton. A small locomotive and a few flat cars were brought here on a barge from Rock Island. This was the first locomotive west of the Mississippi. The engine and cars were used to transport iron and ties for constructing the road. A good many of the ties were made of pine, sawed in the mills here.

I think the junction with the road out of Davenport was some where east of Wilton, at all events the road was completed and formally opened for business on the 20th of November, 1855. A large party came from Chicago and Davenport; Hon. John Wallace who was then mayor of Muscatine, made one of his happy speeches, he was followed by others and a big dinner was served; at night a big ball was given, I think in the wareroom of the Nevada mill on the east side of the Iowa avenue south of Third street. Only a special few in Muscatine were invited to the dinner and it took a five dollar bill to shout "I won't go home till morning" on the occasion of the ball. In the course of a few days the Davenport magnates invited a select few of our courteous business men to their town where they "had a time." Muscatine now had the first eastern railroad connection of any town west of Davenport. The first railroad bridge across the Mississippi at Davenport was not completed until the spring of 1856

When the first locomotive was brought here in 1855 the question of water was quite important. It was just as necessary as coal is to a war ship. For the first few days water was dipped up with buckets at the mouth of Pappoose creek; the company soon got a tank erected on Mad creek near where the stock yards are now located, the water was pumped into it out of the creek by hand. The whole tank was housed in with a double wall to keep out frost and had a stove in it to be used in cold weather, in fact all the water tanks in use at that time were built in that manner and it was no uncommon thing to hear of a water tank being burned down. As the building of the road progressed there were several of these tanks located along the track. I think there was one on the head of the island. I put one up at the slough bridge eight miles out and another one at Ononwa, where a well was bored down some 300 feet without getting a supply of water. Another tank was put up at Clifton, a station some three miles beyond the Iowa river that has now entirely disappeared. These small tanks disappeared when it became known that a covered water tank would not suffer from ice during the winter. Now three tanks answer where five were used in early days.

Here let me say a few words about our condition when the rail road was first built. When Iowa was first settled the local trade of the state followed down the rivers to the Mississippi, the transportation was done with wagons. Crossing streams without bridges was quite troublesome so the travel followed down the ridges or valleys, for instance Cedar, Johnson, Linn, Benton and a part of Jones counties traded at Muscatine, while Washington first named Slaughter county, and the western part of Louisa county dealt with Burlington. When the railroads first began to be built in Iowa they crossed the streams east and west and turned the route of trade their way. Muscatine had an eye on the trade of Louisa and Washington counties and bent an effort to get the railroad across the Iowa river at Columbus Junction, then called the Sand Bank, which they did in 1857 or '58. The railroad stopped a year or more at the Sand Bank where a short side track was made not long enough for more than four or five cars, it led off to a turning table. Only one trip a day was made, and the trains being frequently quite large the switchman's skill came in play sawing cars on the short switch. They had some two hours time at the Sand Bank and quite often the whole time was used up in switching.

By getting the railroad across Iowa river Muscatine gained some trade, and after a short delay an effort was made to push the road on to Washington, which place was reached in the summer of 1859, and the extension of the iron rails greatly increased this city's trade. We had at that time two or three large pork packing houses in Muscatine. S. O. Buttler and LeLand & Co. got their hog supplies in a great measure from Louisa and Washington counties. But few hogs were shipped past Muscatine during the packing season. Summer packing was not followed then, cold storage not having been invented, hence the local packing houses could do business.

After the railroad was completed to Washington the company gave an excursion to that city to the business men of Muscatine and their friends. It was a free ride and in order to reach the people wanted tickets of invitation were issued. Of course our military company, the Muscatine Light Guards, were invited, also the Columbus City company. When the train arrived at Clifton, the nearest point to Columbus City, their company were arranged along the platform; Col. Garner, their commanding officer, undertook to make some backward movement and caught his heel in a tie and fell down, the boys cheered him lustly, he jumped up and got his company on the cars that were already full. The train arrived in Washington in due time, dinner was ready and a good one too; the tables were set in the court square, everybody walked up and helped themselves. It appeared to me as though it was furnished by the farmers as there was plenty of chickens and cake. We returned home in good time with everybody even the Light Guards sober. The compliments did not stop here, the railroad company extended the same invitation to the Washington county people to visit Muscatine. Come, of course they did, the cars were so crowded at Washington that no more could be crowded in; on reaching Ainsworth the platform was crowded and as it was impossible to take the crowd the train did not stop but came on to Muscatine. A dinner had been prepared on the fair grounds big enough for any reasonable number, LeLand & Co. donated fifty cooked hams. I think Joseph Green was chief caterer; when he found what a crowd was here he commenced buying all the melons in the market and all that were brought in; he secured several loads and filled the crowd with melons. The Washington people left here happy and went along finely until they struck the grade beyond Ainsworth where the train came to a stand still, the track had been greased by the disappointed guests left on the platform in the morning. After a couple hour's delay occupied in spinning, scraping, swearing and sanding the train started again arriving in Washington in time for the people to get a late supper.

Recollections of
Early Railroading in and about Muscatine.

BY J P. WALTON.

No. 76.

In continuation of my two last articles on excursions I will venture to relate another one or two. When the Muscatine Western railroad was built across the Iowa river and out along the English river as far as South English, J. M. White and other leading citizens of that place thought it would be a good plan to invite the business men of Muscatine to visit South English. A train was secured and the different business interests of Muscatine were "off to the front,"—the end of the road at South English. It was a cold rough blustering October day. The people of South English furnished a substantial dinner, it was a little on the barbeque order, and it was quite amusing to see some of our epicures enjoying a hunk of bread and a slice of cold beef but hunger treated all alike and when appeased all appeared to be happy.

A great number of country people living in the vicinity of South English came in to enjoy the meeting; of course they brought their dinner and spread their feast in groups by themselves. I looked around and where I thought there appeared to be the most bountiful spread,

I asked if they did not want some help to dispose of their dinner; of course they did, and I helped them. After dinner the crowd collected in the lee of Mr. J. M. White's store and listened to one of John Irish's best speeches.

Our train consisted of a caboose, a smoker, and about three day coaches. When we got started home some of our passengers became very hilarious for some cause not neccessary to explain. This hilarity originated in the smoker and spread its way backwards. I occupied a seat in the middle of the train, yet near enough to hear. There were quite a number of our German acquaintances on the cars, and they made the welkin ring in true Teutonic style. Although it was late before we got home we did not get sleepy.

In former years if the people of this city got up a railroad excursion to Davenport a train could be hired and be hauled at any time desired. The price, if I recollect aright, was $60 for one car or $50 each for two or more for the round trip. On one occasion the republicans of Davenport got Robert Ingersol to speak and also had a grand torch light display, and the republican of this city wanted to hear the noted speaker. The fare by way of Wilton was about $2.50 for the round trip. Dr. Farley and a few others commenced to canvass for the sale of tickets at $1 and soon found they could sell one hundred so they secured two cars. This did not include the caboose car. When starting time came there were some 250 people on hand, they filled the cars and the caboose standing full, and when the train got to Wilton more people climbed on. Dr. Farley had made the arrangements and got the crowd, but did not provide a conductor. It finally fell to my lot to act as conductor, I had no punch but was quite well known and could shout "tickets." I tore off the corner of each ticket in place of punching it, when a man had no ticket I supplied him one for his dollar. I collected considerable money and some straight railroad tickets bought by mistake. I turned the funds over to Lyman Banks, captain of the republican club. We got to Davenport all right, and there was a universal clamor for another car to return in; Farley and some one else went to Mr. Kimbal and asked him to accommodate them. Kimbal offered to do it if they would pay for another car. Farley and his companion came back very much disappointed, and at the suggestion of the republican central committee I was requested to go and see Mr. Kimbal as I was better acquainted with him than any of the other managers. I consented to go in company with Hon. John A. Pickler. We went to the railroad official's office; he thought it was proper if he turned out another car for our use that he should have pay for it. It is hardly necessary to relate the arguments we used, it is enough to say that when the train pulled up to the station for us to return on there was another car attached. A vote of thanks was tendered Mr. Kimbal for his generosity.

Sunday School excursions by river are of very recent origin. I think the Methodists first introduced them about 1870. They sent some one to the Rock Island arsenal and got permission to have a picnic dinner on the island. I joined the party for the purpose of visiting the grounds; before starting I secured a letter of introduction to Gen. Rodman, who was in command. As soon as the boat landed I with two others started for headquarters which was in the old Col. Davenport residence. The general was on the front porch, we introduced one another. The rest of the crowd were on the look out for picnic grounds where they could have their dinner, they received their instructions where to go. I presented my letter of introduction, it was well received and we were treated finely. He informed us that he was looking for material to build the present buildings and that he had just been to Joliet to examine the stone but he had heard that Muscatine had very fine brick and if he could secure good brick he would use them in place of stone. I was not in the brick business, neither did I have any idea what he was going to build or of the number of brick he would want. I came home and mentioned it to some of our brick makers and tried to get them interested in it but to no purpose, there did not seem to be any one to look after it.

I had visited Rock Island to see the wonders, etc., and, of course, if there was any place that visitors were not admitted that was the place I wanted to go. Now, it so happened that the island of Rock Island had been used during the war of the rebellion as a rebel prison, the barracks and yard were yet standing, all of which were supplied with wells. The yard was used to store captured rebel ordinances, etc., and was closed to visitors. My brother, who had been there shortly before, informed me that in that yard was the most interesting articles on the island, but it took a special permit and a guide to get in there. I applied to the general for a permit for myself and a few friends, he informed me that if I would report at the office after dinner with a list of those I wanted to go with me the request would be granted. While in the office in came one of the men in the government employ stating he had located the picnic party on the ground, designated and would like to know where they would get water, stating that a dead rabbit was in the well where they were. Gen. Rodman's reply was "that rabbit must be taken out." After a pause of quite a while he said "you station some one at the gun yard gate and pass water out for their use "

It so happened I had no writing paper with me and as my application for admittance to the gun yard with the list of my friends had to be made in writing I applied to W. S. Richie who tore a leaf from his memorandum book to write the names on. I wrote the names of a few friends and presented it to the general, he read it and ordered a certain man to accompany us. It no sooner leaked out that Walton had got permission to go in the forbidden grounds than nearly all the school wanted to go, so we took the permit and wrote thirty or more names on it, and they and twice their number presented themselves as Walton's friends and all were admitted.

This first Sunday school excursion to Rock Island was a profitable one, and other excursions soon followed.

Recollections of

Railroad Building in the Early days of Iowa.

Published in the Muscatine Saturday Mail July 16, 1898; written by J P. Walton.

No. 77.

I have been requested to write my recollections of early railroad building.

In December 1852 the Mississippi & Missouri Railroad company was incorporated under the laws of Iowa. The incorporators were John B. Jarvis of New York Jas. E. Sheffield of New Haven, John M. Wilson, Henry Farnam and N. B. Judd of Chicago; Ebenezer Cook, James Grant, Hiram Price and John P. Cook of Davenport. The railroad company organized a construction company consisting of Henry Farnam and others mostly of their own men thus keeping everything in their own hands. The railroad company would go to a county or town along the line and say to the citizens, you take stock in the company to the amount of one-third of the cost of building the road, estimating the same at $10,000 a mile, and the company will build the road. The stock could be taken by private subscription or by issuing bonds by the county and city for a part of it. As soon as the funds were raised the railroad company would contract with the construction company to build the road for $10,000 a mile, one third would be paid by the proceeds of the subscription, and railroad bonds were issued by the M. & M. railroad company and turned over to the costruction company for the other two-thirds.

With our road everything was turned over to the construction company to locate and build it. The company made several surveys, as railroad companies are proverbial for doing; they run a line down the river from Davenport west of where the southwestern branch of the C., R. I. & P. road now runs, another from Muscatine west a little south of where the Muscatine Western now runs, and another from Davenport west along where the the main line of the Rock Island now runs. In order to secure support from the leading points they had to interest some of the leading business men by giving them advantages that the outsiders did not know of. In Davenport, Cook and Sargent were the favored men, perhaps Hiram Price may have been one of the selected few. In Muscatine, Green & Stone were the choice, they knew where the towns and depots were to be located in time to purchase the lands. The towns of Wilton and Ononwa were alloted to Green & Stone, while Cook & Sargent were better provided for in the choice to enter government lands with warrants to the extent of several thousand acres. The other railroad men got the remainder of the wild land along the main line from Wilton to Davenport.

This new prairie land was very rich but was so far from timber that no one entered it or cared to venture out on it. After the railroad was built the small towns started, the farms began to be developed, and by the time of the breaking out of the war in 1861 quite a population had settled along the line and had raised good crops of corn In 1862 I had occasion to go to Durant to move the depot for the railroad company; I had to board with a farmer; it was in the fall, the farmer got out of coal and had no money to buy more of it, he was also out of wood and would have had to haul it six miles if he got any so he burned corn for fuel. He claimed he could make money by staying at home and gathering his crop instead of going away for fuel. It looked somewhat hard to us, but I think he was correct, corn was worth only 10 cents a bushel.

To provide funds and build the railroad, subscription papers were started for stock, this was all to be paid in installments but no stock was to be issued until it was all paid. A considerable amount was taken and much of it paid for. The Rock Island railroad from Chicago to Rock Island had been built in a similar manner and had proved to be a fair investment to the stockholders. The county was called on to vote to issue bonds to take stock in a railroad.

We make the following extract from the old Muscatine City Directory published in 1856, on page 24: "At the April (1853) election, the question of loaning $55,000 to the Iowa Western Railroad company, to aid in the construction of a railroad from Muscatine to Oskaloosa, was decided in the affirmative, notwithstanding the strenuous opposition to it in Wapsinonoc and Moscow townships. A similar propositon had been lost the preceding year, on account of some misunderstanding. In June, Messrs. Farnam and others, representing the Mississippi and Missouri Railroad Company, proposed to the officers of the Iowa Western Railroad Company to build three lines of railroads from Muscatine—viz: to Oskaloosa, to Davenport, and Cedar Rapids—provided one-third of the means for their construction should be raised by local subscription and taxation. This proposal was accepted, and on the third day of October a loan of $150,000 for the purpose was voted by the county. Feb. 8, 1854, ground was broke on the Muscatine and Oskaloosa railroad by the M. and M. R. R. Co."

The bonds were issued and handed over to the railroad company, they in turn were passed into the innocent hands of the construction company, who disposed of them as they chose, but to make them more valuable, the railroad stock was left in the hands of a trustee. I think John A. Dix, of New York, held the stock as vouchers and that the interest and final payment of the bonds were made according to agreement. One would naturally ask why such a foolish deal was made. The fact was the people were crazy for a railroad and were willing to do anything to get one from any where, and the railroad company knew it and acted accordingly.

After the panic of 1857 we had nothing but wild-cat money in circulation. Exchange on New York was worth from 5 to 10 per cent premium and frequently more. During the years of 1857-58-59 I worked for the railroad company building bridges, tanks and station houses. The pay days were very irregular, frequently a paymaster would come around with a supply of money and pay off the men and contractors. Usually before they could realize on the money the banks that issued it were at a discount of 50 or 75 per cent—the money had been sent out to unload on the railroad employes. I never lost much but I had usually to wait from three to six months for my pay.

The interest on the bonds had to be paid in New York and it became quite burdensome to pay it, for the city had a similar amount in a similar condition, and the tax-payers began to complain.

Now, it so happened that we, like many other communities, had a lot of "professional" men who were willing to and did help us to get in debt and were willing to help us get out of paying it in any way but a straight one, provided they got the lion's share for doing it, but their share had to come any how. They were loud talkers and had meetings called and generally denounced the railroad swindle and all that were in it, and a general repudiation of the bonds followed.

They soon got into the courts and so manipulated the state courts as to get adverse decisions. The people of Muscatine thought they were out of the scrape, but a law was passed by congress to collect some of the repudiated debts in the southern states after the war of the rebellion and that caught us.

It so happened that the Chicago, Rock Island & Pacific railroad gobbled up the M. & M. road and in the process the M. & M. went into the hands of a receiver, B. F. Allen, of DesMoines. Muscatine county had some stock that had to be disposed of in some way and finally something less than $20,000 was paid into the county treasury. The city never got anything back. As near as I can figure it out the railroad cost the county somewhere between $250,000 and $300,000. The county received annually in taxes about $12,000 which was nearly 4 per cent on the cost. The city has a debt of $300,000 hanging over it that was the result of this M. & M. railroad deal. It was well enough for the city as we could not get along without the railroad but we paid dearly for it.

Had the people of Muscatine been a little more independent and not voted so liberally, the main line of the M. & M. railroad could have been forced down along the river, or we could at least have stopped its being constructed through Durant, Walcott, and other towns, for we put in about all the money the company had. Davenport and Scott county put in less than $60,000, that is if I have been correctly informed, and the city of Davenport eventually got its money back in paved streets.

Our city debt is very much reduced and is being reduced all the while.

Recollections of

SUEL FOSTER.

Published in the Muscatine Saturday Mail July 23, 1898; written by J P. Walton.

No. 78.

On the west side of Walnut street north of the alley, near the end of the high bridge, stood a small brick building; it was erected about 1846 or '47 and was the home of one of Bloomington's most prominent citizens, SUEL FOSTER. He was a native of Hillsboro, N. H., born on August 26, 1811. He was a descendant of the early colonial families of Massachusets, his mother being a first cousin of the historian, George Bancroft, Suel himself had a great faculty for writing and relating historical items, although few if any have ever been compiled and published. He was the son of a farmer, who with hard work among the New Hampshire hills, succeeded in accumulating enough to give his son a common school education. At the age of 20 he started out for himself, went to Rochester, N. Y., worked on a farm for one year for $11 per month; he then took his accumulated wealth and laid in a peddler's stock and followed the peddling business for some three years in that locality.

Here let me say that the Yankee peddler over run all the northern and some of the southern states, in the eastern states it was considered a very reputable occupation, while in the western states, where the Yankee school master had not been, their reputation was not so good. I think it was more the want of education than the fault of the peddler. Since peddling has passed into the hands of the foreigners few are willing to own that they were ever engaged in the business.

In 1835 Suel Foster spent a year in school, studying bookkeeping and surveying, and in the spring of 1836 he, in company with his brother, Dr. John H. Foster, started west; at St. Louis they separated, the doctor went to Chicago and became very wealthy by the advance on real estate, and Suel went to Rock Island. In August, 1836, Suel and his brother made a visit to Bloomington (Muscatine) a town recently laid out, and they purchased a sixth interest in the town of Captain Benjamin Clark, father of the present Captain Clark of Buffalo, for the sum of $500. The town had been surveyed but a few weeks before and was half a mile square. At that time there were but two houses in the town.

James Casey had laid out his town of Newburg which joined Bloomington on the southwest. I presume it had one or two houses.

Suel Foster came here to live in February, 1837, and remained here until the day of his death, January 21, 1886, except a short time of about a year that he spent in California. In 1842 he engaged in the mercantile business with J. W. Richman and continued in it for four years until 1846. They built a two-story frame building about 20x40 feet on Front street just above the avenue. At one time the firm of Foster & Richman were among the leading merchants of Bloomington. Suel Foster was the gallant of the town in its early days, being sharp, quick witted, a fine talker, and agreeable to every one, more especially the fair sex. He had several rivals, however, such as T. M. Isett, Chester Weed and some half dozen more. Suel was finally captured by Miss Sarah J. Hastings, sister of Hon. S. C. Hastings. Their marriage occurred on October 8, 1847; they commenced housekeeping in the brick building first described and remained there until Suel went to California in 1850. After his return he located on the land where he died, and where his widow now lives.

In stature Suel Foster was about 5 feet 11 inches high, weight about 150 pounds, a tall, angular man. The boys about town used to say that there was but one homlier man in the place, and that was Theodore Parvin. Foster was a great walker, on one occasion he was in Des Moines, the roads were very muddy, the only manner of conveyance from there home was by stage to Kellog and rail from there to Muscatine. Trains run but once a day and the stages tried to connect with them. Suel had some disagreement with the driver who would not let him on, and wanted him to wait until an extra was made up. Suel concluded the extra would not start until the next day so he started on foot and traveled the forty miles to Kellog and made his connection with the train while the stage did not.

After Suel Foster went out of the mercantile business he went into the land business, he bought largely but did not sell as he expected to and soon found himself "land poor," without means to improve, and with interest and taxes piling up against him. His selections were good and he got out without serious loss, but had his confidence in land speculation lessened. He had a great faculty for conceiving new schemes for the public good. When the state fair met here in 1856 the directors and superintendents had a meeting one evening to arrange the business of the State Agricultural Society. Suel Foster was present and offered a resolution asking the legislature to use its best efforts to secure an appropriation of lands for an agricultural college. Suel explained his idea, it was new to all present but it passed all the same. Suel Foster followed it up and the Iowa State Agricultural College was the result. He was on the board of directors and its president for some five or six years. While Suel Foster made little or nothing out of this scheme the state has gained immensely from its benefits.

Suel Foster was always in for improvements, he took an active part in our various railroad schemes and was a strong advocate of the Hennepin canal. Shortly after his return from California he went in with Chas. Negus in the nursery business. They occupied the land on the north side of Eighth street east of Mulberry. When the firm of Foster & Negus closed up, Suel started the Fountain Hill nursery out in the west part of the city. He expected to run his fountain with a hydraulic ram placed in the west branch of Pappoose creek, the stream was small and the lift near 150 feet. The water came very slow, being a mere dribble, only about five or six barrels of water were raised in a day. The ram stood down in the creek with no one to watch it and every boy that passed along and hearing the pounding noise had to investigate it, these investigations kept it out of order and Foster had to give up the fountain. I think Foster never made much on the nursery but while in the business he introduced the Catalpa tree as an ornamental tree. I think Foster made some money on this scheme but the buyers never did. In order to introduce his Catalpa trees he claimed they were very durable. He got permisson of the board of supervisors to plant two posts, one Red Cedar the other Catalpa, in the west corner of the court house square. The Catalpa rotted off in three or four years but the Red Cedar stood until it was removed for stone steps some fifteen years later. While engaged in the nursery business Suel Foster introduced many varieties of fruit. The Wealthy apple was brought here by him and seems to stand the test of cold winters and time as well as any other apple introduced by any one. He built a conservatory and started to raise plants for market but was not very successful as a gardener and had to give it up. Mr. Foster could be considered a reformer. He was a strong temperance.man and though he was compelled to make cider from the waste apples he never permited it to get hard, either boiled it or made vinegar. In order to use his waste apples he put up an Aldan dryer, the building is still standing, but I think it was not used to any great extent. He was a member of the Congregational church and sided with Rev. A. B. Robins on the anti slavery question, and, of course, was a republican.

Mr. Foster was not always successful in his reformations. He made one attempt that proved too much for him. that was the bar. He claimed that there was not a bigger set of genteel rascals left out of the "pen" than the lawyers. He wrote articles condemning the legal practices and appeared in court and presented his grievances and charges, and asked the court to make reforms in its manner of dispatching business. Of course, it amounted to nothing— only a laughing stock for the profession. I have often thought if Mr. Foster had adopted the style that Captain Marryatt did in his midshipman esay to reform the British navy or as Charles Dickens did in his Pickwick Paper to reform the prison life, he would have accomplished the needed reform.

Recollections of
SUEL FOSTER.
Continued.

Published in the Muscatine Saturday Mail July 30, 1898; written by J P. Walton.

No. 79.

In our last we stated that Mr. Foster was a cousin of the historian George Bancroft, and possessed the faculty of writing history. As one of his productions we publish the following:
FIRST PROPRIETORS OF THE CITY OF MUSCATINE.

"At the close of the Black Hawk war in May, 1833, George Davenport, the Indian trader who lived on Rock Island, sent a small stock of goods down here by a Mr. Farnham, who built a small double log cabin. This cabin stood on Water street, just above Iowa avenue. The place was called Grindstone Bluff. Mr. Farnham died in about two years and Major Davenport sold the claim to John Vanata. I am informed by J. P. Walton that the date of the Davenport quit claim deed to John Vanata was February 20, 1835. It is doubtful whether Mr. Farnham should be considered an actual settler as he was only the agent of Davenport. Mr. Vanata sold one half of his claim to Captain Benjamin Clark, of Clark ferry, with a view of laying out a town here. This claim was half a mile square and a quarter of a mile up and down the river from the trading house. Mr. John Vanata was a soldier in the Black Hawk war, after which he was for a time with Major George Davenport Mr. Vanata moved from Rock Island here in the fall of 1835. About that time J. W. Casey came from Cloverport, Ky., and made a claim immediately below Vanata's, the division line of which was near the lower end of the present freight depot, 100 feet east of Spruce street. Mr Casey put up a log cabin in the fall of 1835 under the bluff, on a high bank of the river, just below the foot of Broadway, making his home while at work at his cabin at Mr. B. Nye's at the mouth of Pine creek, twelve miles up the river. Benj. Nye was probably the first actual settler of the county, having settled at the mouth of Pine creek in 1834.

"The first survey of the oldest claim of Muscatine into town lots was made in May, 1836, by Maj. Wm. Gordon, who lived at the mouth of Pine creek, who was a military educated man and a surveyor. The proprietors named the town Bloomington.

"The Black Hawk purchase, a new district of country was just opened for settlement on the west bank of the Mississippi river, extending 250 miles north from the state of Missouri, and from 40 to 80 miles in width. It was a land of great attraction for new settlers from Indiana, Ohio, Kentucky and Pennsylvania. Many of them coming with their wagons, families, stock and movables, and crossing the river at Clark's ferry, induced the proprietor to believe that he had a better place for a town site than Bloomington was, and accordingly Capt. Clark sold his interest in this town, myself being the purchaser of his last interest, August, 1836, it being one undivided sixth part of the central quarter section, my interest being about 90 lots for $500. On the same property there was a tax in 1839 of $2,800 for the purpose of building a court house I am not able to give the names of all the joint partners as first proprietors of the city, but can name the most of them. It must be recollected that the settlement was begun three years before the land came in market, and when our title was only a claim, which was considered to be a privilege to buy the land at $1 25 per acre when it came in market. In the central and oldest part of the town the following persons were the principal proprietors: John Vanata, T. M. Isett, Suel Foster and J. W. Nealley, each owning one-sixth part. Those owning smaller shares were Moses Couch, and several others at Burlington, and Wm. D. Abernathy, of Illinois. Proprietors of the lower addaition were Lyman C. Hine, Wm. St. John, Henry Reece and brothers, J. and G. Pettibone, A. Whiting, Alex. Smith, and Breese & Higinbotham. Upper addition: Chas. H Fish, Chas. A. Warfield, Dr. Lewis McKee and others. Titles were obtained of the government at a land sale in Burlington, November, 1838, for that part of the city in township 77, north; and that part of the city lying in 76, north, the land sale was in March, 1839. We had a book of records of our claims, which the legislature of the territory legalized, and made such claims property—real estate—subject to execution. Many a serious and bitter quarrel arose between the neighbors, on account of conflicting claims. Several circumstances caused these conflicts. One was that the claims were made before the government surveys were, and when the section lines and subdivisions were made they often ran through towns, farms and claims. These difficulties were settled by arbitration of three men or before a justice's court and jury, either of which was made legal by statute of law. Another source of conflict was, what amount of improvement constituted a good and valid claim? and what time of residence or what time of absence, should forfeit the claim.

"Among the first settlers of the county was Benj. Nye, Esq., who settled at the mouth of Pine river, in the year 1834 or early in 1835, which was previous to any permanent settlement at Muscatine. There were three or four settlers down the Slough road in 1835, and early in the spring of 1836 many settlers came in—among them Thomas Burdett, Samuel Gilbert, James and William Chambers and Mr. Franklin, who settled at Fairport, and Barkalow who settled near the north corner of the city and had a corn field on the level ground on both sides of the east end of Eighth street, in 1836—having made his settlement in 1835—and he, with his son and son-in-law, Mr. White, claimed one mile square, including the upper addition to the town, the Smalley lands, the Ogilvie lands, and a part of the Isett and Weed lands."

The old claim cabin which Barkalow built is still standing and is occupied.

Mr. Foster's version of the origin of the name of Muscatine, as published in the April, 1872, number of the Annals of Iowa, is likely correct in the main. Mr. Foster says:

"On reading Bancroft's History, some years ago, in it I found a tribe of Indians of this name, and I have no doubt the name was brought here by them, before the Sacs and Musquakies came here. He says: 'At the last village on Fox river ever visited by the French, were Kickapoos, Muscoutins and Miamis who dwelt together on a beautiful hill in the center of the prairies and magnificent groves, * * * Marquette begged two guides of these Indians to pilot them to the portage from the Fox to the Wisconsin river, when he and his companion Juliet went on their voyage and first discovered the upper Mississippi river.' They 'were the first white men who trod the soil of Iowa,' June 25, 1673. I conjecture that a remnant of the Muscoutins, soon after this, were driven from Wisconsin, and formed a lodge upon the beautiful plains of Muscatine Island. The Sacs and Foxes knew nothing of the origin of this name."

When we went on the Muscatine Island in 1842, there were remains of an Indian village of much older date than the last Sacs and Foxes, some two miles below the city. I have many of their trinkets that I picked up here.

Recollections of
Suel Foster, with History of Bloomington.
Continued.

Published in the Muscatine Saturday Mail August 6, 1898; written by
J P. Walton.

No. 80.

Suel Foster was a voluminous newspaper writer. He always signed his name to his articles. Many of the articles were on Farming, Horticulture and kindred subjects, and were quite readable for those in these lines of work, while to others not interested in the subjects the title and the author's name were all that was read. He would frequently write articles on the weather, and on one occasion he condemned the ground hog theory so popular among the Pennsylvania Dutch. A gentleman of our city took him up and quite a newspaper controversy followed. We had a comic artist in our city by the name of John McGreer, who was in the hat business; he took every occasion to advertise his business by painting comic pictures on barns and fences all over the county. This ground hog controversy gave him a good opportunity to delineate it, which he did by drawing a charcoal sketch of "Foster watching for the ground hog to come out," and hung it up in the post office lobby, where everybody could see it. It made talking material for quite a while, and many who were not familiar with the controversy thought Foster was a believer in the ground hog theory

All public meetings of every description were visited by Suel Foster, he lived out in the suburbs of the city, on "Fountain Hill," as he was pleased to call his residence. After doing a day's work it was quite frequently late before he could get down town, he always took it on foot and frequently at quite late hour he could be seen hunting his way home in midnight darkness; he never seemed to care about company in his homeward tramp. He was a regular attendant of the meetings of the Academy of Science and always took part in the discussions with the other members, many of whom were intellectually the strongest men of our city.

Mr. Foster could be found at the temperance meetings. On one occasion a revival meeting was being held in one of the halls. Foster came down town quite late, the first man he met was Santa Eichelberger, a newspaper reporter of whom he asked if there was a revival meeting going on. Santa said yes, and Foster asked, are you going? Eichelberger answered yes, come on! and he led the way. It so happened that a minstrel troupe held forth in one hall and the revivalist in the other on the same night. Santa led the way to the minstrels, he knew the door keeper and went in with his friend Foster without any challenge and took their seats well down forward. The curtain was down, Santa excused himself for a minute and went out and informed the troupe who was there and how he came. The curtain soon went up and the show began with a conundrum between the end men; it was "What is the matter with Suel Foster?" The answer was "he is in the wrong pew." Of course, the audience cheered, but Suel sat still and staid till the end of the performance. Eichelberger had a local item at Suel's expense; it mattered not, for Suel could enjoy a joke as well as any one, and he would never spoil a joke "for relation's sake."

Suel Foster was an out spoken, candid man; he denounced any evil that occurred without regard to persons. He was too independent to hold office; he was one of the town trustees in 1841 which is the only time his name occurs among the town or city officers, although an extensive tax payer and a public philantrophist. He has written more local history than any other of our early historians, some of which we may reprint. Of the Indian war Mr. Foster wrote:

"The first winter I spent here, 1836-7, there were many Indians about, but they were only troublesome as beggars and thieves, not belligerent; for only four years previous they had been taught by dear bought experience the lessons of the Black Hawk war. A lodge of them lived across the river opposite the lower town, with White Hawk, their chief. White Hawk was famous for playing checkers, but Jonathan Pettibone was a full match for him, and used often to beat him. Some of our young men would play with him for whisky, and sometimes for money. The old chief would often draw them on by letting them beat him. Some of the Indians could play cards, some shoot at marks, some run races. The Indian boys' favorite sport was shooting at a real or picayune, with bow and arrow, stuck up in the top of a split stick, which piece of money we would take turns in putting up for the sport. These Indians afforded a great deal of company for our social circle. There was one Doctor Jim, who had his arm shot in battle, and some three inches of the bone was taken out just above the elbow; the flesh healed over, and when he raised his hand that part of the arm would double up like a soft cotton bag. He could talk some English, and was full of his jokes and witticisms.

"The Indians liked whisky. Sometimes they had a little money, but usually they traded skins and furs for whisky. One old man named Maine then lived about two miles down on Muscatine Island, and kept a barrel of the article to trade with the Indians—what little he did not want to drink himself. One day on a noted occasion, the old man Maine took a little too much, while his wife was in bed, and mother Stark was there helping her in the increase of her family. Several Indians about there, having drank enough to feel a little quarrelsome, insisted on having more whisky, but Maine refused. The Indians threatened him, and he ran towards town for help. As Maine left one of the Indians fired—at the whisky barrel and tapped it in the head. The crack of the rifle brought mother Stark out of the house to see what what the matter was, and found one of the Indians sucking at the bullet vent of the whisky barrel. She caught up a nigger hoe and drove the Indians off, and set the barrel up on end and saved most of the whisky. But the affrightened Mr. Maine, heard the rifle and imagined that his family and the woman there were being murdered, and he alone escaped to tell the tale. The nearer to town he got the faster he ran and the louder were his piteous cries for help. The villagers were alarmed and when Maine could get breath so as to utter an audible word, it was 'The Indians have murdered all of my family and as I ran they fired at me; but I have out ran 'em. Go down—go down!' Some guns were gathered up; some with sticks, and some stayed to guard the village. But our good landlord, Robert C. Kinney, the fattest, laziest, quietest, can't run man in town, said: 'Gor almighty, what shall we do! John Camp, take my horse and go to Moscow, and give the alarm that the Indians have killed all the folks on the Island, and we will run in that direction and they must come and meet us.' But those brave fellows who made the charge on the whisky barrel on the Island got shot in the neck, set fire to the rank grass on the Island, fired guns, screamed and yelled louder than Maine did, and on this alarm Mr Kinney fairly trembled in his boots. No Indians were seen. Their canoes being at hand they put for Coa-Mack Island, opposite town, at the suggestion of Mrs. Stark's nigger hoe."

Recollections of
SUEL FOSTER.

Concluded.

Published in the Muscatine Saturday Mail August 13, 1898; written by J P. Walton.

No. 81.

We hope the readers of the SATURDAY MAIL will not get out of patience with us for occupying so much time with Suel Foster. Our excuse for doing it is that Mr. Foster was one of our common men in appearance but he was possessed of a very strong character—wherever he was, his influence was felt. Had he served himself as well as he did his neighbors he would have died a wealthy man. There was hardly a convention in the land, that Foster thought to be advantageous to the community, that he did not attend. His habit of writing for the newspapers was considered foolish by many, but his historical sketches, from which we have ventured to make a few extracts, contain more history of early days than can be had otherwise. His account of the early inhabitants is worth reprinting. We have changed some local names of Mr. Foster's time to those of the present:

SOME OLD SETTLERS.

"It appears, according to dates, that J. W. Casey was the first settler at Muscatine, having moved from Cloverport, Ky., and built a cabin in the fall of 1835 In locating towns on the banks of the Mississippi, it was a great object to find a place where there was depth of water enough for boats to make a good landing in time of low water. Mr. Casey had sounded the water along here and found that the boldest shore was opposite the high bluff, and extended nearly down to the head of the Muscatine Island; so he made his claim next below the Farnam claim. Mr. Casey was a small man, quick, active and resolute. Mr. Vanater came in the spring of 1836 and took Mr. Farnam's place, and a strong competition was carried on between Casey and Vanater, as to the best place to build a town. Mr. Casey having the advantage of the best water and Mr. Vanater the best land. As the claims began to be valuable, a dispute arose as to where the line should be between the two claims.

"Major Wm. Gordon, then living at Rock Island, and having a claim adjoining Benj. Nye, Esq., above the mouth of Pine river, was called upon to survey the town of Bloomington into lots. Vanater's claim was a quarter of a mile up and down the river each way from the log cabin, but as the log cabin was a double one, some 32 feet in length, the surveyor must have a definite point to start his measure from, and Vanater told him that the outside of the stick chimney at the west end of the cabin was the starting point. So Major Gordon obeyed orders and Vanater's part of the town was surveyed and platted accordingly, encroaching about twenty feet on Mr. Casey's claim. This claim line commenced on Water street twenty feet west of the east line of lot 2, block 9, and thence through the center of the Butlerville road to Morford farm. Hard words passed. Vanater was a very large, strong and active man, about three the size of Casey, and both of them carried deadly weapons, but no fighting occurred and the town plat held the claim. Soon after this the claim law was established and the committee of arbitration appointed.

"Mr. Casey died in the fall of 1836 and was buried on the high elevation where school house No. 1 (now Third Ward) now stands. This was the first burial. Afterwards Charles H. Fish laid off the upper addition, and reserved that square as a cemetery. which was retained for that purpose for nearly ten years, in which time there were a good many interments. Charles H. Fish, whose native place was in New Jersey, near Philadelphia, Pa., moved to Cincinnati, thence to Burlington, and thence to Muscatine in 1837 with his family consisting of his son William and two daughters, Emmeline and Caroline. Few persons were more servicable in the new settlement than Mrs. Fish in taking care of the sick and occasionally boarding the homeless. With her two beautiful daughters her home added greatly to the life of our social circle.

"Moses Couch came from Burlington here in the fall of 1836 and his wife in the following spring, who also rendered great service in taking care of sick and boarding the homeless. A family by the name Dana came here as merchants in 18— and opened a store and boarded at Mr. Couch's, with his wife and a beautiful boy of five years. Few, if any, persons have lived in this city since who carried with them the same high qualities of refinement, education and intelligence. Mr. Dana died of fever and the boy followed him the next day. Alone, among strangers, Mrs. Dana bore the affliction with becoming fortitude, as few ladies can. Mary S. B Dana was the daughter of Rev. Dr. Parmer of South Carolina; she was the author of 'Passing Under the Rod,' also a volume of poems, and other literary productions.

"The assignees of J. W. Casey, the Lower Town Claim Co., had built a good sized double house up in the neck of the bluff near the foot of Broadway, and the Reece family moved in there in 1837, and kept boarders and a hospital for the sick also. Then this was not a very healthy place. Few, very few, escaped the bilious fever, ague or typhoid fever. The summer of 1839 was excessively dry and hot, the river was low, and the water of the river, although it continued to move on in its sluggish course, turned green from shore to shore. This, with the drying sediment of the previous spring, filled the air with miasma and bilious breath. The able ones were mostly employed in taking care of the sick, and when one set got better their assistants came down. 1839 and 1840 were the trying times for our new place, new settlers crowding in and no place to go; some lying upon the floor, some in wagons and cooking by the side of a stump.

"Robert C. Kinney was the first landlord who put up a sign and kept tavern. * * He was one of the best men we ever had here, he kept travelers, boarders and hospital. * * * Mr. Barten [likely Barten Lee] kept boarders in 1837-8 in a log cabin which stood near where Jos. Bridgman now resides. John Vanater built the second hotel early in the spring of 1838 on the southwest corner Iowa avenue and Second street."

Recollections of
STEPHEN WHICHER AND HIS MANSION.

Published in the Muscatine Saturday Mail August 20, 1898; written by J. P. Walton.

No 82.

On the northwest corner of Locust and Second street stands a venerable structure that was erected in the spring of 1839 by Stephen Whicher. It is now owned by Dr. Charles Robertson. I dont know who lives there now. The lumber used in building the house was largely brought from Cincinnati and probably from the pineries of Pennsylvania. The framing timbers were cut and hewn from the trees growing within the city limits. It was built with an old fashioned hip roof, the lower part being steeper than the upper, having three ridges running lengthwise. The gable ends were finished with battlements. It was an old castle in ever sense of the word. Mr. Whicher had this roof and the battlements removed in 1849, robbing it of its feudal appearance. Whicher owned the whole block and had it planted out in apple trees. The boys of that time living on the hill recollect that without much trouble. Mr. Whicher brought those trees with him when he came west; they were probably the first fruit trees brought here. The Silverthorn cherry that is now quite popular was brought in this collection. Stephen Whicher came here, with his house, from Dayton, Ohio, landing here on April

3, 1839. He was born in Rochester, Vt., May 3, 1798; was the second son of a family of fourteen children, and was a descendant of Thomas Whitcher, who settled in the New England states in their early days. Stephen Whicher, like many of the young Yankees of those times "came west" at the age of 18 years and taught school in Lexington, Ky. He studied law in the office of Henry Clay and later at Lawrenceburg, Ind. He was admitted to the bar in 1823, and moved to Dayton, Ohio, where he married Miss Eliza Venable in 1826. At the time of coming to Bloomington in 1839 his family consisted of three sons and one daughter. The youngest son and daughter are still living.

Mr. Whicher was tall, 6 feet 1 inch, slim and dignified; he usually wore a tall hat that added to his height and dignity very much in our estimation. At that time as a lawyer he had no superior; he always managed to have a comfortable living but never became what would be called wealthy. He was one of the leading men of our town. At public meetings he was usually president, or chairman on resolutions. Sunday would always find him in his seat in the little church on the hill. He was noted for his pungent wit. Whicher's witty sayings are still remembered by many of our old settlers. One story told of Mr. Whicher is too good to be missed. In early times all steamboats on the Mississippi river carried bars and were said to have the best of liquors. At that time liquor drinking was practiced by almost every one and to get it where the best could be had was considered "all right." When a steamboat landed a score or more of thirsty fellows could be seen rushing aboard the boat; their business was generally with the barkeeper. Mr. Whicher rarely drank much but once when he wanted a drink and seeing a large number going aboard a boat ahead of him he concluded to keep up with them. Placing his hand on his stomach and leaning a little forward he walked leisurely up to the bar and asked, have you any good brandy, sir? The barkeeper's sympathy was excited and he promptly replied, "yes sir," sitting out his best bottle. Have you a tablespoon? asked Mr. W. No, but I will get you one, answered the barkeeper, starting for the pantry. When the spoon was procured our friend held it over his glass and commenced to pour the brandy into the spoon, and continued to do so until the glass was sufficiently full to meet his requirements, he then majestically staightened up and drank it all down. Sitting down the glass he produced his money enquiring, "How much is the charge, sir?" "Nothing," was the reply, "I never charge anything for a spoonful of brandy." Our friend thanked the barkeeper for his generosity and left the boat amid the roar of the bystanders. After that a large measure became synonomous with Whicher's spoonful.

At one time Jacob Butler occupied the front room in the second story of a building on Second street, for a law office. Whicher had a desk in the office. According to the agreement Butler was to keep the room swept—a thing he very rarely did. It so happened that a number of young men who styled themselves "The Killers," occupied the room in the rear. Butler owned the building and Whicher concluded that in order to stop the trouble if he could get up a rumpus between him and the boys Butler would attend to having the sweeping done, so he went to work and did the sweeping himself and swept the litter up to the door of the Killers. He did this two or three times before any attention was paid to it. At last the boys heard him sweeping, they started for the door swearing they would kill the lazy fellow that was sweeping his dirt up to their door. Whicher was on the look out and hid his broom. He blamed it on Butler. It got out and Butler attended to the sweeping after that.

Mr. Whicher did not trust every one with his confidence. He was usually on the defensive, but he formed a few close acquaintances who would stay by him through thick and thin. There was a young man in our town who became perfectly infatuated with Mr. Whicher. This young man was employed in freighting from Bloomington to Iowa City; he was engaged to a young lady living in Pike township, the most direct route was through West Liberty, he frequently came down through West Liberty and returned to Iowa city through Pike. On one occasion when he was coming through West Liberty he happened to meet the stage and there found the driver abusing Mr. Whicher. The young man "mixed in" and the stage driver came out considerably worsted. They all came to Muscatine, and while here the stage agent informed the young man that when he went back to West Liberty they would give him a thrashing, meaning the drivers. The young man was in a fix, he had made an agreement to return by Pike township, if he did so the stage drivers would call him a coward; it was a question which should prevail love are honor. He chose the latter and returned by way of West Libery without any trouble from the stage drivers, but the love part did trouble him. The young lady said if he would cancel an engagement to fight a stage driver she wanted to cancel her engagement with him. It is possible the young man might have made the matter all right in some way but before he reached that point he found another young lady who had considerable money, to take her place. All of this love trouble was traceable to Stephen Whicher's independence in not complying with the stage driver's wishes.

RECOLLECTIONS OF

STEPHEN WHICHER AND HIS MANSION.

Concluded:

Published in the Muscatine Saturday Mail, Sept. 27, 1898; written by J. P. Walton.

No. 83.

The Whicher family always attended church and no one knew it better than I did. I had been in the habit of attending the Methodist church. Then the men always sat on the right side and the women on the left. The Congregationalists had built a small church on the then hill, where the Episcopal parsonage now stands. On my first visit to the church I went early, taking a seat on the right side about half way down the aisle, and in order not to take more room than one should I sat well back to the wall. Shortly in came Mr. and Mrs. Whicher and sat in the seat with me. I was caught in the wrong pew that time, and I was terribly embarrassed. I did not attend that church again for a long time.

Mr. Whicher did not go off on excursions or outings as they are called now. He had a studious turn and if leisure occurred he devoted his time to reading or studying. In his legal practice he was fearless and would take any man's case whether he got pay or not. A friend of ours was once expostulating with him for defending the Coruthers boys in different prosecutions. They were frequently arragined before the court for horse stealing and other offences and it was known that he did not get much pay from them. His reply was that if he did not defend them some one else would, and that such men made business for lawyers. When he took a case he stuck by it through thick and thin, and generally came out a head. As an advocate he stood at the head of the bar; his best success was with the jury. If his case was a doubtful one, like Lincoln, he got them to laughing before closing; if he could not reach that point he would tell an amusing story in a way that brought the answer.

Mr. Whicher was a gritty man and had a great deal of bluff about him. On one occasion he detected a man in some act of wrong doing and seized him by the collar and started him down the street to the magistrate's office, ordering him to move on by telling him he was in the hands of a powerfull man and must go. The man went, but had he made an effort to resist it would have required two men like Whicher to have taken him.

The Whicher family used to enjoy themselves in a very unusual way or at least it would look so to us at this time. On one occasion when there were a great many Indians around here, probably it was on one of their annual trips to Fort Armstrong on Rock Island to get their annuity, Mr. Whicher conceived the idea of having an indoor war dance. Suel Foster described the event as follows:

"In the spring of 1839 Stephen Whicher, Esq., made a large social party at his house, northwest corner of Second and Locust streets, at which was present about twenty Indians with their squaws, in calico breeches, roundabouts, moccasins ornamented with beads and trinkets. The Indian men were dressed for the party also, with faces painted and gay blankets, with war trophies on, jewels in their ears and noses, brass bands on their arms, long ornamented pipes, weasel and skunk-skin tobacco pouches, war clubs with feathers attached to them, bears' claws and tusks, buckskin breeches and waumises highly ornamented. All the elite of town were present—ladies and gentlemen, young and middleaged (we had no old folks then). George Lucas was there, Ralph Lowe, Esq., and his wife, Matthew Mathews and his daughter, H. Mathews and wife and two daughters, M. Couch and wife, etc.,—a social and jolly company indeed. The center of the large front room was cleared and an Indian war dance introduced. They lacked music, and

Mrs. Whicher brought out some tin pans and the fire shovel and tongs, with a few sticks made the music. Kishkekosh, the noble chief, stepped out on the floor alone, divested of nearly all his garments, a most splended figure of human form and led the dance in majestic savage style. Shortly one after another of the men joined, until the floor was nearly filled, the whole circling around in all sorts of savage and frantic shapes and forms of attitude, keeping time with the ding of the pans and tongs, at the same time uttering low gutteral sounds—hew-wa-wa hew-ha-wa we-ho-woo—which increased in loudness and tone until it became a savage howl, and they charged upon each other until the ladies were greatly frightened. The door was guarded so as to not let any escape, and the tumult became very general all around, whites and copper. The squaws did not dance, but laughed to burst to see the pale faced women so frightened. The dance gradually subsided when suddenly one of the Indians sprang at one of the fairest of the fair ladies to kiss her; but she would not let him and screamed a scream. As compensation for this most excellent and extraordinary entertainment—the best ever witnessed in Muscatine—the Indians insisted on a dance by the whites, and more especially by the white 'squaws.' So a good violin was tuned, and the dance performed in most excellent style, at which the Indians appeared equally delighted as the whites did at their dance. Thus ended one of the most brilliant occasions in the history of our city. The party dispersed at the small hours of the night. The whites to their log cabins and the Indians to their whisky, up Pappoose creek, each in their peaceful and happy homes."

When the Missouri war broke out in the winter of 1839-40 and when the armies of Iowa and Missouri were marching to deadly combat, Gov Lucas appointed Mr. Whicher as one of the commissioners to arrange terms of peace which was done by agreement to submit the question at issue to congress for settlement. When the Whigs got control of the government by the election of Taylor and Fillmore, Whicher was appointed United States District Attorney for Iowa by President Fillmore.

Mr. Whicher died February 13, 1856, at Iowa City. Mrs. Stephen Whicher died in Cincinnati, at the home of her daughter, Mrs. Charles Brown, in the early part of May, 1880. Her remains were brought to Muscatine for interment. Both died away from home and both were brought here for burial.

Pioneers' Anniversary.

AT THE FAIR GROUNDS, TUESDAY, AUGUST 30, 1898.

President Walton's Address.

Published in the Muscatine Saturday Mail Sept. 3, 1898; written by J P. Walton.

Ladies and Gentlemen, Old Settlers of Muscatine County:

I was asked the other day if I could tell how many of the first settlers were yet living. Those originally called old settlers were those who came here prior to 1840. That question induced me to look up the history of this society. I found in the record books that on February 4, 1856, the old citizens of Muscatine met at Hare's hall to take action on the death of Hon. Arthur Washburn, our first county judge. Pliny Fay was chairman, and Jos. Bridgman was secretary. After transacting the business for which it met, on motion of T. S. Parvin, the meeting adjourned to meet on February 9, in the lecture room of the Congregational church.

At the adjourned meeting Hon. Joseph Williams was called to the chair. There were present Joseph Williams, T. S .Parvin, Pliny Fay, Joseph Bridgman, Suel Foster, H. Q. Jennison, H. H. Hine, Zeph. Washburn, G. W. Humphreys, J. S. Allen, Myron Ward, Wm. Chambers, Giles Pettibone, A. T. Banks and J. P. Walton, fifteen in all. A committee was appointed on constitution. They reported at a meeting held in the lecture room on February 16, 1856, when the constitution was adopted. The officers elected were Joseph Williams, president; Thomas Burdett, vice president; T. S. Parvin, secretary. Article 1 fixes the eligibility to membership to those who settled in Iowa prior to the first day of January, 1840, or their descendants for all time to come. This article was found to be too narrow and the time was extended to 1846. Later it was again extended to 1861.

On February 23, 1856, the society met and adopted a long code of by laws and were in order for business.

Now this society was like many other societies that we have helped to organize. When its organization was all perfect it came to a standstill, so far as records show.

After a lapse of almost nine years the records show that a reunion of the old settlers of Muscatine was held at the residence of D. C. Cloud on January 6, 1865. Peter Jackson acted as secretary. Here it was voted to attend a meeting that was to be held at the

Eichelberger house on Jan. 20, 1865, to revive the Old Settlers' society. Here the name seems to have been changed from "First Settlers" to "Old Settlers," more by common consent than any other way. At this meeting the husbands or wives of old settlers were made eligible for membership. A motion was made and passed, appointing P Jackson and J. P. Walton a committee to wait on Joseph Bridgman and secure the books of the society. From this one could conclude that Joseph Bridgman was secretary during the nine years. At this meeting William Leffingwell was chosen president, Suel Foster vice president, and Peter Jackson secretary. Peter Jackson has served as secretary ever since January 6, 1865, thirty-three years.

On March 15, 1865, the quarterly meeting was held in commemoration of the first settlement of the county by Benjamin Nye on March 15, 1834, at the mouth of Pine Creek. There was nothing small about the old settlers at that time. They attempted to hold quarterly meetings.

The next record of a meeting was April 10, 1869, some four years later. At this meeting Samuel Gilbert stated the first boarding house in the county was kept by J. G. Coleman, in a building of rails, in the summer of 1836; meals 50 cents.

On May 8th the by laws were revised again.

On June 29, 1869, an anniversary meeting was held in the court house square. The tables were set under the trees, but in anticipation of rain the tables were moved to the court house. The speakers on the occasion were D. C. Richman, John A. Parvin, Pliny Fay, Suel Foster, Judge Woodward, Col. Kincaid, John Mahin, Richard Cadle and Ben Mathews, the latter a colored man. John A. Parvin was elected president, and Suel Foster vice president. We think that this was one of the most interesting anniversary meetings we ever held.

On September 6, 1870, a meeting was held at the court house. General J. E. Fletcher was elected president and Col. G. W. Kincaid vice president.

On April 4, 1876, the old settlers held a reunion at the residence of Marx Block.

At a meeting held October 31, 1876, the time of admitting members was extended to all settlers here prior to 1861. At this meeting two resolutions were passed. One was for permanently fixing the date of our annual meeting, which has not been adhered to since I have been your president. We have complied as near to it as we considered expedient. Another was that a collection should be taken up to defray the expenses. We have tried to comply with this resolution, but frequently the collections do not reach. If you could help us a little more liberally perhaps they would.

The annual meeting of 1879 was held in the grand jury room and was quite lively.

The annual meeting of 1880 was held October 9, at the court house. Joseph Bridgman was elected president. Dr. Robbins and Suel Foster were elected vice presidents. Sixty gentlemen and 52 ladies were reported present.

The annual meeting in 1881 was held in Armory hall (Hare's hall) on October 5. It was one of the most extensively reported meetings ever held. P. Fay, Geo. B. Denison, J. Scott Richman, John A. Parvin, and John Mahin were among the speakers.

The meeting of 1882 was held on September 27th, at the Hooks' hall, (in the Hotel Grand). Among the speakers of the occasion was the president, Joseph Bridgman, H. H. Benson, Rev. E. P. Smith, Z. Washburn, R. M. Burnett, Rev. Mr. Hayes, Rev. J. H. Barnard, and Mrs. Laura (Nye) Patterson. Suel Foster was elected president, William Gordon, vice president, P. Jackson secretary, and Mrs. Peter Jackson treasurer,

The old settlers' meeting in 1883 was held in Hare's hall on the 26th of September. About 200 were present. I was in Burlington at the time. You may imagine my surprise when being informed of my election as president. I appreciate it. I have been elected for fifteen consecutive times and have appreciated it every time since then. But now I feel that it would be better for the society and I know it would be better for me, if some else were elected as president.

Our meeting in 1884 was held at the mouth of Pine Creek, where the first white settlement was made. Judge S. C. Hastings was our principal speaker on this occasion. A boat excursion was introduced that was very pleasant. Since this meeting we have had reports of the meetings printed and bound. A few copies can yet be had.

Since it has been our good fortune to preside over this society of old settlers, we have had our annual meetings. The first, in 1884, at the mouth of Pine Creek, the second at Captain Clark's at Buffalo, the third on September 8, 1886, a steamboat excursion to Pine Creek; the fourth at Cherry bluff near Moscow, the fifth at the court house square in 1888, the sixth at the fair grounds, the seventh at Wilton in 1890, the eighth at Hitchman's Grove in Pike township, the ninth in 1892, by a steamboat excursion to Wyoming Hills; the tenth and the eleventh at Park Place, the twelfth in 1895, and all since, have been held on the fair grounds.

A short description of those fifteen who first organized the society will not be out of place.

Joseph Williams was a native of Pennsylvania. He came here as one of the U. S. judges. He was a prince of a good fellow with hardly as much dignity as one would expect to find in a supreme judge. He would engage in almost any kind of fun that the boys were engaged in. He could play the fife, beat the drum or saw the fiddle, with most any one. He was a methodist exhorter if he happened to be among the Methodists. He was connected with many of Bloomington's early schemes, such as the ferry franchise, etc.

T. S. Parvin now lives at Cedar Rapids and is quite well known among the old settlers. To T. S. Parvin the credit of this organization belongs in fact, he was a good organizer; he is a native of New Jersey, studied law at or near Cincinnati, and came here as private secretary of Governor Lucas on July 4, 1838. He lived in Muscatine until 1860, when he removed to Iowa City and later to Cedar Rapids. He is grand secretary of the Grand Masonic Lodge of Iowa, and has charge of the Grand Lodge library at Cedar Rapids, under whose supervision the best library in the state has been built up.

Pliny Fay was a native of New England. He came here in 1837. He was a quiet, modest, intelligent man—one would think too refined to be found on the frontier. He was one of the leading men, always cited as a standard of honesty. His health gave out and he went to California and after some years died there.

Joseph Bridgmen is a native of Massachusetts. Came to Bloomington in 1837. He is yet living with us at the advanced age of over 80. In his younger days he was engaged in the mercantile business. He was one of the few prominent men of the town.

Suel Foster was born among the New England hills. He was the best sample of a Yankee we had with us; always outspoken and ready to share in anything for the public good, and was always to be found at the head of all our important public improvements. He worked better for the public than he did for himself.

H. Q. Jennison was an eastern man. likely New England—a civil engineer by profession, although he engaged in farming, and in mercantile pursuits. He was also quite a prominent man, but his disposition to keep well to the front took him west, to Colorado I think.

H. H. Hine—well every one knew Hick Hine, one of the earliest carpenters. He is credited with coming here in 1837. He worked at his trade a large part of his life. He was elected sheriff and served one or more terms in that place and likely filled other places of trust.

Myron Ward was a complete specimen of a pioneer—a large frame, coarse in appearance, a stone mason, if I am correct, but he filled his place as a leader among the common men very successfully. When last heard from he was living at Seattle, Washington, and loaning money for a livelihood, and had accumulated wealth.

Zephaniah Washburn was another mechanic. He did not work as closely at hist trade of carpenter as some others did, but nevertheless he was always on hand if some improvement or reform was being made. He was the first mayor the city had; elected by the "boys" as much for fun as anything else. He was a leading man at the Methodist class meetings, was respected by all and a temperance reformer.

William Chambers was a native of Indiana. Came here in 1836 and went on a farm with his father near Pine Creek, and afterwards moved to Muscatine and engaged in the saw-mill and lumber business. He was a reliable, straightforward man.

G. W. Humphreys came here in 1839, and was engaged in the mercantile business. From 1844 to 1876 he served as sheriff. What eventually became of him I don't know.

J. S. Allen—I recollect Jim Allen, but I don't remember what he did for a living or what became of him.

Giles Pettibone came here in 1838 and went to farming. He sold out the farm and engaged in the ferry business at Muscatine, at which he was not always successful. He finally fitted up his old boat for a packet on some of the small rivers in the south, where it was sunk.

A. T. Banks was a native of New England. He came here in 1838. He served as county treasurer from 1851 to 1855. He was esteemed by every one. In 1856 he was engaged in the livery business, with a man by the name of Morton.

Of the last mentioned signer to the list, J. P. Walton, we have no remarks to make. We will say that he was born in the state of New Hampshire on Feb. 26, 1826; came to this county when but a mere boy, on June 11, 1838, and has been here ever since.

The Pioneer Doctors,

AS SEEN BY THE VENERABLE S. W. STEWART.

Notes by J. P. Waltou.

Published in the Muscatine Saturday Mail, Sept. 10, 1898; written by J. P. Walton.

No. 85.

Some weeks ago Mr. S. W. Stewart, of Wilton, an old settler who came to this county in the spring of 1838, wrote me that he intended to be present at the the recent reunion of the old settlers held on August 30, at the fair grounds. At my suggestion he prepared a reminiscence of "Our Pioneer Doctors" which he was to relate at the old settlers' meeting, but as the meeting adjourned before Mr. Stewart had an opportunity to read it we present it in these columns. Permit me to make a few corrections on the early history.

The jurisdiction of Michigan was established in 1834 by the organization of Des Moines county. It extended from the mouth of Rock river to the mouth of Des Moines river. In 1836 Wisconsin territory was established in place of Michigan with another county, Dubuque, added. On October 25, 1836, the first legislature met at Belmont. Dr. Eli Reynolds was one of its members. Dr. Reynold's mill was built in 1837 The same year Weane Long built a mill on Sweetland creek, and Benjamin Nye on Pine creek.

Dr. Eli Reynolds came here in 1835 and spent his life here and near here. He died at Drury's Landing, Mach 10, 1873. He was a practicing physician for fifty-six years. J. P. W.

OUR PIONEER DOCTORS.

In our rambling talk we will use the word doctor, it is not so elegant but it is easier written than physician and more familiar to the ordinary denizen of earth. Our early doctors were a mixed multitude, they were all alike at some points—very different in others—some were good as the word goes, others would not be cannonized as saints. All were open hearted and worked as honestly for those from whom they expected no reward as for those from whom the fee was certain. If we are right, our first doctor was Eli Reynolds. He built or had an interest in a saw mill, built at Geneva three or four miles above Muscatine on the river. It was the first mill in the county, when built it was in the Jurisdiction of Michigan, then in Wisconsin and last in Iowa, and did not change its location; it was built in Dubuque county and did most of its work in Muscatine county.

Dr. Reynolds with four or five others, was elected to the legislature of Wisconsin from Dubuque county. They first met at Madison, Wis., and adjourned to Burlington. At that session of the legislature they divided the forty mile strip, or the Blackhawk purchase, into counties as far as it went. The strip was not wide enough to give Cedar and Washington and some other counties their full size. Reynolds was free hearted and free handed, he made money and spent more than he made; he dearly loved his toddy, being very sociable and had a dislike to dinking alone; he loved a horse race, never failing to be on hand; he was a faithful student in the class that studdied the history of the pasteboard kings and queens; he was a faithful friend, a good citizen in his day, he had the reputation of being a good doctor, he served the poor as cheerfully as the rich.

In addition to Dr. Reynolds we had Dr. Olds, Dr. Reeder, Dr. Blades, Dr. McKee and Dr. Dayton; later we had Dr. Hastings, Dr. Prichard, and Dr. Fulliam. They were all orthodox calomel doctors but Prichard and Fulliam. Prichard used water, Fulliam roots and yarbs, lobelia No. 6 and composition powders. Prichard would wrap you up in a wet sheet, take you out and pour a bucket of cold water over you. The regular when called to a case would look wise and dignified, feel the pulse, look at the tongue, pull out his watch and look as if he was in a brown study, then give a dose of calomel and leave some Dover's powders for the patient when the calomel had performed its office. That was for fever; if the patient had ague they gave a dose of calomel and perhaps of Julup, then lelt ten or fifteen doses of quinine or some peruvian bark. Strange as it may seem many of the victims survived—they never were well but lived a time.

Dr. Olds was the brainest of the crowd, he retired from the field early in the 50s, he was very pleasant and agreeable in his social intercourse. Hastings and Dayton were both afflicted with weariness from away back. back. They were both good and upright men personally, of more than fair ability, peaceable, quiet, good citizens and an honor to their friends. McKee was a sharper. Blades was an all round good fellow when he was sober; no polish was wasted on Blades. McKey and Fulliam were born rough, age only added to the original. Reeder was called a "finehaired doctor," he was employed by the upper ten, he was fastidious in his habits, kept himself clean and presentable every day in the week, he was a good man and honored his profession.

There were other doctors in the county, most of them were birds of passage. Moscow had two, Randle, a regular, and Langdon, a mixture of all sorts.

All the doctors we have mentioned were open hearted and handed. A large part of their service was for the love of God or the good of humanity, they got no pay and did not expect any, yet it was given freely. They were a benefaction to the community, any moral shortcoming may well be written in the sand. We were all poor and sure to be sick in the fall. If they had demanded money many of us would have done without their help. There was no money, no employment; our exchange was by dickering. The pioneer doctors deserve a tribute of gratitude and a warm place in our appreciations. The doctors who have taken the place of the pioneers are as kind and generous as they were. If our observation is correct no class of men do more work for which they expect no material reward than our doctors, not even ministers of the gospel.

THE EARLY FINANCIAL RESOURCES OF OUR CITY.

Published in the Muscatine Saturday Mail, Sept. 17, 1898; written by J. P. Walton.

No. 86.

Quite recently the treasurer's book of Bloomington, now Muscatine, came into our hands, hence the following:

The town of Bloomington was first organized in March, 1839, with Hon. Joseph Williams as president; Arthur Washburn, Henry Reese and Benjamin P. Howell trustees; Moses Couch recorder, and Giles Pettibone street commissioner. They did not seem to have any treasurer. The next year, 1840, they appear to have been in better shape so far as town officers were concerned, for they had John Lilly (father of our B. E. Lilly) as president; Henry Reece, John W. Richman and R. P. Low (who was afterwards governor) as trustees; E. E Fay recorder, Mathew Matthews street commissioner, Hiram Matthews marshal, and D. J. Snyder treasurer.

If D. J. Snyder ever acted as treasurer he did not keep any account. John A. Parvin appears to have been the first acting treasurer, his account commences with September 16, 1840, when he received cash from H. Matthews, the marshal, $13 06 for taxes collected. In 1841 John Marble collected the taxes as marshal. The money receipts of the town, all told while Mr. Parvin acted as treasurer, were $338.66. The expenses were $334.56, leaving a balance of $4 10 to be paid over to his successor, John W. Weller. Out of the amount Susan Parrott paid $25.00, a Capt. James Parmer $25.00, both for tavern licenses, and $75.00 was paid for c. house licence, in all $125 for licenses. The c. house license meant coffee house license what would be considered a restaurant at this time. Of course whisky was kept.

The second statement for 1842 to March 1843, the total receipts were $705.82. In 1843 John

Ziegler appears to have been the treasurer. The receipts that year were but $536.35. That year Captain William Fry paid $25.00 for a tavern license, he was the successor to Susan Parrott; she succeeded Robert C. Kinney, the first tavern keeper in our town, on the west corner of Chestnut and Front streets. Daniel Ball paid $25.00 for a grocery license for one year. Daniel Ball kept a model grocery—nothing but liquor, whiskey, brandy, etc. The name saloon did not apply to such places of business until the German came. One entry reads thus: "Received of J. C. Baldwin in county orders $12.50, in cash $3.00 in corporation orders $3.75, total $19.25, for license to sell spirit liquors." Another entry reads thus: "Aug. 28, 1843, received of A. Blanchard for tax on dog, 75c." This was the first account of a dog tax being collected. On the next day, Aug. 29, 1843, Howe & Mabie paid $5 for a circus license. The grocery licenses seem to have been divided with the county, for on the 21st of Sept. 1843, Mr. Ziegler is credited with paying $37.50 over to the county on grocery licenses. In 1843 the lots in the old part of the present city cemetery were first offered for sale and a great many were sold at $5 for the best ones. A draying license was collected on the 28th of February 1844. The treasurer is charged with note of C. Weed and Benjamin Weed, his father, for $33.14, given for taxes by order of the trustees. I presume if a man was good but hard up he could get time on his taxes; it appears that way. The treasurer's account contained four similar notes agregating $69.60. The Weed note was eventually placed in the hands of the marshal for collection and paid with interest of $1.99. In March, 1845, after the Weed note was paid, there remained eight similar obligations, many of which were never paid.

The town collected two day's road tax of every voter under 45 years of age. Public opinion forced the payment in work on the roads. Now, as a rule, the fellow that does the voting never pays any road tax unless he should happen to own a little piece of property to tax it up to. I always paid my road tax and wish that others had to now.

The revenue of 1845 reached $561.70. On June 1. 1846, the revenue for all purposes during the previous year was $1075.00. This does not include the two day's road work. The seven unpaid notes were considered as assets, and a considerable of the amount accrued from the sale of grave yard lots, the best selling at $5 each.

While our town was small we had "groceries" enough. During the months of October and November, 1846, there were six licenses issued at $6 25 for three months, in the next two months four more were issued making ten in all. There were also ten dray licenses issued that year.

In the year 1848 the gross revenue that passed through the treasurer's hands was $1125.15 including the notes. I notice the first billiard table license was issued in 1848, and also the first ten pin alley license. On Sept. 15, 1948, the I. O. O. F. bought six lots for $30. The same year the sale of lots amounted to $120.

In 1849 the wharf master paid in to the treasury $253.75. This was the first item of any large fund received from the wharf. In 1849 the lumber dealers had to pay $15 a year as a license. The revenues of that year took a boom, amounting to $4,123,51. It was raised largely by taxes.

In 1850 licenses took a jump, four dealers paid $100 each for "grocery" license and others paid $25 each for beer license. John Adair paid $5 for an auctioneer's license. Not all the revenue was raised by licenses, the tax for the year 1850 was $4,720.33, from all other services it was $706, a portion of which came from the sale of grave yard lots and wharfage.

This carries the accounts up to the incorporation of the city of Muscatine and if the readers will forgive us for following the record thus far we will promise not to do so again. At this time (1850) there was no city debt, our orders were at a discount both in the city and the county. Any one having an order could present it, if no money was on hand to pay it he could have it endorsed on the back as presented and not paid for the want of funds, the order would then draw interest until paid. But little interest was paid to any one, for the tax payer could trade for orders to pay his taxes much easier than he can now.

The citizens in those early days as a whole took much more interest in our city than they do now. Before any great and important undertaking was begun the interest of the tax payer was considered. The custom of taxing the property holder to make work for the laboring man was not followed at that time. On the contrary it was difficult to get the laboring man to work for the pay the city had to offer. There were several entries in the treasurer's book of 75c for a day's work. Of course, this was in orders or paid with orders for road work not worked out. It was the custom if a man was so situated that he could not work on the road to hire some one to work for him; he could hire a man for 50c a day or a man and a team for $1.00 to $1.25 and pay as best he could, if he did not do the work he had to pay 75c a day.

THE MILITARY SPIRIT OF IOWA IN BY-GONE DAYS.

Published in the Muscatine Saturday Mail, Sept. 24, 1898; written by J. P. Walton.

No. 86.

As these are military times it has been suggested to us that we review some of our early recollection of the early war footing of Iowa.

The legislature of 1842-3 passed what is known as the "Revised Statutes of the Territory of Iowa." In this revision the military law was revised. Section 5 of chapter 96 provided for the enrollment of all free white male persons between the age of 18 and 45 years, residing, or from time to time coming to reside, within the military district. I think the assessor generally did the enrolling, although the law required the clerk of the commanding officer to do it. The law also required them to rendezvous once in each year between the 10th of September and 15th of October for the purpose of inspection, review and martial exercises. They were to be notified by leaving a notice at the place of residence, and in case no person could be found in the house the notice was to be posted on the outside of the outer door of the house. These notices required the person subject to military duty to appear at "such parade or place of rendezvous, armed and equipped as the law directs." That was where the fun came in, the arming and equipping was immense. We recollect visiting one general training held in the autumn of 1843 or '44. It was held out in Kecklerville, there were no buildings in the way. There were probably two hundred men gathered there, they met in the forenoon and organized and adjourned for dinner, after which the colonel came out to review them. Irad C. Day was the colonel, he was a very small man, much less in stature than his son Ebenezer. He came out mounted on a very large charger so large that his short limbs would little more than reach down to the sides of the large horse; he undertook to gallop his horse and he bounded like a kid in a baby-jumper. He had a nice uniform on and was armed with a sword which had been presented by Gen. Lafayette to an ancestor of his who served on the staff of the revolutionary general. (I have the sword now.) The colonel held his review. The rank and file were armed with sticks, wooden swords and corn stalks; a few of the rural militia took every thing as it should be and bought their rifles with them; they had the post of honor, while the corn stalk boys were placed in the rear. The drill in the afternoon lasted about an hour after which the militia were by order of the colonel discharged for the day. The brigadeir general, J. E. Fletcher, was on the ground, but as it was only a regiment muster he had no authority. I don't think that any more musters or trainings were held here. Shortly after, say in 1845, the Mexican war broke out, when a man by the name of John R. Bennett enrolled a company but I think they did little drilling. This company was composed largely of river men—raftmen. All the lumber and logs were floated down the river in rafts manipulated by hand, no steamboat towing was done then, hence a great number of strong athletic men were to be found along the river, just what were needed to make soldiers. Of this company of more than a hundred men that went off but two ever returned; they were mustered out elsewhere and had no especial incentive to bring them here, not even the captain came back.

When the war of the rebellion broke out the Kecklerville flat came in for its share of attraction. There the gallant captain, afterwards General Edward Hatch, mustered his company of the Seccond Iowa Cavalry; there they did their horseback drilling. I recollect loaning my "old yellow horse" to Lieutenant Metcalf on several occasions, the old horse possessed all the requisits of a good driver but as a rider he was terribly rough, he came near running away with the lieutenant several times.

After the war of the rebellion was fairly under way the people of this city were startled by the report that a rebellion had broken out in Keokuk county, known afterwards as the Skunk war. Our military company was ordered to the front and were gone a week or more. They went by rail to Washington, and from there by wagons to Sigourney, where the court house was their headquarters and barracks. Their living was fine. The thought of going to war kept them duly sober on the outward trip, but such was not the case on the return as some were very sick. One fellow in the returning ambulance was laid with his head hanging out at the back to keep him from despoiling the wagon. It proved a bloodless affair so far as our Light Guards were concerned. We are not going to give the names of the veterans of the Skunk war for we were not there, but if one would inquire of Harry Canon he might get the roll.

The Missouri war that occured in the winter of 1839-40 has been written up, so no further mention will be made of that.

EARLY DAYS OF STEAMBOATING ON THE MISSISSIPPI.

Published in the Muscatine Saturday Mail Oct. 1, 1898; written by J P. Walton.

No. 87.

From 1836 to 1856 almost all the traffic of the states and territories lying along the Mississippi river between New Orleans and St. Paul was done by steamboats. The river was known as the Upper Mississippi and the Lower Mississippi. St. Louis was the dividing point. The steamboats were of all sizes, being from 50 to 2,000 tons burden; the larger ones run on the lower river. The boats, as a general rule, were all constructed for freight and passengers, a combination hard to reach, especially in low water. The boats used up this way were mostly all side wheelers, similar to the Gen. Barnard or the Quincy. In the forties but few sternwheel boats were used, they were considered to slow and unhandy. I don't know as I can give any better idea of the best early boats than by describing the one I came to this territory on in 1838, the Brazil (Old Brazil) with Capt. Orin Smith master. It was built at Cincinnati for the Upper Mississippi trade and went up to Pittsburg for a load, considerable of which was government supplies to be taken to Fort Snelling, at or near St. Anthony Falls. The Ohio and Mississippi were high. The Brazil was a fast boat and it was one continual race from Pittsburg to Muscatine. The river was alive with steamboats and we would hardly get clear of one before we would be in sight of another; of course, the same excitement occured again. I recollect our getting after one boat, I think its name was Columbus, and running all day before we got away from it. Of course, both boats had to stop and do their business and take on fuel (wood). The excitement was so great that the passengers all took a part in wooding. As a rule, all the boats could work off steam faster than they could make it, especialy if they had to use green wood, which was more abundant than dry, so they usually carried along a lew barrels of rosin to urge up the steam. Boats on the lower river frequently kept a few cords of yellow pine knots stored away for such occasions. Coal was not in use at that time. When we saw a black smoke coming out of the chimneys we knew it was rosin or pine knots that was being used. But to the description of the Brazil, she was a large side-wheel, single engine boat with two double flued boilers; these boilers were probably four feet in diameter and 28 or 30 feet in length; the engine was situated in the middle of the boat, had a large fly wheel and could uncouple either paddle wheel or both. The pump for supplying the boilers was attached to the engine, when the water got low the wheels were unshipped and the big engine run to "pump up the boilers." It had no doctor, the injectors were not known at that time. Like all other boats the Brazil had a crooked hull, that is to say, the bow and the stern stood up high while it was low amid ship or in the middle. It was very common to load the boats down so much that the guards amid ship were under water. I recollect seeing the steamer "Uncle Toby" going down the river loaded so deep that the water would frequently run across the deck of the boat just forward the engine. It took its load through to St. Louis all right though.

Boats then carried large spars to push them off from bars in shallow places in the river. These spars were usually laid away when the water was high and only brought out as the river fell. The process of sparring off a sand bar was frequently quite tedious. I recollect being on a boat that got fast below Keithsburg and staying for over twelve hours before getting away. In those days the stage planks were all moved by hand, no swinging stage planks were in use. The early boats had no extra pumps, doctors as they were called, for pumping out the boat or for filling the boilers or no small boilers for filling the large ones when empty. They had no steam "nigger" for running capstan. The steam escaped through a perpendicular heater and thence out of the escape pipe—never into the smoke pipes as now. These escapements were so loud one could not talk with ease if on the upper deck near the pipe. They could be heard for miles under favorable circumstances. We had a boat, the Osprey, that run up here; on a still evening it could be heard for two hours before it arrived, long before it could be seen from the top of the hill. Upon the introduction of the horizontal heaters the nuisance was very much reduced. The introduction of the escape steam into the chimneys, as is now in use, also modified it still more.

Before the introduction of steam whistles the bell was the main thing used where whistle and bell are now used; hence they had some very fine loud toned ones. A five or six hundred pound bell was very common. Most of those in use were made at the Buckeye Bell Foundry at Cincinnati. We ran against one of these old bells on the steamer W. J. Young. It is the personal property of Capt. Blair; and only loaned to the boat. It has an excellent tone and was cast by C. W. Coffin at the Buckeye Bell Foundry in 1849. Around the top are allegorical figures of the seasons of the year, etc. Its history is not known farther back than the old steamer Muscatine, that run here during or very soon after the war of the rebellion.

Speaking about steam whistles on steamboats, they appeared here as near as I can recollect about 1844-45. The old Glaucus had the first one, and it seemed to me the loudest one of any. When it blew it would terrify almost any of the uniniated. We recollect hearing an acquaintance of ours, James Marshall, tell of being at a house on the bluff accross the river watching with a dead person during the night in company with an aged man by the name of Essex, when the old Glaucus, or some other boat, blew its whistle. It was the first time either of them had heard one. They were both somewhat startled. Essex suggested that something awful would be the result, and suggested that they have prayers; which proposal was agreed to.

Soon after steam whistles were introduced the calliope followed. At that time all the lumber and logs that came down the river was floated down in rafts, it took from 12 to 20 men to a raft; these men had to return to the pineries by steamboats and the boat that picked up a raft crew increased its passenger list considerable. In order to catch the raftmen bands were carried on the boats. One steamer, the Denmark, put on a calliope, they had more than their share of raftmen during the reign of the calliope. After a year or so it became an old story and was laid away.

EARLY DAYS OF STEAMBOATING ON THE MISSISSIPPI.

Published in the Muscatine Saturday Mail Oct. 8, 1898; written by J P. Walton.

No. 88.

We stated in our last that most of the traffic of the states along the Mississippi river was done by steamboats. Such was the case until the railroad reached the river. The products of this part of the country were stored during the fall and winter, waiting the high water in the spring for shipment. As soon as the ice moved out the steamboats were here in abundance. I have seen a dozen boats in a day, they were going up and down the river. Those going down during the spring months were usually loaded quite heavily. They were generally of a large class of side wheel boats, something like the Quincy of the present time; they were both freight and passenger boats, good runners and good carriers. As the season advanced the up stream freight was more abundant, merchants were bringing on their yearly supply of goods.

The heaviest article brought here was salt. The "meat" was packed here, no live hogs being shipped away at that time, hence the loading in the hull below deck was salt. It was a cheap commodity and quite heavy making a desirable freight; the steamboats would frequently load with it at St. Louis and leave it to be sold on commission. The salt mostly came from the Kanawha river in western Virginia, and came in barrels. It was a very common thing to see salt piled up by the cord with a few boards to cover it. The salt was brought here on speculation.

When the river began to fall in the autumn the large boats had to draw off and a smaller kind had their day, they towed barges to carry their freight and were very familiar with sand bars. In order to meet such emergencies they carried heavy spars to lift the boat into deep water; using these spars was quite a skillful piece of work, it was usually under the supervision of the mate; when the river was high these spars were laid away and nothing but the derricks were to be seen. The derricks were used for swinging up the large staging.

The greatest drawback to navigation was the lower rapids above Keokuk especially in low water. The river frequently got so low that not more than 18 inches of water could be found on some of the chains. The upper rapids were not so bad. I recollect coming down over the upper rapids when the the boat drew fully six inches more than there was water on one of the chains, the rock must have been quite smooth as the boat took a run for it and slid over. We could easily see that it raised the boat while going over. I don't think a boat could run up over the chain drawing as much water as that one did. At these rapids there were companies that kept lighters to take freight over, and while the low water prevailed there were two classes of boats that run on the upper Mississippi, the larger ones ran from St. Louis to Keokuk, and the smaller ones from Montrose at the head of the rapids to Galena and Dubuque. Freight was frequently loaded on barges at Keokuk and towed over the rapids by light draft boats. I think horses were used in towing to a certain extent to Montrose, thence by steam up the river. On the return these barges were loaded and returned to Keokuk. Most of the boats had barges of their own to assist in carrying freight.

Here let me say that those were good democratic times, the slogan was "no national improvement on the western rivers." If any was made the states should make them and the states could not, so they were not made. Now the river is comparatively of little value, the government is squandering money by the millions in putting in wing dams and the like when there is very little call for them. For our part we have given the river commerce up as a thing of the past and not to return any more. If the money that is spent putting in the wing dams was put on the banks as levees to keep the river within its banks it would be of vast advantage to those residing in the low bottoms that are washed out every three or four years, or at least if the system of wing damming is to be continued, the banks of the river should be raised high enough to keep the water held back by the dams from flowing over private property which it does now in many places. I understand that the last congress appropriated some $600,000 for such purposes on this upper river and that there is some ten or twenty dams anticipated between Muscatine and New Boston. This is quite interesting for the Muscatine Island and the Illinois bottom residents. The government engineer claims that to dam up one-half of the river at low water won't effect it at high water. I don't think so.

But to return to steamboating on the Mississippi river between the years 1845 and 1855. I think that was the zenith of steamboating in the then west. As before stated the fuel was all wood, coal was not in use. Along the bank of the river there were great piles of wood which was mostly cut in the winter for the use of the boats in the summer. Some of the more prosperous woodmen kept flat boats to sell wood out of. They would load the wood boats and let the steamboat tow them up stream until the wood was taken out. This was considered a great advantage to the boat and it was a greater advantage to the seller in the way of cording his wood. A skillful piler would make three-quarters of a cord pile a cord, and no questions asked.

During the time that navigation was open, the arrival of a boat was quite an event and especially during low water when they were a little scarce. The hotels all kept a boy whose principal business was to announce the "coming of a boat." Our first recollection of Adam Reuling was when he was "boat boy" for the Iowa House in the spring of 1843. I tried to get the place but Adam beat me. Martin Bitzer was "boat boy" for the Park House kept by one of the Neidigs. When a boat was announced there was a lively time at the hotel, in the getting off the guests and getting more in. In fact the whole town was alive, we did not have boat agents so every merchant had to look after his own goods and pay the freight on them.

All steamboats had a bar, and, of course, a class of drinking men, the number was not small, went aboard the boat for a drink, while the boats were at the wharf, the price was double that of the price charged at the "grocery" in our town. Speaking about the "bar" on the steamboat, it was the most profitable interest about the boat, if properly managed. They all had them. The privilege was usually rented out to the bar tender who paid liberally for it; and two prices for his whisky, and two windows for its sale. I think the one inside sold for 10c a drink and the one on the outside at 5c. The one outside was patronized by the deck hands and the niggers, of course they had to have it cheaper. The bar keeper never lost anything at that price for his whisky did not cost him to exceed 10c a gallon.

But to turn back to the manner of handling freight, we never had any warehouse on the wharf until the Northern Line built the present one about the close of the war. All freight was put on the bank of the river, where a lot of dunnage could be found; who put it there I don't know. It was made of two pieces of timber say 4x4 12 feet, fastened together about 12 inches apart with about three rounds. This dunnage was laid up and down the slope of the bank and the freight was piled on it, having an open place underneath for water to run. If the freight was landed in the night and no drays ready to haul it, it was covered with a tarpaulin and the edges weighted down with cord wood taken from the boat if no other was handy.

When grain was shipped it was hauled down to the river in sacks and piled on this same dunnage and covered up. A watchman had to be kept by the shipper to keep off the hogs that were allowed to run at large greatly to the annoyance of every shipper. Those hogs "got onto their business," it was quite difficut to weight down a tarpaulin so secure that a hog would not root it up and tear open the sacks of grain.

EARLY DAYS OF STEAMBOATING ON THE MISSISSIPPI.

Published in the Muscatine Saturday Mail Oct. 15, 1898; written by J. P. Walton.

No. 89

We are very loathe to give up an industry as important to the early settler as the steamboat interest was. While there was an immense amount of money invested in the river traffic but a small amount was held in our town or city. Captain Clark L. Phelps, better known as Jim Phelps, was a river man and was interested in several boats at diferent times. I recollect but one, the old Lamentine. He never got very rich at the business. Captain T. S. Battell sold out his hotel, the American House, that was the best property in the town—it stood on the northwest corner of the Avenue and Second street—and bought the Oswego, a large sized side wheeled boat, rather slow. He run it perhaps one or a part of two seasons and sunk it, taking about all Battell had with it. I think Joseph Bennett lost some in the old boat. About the close of the war an old boat laid at our wharf all the season. I think Luke Sells had something to do with it. I have forgotten the name.

When the 35th regiment came home from the war Harry Compton and some of the other patriotic men of our place circulated a subcription paper and raised money enough to purchase fuel for the old boat and secured an engineer to go down and meet the boys. Charlie Chaplan, an old river man who was then engaged in running an engine in the Bennett mill, was secured to run the engine of the boat. A crowd got on board the boat and started down the river and when ten or twelve miles below the city they met a boat coming up with the 35th on board. As soon as the boat came along side every one jumped on board and left Charlie Chaplan and his old fireman, Joe, in charge of the boat. Even the pilot left his post. I think they run the boat ashore first. The boat having been laid up awhile the seams above the water line were all open and when the load got on, it put the boat down in the water and it commenced to leak, and the boat nearly sunk before the men got off from it; nothing but the tact of the engineer saved it.

Previous to the war of the rebellion there were but few regular lines of boats. Of course, some general regulation applied to all; for instance, while all boats run on Sunday and did their business on Sunday but few left St. Louis on that day, and but few in the mornings. At meals on the boat the captain sat at the head of the table and when he sat down the others were at liberty to do so. If any especial or noted guests were on the boat they were seated near the captain, chairs were turned down for them, and woe be it to the greenhorn that got into one of these chairs. We did once, and, of course, had a rumpus with the waiter, but held the chair all the same.

On the old boats the front end of the cabin was set apart for business, a curtain was drawn across just back of the clerk's office and the bar; this was called the "social hall," The principal business on most of the boats while they were under way was gambling. There were a class of gamblers that traveled on the boats most of the time that were experts in their business and woe be it to the unfortunate fellow that fell into their hands. It was charged that the boats were interested in a share of the gambler's profits, it certainly looked so to an outsider.

We take a few extracts from a paper published by Captain L. Parkhurst, an old timer in the steamboat line on the upper river:

Take ten years reaching from 1835 to 1845 and we call to mind ten or a dozen first class boats, such as the "Brazil," Capt. Orin Smith, afterwards president of the Minnesota Packet Co., and after relenquishing steamboating, president of the first street car company of Chicago. The "Brazil" was a fine appearing, commodious, attractive boat, owned by parties then in Cincinnati. She would compare well with the St. Paul; not quite so strong, but more beam or breadth. There was the "Osprey," "Rosille," "Empress," "Amarath," Captain John Atchison; "Iona," Captain Pierce Atchison. On the latter our esteemed and long since deceased neighbor, Captain Dodge. first became initiated in handling the rudder and tracing the channel of the river. Many others I could name, such as "Emerald," sunk and wrecked on Sycamore chain. She was loaded principally with stoves and castings for Galena from Cincinnati for a man named Dowling, who had a large trade in that line of goods. Having no insurance, the man was nearly crazed over his loss, and for days he would walk up and down from the boat to Port Byron, singing "Racoon on the Rail," oblivious to everyone and to everything. All had sympathy for him, too. There was the "Admiral" and "Arabia," both side-wheel boats and of an attractive and imposing appearance. The "Tempest" was another—a regular racer. In her later years she was employed in the transfer business between Alton and St. Louis, when the Alton and Chicago road was first opened to the river. There were several stern-wheelers, also mentioned in the list. There was the "Adventurer," Capt. Van Houton, the boat on which James B. Eads introduced himself to the western waters. He became famous as an engineer in later years. While mentioning some of the more ancient class we must remember that during all this time boats were being rapidly constructed to ply in all the western streams. Even the Des Moines, Iowa and Cedar were thought to demand the utility of a smaller class of boats. Wisconsin, Black, Chippewa and the St. Croix were streams inviting the enterprising spirit of western navigators, and the next ten years, reaching from 1845 to 1855, developed surprisingly the magnitude of travel and traffic demanded on the western waters. Companies began to form and talk up systematic schemes to supply the wants of the traveling public. There was a heavy emigration up the streams, and all were interested, as navigators were desirous to bring about some regularity in the arrivals and departure of the boats, and to avoid competition among themselves.

EARLY DAYS OF STEAMBOATING ON THE MISSISSIPPI.

Published in the Muscatine Saturday Mail Oct. 22, 1898; written by J. P. Walton.

No. 90.

(Continued Extracts from Capt. L. Parkhurt's letter.)

The Keokuk packet company was organized about 1845; the traffic between St. Louis and Keokuk was of immense magnitude, and the boats were of the most majestic, attractive and popular class. The stock was bought out and eagerly sought. At the same time the traffic between St. Louis and Galena was of equal or similar proportion, and a daily line was proposed and a time effected, composed of the W. L Ewing, Tucker, Sucker State, Danube, Bon Accord, of which Hiram Bersie, of Scott county, a companion of LeRoy Dodge, was part owner. Canada and Minnesota, each taking a certain day designed in the week. This arrangement was well intended but proved abortive when low water occured. The unimproved state of the rapids and sand bars at that period, no canal around the lower rapids, the boats were brought in confusion, and the regularity destroyed. It was during this period that the two upper companies—Galena, Dunleith and Minnesota Packet company and the White Collar line—became visible competitors for the upper trade from Galena to St. Paul, in connection with the railroads tapping the river at Dunleith, Paririe du Chene and LaCross—the White Collar line from the latter place up and the Minnesota Packet company from Galena first and latter from Dubuque and Dunleith when the Galena and Chicago Union road was extended to Dunleith. In the meantime, while these companies were growing into visible factors for the commerce of the upper Mississippi, it was found necessary, on account of the two rapids, in order to epediate the travel, to have short lines of boats running between the rapids above, from Rock Island to Galena and Dubuque, and to Keokuk below. The railroads opening to the river, traffic at Rock Island in 1854 was phenominal, both in freight and passengers, and a daily line was inaugurated and afterwards called the Rapids Packet company. The names of the boats may be recognized in the list herewith, such as the Campbell, Tishomingo, Jennie Whipple, Jennie Lind, Kate Kassell and later on, the New Boston and Keithsburg. The company held their position, in their daily arrivals and departures in the estimation of the public until August, 1864, when they sold to the Northern Line Packet company for $95,000 cash. Benj. H. Campbell, who but a few years since committed suicide in Chicago by drowning, was the principal owner when the sale was effected. The writer was then employed on one of the boats, and was immediately transferred to the Muscatine, and from the middle of August to the close of navigation, November 22, cleared $10,000.

The Galena, Dunlieth and Minnesota Packet company saw the necessity of making a connecting link between this short line, and in 1854 contracted for the building of four new boats and the season following, gave the people of the upper Mississippi a fleet of side-wheel steamers that have never been equalled, being attractive, commodious, light; and yet carried all the freight reason dictated, while thronged with human life, as they were, during a period of heavy emigration. They were called the Key City, Itaska, Milwaukee and Northern Light, and four finer boats never floated the waters of this grand highway. They ranged in length from 225 to 245 feet, were of uniform breadth and their cost was from $50,000 to $60,000 each. Capt. Orin Smith, spoken of heretofore, in connection with the old Brazil and later new Brazil, was the constructor and superintended the building of the same, and our worthy and esteemed neighbor, Captain Gabbot, commanded the Northern Light.

The addition of these boats enabled the company to make the connecting link with the Rapids company without crippling the business of the upper line. The Alhambra and Fanny Harris were placed in the Rock Island and Galena trade which prospered. The Royal Arch, a side wheeler, being detailed to fill the place of one of the boats in the spring of 1858, was sunk in the bend just below Sand Craine by the Eclipse, a stern wheeler, on the 30th of May, up to which time, from the 20th of March, she had cleared $13,000. Being in charge of the office myself I witnessed the transactions and scenes on board. There were about one hundred cabin passengers, six mail bags, and several thousand dollars in the safe. I stuffed my pockets with the money, gobbled up the mail bags, and with all the passengers sought the hurricane roof for safety. The boat settled to the bottom in fifteen or twenty minutes, in about fifteen feet of water, reaching about half way from the lower deck to the cabin floor. She happened to lie straight on the sand, however, and with the aid of a barge was raised and brought down to the ways at Rock Island, repaired and resumed business in about two weeks. There were two or three disasters in this trade following that, one by the Fanny Harris and the City Belle, both by collisions with the old bridge at this place. The Fanny struck the little pier on the larboard side, sheered off toward the draw pier, striking the lower end on her starboard side and brought her stern end in contact with the little pier, by which time there was terrible excitement in the cabin with the passengers, of whom there were about 100. The stove upset, the lamp in the office was knocked over and the bright blaze trailing up the ceiling threatened destruction by fire. The pilot rounded to at the foot of the island and about twenty passengers jumped off rather than to risk the result further. The captain finding the water too deep to let her sink there, which she was doing rapidly, ordered the pilot to back her on the bar, upon which she settled, the water covering the lower deck about two feet. By the time she was well settled the ferry boat came to us and took the passengers off. The City Belle was more fortunate, as she managed to get to the shore at Davenport, but lost very near her whole starboard side wheel and guards. Of course, she was lop-sided, but she effected a landing.

EARLY DAYS OF STEAMBOATING ON THE MISSISSIPPI.

Published in the Muscatine Saturday Mail, Oct. 29, 1898; written by J. P. Walton.

No. 91.

(Continued extracts from Captain L. Parkhurst's letter.)

While these two decades [1835 to 1855] made good returns on the capital invested, the next ten years brought about the climax of prosperity to the navigators of the upper Mississippi, although several fine boats left their wrecks scattered up and down the river. The Northerner was burned, the Burlington sunk below Wabasha, the Nominee sunk at Crooked Slough, the Northern Light, likewise, and the Brazil on a big boulder off the foot of Camp McClellan from which it was called Brazil rock, up to the time the government blasted it out. The season of 1865 turned out a net profit of over $500,000 to the Northern Line Packet company. Their stock was buoyant at 3 to 1 and and surely it was then the proper time to unload. The transportation of troops had ceased, travel diminishing, railroads were becoming too numerous and paralleling the river and all kinds of traffic falling away from the river lines. Bridges were coming forward rapidly to obstruct the passing of boats in the night, in fact they are an obstruction to the freedom of navigation in any light they may be considered. Time is money and all bridges cause loss of time with anything floating on the river! As to profits of individual boats, 1865 was something remarkable. The Muscatine, costing probably $40,000, cleared over $71,000; the Keithsburg and New Boston in this short time netted some $24,000 to $30,000 each. In one trip the White Cloud cleared over $10,000. On this trip the writer had an experience which exemplified the precarious state of our currency at that time (1857). We had a freight bill to collect at Omaha for the transportation of an iron safe and vault, over $500 in amount. It was paid in new bills, one package of $500 being on the bank of Brownsville, Nebraska. Stopping there the next morning, we went to the bank about 10 o'clock and drew the gold. Next morning the failure of the bank was announced in the St. Louis papers, but that was a famous year for the tumbling of banks all over the country.

When we look back over the past fifty years and comprehend the vast amount of capital that has been invested to properly navigate the western waters, and then view our present surroundings, the accumulated improvements of the age and prospects of further advances, we can only estimate the value of such capital by the good it has accomplished. It has settled up the country and opened the way for railroads to clip the traffic therefrom, and, in the language of Shakespeare, "Othello's occupation is gone." There is no dispute, however, that water highways are a leveler of rates of trasportation. Following are the different packet companies and their boats:

St. Louis and Keokuk Packet Co—Andy Johnson, City of Quincy, City of Louisana, City Warsaw, Des Moines, Golden Eagle, Hannibal City, Jennie Dean, Kate Kearney, New England, Rob Roy, War Eagle, Sam Gaty, Stephen Bayard, J. H. Johnson, Di Vernon, Lucy Bertram, Edward Bates, Monongahala, Cambria, Mary Stevens, New England.

Minnesota Packet Co.—Itasca, Northern Light, Northern Belle, Milwaukee, War Eagle, City Belle, Greek Slave, Alhambra. Galena, Gray Eagle, Kate Kethsell, Key City, Royal Arch, Fannie Harris, Flora.

Northern Line Packet Co.—Burlington, Clinton, Canada, Denmark, Davenport, Dan Hine, Henry Clay, Hawkeye State, Keithsburg, Lake Superior, Minnesota, Muscatine, Minneapolis, New Boston, Pembina, Petrel, Red Wing, Rock Island, Sucker State, Savana, W. L. Ewing, Dubuque, Northerner, James Manes, Fred Lorenz, Charlie Cheever, Bill Henderson, Reserve, Metropolitan, Little Giant.

White Collar Line.—Annie Johnson, Addie Johnson, Alexander Mitchell, Frank Steel, Gem City, Moses McClellan, Northwestern, Phil. Sheridan, S. S. Merrill, Favorite, Enterprise, Flying Eagle, Dexter, George S. Wicks, Countess, City of St. Paul, Belle of LaCrosse, S. S. Merrill, Jacob Fraber, Alex. Kendal, G. H. Wilson, Grand Pacific, Jennie Baldwin.

Diamond Jo Line.—Arkansas, Bannock City, Diamond Jo, Ida Fulton, Josephine, Josie, John C. Gault, Libbie Conger, Imperial, Mary Morton, Pittsburg, Sidney, St. Paul, Tidal Wave, Gem City, Martin Walt, Sligo.

Captain Parkhurst gives the names of some 250 independent boats, most or all of which run here during the period of twenty-five years from 1840 to 1865. It can be easily seen how we got our dozen boats a day as mentioned in one of our early communications.

To an outsider it now looks as though those short line boats that do the passenger and freight business of the river were only feeders for the railroads, and what through boats that are left, not more than three or four, run for outing travel during the summer months and are laid up during the spring and autum. Of course, this does not include the raft boats that are used in the lumber business.

Recollections of

PERSONS AND EVENTS CONNECTED WITH OUR SCHOOLS IN EARLY TIMES.

Published in the Muscatine Saturday Mail, Nov. 5, 1898; written by J. P. Walton.

No. 92.

When our high school building burned down nearly three years ago, all the records then known to exist were burned, even those of the last meeting before the fire. So the writers of history could have a clear sailing with little or nothing to contradict them. Such is not the case in a literal manner, for quite recently a few fragments of the records of school districts, Nos. 1 and 2, came into my hands. They were rescued from the old building used by M. Block as an office, it stood where the Oat Meal Co. are building a new elevator. These old books contain the records and accounts of school district No. 1 from May 1854 to May 1859, and the records of district No. 2 from March 8, 1850, to March 28, 1858.

The city was divided, by whom or when I don't know, into two districts. Sycamore street was the dividing line—No. 1 on the northeast side, and No. 2 on the southwest side. School house No. 2 was built in 1849-'50, at a cost of nearly $5,000; it was a 40x45 feet, two story, brick building; it stood where the present First ward school house now stands.

School house No. 1 stood where the Third ward school house now stands. It was a two-story brick building, much larger than the other, 45x65 feet, and was constructed in 1851-52. It cost over $7,000.

The school year in No. 1 was divided into two terms a year and was opened March 7, 1853, with D. Franklin Wells as principal, Miss Margaret M. Lyon first assistant, Miss Henrietta A. Mikesell second assistant; Miss Kate P. Foster, a neice of Suel Fostor, was connected with the school in some manner for she was paid two orders of $50 each. In 1854 Miss M. L. Davidson's name appears for a $100 order. In 1855 the following names occurs on the treasurer's book as drawing money for teaching: D. Franklin Wells, $250; Miss M. M. Lyon, $125; Miss Mikesell, $75; Miss Davidson, $75; Miss Lane, $100, Miss M. E. Barrows, $81.80.

D. Franklin Wells came from Oneida county, New York; he was a graduate of the State Normal school at Albany, N. Y. At the time he came here, in 1853, Hon. T. S. Parvin was president of the school board and interested himself in securing good teachers; through his influence Prof. Well and Miss Lyon were induced to come here. The professor staid here four years and had a professorship in the state university at Iowa City offered him and he accepted it. He was afterwards appointed and elected state superintendent of public instruction. He died at Iowa City, leaving a widow and some four children.

The first assistant, Miss Margaret M. Lyon, was a native of Herkimer county, N. Y; she a was graduate of the State Normal school, class 3. She taught four years and retired at the time Prof. Wells did, concluding some other vocation was more to her liking. After spending a few years with her friends she married Mr. George B. Dennison, a former principal in district No. 2, who died some years ago. Mrs. Dennison now lives at 409 east Fifth street, and looks quite as pleasant and about as young as she did near fifty years ago when I first saw her.

When the school was first opened there were two other assistants, one was a Miss Emeline Fisher, who married Mr. John Wilson; they lived in Chicago but a few years ago. The other assistant was a Miss Griffing. I don't know what became of her, I presume she got married and lost her identity, which was the lot of many of our lady teachers.

Miss Henrietta Mikesell came here with her parents while quite young, and by hard study filled her place as a teacher with entire satisfaction until she married John Miller and raised a family of two daughters and perhaps others. She is now dead. Miss Davidson married and moved west, had a family, but was said said to have been killed by the Indians. Of Miss Lane I know but little.

Miss M. E. Barrows was a native of Oneida county, N. Y., was a graduate of the Clinton Liberal Institute, class of 1854. After teaching a year in old No. 1 and a year in county schools, she returned to her home in Oneida county, where she was married in June, 1857, to J. P. Walton, and returned to Muscatine, and has been the mistress of Evergreen Nook for more than forty years.

In 1856 Miss Fannie Adams was employed as an assistant teacher. She was the daughter of Samuel Adams the Quaker brickmaker. She taught a year or two and, if I recollect aright, when her father moved to Indianapolis she went with him.

In 1857 the account book shows Thomas Beham as principal, Miss Mary Williams, Henrietta Mikesell, Fanny Adams, and Tempy Seeley were the board of school teachers. Their salaries ranged from $200 to $800.

Miss Mary Williams was a sister of Judge Joseph Williams and Hon. Robert Williams. She came from Pennylvania, was a good teacher and very popular with the smaller grades pupils, but as a scholar she was not very proficient. Her popularity kept her in the schools a long time. She was an exception to the rule for female teachers, she never got married.

On December 19, 1857. an order was drawn to pay Miss D. E. Payne for teaching the tenth term just then ended. There being two terms a year this order would indicate that the school had just closed its fifth year,' which was a fact. Where Miss Dela E. Payne came from I don't know, but she married Hon Ed. H. Thaeyr, now of Clinton, Iowa. During the tenth term a Miss Tabor and a Miss Julia Beard taught school. I don't recollect any thing about them.

On March 15, 1858, Dr. D. H. Goodno was employed as a teacher at a salary of $900. Dr. Goodno held this position until the second year of the war, in 1862, when he was appointed adjutant of the 37th regiment of Iowa volunteers, the grey beard regiment. After the war was over he got a position in the Interior department at Washington. He died some four years ago.

The record book commences April 4, 1856. E. Klein was president, Wm. Leffingwell treasurer, and Richard Cadle secretary.

There are many interesting entries in the book. In June, 1856, occurs the following: "Complaint has been made to the directors of school district No. 1 that undue severity has been used in said school by the correction of scholars by whipping them with a rawhide; therefore, be in resolved by the board of directors, that from and after this day and date the use of a rawhide in the schools will not be tolerated." On September 18, 1856, Mr. Edward Couch was appointed principal of the school at a salary of $275 a term. On October 15 appears the following: "Edward Couch for teaching two weeks $25, and Thomas Beham is employed to teach the balance of the term." We never knew that Ed. Couch tried his hand at teaching. This was before he went into the army.

In March 1847 a resolution was carried requiring the principal to keep an account of the time that the teachers were absent and to have the same deducted from their salary. In July 1857 it was ordered that the principal of the school shall employ his own assistant at such price as the board shall allow. I think this rule was in force while Dr. Goodno remained.

In our next we will review some of the records of school district No. 2. While it did not have near as many scholars it perhaps has more interesting history.

Recollections of

PERSONS AND EVENTS CONNECTED WITH OUR SCHOOLS IN EARLY TIMES.

Published in the Muscatine Saturday Mail, Nov. 12, 1898; written by J. P. Walton.

No. 93.

As I before stated most of the records of our city schools were destroyed at the burning of the high school a few years ago. The only remaining fragments left were rescued from a pile of old papers in M. Block's old office. How the school districts in Muscatine were organized is a little problematic. In the Muscatine county history, on page 420, occurs the following:

"The board of county commissioners constituted school district No. 1, November 4, 1839, embracing the limits of township 78, north range, two west." [This was undoubtedly 77 north.] This organization was used to draw public money for school purposes. Later there was a school house built by private enterprise and used for the town school, it stood on the ground where the Journal printing office is now located or on south end of lot 5 in block 34. This school house was 'gobbled' by the Methodists for a meeting house and a new school house had to be secured.

When district No. 2 was organized I am unable to ascertain, at all events it occupied that part of the city west of Sycamore street, and in 1848 they commenced to advocate the building of a new school house. A tax was levied and litigated and decided illegal. Then another effort was made with better success. The old record begins with the following entry:

"Muscatine, Ia., March 8, 1850. The first meeting of the board of directors of school district No. 2, Bloomington township, Muscatine county, took place this evening. The present board consists of G. S. Branham, president; Alfred Purcell, treasurer, and M. M. Berkshire, secretary. The first business before the board was the settlement with Z. Covel, the former secretary. Mr. Covel had collected of the tax levied to purchase a site for a school house and to build a house thereon, $1,080.21, and was allowed his percentage thereon." The District was undoubtedly organized and running a year or more before this record commenced.

On April 5, 1850, the assessment on Joseph Bennett's mill was reduced from $22,902 to $18,000. At the same meeting a mention was made of the receipt of $140.06 from the state school fund for the year 1850. On Aug. 3, 1850, Daniel Mauck was allowed $875.24 for brick and stone work on the school house. We conclude by this and similar bills the school board did not let any one man have the contract of the whole house but divided it.

At the meeting of Dec. 21, 1850, J. C. Irwin was given the contract to make the seats for the new school house; he was also authorized to measure the plastering. On January 10, 1851, the secretary, M. M. Berkshire, presented his bill for collecting the tax for 1850. Then all school and city taxes were collected by special collectors. On February 5, 1851, M. M. Berkshire tendered his resignation and Henry O'Connor was appointed secretary. From Feb. 5, 1851 to May 5, 1852, there is no record.

At the meeting, May 5, 1852, J. C. Irwin was president, Pliney Fay treasurer, and Henry O'Connor secretary. At a previous meeting G. B. Denison was employed as principal at a salary of $500 per year. Lydia E. Denison was also employed as first assistant at $250, and Mary A. Stiles as second assistant at $225. The school year was divided into three terms.

On May 23, 1852, the officers were John C. Irwin president, Wm. St. John treasurer, and M. Berkshire secretary. On August 3 a resolution was passed instructing the teachers to assess against each scholar as a tuition fee from $1.50 to $2 per term, but no provisions were made for collecting. By November 18 there had been several changes in the board. M. Block was president, Wm. St. John treasurer, and Joseph Bridgman secretary. A resolution was passed instructing the secretary, Jos. Bridgman, to secure the papers and money belonging to the district in the hands of Mr. O'Connor.

At a meeting held on January 3, 1853, the teachers' salaries for the last term were allowed amounting to $325, also a bill of G. B. Denison for cash paid for sundries amounting to $37.24. There had been several of this kind of bills. I think Mr. Denison must have been their banker, as he appears to have advanced for them in money at other times.

A move was made on March

11, 1853, to reorganize the district under the new school law, and on the second day of May a meeting was called to vote a tax to pay off the debt of the district. A new board of directors seem to have been eletced who were Rev. A. B. Robbins to serve three years; Joseph Bridgman, secretary, for two years, and James S. Hatch, treasurer, for one year. At a meeting held on April 18, 1853, Mr. G. B. Denison was elected principal, Miss Emma Lincoln for the second department, and Miss Charity N. Merrill the primary department. There was an order issued to the patrons of the school that the unpaid tuition must be paid immediately to the treasurer.

On May 8, 1853, Jacob Butler, J. P. Freeman and F. Thurston were admitted to the board, they having been elected on the 2nd. At this meeting it was voted that no children under 5 years of age should be admitted; it was also voted that no children outside of the district should be admitted without a special permit from the directors, but if any were admitted they were to pay $3 per term for the first department, $2 for the second department, and none were to be admitted in the primary department. Circumstances soon proved that these arbitrary rules were not needed, for district No. 1 had a larger, better and further advanced school than No. 2. No. 1 soon took the lead and always kept it while the districts were separated.

On August 5, 1853, an unusual motion was offered by Rev. A. B. Robbins and passed. It provided that Mr. Hatch be made a committee to see that a branch of study called the "history of the United States" be taught in Mr. Denison's room. I don't know what that meant, but I think that a little friction existed between the president of the school board and the principal of the school, which eventualy developed into a general school revolution that relieved the school of both its Caesars.

At the close of the November term of 1853, it was decided to have a public examination of the schools. It was quite common at that time to have such examinations. The directors and other noted personages were expected to be present and were frequently requested to ask questions of some of the more brilliant scholars. I recollect being present at one public examination and asking a very simple question of a class in arithmetic, it was a little out of the ordinary and it made a "fearful break." I did not have a chance to ask any more questions in that school. These examinations had the effect to bring the scholars, the teachers and the directors into some kind of prominence. I think it is many years, at least thirty, since we have had any of those public examinations in our city schools.

At a meeting held March 28, 1854, Rev. Robbins reported that he had conversed with Mr. Denison about teaching one term longer, and that Mr. Denison declined to do so. There was a motion made and carried, but afterwards rescinded, to employ two female teachers in the place of Mr. Denison. On April 21 Mr. Butler was instructed to correspond with Mr. A. B. Tuttle. On the 26th Mr. Tuttle with Mrs. Dennice and Miss Eliza B. Walker were employed as teachers. The selection of these teachers was the culmination of the Denison-Robbins rupture. Denison was out and he was determined that Robbins should go. A meeting of the voters was called to refer the matter to the people; it looked to an outsider who attended the meeting, like a battle between the Congregational church and the outsiders including all the roughs in the town. It was voted by the crowd that Rev. A. B. Robbins, F. Thurston, Jacob Butler and Joseph Bridgman should resign. At a meeting May 1, 1854, they did resign and with them went an interest and a standing that took the school a long time to, if it did ever, recover.

RECOLLECTIONS OF

PERSONS AND EVENTS CONNECTED WITH OUR SCHOOLS IN EARLY TIMES.

Published in the Muscatine Saturday Mail, Nov. 19, 1898; written by J. P. Walton.

No. 93.

Previous to 1860 the free schools, as the public schools were called, were not considered hardly toney enough by all classes. In this state there were a goodly number of western and southern people who thought that free schools were provided for poor persons to attend, they considered their children too good to associate with the poor man's "kids." This was true of the eastern people also to a certain extent; hence the necessity of securing the support of the more influential class in the public school movement.

In continuation of our review of school district No. 2 we find that on the 1st day of May, 1854, four of the six members of the school board resigned, one at a time, commencing with Jacob Butler whose place was filled by Mr. A. Dunsmore; then F. Thurston, whose place was filled by S. B. Hill; then Joseph Bridgman stepped down and out and was succeeded by Mrs. S. G. Stein; lastly Rev. Robbins the president of the board, resigned and his place was filled by Mr. Henry Reese. These men had worked hard to keep the social standing up to a high position and they felt as though they were crowded out by a lot of citizens who had little or no interest in the schools. They then turned their attention elsewhere, they got up a company and built a large frame house on the west side of Iowa Avenue at the corner of 5th street, which was known as the Stone school house; they employed a Mr. Stone and opened an academy. This school was not a paying investment and was closed. Other parties got hold of it and tried to run it, but the public schools proved too much for it. One cold morning when the thermometer was 30° below zero it burned down and was never rebuilt. Many of us recollect the Stone school house and the beautiful lake, Siler's pond, near by, both have disappeared.

But to return to No. 2, the first thing the new board did was to rehire the teachers the old board had secured. At their second meeting they appointed a committee to settle with Mr. O'Connor who had been secretary some two years previous. A settlement was not had with Mr. O'Connor until sometime afterwards, and then the balance was paid in attorney fees in a suit between the two school districts. I don't nose what they were lawing about, the record doesn't tell. Mr. Abel Fry was appointed collector for the district.

In those days the school directors had to do something for the honor of being officers. They got no pay. I notice that on June 5, 1854, a committee of three were appointed to examine the different school rooms, to arrange the scholars and equalize the numbers in the different departments. This was not necessary while Mr. Denison was the principal. I wonder how it would suit our present medical school board to have to put in their time on such an arrangement.

In July, 1854, Mr. Purcell withdrew from the board and Charles Nealey was appointed in his stead. The teachers during the season of 1854 were A. B. Tuttle principal, with Mrs. Dennis and Miss Walker as assistants.

At the November, 1854, meeting a move was made to change the teachers, and on December 9th they employed Mr G. B. Denison as principal, Miss Merrill and Miss Jones as assistants. The appointment of Mr. Denison did not suit the Robbins faction, and December 19th "a remonstrance was presented, signed by more than thirty citizen of the district against the action of the board in hiring Mr. Denison as a teacher." The remonstrance was referred to a committee consisting of Henry Reese and J. P. Freeman, who made their report at the meeting following, it was placed on file, and Denison kept on teaching all the same.

At the April election in 1855, the board consisted of Henry Reece, J. P. Freeman, S. B. Hill, C. Neally, A. Jackson, and J. A. Green. At the first meeting of this board the following bills were allowed for janitor's fees: Ed. Couch $2.00, J. Birkshire $5.25, Aug. Springer $2.62. We may mention something of the character of these boys later,— they were nothing but boys then.

On April 28, 1855, the following teachers were employed: N. F. Hoag principal, Miss Lydia E. Denison and Mrs. Julia N. B. Walton assistants. A list of the text books used were: Cutter's physiology, Mitchell's geogra phy, Pinneas' grammar, Wilson's history's and Parley's illustrated history, Burrit's astronomy, Davies geometery, McGuffey's readers, Ray's arithmetic and algrebra, and Fulton and Eastman's bookkeeping.

August 30, 1855, the board appointed G. B. Denison a committee to settle up the old accounts and fix up a judgment standing in the court brought by LeGrand Byington against M. M. Berkshire. If I recollect aright Berkshire collected some taxes for the district that Byington considered incorrect and got relief by the court. He was afterwards paid $49.

On December 24, 1855, R. M. Burnett took the place of Henry Reece on the board; Charles Neally was elected president of the board, and J. A. Green secretary. A Mr. Gillman taught five weeks in the place of Mr. Hoag who was prevented from filling his term by sickness.

On April 4, 1856, Our Hon. Samuel McNutt was employed to teach the school at a salary of $500 a year, with Miss Upham and Miss Merrill as assistants. On April 25 G. B. Denison and S. G. Hill presented their certificates of election as directors, and Denison was appointed secretary. During that year he was quite exact in some of his entries, for instance "adjourned at 10 o'clock;" the next meeting "at 9 o'clock." He was undoubtedly the best secretary the district ever had. On December 25, 1856, Samuel McNutt resigned—a six month's school was enough for him at that time.

Ou January 8, 1857, Mr. Denison resigned his position as secretary and S. G. Hill was elected in his place. February 21, 1857, Moses Ingals was elected principal. At the end of the year Geo. Meason was added to the board, in whose place the minutes do not say. The records show that the teachers in December were Moses Ingals, Miss Upham, Miss Denison and Miss Maxwell.

January 2, 1856, a report was made that an eastern lady refused to come west and take a position as teacher on the ground of her inability to raise funds to pay her expenses; a draft for $50 was sent to her for traveling expenses and taken out of her salary. She proved a valuable teacher and remained some years. After getting married and leaving Muscatine she resumed teaching in the city of Des Moines for the remainder of her days; she died but a few months ago. At the January 2d meeting the rate of tuition was fixed at $2.50 per term or $7.50 per year for primary department for the intermediate $10.50, and the higher department $15 a year. A motion was also made and carried to expel all pupils who did not pay up.

There seems to have been a little jarring on the board in some way, quite likely between Butler and Denison, for Butler offered a resolution to have some of the entries made by Denison in the school registry expurged from the registry, as being irrelevant and only the opinion of Mr. Denison. The restlution was laid on the table. Mr. Denison was employed to write up the "registry of scool monies" at an expense of not to exceed $10.

The last entry in the old book was a record of the salaries paid to the teachers; Moses Ingalls $266,67; Miss Pepper $65.30, Miss Denison $100, Miss Upham $100, Miss Merrill $21. This was for one term or one-third of a year; while the salaries of the teachers were much lower at this time the expense to the pupil was much more. Then the poor man had to pay for the schooling of his boy, now the rich man pays for schooling the poor man's boy, and in many esses the poor man keeps growling about some imaginary wrong, especially if his boy don't get a good education for the want of time to attend school.

During the period from 1850 to 1860, while the public school system was in its infancy, we had a great number of private schools, frequently several at a time; they were generally quite ephemeral, "but they were here all the same."

Recollections of

Persons and Events Connected with our Schools in Early Times.

Published in the Muscatine Saturday Mail, November 26, 1898.
Written by J. P. Walton.

No. 94.

In our last we promised to say something about the schools of our city previous to 1865. The public schools were being developed, they had just become free schools, in fact, no tuition was collected after that time. The teachers salaries and the running expenses were raised then as now by taxation. In 1865 there were between 600 and 700 pupils with sixteen or seventeen teachers, There are now, during the fall term about 2,300, in the winter term it will reach 2,800, with fifty-seven teachers. The public schools have gained such a hold on the people that no private school in the city exists, save the two parochial schools of the Catholic churches with about 150 pupils, and a Normal school taught by Prof. Leverich of from 30 to 50 pupils—in all less than 200 go elsewhere. The question, how did this come? we will answer by saying that those school fathers, as we will call them, who organized and conducted our schools through their earlier days are undoubtely the parents of this generous school system. In looking over the names of these directors we find the imprint of New England deeply stamped on all of them either by inheritance or by their associations. In district No. 2 the three first directors were probably not natives of the New England states, but before they commenced to run the school it went into the hands of Mr. G. B. Denison, who although a native of New York was said to be a lineal descendant of that old Massachusetts magistrate, Daniel Dennison. Mr. Denison was thoroughly familiar with the free school system of New England which at that time extended over all the Northern states; he was a man of personality and magnetism that would almost always influence any one he associated with to believe that his was the correct way. It was so with this school; the directors were good men, they were willing to let Mr. Denison "run the machine," for they thought he knew how. Results have proven that they made no serious mistake. School matters went along quite smoothly until a man of equal personality was elected on the school board, Rev. A. B. Robbins, then the trouble began. In our extracts from the old school records in a former contribution we have reviewed their differences quite fully.

After Mr. Denison left school No. 2, he was elected county superintendent and served some three or four years. He then went into the school book business as traveling book agent; his duty was to visit all the school houses in this territory and talk school books and education, and to introduce and sell books. In the rural parts of Iowa he found things quite different from our city, the country was thinly settled although an abundance of school houses were built or in the expectation of being built. The land had largely been entered by speculators who did not improve it, they simply held it and paid the taxes on it, The settlers gave them all the taxes they wanted, they assessed the non-resident property up to its full value and built school houses, and supported the schools largely on the taxes. The lands were frequently sold for the taxes, there were always enough buyers, the profits were large and the title good if the proper legal proceedings were followed, which the school boards were careful should be done. Such was the condition of the school system that met Mr. Denison, who undoubtedly ressoned that if the land is going to be sold why not go in for some, and he did quite largely and very profitably.

These western people were not all the parties that practiced taxing non-residents, for while in New England some three years ago my attention was called to a tract of land for sale very cheap. I thought of buying it on a speculation, but on enquiring about the taxes I was informed that the assessment on land like that if it belonged to an non-resident would be double that of a resident. I found that the New England people had acquired the early western way of taxation.

Mr. Denison married Miss Margaret Lyons, a former teacher in district No. 1, and was a resident of this city at the time of his death. He left a wife and daughter, the latter is now Mrs. Edna Denison Blackwell. Both are residents of our city.— Mr. Denison was the most active and prominent school man in our city during the early days of our schools.

District No. 2 had in the person of Rev. A. B. Robbins a most excellent school man; he was a native of Massachusetts, came west shortly after leaving college, organized the present Congregational church, and was its minister for more than fifty years. For the short time he was president of the school board the schools inhaled a moral influence that remained for a long time. While Rev. Robbins was a very mild speaking man, he was in the estimation of many people a good deal of an autocrat. If things did not go his way in the church or in the school, he at once denounced them. I have often heard it remarked that he was the greatest leader in the city; he managed in some way to have the turbulent or unruly members leave the church without resorting to arbitrary measures. It was said that at one time there was not a democrat belonged to his church, Mr. Robbins being an outspoken republican; he was strongly opposed to slavery. I recollect hearing him preach a sermon recommending every one to read Mrs. Stowe's book, "Uncle Tom's Cabin." The effect of this was he soon was known by the cognomen of "Uncle Tom," and the church as "Uncle Tom's Cabin." Mr. Robbins was always a school man, for many years was a trustee of the Congregational College at Grinnell.

On May 15, 1854, four of the board of directors of No. 2 resigned; they were Rev. Robbins, F. Thurston, J. Butler, and Jos. Bridgman. Franklin Thurston was a man of considerable prominence, for many years a bookkeeper for Gen. J. G. Gordon. He married Miss Margaret Reece of our town and raised a family of two daughters, one married Mr. E. H. Dolsen of the firm of Thurston & Dolsen, the other married John D. Hopkinson, and after his death she married Louis Maxson.

Jacob Butler was a lawyer of prominence and, in his time, one of our most public spirited citizens. He was a little hasty and impulsive but a good thinker; he accumulated considerable property and thought our city not large enough, so he went to Chicago, where he was unfortunate and lost most of his wealth.

Joseph Bridgman was the fourth school director to resign; he was a merchant; as I have written him up in a former contribution, I will only say that he was secretary for that year, and that when he commenced the writing was very plain, but as unrest in the district began to develop the secretary undoubtedly began to get nervous—the writing shows it—the minutes of the last few meetings he recorded can hardly be read. For my part as a reader of them I was glad when S. G. Stein was elected secretary. If I recollect aright, all of these four old members were attendants at Mr. Robbin's church. I think the other two remaining members, Alfred Purcell and J. P. Freeman, were not regular attendants at any church. Mr. Purcell was an outspoken man, always willing to advocate his convictions; he was a strong whig and loved to discuss politics. He married a daughter of "Uncle William Parvin, an old "moss-backed" democrat, who was so incensed at the marriage of his daughter to a whig he would not stay in town on the day of the wedding—he went a hunting. The same conditions existed when the other director, J. P. Freeman, another outspoken abolitionist, married another daughter—"Uncle Billy" he went a hunting again.

Recollections of

Persons and Events Connected with our Schools in Early Times.

Published in the Muscatine Saturday Mail, December 3, 1898.
Written by J. P. Walton.

No. 95.

When we began the review of the public schools, we did not expect to devote so much time and space to their consideration. We offer as an apology that, in our opinion, there is no one institution that has as much influence over the public well being as our schools; hence we hope our review will prove interesting to the readers.

On May 1st, 1854, four new directors became members of the school board in old No. 2 district. They were Alexander Dunsmore, S. B. Hill, Henry Reece, and S.

G. Stein. Mr. Dunsmore was a Scotchman and a merchant; he probably came here about 1843 or '44; he kept a general stock of merchandise; his store was on the south side of Second street, west of tne avenue; his residence was on west Fourth street, east of Ash street; his daughter Miss Louisa Dunsmore still lives in the same locality that her parents did many years ago. "Alec," as he was called, was a splendid man, straightforward and honorable in all his dealings. He, like many other merchants of our early time, did not get rich as fast as he wanted to; of course he had to deal largely on credit, for a year's stock of goods had to be laid in while navigation was open, the farmers paying for their goods the following winter with products of their farms. The year 1857 proved a bad year for the farmer; he did not raise much to sell—of course he could not pay. In the fall and winter a panic set in, the merchants could not meet their engagements and large numbers went by the board, and Mr. Dunsmore was one of them.

Mr. S. B. Hill was a native of New England, a carpenter by trade and a contractor by occupation. His first job was building the dwelling on the northeast corner of Third and Cherry streets for Messrs. Green & Stone; he also built many valuable buildings. He died quite recently, leaving a widow and one or more children.

S. G. Stein came here about 1852 and bought out S. S. Branham's lumber yard on the corner of Pine and Second street, which has been known as Stein's lumber yard ever since, at least 46 years. Since the death of Mr. Stein, his son, Dr. S. G. Stein, continues it.

Henry Reece, who was elected president of the board, was a native of Eastern Pennsylvania or New Jersey; he come to Bloomington as early as 1836, perhaps 1835. He was one of three brothers and two sisters, that came here with their mother, who, I think, was the first white woman that came to our city. Henry Reece was a carpenter; he and his brothers built a good sized two-story frame house for the family to live in; it stood between Front and Second streets, near Broadway. I think it was the first frame building in the city. After standing some ten or twelve years, the ground commenced to slide towards the river, it soon got on some other man's lot and the house stood at a very undesirable angle and had to be taken down. Mr. Reece occupied various places of trust; he served a term as postmaster; he kept the postoffice in Freeman's old frame builing on the southeast corner of Sycamore and Second streets. He raised a family, of which only one or two children survive him.

Let me say right here that I consider the Reece family, consisting of "Mother Reece," her three sons, Henry, John, Joseph, and two daughters, Margaret Reece and Mrs. Beaumont, were the best fitted to build up a new town in a new country, of any family in the town. They were large sized, strong, healthy, pleasant and accommodating. When four out of five persons suffered with sickness they were the fifth ones and did not suffer. Their helping hands were always extended to the needy. I don't know but we are getting away from the schools a little, but we are in the town all the same.

The teachers secured to succeed Mr. Denison were Mr. A. B. Tuttle, Mrs. Dennis and Miss Walker. Of the two latter I know nothing. Mr. Tuttle was a native of Herkimer county, N. Y.; his parents were natives of Connecticut. He graduated from Hamilton college in the class of 1851; he came to Muscatine in 1854 to accept the principalship of school No. 2. He was admitted to the bar here. In 1856 he settled in Clear Lake, Iowa, in company with a younger brother. In 1863 he moved to Mason City, Iowa, and went into the mercantile business. He died there September 29, 1898.

The two next directors elected were Charles Neally and Henry O'Conner. Charles Neally was one of our early settlers: he probably came from New England. I think he tried farming a short time out on the Lucas Grove road, but gave it up and came to town to live. He was engaged in the boot and shoe and leather business in 1850, on the north side of Second street, west of Sycamore. He lived in one of those two story brick buildings on Third street, west of Sycamore. While acting as school director he was serving the city as alderman from the Second ward. He was one of the substantial members of the Presbyterian church; when the present church was being built in 1856 and '57, he paid the bills. I have understood he paid out money faster than he collected it—advanced for them—and it was a long time before he got it back. He continued in business for some ten years. I find his name in the directories of 1856 and '59. In 1869 he is not mentioned; his son Charles was in the notion business at that time. He had a daughter Clara, who married Thomas Vail, the son of Bishop Vail of Kansas. They lived in Topeka. Mr. Neally was a tall, dignified man; he never mingled much with common people; most of his time was devoted to his family.

We must make a mention of Henry O'Conner. He was an Irishman by birth; in early days he followed tailoring for a livelihood. At the age of 20 he came to America. My first recollection of him was in the law business with D. C. Cloud, the firm name being Cloud & O'Conner. This firm at one time, say from 1850 to 1860, did about as much legal business as all the other lawyers: it was seldom that a case occurred that they did not appear in it in some way. As a school director O'Conner was a failure. He was secretary for near a year. If he kept any minutes they do not appear in the record book. For a brief review of his public life I make this extract from Burrell, of the Washington Press: "He served as private in the civil war, in the First Iowa regiment, and became major in the 35th. He was district attorney, for six years attorney general of Iowa, and solicitor for the state department in Washington under Garfield & Arthur. He was brilliant, witty, whole-souled and eloquent." Mr. O'Conner married a sister of S. B. Hill, and raised a family of children, one of whom is living in Sioux City. Mr. and Mrs. O'Conner have recently resided with them.

Recollections of

PERSONS AND EVENTS CONNECTED WITH OUR SCHOOLS IN EARLY TIMES.

Published in the Muscatine Saturday Mail, Dec. 10 and 17, 1898; written by J. P. Walton.

Nos. 96 and 97.

We notice among the directors of school No. 2 the name of Hon. George Mason. He was a native of Pennsylvania, a brother-in-law of Hon. Jeseph Williams and Hon. John H. Wallace. Mason was our County Judge for some time. His family consisted of one son and six daughters. Mr. Mason very sensibly concluded that duty called him to Iowa, and here he came—a good place for a man with such a family. The daughters all married in due time, giving him the following list of sons-in-law: Col. Ben. Beach, Fred Bridgeman, Alien Broomhall, J. E. Coe, S. E. Whicher and F. E. Blackman. Mason was in good shape to be elected to any office, and was elected to the office of mayor in the years 1858, '59, '60, '61, '62, and '67. His first election was not due to his sons-in-law, the daughters were not married at that time—it came about in this way: Politics at that time did not always control the voters in the city election. John G. Steine, the incumbent, was a very coarse and unpopular man with some classes; he was a democrat in every sense of the word, so far as he knew how to be; he drank his share of the democratic beverage, smoked and always kept his white shirt bosom covered with tobacco saliva. There was another democrat by the name of General Humphreys who wanted the place and he had some following. Mason was a republican. Then any one could run for office if he paid a dollar to pay the newspaper to have his name announced. In this case a couple of republicans paid for announcing Humphrey's name—this divided the democrats and Mason was elected. He made a desirable mayor and retained the office longer than any one did before or since.

In one of my former articles I promised to mention the young men who drew pay for attending to old No. 2 school house as janitors—Edward Couch, John Berkshire and Augustus Springer. The latter was the son of Louis Springer, one of our early plasterers; he was a native of Germany and came here when quite young; as soon as he was large enough he went to work at engineering, for a long time living at Des Moines but now is farming in northern Dakota.

"Ed Couch" was a native of our city, an active energetic boy but quite wild and impulsive; would go into anything he took a notion to, irrespective of the possible results. He undertook the principalship of school No. 1, so the records say; after two week's trial he gave it up. When the civil war broke out Ed. enlisted, served full time and came out without a scratch or a day's sickness. As a soldier he was a hustler, one of the best bummers in the army. In his later days he followed selling agricultural implements for the various dealers in our city. He died recently.

John Berkshire was a native of Sweetland township in this county, born in 1839; he was the son of M. M. Berkshire, one of the first secretaries of school district No. 2; he got his education in our town, and when old enough he commenced to learn the trade of running an engine with Mr. Charles Chaplin, the veteran engineer of our city; During the war he was an assistant with him on the Missouri river, Mr. Chaplin tells the story of John's return to Muscatine about this way: John had worked a while in the Hershey saw mill before going with Mr. Chaplin to run on a steamboat on the Missouri river, where Mr. Chplain succeeded in getting him a second engineer's license. They run on the Missouri river one or more seasons, when Mr. Chaplin concluded to return to Muscatine, he went to the inspector at St. Louis and secured John a head engineer's license. John then arranged to run the boat they were on as cheif engineer, but had to lay off a few days and come home. He was not 21 years old. Mr. Chaplin says that first-class papers were never given to so young a man before. While here he met Mr. Hershey, and boy like, he commenced to brag of his job. Mr. Hershey heard him until he got through, when he said, "John, what will you take and come and run my mill?" John answered he did not know, and asked how much he would give. Hershey's reply was I "will give you $2,000 a year and board you." John staid with Mr. Hershey, and as fast as he earned money he took stock in the Hershey Lumber Company, and had charge of both mills. After the death of

Mr. Hershey he sold his stock and invested in a hard pine saw mill in Winona, Mo. He is the principal manager and resides there. John's steamboat run on the Missouri was not the only thing that interested him in that direction, a good looking dark eyed girl claimed a share of his attention. On one of John's visits to Missouri she returned with him and put a stop to his boarding with Mr. Hershey. They have two children, a son whom he has educated very highly in Technology, he is a fine mechanic; and a daughter that is married to Mr. Cherry of What Cheer. From the janitorship of No. 2 school to the superintendency of a plant like Hershey Lumber Company's is a wide step for one poor boy to make, but does occasionally occur in this liberal land of ours.

There were a number of teachers—a Miss E. Jones, Miss E. N. Merrill, Mrs. Julia N. B. Walton, Miss Upham, Miss Maxwell, Mr. N. F. Hoag, and perhaps others—that I can't tell much about.

Miss Lydia Denison, a sister of G. B. Denison, taught several terms in old No. 2. She was one of the best teachers that the school ever had. She married Whitney Olds. She died in Chicago in 1865. Miss Clarissa Denison, another sister of G. B. Denison, taught in our schools and married Mr. James M. Coleman and went to the state of Washington to live, where he recently died.

Mr. Moses Ingals taught as principal for two or three years with fair success. He left here and went to St. Louis where he went into some other business.

No. 2 school had one teacher we should not overlook, Hon. Samuel McNutt. He was born November 21, 1825, in Londonderry, Ireland, of Scottish decent. When only a small boy he came to Delaware; after obtaining an education he commenced teaching and studying law, and in 1851 he came west; later he held a professorship in a college in Mississippi. In 1854 he came to Muscatine and taught in old No 2. His next business venture was in the Democratic Enquirer of the firm name of McNutt & Biles. I recollect Mc's debut here, it was in a lyceum or debating society; it was held in the third story of the old Masonic building on Second street. He was one of our champions, as he was about the only professional man in the society which was composed of common men. After McNutt left here he went to Dubuque and took an interest in the Herald and later the Times. In 1862 he came back and went to farming. He served ten years in the state legislature; since then he has filled several places of trust, having been appointed U. S. Consul to Maracaybo, in Venezuela, South America. After making a trip there he wisely concluded he was not suited for the place and resigned. He is now filling the place of Justice of the Peace. In 1857 he married Miss Anna Lucas, a niece of Robert Lucas the first governor of Iowa. They had three children, William, Samuel and Robert; the latter is now in the dentist business in our city.

Previous to 1858 the two school districts, Nos. 1 and 2, were separate, Sycamore street being the dividing line. Both of the schools started out under favorable circumstances. No. 1 had Prof. D. Franklin Wells as principal. He was followed very shortly by Dr. D, H. Goodno. No. 2 had G. B. Denison for some four years. After his retirement the school had a variety of teachers. The result was, No, 1 stood a long way ahead educationally. No. 2 had a financial advantage over No. 1. It had twice the taxable property and not more than perhaps half the number of scholars. As a result No. 2 had a smaller schoolhouse and considerable money in the treasury, while No. 1 had a much larger building and larger number of scholars, with a debt. We in No. 1, expected when we united that we would have a common interest with No. 2, but such was not the case. No. 2 succeeded in getting a majority on the board of directors, who levied a special tax on No. 1 to pay their debt, and instead of dividing the surplus money that No. 2 had. they managed to use it up for some imaginary need on their school-house or grounds.

We have managed to keep politics and religion out of our schools quite well. During the war of the rebelion the democrats got control of the school board and removed most of the outspoken republican teachers, especially those who had taken a part in the Soldiers' Aid Society, and supplied their places with democrats. "When Johnny came marching home" the former teachers again got their places.

The directors at this time were H. W. Moore, president; J. H. Wallace, secretary; M. Block, treasurer; J. B. Dougherty, S. Smalley, G. A. Garrettson, and Charles Page, all democrats but Dougherty. W. H. Hoopes was employed as principal in No. 2. The Hoopeses at that time were all democrats, but strange to say, many of them have changed their political faith since.

The law allowed the negroes to send their children to the public schools. The board as yet had failed to provide a special school for them, so Mr A. Clark, a prominent colored man of our city, sent his children to Mr. Hoopes to school. The darkey did not trouble William very much, but several of the patrons did object, so William went to one of the directors, Mr. Garrettson, who said "If Clark sends his children there, kick the d—d niggers down stairs, and I will pay the bill:" The directors then rented the colored church and opened a colored school and compelled the colored patrons to send their children there. Mr. Clark got tired of that and sent his children to the other schools. Of course his case soon got into the courts, where the darkey came out ahead. The school board concluded that if they could not force the darkies to go to a special school they would not keep one up for them, therefore the school was abandoned much to the relief of the tax payers. They were generally seated by themselves and no further objections were raised to their attendance in the common schools.

At one time the Methodists got control of the school board to such an extent, that is was almost impossible for any but Methodist teachers to get places. A year or two rectified that error, if it was one.

The law requires two directors to be elected each year to serve for a term of three years. At an early time the school boards were quite harmonious and they did not want any change, so they got into a habit of printing the tickets always continuing themselves in office, and calling on the voters to elect them. This scheme was worked for several years. On one occasion a party of voters concluded they wanted a change, so they selected a couple of good men as candidates, got tickets printed headed "The New School Directors." They did not show them until the morning of election. When a man came up to vote he had his choice, the old ticket or the new one. Almost every one voted the new one, and the new ones were elected, much to the chagrin of the old ones, especially to one that was a merchant, who had been in the habit of trading goods for teachers' orders and presenting them to the treasurer and having them accepted, so as to draw interest until paid. He had managed it so as to handle a large amount of the teachers' fund. When he was out his jig was up. The new directors went to the bank and arranged to have them cash the orders and draw the interest. Ever since that time the teacher has received the cash as soon as it was earned. Previous to that time they got but little or no money without they sold their orders at a discount. A teacher that would not trade out her orders stood a poor chance of continuace.

Old No 1 school house was a two-story brick building, 42x65 feet with a square bell tower. It had a brick turreted cornice and deserved the name of castle rather than temple of learning. D. Franklin Wells was its first principal, who left and was followed by others, as before stated. On March 22. 1858, Dr. D. H. Goodno was employed. He taught until the breaking out of the war, when he was appointed adjutant of the 37th regiment of Iowa volunteers, probably in 1862. Dr. Goodno was a dentist by profession; he had practiced dentistry in Boston, Mass.; was a staunch Methodist although his wife was or had been an Episcopalian; he was probably the strictest disciplinarian of any teacher the city ever had. Even the soldiers of the 37th (Graybeard) regiment, called him an old tyrant; but as a teacher he was a success. He held the position of county superintendent for two or more years.

Dr. Goodno was succeeded in No. 1 by Daniel W. Lewis, who afterwards went to Washington, Iowa and took charge of their schools for several years.

On July 2, 1868, old No. 1 was struck by lightning and burned down, having some $8,000 insurance. The companies declined to settle at once, and some delay in rebuilding was the result. The city then had to depend on renting. The old pop factory, a building standing on the south side of Fourth street, east of Orange, was used.

The ground occupied by old No. 1 was originally a burying ground for the city. There were from 50 to 100 graves scattered around on top of the hill, that had not been removed. The school house was set on top of the ground without disturbing them. When it came to rebuilding the school house it was considered necessary to grade off the top of the hill some twelve feet or more. In the process a great many bones were exhumed, which were gathered up and reburied in the present cemetery. The present Third ward school house was built on the former site of No. 1 in 1870 Since then it has had the roof and third story burned off and replaced. After grading 12 or 15 feet from the top of the hill, it is yet too high, according to the ideas of our city authorities, who seem determined to make a prairie town out of a hilly village. They have cut the street some twelve or more feet in front of the school house for really no benefit to any one but the builder of a huge hump backed stone wall. This stone wall is one of the most outrageous architectural abortions ever erected in our city. We do not know who is responsible for it. Not the builder, for it cost him nearly double the work to build it in that shape to what it would to have run the courses straight, without the hump, making square offsets when necessary. The wall will stand; it is a pity it will, for the sooner it falls down the sooner we will be rid of a bad architectural educator.

Recollections of

PERSONS AND EVENTS CONNECTED WITH OUR SCHOOLS IN EARLY TIMES.

Published in the Muscatine Saturday Mail, Dec. 24, 1898; written by
J. P. Walton.

No. 98.

We had intended to confine ourselves to the public schools, but one other school figured largely in our educational work—the Greenwood Academy. This building stood on the corner of Fifth street and Iowa Avenue. It was first erected by a joint stock company and was known as the Stone School House. It was a large two story frame building. A Mr. Stone first opened school there—it was built for him. He could not make it pay and had to give it up and leave the city. For a while it was used for a Universalist church.

In the summer of 1860, Mr. James L. Daymude came here, probably through the influence of Rev. John Ufford, the Episcopal minister, who was desirous of having an advanced school in our city. Mr. Daymude had just graduated at Kenyon College, Gambier, Ohio.

Mr. Daymude started his school in the autumn of 1860 and called it Greenwood Academy, in honor or Miss Grace Greenwood, a lady of some literary ability.

Its instrutors were—
J. L. Daymude, A.B., principal.
T. Brown, A. B., Geo. E. Fawcett and Willis Davis, assistants.

T. Brown was a graduate of Kenyon in the class of 1861, and like Daymude, came west at once and went to teaching. He is practicing law here at this time. After conducting the school for two or three years. Mr. Daymude left here and went into the insurance business in Davenport. When last heard from he was in Boston, Mass.

The school was what interested Muscatine the most. It was certainly a good one. Financially it was not a success, as it had to run against a public school where nothing was charged. It cost from $25 to $50 a year for tuition to attend this school. Was it worth more than a public school, was the question to be considered by most of its patrons.

Daymude had a very creditable catalogue published. As references he gave the names of twelve or fourteen of our most literary citizens. As an examining committee, he had enlisted several preachers and lawyers, and strange to say, many of them attended and engaged in the quarterly examinations.

The tuitions were per quarter, four terms a year: Primary, &c., $6.00; scientific, $8.00; collegiate preparatory, $10.00; music $12.00. "Boarding at private houses from $2.00 to $3.00 per week. Students can board themselves at a much cheaper rate."

Among the students now living who attended this school, we find such persons as John Bell Dougherty, Jesse C. Adams, William Barnard, Audley G. Butler, William Norman Butler, Charlie Cadle, William S. Chambers, Marshal Chambers, Frank W. Eichelberger, Hamilton Fay, Frank Freeman. Abe S. Funk, William Henry Hoopes, Edwin Webb Norton, Will H. Hughes, Charles B. Ogilvie, William H. Reeder, Com. U. S. N., Clayton Scott Richman, Com. U. S. N., Horace Robbins, Albert Sibley, Niles S. Sherfey, George R. Warfield, Lisle Cummins Waters, David Worsham, Willie Block, Gardner Gordon, E. Frank Richman, William Ziegler, Charlie O'Connor, Charles Nealley, and others we cannot locate.

Among the ladies who are now living, perhaps having different names, are Ada M. Gordon, Mary Gordon, Hattie A. Garlock, Magie Kincaid, Willie A. McCormick, Lepha R Woodhouse, Ella B. Woodward, Nellie M. Barrows, Hattie A. Barrows, Sarah A. Chambers, Maria A. Dunsmore, Ella Fay, Rebecca Hoopes, Clara Isett, Ella F. Lemp, Clara M. Martin, Emma Olds, and Mary L. Brent.

The first annual catalogue contains the names of 52 students, and the second has 106 names. The school terms closed June 26, 1863. I don't know when the school finally closed, but am inclined to think it was running until the High School was started in 1864. When Mr. Daymude gave up school teaching, Greenwood Academy was ended.

When the City High School was organized in 1864, it occupied this building for one year.

In the directory of 1866, I find that a stock company was organized under the name of Muscatine Academy to occupy this building, with T. Brown as principal, J. B. Dougherty, sr., as president. T. Hanna, sec'y and treasurar, and J. Butler, J. P. Ament and S. Foster as trustees.

One cold morning, Feb. 10th, 1868, while the thermometer was

23 degrees below zero, this building burned down. But the Muscatine Academy seems to have been kept running, for in the directory of 1869 we find it occupying the third story of the building on the northeast corner of Iowa Avenue and Second street.

It is enough to say that when Greenwood Academy was in existence, it turned out some of our best men and women of the present time.

Among the students of Greenwood Academy was John Bell Dougherty, now Col. Dougherty. He is unmarried, and we are not going to examine the church register to find when he was baptized or to inquire how old he is. It is enough to say he was born in Muscatine, attended Trinity Sunday School and Greenwood Academy. He attended the sunday school because he loved his teacher and it was a pleasant place to go. He belonged to a class of some twelve or fifteen boys that did not have to go to Sunday school unless they wanted to. Some of them would have been considered a little wild; they always sat near the door, hadn't piety enough to venture up very far. They styled themselves the mission class. There was not a dull one among the lot. Sometimes the teacher was put to his wits end to keep ahead of them. On one occasion the teacher took a notion to go east, and was gone some three weeks. He promised his boys if they were good and attended sunday school while he was gone, he would remember them when he came back. On the Sunday after he got back they were all in their places. The teacher knew better than to inquire about their past conduct or attendance; enough for him to know that they were there. He remembered them with a Bible apiece, which he purchased in the east, and they all appreciated it. Col. John Bell Dougherty has his now, and says "it is nearly as good as new."

When John got through with Greenwood Academy he went to Chicago to complete his education. His school was some three miles from his boarding place, and he had to make the trip at least once a day. There were no street cars then, an omnibus line being the public conveyance, which took money, and John's purse became exhausted. The stipends sent from home got low, and many a time he had to walk for a whole week, being minus the omnibus fare.

When John started from home, his mother fitted out his trunk, putting his Bible therein, and received a promise from her boy that he would read it, which of course was made in good faith. After his return she examined his trunk and in his presence opened the Bible, and to John's surprise found a five-dollar bill that she had put inside of it before he started. She always had doubts about his reading it while away. Her mind now was entirely clear on that subject.

Well, Johnnie is now a man. He learned to make pills from his father, in the drug store run under the name of J. B. Dougherty & Son, later becoming known as J. B. Dougherty's drug store. He eventually became Colonel Dougherty, holding a commission on the Governor's staff,—and I never knew that his head was in any way disturbed by the appointment. He is a director of the First National Bank, and has often been spoken of as a candidate for some of our municipal offices, but has invariably declined —being too modest to assume the honor, I suppose.

Recollections of
Some of the Leading Families of the County.
THE STEINBERGER FAMILY.

Published in the Muscatine Saturday Mail Dec. 31, 1898; written by J P. Walton.

No. 99.

On the 4th day of July, 1838, Iowa became a territory, and to it came a governor in the person of Robert Lucas. He was a native of the Shanandoah valley in Virginia somewhere, near Harper's Ferry. Shortly after his arrival, his sister, Mrs. Levisa Steinberger came, about the year 1840, and with her, five daughters. These daughters all married, some being married before they came. The oldest one, Elizabeth, was married in Ohio to George Porter; the second, Mary B. to H. Q. Jennison; the third, Rebecca, married William Miller; the fourth, Levisa, married G. W. Kincaid, the fifth, Joanna L. married David R. Warfield.

The name of Steinberger in is spelled four or five different ways. I presume each son-in-law spelling it differently, in fact each family of the descendents of the old lady spell it in a different way. The Kincaids spell it Steinberger.

Mr. Porter's family came here probably about 1845, and he opened a store under the name of

Porter & Lucas. John W. Lucas, his partner in business, married his daughter Mary in Ohio. Mr. Lucas evidently came from Virginia. He had been reared in the F. F. V. style and had not been away long enough to wear any of it off if he had desired it. On the contrary, he put on all the style his circumstances would permit of. I don't think the store run a great while, probably two or three years. Lucas, who should have managed it, did not appear to have been suited for it. He was a staunch democrat and was on hand to share in the good things of the party. He secured a position as clerk in the surveyor general's office and was holding it in 1856. From 1858 to 1862, four years, he held the office of county treasurer and recorder, the two offices then being filled by the same official. His chances for making money were in many instances quite good, but his mode of living prevented his acquiring much property. He died some ten or fifteen years ago, his wife having preceded him.

Mr. Porter had another daughter, Miss Levisa S., who married a Mr. Mull and went to California, I think, where he has since died, leaving his widow in good circumstances.

Mr. Porter also had two sons, Charles S. and G. W.

Charles S. followed book-keeping. When the civil war broke out, he went into the army as a lieutenant. At the close of the war he engaged with the boot and shoe firm of Davidson & Roach. In 1876 we find him engaged with T. S. Stewart under the title of Stewart & Porter, in the boot and shoe business; in 1886 he was in the same business by himself; in 1888 he appears to have gone out of business and left the city. I think he went into the banking business with his son-in-law, Frank R. Lewis, at Algona, Iowa, and later in McPherson, Kansas, where the son-in-law has since died.

His younger son, G. W., we have here with us, in the newspaper business and can speak for himself. While he is but a grandson of the Steinberger family, we will venture to look up his record a little, at least we have consulted our old directories. We find him in 1874, a printer residing on Fourth street west of Linn; in 1876 we find he has moved to 108 East Seventh street, still following printing; in 1879 we find him located at the northwest corner of Sixth and Orange streets, having thrown away the printer's stick and taken up a wooden one, gone to dealing in wood. If we recollect rightly, we used to see him hauling pine wood with a beautiful team of light grays. In 1885 he has changed his residence to 616 E. Seventh St., and is known as contractor. In 1891 we find him still living on Seventh street, but is put down as business manager of the News-Tribune. He has struck a better job and has his name in bold black letters, which is an indication that he has subscribed for a directory, the way a directory maker has of rewarding his subscribers. He is still with the News-Tribune, but has changed his residence to 605 East Sixth street.

When young, William got the name of being quite wild—nothing mean about him, but he was unforunate in being the younger son of an old Methodist class-leader, who possessed little or no gift of providing wholesome amusement for a young irrepressible boy. At the death of his father he was under the influence of an older brother, who had little time and inclination to devote to William, who was allowed to "grow up" as best he could. His first work was carrying newspapers, from thence to "Devil" in the office, and then printer. He married Miss Laura Van Buren and has a family of children, two boys and two girls. The eldest son, Lemoyne, is now bookkeeper for the Muscatine Oat Meal Company, The youngest, George, is bill clerk at the Muscatine Sash and Door Company's plant.

As before stated, George Porter was a native of Ohio, and inherited the Virginian characteristics of his ancestors, but had mingled enough with the outside world, not to show it. He was a man of some means and was disposed to take care of it when allowed to. After retiring from business, he took upon himself the management of the Methodist church, and for a long time he could have been seen stubbing around the street, cane in hand, buying wood, etc., for the church. At church he always sat in the "Amen corner" to lead in the singing for which he had no equal.

We find Mrs. Elizabeth Porter living on Front street, east of Cedar in 1875, her husband, George, having died in January, 1867. For the time that he had lived here, nearly twenty years, but few if any citizens were better known or more respected than George Porter.

The second Steinberger daughter married H. Q. Jennison, a native of Vermont, who came here at a very early day, probably 1839, bought a farm out along the Lucas grove road and perhaps lived there a while. Later he built a house on the south side of Second street, west of Cedar, and lived there. In 1855 he built the house east of the Episcopal church, now belonging to Mr. Echol, and lived there until he left the city.

When he first came here he was connected with F. H. Stone in the mercantile business. He was a topographical engineer by profession and was engaged in making surveys for some of the wild cat canals and railroads which Indiana and Illinois were going to build at the time he came here. He was engineer in charge of the first grade established by the city. It did not include the entire city, but was a satisfactory grade. Succeeding engineers and officials have changed it out of existence.

If my recollection is correct, he had a son, Charlie, and another, Walter, and a daughter Rebecca, who married a Mr. Cass who subsequently died in Chicago, and perhaps another child. H. O. Jennison and the son, Charles, are both dead. I am of the opinion that Mrs. Mary B. Jennison died in 1885 in Colorado. Walter is living in Ottawa, Indian Territory.

The third daughter, Rebecca Steinberger, married William H. Millar and came here about 1840; settled under the bluff about three miles west of the city; raised a family consisting of five children. The eldest, Charles S. Millar, lives on a farm in Seventy-six township. He married a daughter of Hon. G. D. McCloud and has a family of children. The second, John W. Millar, occupies the old homestead. He married Miss Henrietta Mikesell, who recently died. They had several children, two daughters who have some musical distinction, and now living in Chicago.

The third son, A. H. Millar, has five children, two sons and three daughters. He resides in the city and is engaged in the express business.

The fourth child, Polly, married Rev Emory Miller, and lives in Des Moines. They have two or more children.

The fifth child, Lou, married a Mr. Shade, and they live in Sioux City.

William Millar was a fine appearing, intelligent man, a native of Ohio, and supposed to be of Virginia stock, although the way of spelling the name with an "a" makes it difficult to locate nationality.

Mr. Millar occupied the position of Muscatine Island Levee Commissioner, to apply the funds arising from the sales of swamp lands on the Muscatine Island district, under an act of congress passed in 1850. He was a straight forward, fore-handed farmer. Not a man who desired a prominence he had not earned. He was a man respected by all who knew him. His wife died in 1880 and he followed her in 1885.

Recollections of

Some of the Leading Families of the County.

THE STEINBERGER FAMILY.

Concluded:

Published in the Muscatine Saturday Mail Jan. 7, 1899; written by
J. P. Walton.

No. 100.

Mrs. Steinberger's fifth daughter, Levisa S., married Colonel G. W. Kincaid January 18, 1838, came to Iowa in 1839, and commenced farming in Seventy-six township. Among the pioneers the place was known as "Fishing Gut." Mr. Kincaid was prominent at all of the public gatherings, and always had something to say. He usually spoke his convictions, although frequently making himself unpopular by so doing. While living at the "Fishing Gut" farm, he had a boy whom he had taken to raise. The boy ran away and nothing could be heard of him. Some evil disposed person perpetrated a huge joke, on both Kincaid and the neighbors, by starting a story that Kincaid had killed the boy and buried him in a corner of his field. This started the neighbors to digging in the corner to find the remains, which was continued for quite a while with —no find. This worried Kincaid and his family considerable, but as there appeared to be no remedy for it they were obliged to live it down. When the neighbors became acquainted with Kincaid they found that he was not dangerous, and they did not think it would take a very large field for his burying ground. They had "got on" to his way of talking, that gave rise to the sell that was perpetrated on them

Some twenty or more years later I happened to stay over night at a house in Cedar county where a young man was working. The young man discovered that I was from Muscatine, and after supper he called me aside and stated that he was the boy that ran away from Kincaid, and also told how he managed to get away and where he went. He requested me to inform Mr. Kincaid, which I did the first opportunity that offered, much to the apparent delight of the Colonel.

The Colonel lived some eight or ten years on the Seventy six township farm, and in 1843 he moved to what is now known as the Kincaid farm, some four miles west of the city. It suited the Colonel much better, as it was much nearer town, and he managed to have some business to bring him in every day or two. The fact was, that he was very sociable and the farm did not afford society enough.

When the civil war broke out, he took advantage of the Steinberger connection and obtained permission from Governor Kirkwood to do a thing never heard of before or since, to get up a "Gray Beard" regiment, which he did with good success. This regiment was composed of men over forty-five years of age, and was recruited from about every county in the state. It was my lot as commissioner to take the vote of the 37th or gray beard regiment while at Alton, Ills., doing guard duty in the old Illinois penitentiary. The voting was done in a single day, but the counting and making the returns took two more days. There were votes from about every county in the state, and returns had to be made for every county separately. The judges of election went back on the job, and I had to hire them to do it, paying them out of my own pocket before getting the returns completed.

When the second attempt was made at building a levee on the Muscatine Island from the proceeds of land sold under the swamp land act of 1850, Mr. Kincaid had the contract. Nearly the whole island had been sold at from fifty cents to one dollar an acre which rasied considerable money. For land that had been previously entered, warrants were issued to the levee fund, and they could be located on any other vacant land. Most, or all of them were located in the name of the county and were sold, the county taking the proceeds. Kincaid got some of it for his work. I doubt very much if he got all of his pay, but the price was large enough so he could stand a small loss. If there was any thing that had to be done where there was little or no financial remuneration connected with it, Kincaid could be relied on as taking a foremost part.

Mr. and Mrs. Kincaid have both acted on the board of trustees of the state asylum at Mt. Pleasant. I am of the opinion. that she was appointed after his death which occurred October 20, 1870.

Mrs. Kincaid was the youngest of five sisters, being born in 1819 in Ohio. She died quite recently in our city.

Their children were Joanna E., who married G. D. Magoon; Margaret L., who married J. A. Bishop; Charles S., William M. and Warren E.

The Kincaid family are recorded in three or more biographies that enter more minutely into the family records than we have space for.

The fourth daughter of Mrs. Steinberger, Joanna, married David R. Warfield in 1841 or '42, which event I think occured at the Kincaid farm in Seventy-six township.

They had five children, four of whom are now living: Alice C., who married Daniel Hayes; Geo. A., Frank and Charles L. who is now living in California. The first three are now residents of this city.

In David R. Warfield we had one of the pioneers in every sense of the word. He came to Iowa then the Black Hawk purchase of Wisconsin, late in November, by steamboat as far as Burlington, where the boat was stopped by ice in the river, and the trip to Bloomington, now Muscatine, was made overland. He was accompanied by his cousin, Asbury O. Warfield. Shortly after leaving Burlington David purchased a horse with saddle and bridle, which they took turns in riding. One would ride ahead and hitch the horse for the second one and then go ahead on foot, the second one taking the horse and riding until he came up with the first, and so on until Bloomington was reached, it taking some four days. After arriving here they began to look around for some investment. They selected a mill site on Mad creek above Tenth street, put in a dam and built a mill, but had hardly got it in opperation when the dam washed out. It was rebuilt but was washed out the second and third time. Asbury informed me that they had sunk $8,000 in the dam and mill before he gave it up. David R. kept it for some time, but eventually had to do as his cousin had done—sell out. It passed into the hands of the Brooks Brothers, Sherman and Hiram. They were mechanics and ran it with better success until the flood of 1851, which washed out so much of the dam that they never replaced it.

David R bought and improved a very fine farm adjoining the present county farm on the south; he also bought an out lot on Mulberry street, where the residence of Fred Daut and other buildings are located on Ninth street, including the Cedar Street School house. He had another cousin, Charles A. Warfield, who formerly owned the Chester Weed farm where Park Place is now situated.

This family of Warfield brothers brought the first colored people here, they were formerly slaves in the Warfield family in Maryland but were set free and brought out here. I think there were four men with their wives and children, if they had any. Most of us recollect old Ben Mathews, I think he had two brothers, Joe and Ed, and old uncle Daniel. They were all hard working and industrious colored citizens.

But to return to Mrs. Steinberger. She made her home most of the time with her daughter, Mrs. Kincaid. Not wishing to be dependent on her sons-in-law she had a small house built for her convenience on the farm of Col. Kincaid near the city, where she spent her declining years. She was the mother-in-law of five of the prominent persons of our community—while they are all gone their connections by marriage and their descendents number more people than any one family in our vicinity.

The following is an extract from an article prepared by Suel Foster:

"In December, 1836, I think it was near Christmas, I returned to Bloomington from a temporary trip, and was told that three men had been on the other side of the river for several days, and were anxious to get over. The ice was running so thick, that no one could cross. I found two men who were willing to venture in a skiff, to bring the three new settlers to Iowa. By this means, A. O. and D. R. Warfield and Captain Dunn were brought across in safety, and from that day became residents of the county. A. O. Warfield remarked that he and David had been in Bloomington a few days before the period of which I write, having walked from Burlington, the boats having stopped running. They had crossed over into Illinois, for provisions, preparatory to setting up bachelor's hall. They were on their return, laden with pork and other necessaries, which they had obtained of Stanton Prentiss, near the mouth of Copperas Creek, when the ice prevented their crossing. A. O. and Charles A. were brothers. D. R., the cousin, became interested with them in valuable tracts of land. In the spring of 1838, Asbury and David built a sawmill on Mad creek, near the northeast part of the town plat, where considerable lumber was sawed. During the 'Missouri War, Maj. D. R. Warfield was called out to defend his country, and he and I were messmates. In 1841, the Major married Miss Josephine Steinberger." The notices of the Major's life and death are uniformly eulogistic of a man who ever exerted a wide and beneficial influence. The last years of his life were devoted to farming. He died in April, 1872. Mrs. D. R. Warfield, wife of the pioneer, died January 8, 1875. She was one of the Steinberger sisters, a niece of Gov. Lucas, and filled a most enviable and admirable place in the society of early times. She came to Bloomington in 1840."

NOTE—The manner of spelling

the name prominently mentioned in the foregoing article, seems to have been a mooted question. Mrs. G. D. Magoon says she has talked with her grandmother about it, and the old lady spelled it "Steenbergen."

Recollections of

Some of the Leading Families of the County.

THE MAGOON FAMILY.

Published in the Muscatine Saturday Mail Jan. 14, 1899; written by J P. Walton.

No. 101.

In 1840, Isaac Magoon came here with his family, consisting of his wife Hannah, both natives of Massachusetts, two sons and six daughters. One son soon died, leaving only George D. to preserve the family name. The family strength was in the daughters. While but a portion of them were born in New England, they had the New England ideas of social equality, a fortunate condition for anyone in a new country, where the "previous condition" of a person is rarely if ever looked after. While they went in or made the best society, they were not troubled for fear they would not "get there." They were not wealthy but were cultured. In short, they were just such women as our young town wanted. Their names were Selencia, Maria, Eliza, Mary, Jane and Augusta.

The eldest, Selencia, married Abial Fry at Warsaw, Ills., in 1840, just before the family came here. Fry and his wife did not come here for some four or five years afterwards. She died in 1858, he much later.

Mr. Abial Fry was a very modest man for the business he followed, that of collecting. He collected the school taxes for many years for District No. 2, in which he lived. I think he acted as constable for a while. He was city marshal in 1854. The marshal collected the taxes at that time, but did not collect as many licenses as they do now. The town was glad to have people come here without licensing them for every little thing imaginable as is now the case. In 1862 he was city collector. Previous to the panic of 1857 there was a general credit system and settlements were made once a year if convenient. When settlement was not made promptly, the accounts were placed in Abial Fry's hands for collection on a small commission. He always made prompt remittances and gained a good standing. While the commission seemed quite small, Fry made and saved money. He happened to have a brother-in-law in or connected with the court house in the person of William Gordon, as sheriff, or Richard Cadle as clerk, who furnished him with a good many court house jobs, such as serving notices, bailiff for juries, etc. We find him in 1869 acting as deputy county treasurer.

In looking over our old directories, in 1856 we find him city marshal and boarding on the north side of Fifth street, west of Chestnut, at his brother-in-law's. A. J. Fimple. He appears to have boarded with him until about 1874, when we find him acting as overseer of the poor, with residence on the south side of Fouth street, west of Sycamore, the house occupied by the Episcopal Rectory. In 1859 he is mentioned as being a civil engineer and again boarding with Fimple. I think that engineering was his first occupation. In 1877 he is put down as bookkeeper and his residence at 11 East Third street.

The second daughter, Lydia Maria, married in 1841 a man by the name of Wheeler and lived in Warsaw, Ills., a short time. After his death, she came to Muscatine and married Andrew Jackson Fimple, who came here probably in 1844 from or near Harrisburgh, Pennsylvania.

Mr. Fimple was one of the unusual characters often found in a new country. He was a tailor by occupation, tall, slim and fine appearing, out spoken and a man that considered his honor of more importance than his religion. He had a great respect for his better half who would go to church, she being one of the first members of the Congregational church, organized in 1843. She attended regularly every Sunday, while he would just as soon go hunting. He acted on the old adage, "The better the day, the better the deed," and was willing to let the dictates of his conscience be his guide, often repeating the following quotation from Pope's Universal Prayer:

"What conscience dictates to be done.
 Or warns me not to do,
This, teach me more than hell to shun,
 That, more than heaven pursue."

He was somewhat selfish "all the same." We recollect about a party going with him on a hunting excursion. They were gone three or four days and killed an abundance of small game, squirels and ducks. One of the party killed a wild turkey. While they divided the small game by an unwritten law among hunters, the large game belonged to the one who killed it. The party consisted of some six or more gentlemen from our city. Fimple had not killed the turkey but wanted it. He suggested that they all throw in and buy the turkey, and then shoot it off, which they did. The turkey was owned by nearly every one of the party but Fimple. When he captured it he utterly refused to put it up again He informed them that he had been shooting for the turkey. This was the last act of the hunt as they had to start for home, and row their boat up stream about twelve miles. They arrived home that night, and Fimple had the turkey, but it cost him twice its value. I don't say what day it was, but I am inclined to think that while Fimple was shooting for the turkey Mrs. Fimple was attending Sunday school at the Congregational church. Fimple's tailor shop was the headquarters (club room) for all the liberal thinkers, in their discussions, he usually taking part. He was a fine tailor. At that time we had no ready made clothing dealers. The merchants brought the goods here and the tailor made them up. We recently took a stroll into one of our tailor shops to compare it with Fimple's. The first thing we met was a sewing machine with a tailor sitting at it sewing on a pair of pants at a speed that would have amazed old Andrew J., although he was a very fast workman. In Fimple's shop there was a bench somewhat higher than those in use now, a wood stove and a half dozen chairs, a lot of fashion plates hanging on the wall, but no extra goods. In those days the tailors had to carry their work home with them at night to prevent burglars breaking in and stealing it. Fimple's shop was no safer than others in that respect. Fimple would sponge his cloth, cut out his garment and mount up on the bench, sitting flat down and curling his feet up crossed under his knees, pin his work to his pants and sew all day. His work was not heavy or mentally laborious. He was pleased to have anyone come in and talk with him, which a great many did to the mutual advantage of both.

The first dress coat I ever wore I bought the goods of Chester Weed, and Fimple made it for me. I don't recollect what I paid. I got a pair of pants of another tailor, which at this time I could duplicate for six dollars, and gave him a fresh cow for them. The cow would at this time be worth twenty-five or thirty dollars.

Fimple stuck to his bench for several years and accumulated considerable property, but thinking his health would be better if he should get out a little more, changed his vocation and went into the ferry business with I. C. Day. They got the Apex built at Rock Island. Fimple rode on horseback to Rock Island, taking his horses with him to run the boat down the river. He got aground on a sandbar and it took several days to make the trip. When I. C., Day died Giles Pettibone, Day's brother-in-law bought Day's interest. When they became tired of the Apex, Pettibone went to Pittsburg and bought the ferry boat Muscatine, and loaded it with furniture for S. G. & P. Stein and brought it around. The peculiar build of this boat gave it the name of "The Turtle." A poem appeared in one of the papers, the authorship being attributed to E. Kline, a merchant of our city at that time, who resided on Front street and could see the boat cross the river to and fro.

THE FERRY BOAT.

A score or two of years ago
(I was about your age, I think my boy)
The old "hoss-boat" was found too slow,
And a new one made in the town of Troy.

She was made as strong as strong could be,
All in all the best that money bought—
Her plank were cut from the white oak tree,
The boilers of iron were toughly wrought.

Deck, bolt and pin, beam, rod and shaft,
Pipe, truck and kelson, rudder and wheel;
In truth, she was a wonderful craft
And sound as a dollar from top to heel

They named her—but what's a name,
Be it "Snorter," or "Daisy" or "Myrtle?"
She could and she would go just the same,
So they called her, and dubbed her "The Turtle."

The years moved on, and so did she,
And was very like the "The One-Hoss-Shay:"
The only difference here, you see,
The "Shay" broke down, she never gave way.

Boys grew men, lived and died,
But "The Turtle" ran on from shore to shore,
From bank to bank her trade she plied,
And many a load of teams she bore.

When Gabriel's trump shall sound at last
She will escape the general "mix,"
And still a ferry, staunch, strong and fast,
Will be run by Charon, on the river Styx.

While Mr. Fimple was ferryman he was an early riser. One morning he came down about the " peep o'day" and to his surprise he found his boat sunk with its deck under water. The news soon spread and a number of sympathizers and advisers were on hand. At some one's suggestion, Hobson's air bag scheme that he wished to apply on the Christopher Colon, was applied to the ferry boat in the shape of empty pork barrels. The hold below the deck was filled with them, but to no purpose, it would not float. Walton, with his then light apparatus. was called to its assistance and succeeded in getting it up.

On examination it was found that some miscreant had bored a two-inch augur hole in the bottom. Walton seeing the necessity of having heavier rigging for such work, went to Chicago and secured sufficient apparatus for any such an emergency, and had occasion to use it twice after that on the same boat, but for other parties, and has it yet for such purposes.

I think Mr. Fimple sold his interest to Absalom Fisher, and went to quarrying, hauling and boating stone from his farm some four miles above the city.

Recollections of
Some of the Leading Families of the County.
THE MAGOON FAMILY.

Published in the Muscatine Saturday Mail Jan. 21, 1899; written by J. P. Walton.

No. 102.

I don't think Fimple, who married Magoon's third daughter, brought much money here but he was industrious and saving; he soon accumulated enough to build a brick house out in the woods on the north side of Fifth west of Chestnut street—the house is standing there yet. At that time there was so little improvement that he could not get his house set straight; it stands some three or four feet out of square with the surroundings at the present time. There he took his wife, Lydia Maria, when he was married, about 1850—the relatives say, I thought earlier. Mrs. Fimple was one of the best women living, always pleasant and agreeable, kind hearted and not a particle haughty. She could affiliate with any society quite as well as any woman we ever met. She lived to the good old age of almost 80 years beloved by every one. After the death of Mr. Fimple, March 8, 1880, she lived with her brother, Geo. D. Magoon, until

1891 when she went to live with her son, Andrew W. Fimple, in Duluth, afterwards living in Chicago, where she died on October 14, 1897, and was buried in Muscatine.

Fimple's second building was a three-story warehouse on Front street west of Sycamore; the first and second stories were used for storage, at one time the building was so well filled with wheat it endangered its standing. The third story was used for hall and meeting house. The year the Congregational society was building what is now the old Congregational church, their meetings were held in Fimple's hall. The Universalist society also occupied the hall for a while. Later the Muscatine Light Guards used it for an armory; when they broke up Fimple attached their effects for rent; he had their guns attached but as they were the property of the state he had to let them go. This building was probably erected in 1856, but the panic of 1857 so embarrased him that the warehouse proved a bad investment on his hands, and he never fairly recovered his former financial standing. He moved on to his farm and lived there a year or more but he had to return to the city. After the Front street warehouse had passed into other hands it was converted into a sash and door factory and finally burned down. Mr. Fimple was a prominent member of Iowa Lodge of Masons, he took a great deal of interest in its work and welfare, and while most of the other members attended lodge meetings in their everyday clothes Fimple would always put on his best, I think he never occupied any prominent office. His family consisted of three children; they are all dead, the last one, Andrew Wheeler Fimple, died Nov. 20, 1897, in Chicago, about one month after his mother; he was born in Muscatine, was in the insurance business in Des Moines, in Duluth, and in Chicago. While residing in Duluth he married Miss Gorgia Bruse who with one son survives him.

Eliza Hannah was the first Magoon girl to marry in our town. She was married to William Gordon October 21, 1840. She could not have been here more than six or eight months before the wiley Scotchman fall a prey to her beauty and charms. She was undoubtedly the most beautiful young lady in our village; tall, handsome, with fine form and bearing, and good address. The same could be said of both. He was fully six feet high and well built, and a good talker. He was a native of Scotland, born June 12, 1812, while she was a native of Massachusetts. They have had five children. The eldest, William A., died on July 8, 1866, from the effects of a wound received at Shiloh on April 6, 1862. The second child, Addie M., married Col. John H. Munroe; the third married Martin L. Mikesell; the fourth married William M. Kincaid; a fifth child died young.

Col. John H. Munroe was a native of Quincy, Ill. His father was a native of Lexington, Mass., and a relative of Lieutenant Munroe, who was killed at the battle of Lexington. John is of Scottish descent, probably of one of the four or five hundred Scottish prisoners sent to Massachusetts a little later than 1650 by Cromwell, but his Scottish blood don't hurt him much as two hundred years among the yankees has diluted it to almost extinction. He still retains the desire common to the celtic race for holding office. He recently allowed his name to appear on the Republican ticket for representative to Congress for the Second Congressional District of Iowa, hence the title of honorable. He has been candidate for mayor and served some twelve years as county clerk, a term longer than any other man. He is a little too out-spoken for a successful politician, recently venturing a criticism on the president that but few of the more fortunate officeholders would have dared to make. He has several children: William, who married Carrie Dolson, is now in the insurance business in Philadelphia, Pa.; another son, Frederick, who is in the insurance business with his father. During the recent war with Spain, Frederick was a lieutenant in Company C, of the 50th Iowa volunteers. Col. John H. Munroe is now engaged in the insurance and land agency business with office on Iowa avenue. His biography is quite extensively published in the Muscatine Biographical Album, to which we refer our readers.

Martin L. Mikesell, now the delivery clerk at the postoffice, came to Bloomington a small boy probably in 1841 or '42. His father was a blacksmith. He is better known as Doc Mikesell. How he got the title no one seems to know. The only professional occupation I ever heard of his having was that of a steamboat engineer. Mr. Mikesell has had to earn his own living, he commenced when a mere boy in the post office under Richard Cadle and later with Henry Reece. After spending some four or five years in the post office he went on a Mississippi river boat as engineer and pilot. When the civil war broke out he joined the First Iowa volunteer infantry and later the Eleventh and served through the war. After serving a term as county treasurer he was superintendent of a railroad in the state of Iadiana. He returned to Muscatine about 1872 or '73 and went into the post office where has been ever since except about four years that he was engaged with the gas company. He has the reputation of knowing and recollecting more persons than any man in the city. Mr. and Mrs. Mikesell have one daughter who is married to Sam F. Lewis and they have several children.

William M. Kincaid, who married Miss Agnes Gordon, was a native of this county, born in 1846. They had one daughter who married Frank Parham, manager of the Postal Telegraph office at Muscatine. Mrs. Agnes Gordon Kincaid died some years ago and the daughter, now Mrs. Parham, was cared for by her aunt, Mrs. G. D. Magoon, for many years. William M. Kincaid is now connected with G. D. Magoon in the building business.

Recollections of

Some of the Leading Families of the County.

THE MAGOON FAMILY.

Published in the Muscatine Saturday Mail Jan. 28, 1899; written by J. P. Walton.

Nos. 103 and 104.

But to return to William Gordon, the first one to marry a Magoon girl in our village. He had any amount of self-esteem and a good supply of conversational powers providing he was the subject of discussion. He was industrious, although he would rather observe another work than do it himself. While one biographer claims he was an extensive builder; he certainly was not a successful one financially as he was a little too generous with his promises, to succeed, frequently anticipating more than he realized; but for all that, as a citizen he was courteous, generous and well liked. He liked office and held that of sheriff from 1856 to 1862. Here was where the Magoon family came, such a host of brothers-in-law with their influence, was a big starter. He was a democrat but managed in someway to get the "Know-nothing" vote to help him. When the war began to thicken, the democrats soon lost their prestige and Gordon went out with others. These terms of office cured his propensity for work and he did but little afterwards.

During the six years that he had the sheriff's office, he accumulated considerable property and built for himself the large two-story brick building on north Mulberry street, now belonging to J. K. Miller. This he traded for property on Second street, with a defective title and his loss on the deal was considerable. He then built the frame building and brick barn now belonging to T. R. Sawyer. It cost from $6,000 to $8,000 exclusive of the land, some ten or twelve acres, that was worth at least $2,000 more. The house was so badly located, away from the road, that anyone having money to purchase would not look at it. He was admonished not to build there, but he was building for himself and did not care whether anyone else wanted it or not. As a result he became embarrassed financially, and the property was sold to pay for borrowed money, and was eventually sold for less than $3,000 for land, house and barn.

Mr. Gordon was very unfortunate in getting lime in his eyes and became nearly blind and helpless for a number of years. Mrs. Gordon died Aug. 8, 1873. After his eye sight became impaired he lived the most of his time with his daughters. He died some few months ago.

William Gordon came here on Aug. 11, 1836, and worked at the carpenter trade. Soon after he was married, he bought a large farm on Muscatine Island of Adam Ogilvie, it included the present property of Wm. H. Hoopes, T. B. Holcomb, the Barrows brothers, and the Sheperd place. The Ogilvie farm had a comfortable frame house on it, and in the spring of 1842 Gordon with the Magoon family moved into the house. I don't think Gordon stayed long on the Island: he secured a lot on the south side of Fourth street, between Pine and Linn streets, and built a small frame house. In 1854 or '55 he built the brick house now occupied by the Erb family. (This we lowered some two years ago.)

During the cold winter of 1842 and 1843 Mr. Magoon and his son George, went across the river where they cut and hewed a set of cotton wood logs and hauled them across the river. In the spring they put up a large cabin near where T. B. Holcomb's barn now stands, and the Magoon family moved in there in the year of 1843. The fourth daughter married George Martin, a carpenter by trade, who came here from Dayton, Ohio. If I am correct, he bought a part of the farm, and Gordon moved to town. Martin farmed the place for a year or two when he moved to town and went into the building business with Sherman Brooks. The firm of Brooks & Martin did considerable building and some house moving, they had two wooden bed screws, as they called them, to raise buildings with, they were about six inches in diameter and four feet long, they set in a nut about eight inches thick, two feet wide and four feet long; they were made by Isaac Magoon. In 1851 George Martin and family moved to California, where Mrs. Martin died in 1886, he died in 1896. They left three sons living in California and Idaho.

John T. B. Martin, a brother of George Martin, came here about 1845 and married Augusta Magoon in 1846. They had one child, now Mrs. Clara Kerns of Rock Island, her mother Mrs. Augusta (Magoon) Martin lives with her. Mr. Martin died some years ago. After their marriage John and Augusta lived in Muscatine, he was engaged in house building and in 1851 he went to California where he succeeded in getting money enough to come back with. I think that was about all he got. He returned in 1855 and built a house on the top of the hill on lot 6, block 122, south side of Seventh street west of the Avenue. John was a great society man, most of the parties and "balls" had his name down as one of the principal men; he was well liked and respected by all who knew him.

The last daughter of Isaac Magoon to marry was Jane Sarah, in 1847, to Richard Cadle, a young man that came formally from the city of New York. He was a carpenter by occupation and worked at the trade considerable. He was a brother of Cornelious Cadle who built the first saw mill in our city. Dick as he was called was an immensely popular man, kind, courteous and agreeable. He, like his brother Cornelius, was a great joker or punster; he, of course, was popular, especially in society, where he could be found quite frequently. I don't think Dick was much of a dancer, he depended on his wit rather than his feet for his standing in society. In 1848 Dick was elected County Clerk and served two years, then again in 1854 and served four years; he was afterwards Deputy Clerk for some five years, having been in a county office near eleven years, he also served six years as township clerk. This Magoon family seem to have taken kindly to public offices as some of the sons-in-laws or their descendants by marriage have held positions in the court house for fully thirty-five years with little or no intermission. During Fillmore's administration Richard Cadle was postmaster for a full term of four years. After leaving the post office he went in with J. S. Patten in the sash and door business, for a couple of years. In October, 1861, he went into the army and served three years in the quartermaster's department as first lieutenant. On returning from the war he went into the sash, door and blind factory of Cadle & Mulford which business afterOard developed into the Huttig Bro's. Manufacturing Co., with which he remained some time. Not wishing to devote all his time to the public he went out on North Mulberry street and bought a tract of land, perhaps eight or ten acres, and built a fine house and out buildings, and started to educate chickens and raise raspberries. This, of course' made him a Granger and when the Grange Wagon Factory was built he put in some money and got a position in the office. While he probably got his pay for the time he was with them I presume he never got his money back on his stock. Richard Cadle had two children, George H. and Eva. He, with his family, moved to Monta Vista, Colorado, some six or seven years ago. He died there in 1896, his widow and the two children are there yet.

> It is well to remember the "larks" of our boyhood,
>   At the eve of old age, we recall them anew,
> On the river, and the fish pond, the timber, and Sand Mound,
>   With the broad spreading Island yet plain in our view,
> Where we boated, and hunted, and wandered around,
>   When in search of adventures, there to be found.

Our acquaintance with George D Magoon, the son of Isaac Magoon, commenced in the spring of 1842. We both moved to Muscatine Island about the same time and lived about three hundred feet apart. I don't know how I can tell George's boyhood history without telling my own—a thing I have a great reluctance in doing. George, my brother and myself were the boys of Muscatine Island for the year 1842. We swam, boated, fished and hunted together. That is to say, we put in our spare time together; we had to work and got but little time besides Sundays. There were no meetings or Sunday Schools on the Island, and the boys were not required to go to town to meeting. I am inclined to think we did not have clothes nice enough to appear in a town church and this was one of the reasons for not going. Well, we did not want to go, our parents objected to our going a hunting on Sunday, but would allow us to go visiting. We managed to take a great many strolls together; when the the river became high we had to do our traveling by boat, with which we soon became expert managers. We did not indulge in any of the games played by the town boys, we were in the company of men and had to use men's recreations. In the spring of 1844 another boy came on the Island, by the name of James D. Reeder. This made a quarette, and occasionally a fifth one joined them by the name of Amasa Brooks, who was about as sharp as boys generally are. James Reeder was a common boy, but his parents considered him very much better than we were, and kept him much finer dressed and would frequently talk about it. Jim was a good fellow, but no leader, while Brooks was. Card playing was especially indicted by our parents. Of course we had to play cards, and when the river was high it was difficult to find a place to play out of sight of the old folks. On one occasion we were playing in an old open house that had four or five upper joists running across, overhead. We happened to look out and see my mother approaching. We had no time to retreat, so gathering up our cards, each one climbed up on a joist and stretched out length wise on top. Mother came in and looked all around, but did not look up. and exclaimed. "Well, I saw those boys here, where could they have gone." She went away without knowing, and we went on with our game. On another occasion when wild strawberries were very abundant on the Island, so thick as to make the ground look more red than green, we gathered a fine lot and resorted to the pantry and helped ourselves to cream and sugar while the old folks were in town attending meeting. After enjoying our repast we adjourned to the attic to engage in a game of seven-up. When it was nicely in progress, the old folks returned, and found us "treed" in the attic. We got down and departed in the best manner we could, leaving George to make matters right. How he got out of it, I have forgotten.

Our passion for card playing did not last very long, as we knew it was disobeying orders and did not afford us much pleasure, so we quit it.

Our desires to get out and see something took the preference. On one occasion we went down to the Sand Mound, and saw a big wolf run into a hole. We detailed a guard over the hole and dispatched others for shovels to dig the wolf out. We commenced digging and soon reached its nest and other fresh signs, and could hear what we thought was the wolf digging away from us. We dug a long way but got no wolf. The wolf if there, and we were sure it was, likely went into some side hole and filled it with earth so we missed it.

When we went on the Muscatine Island 50 or more years ago, the prairie wolf was very abundant. The Sand Mound was a favorite haunt for them, where they made their dens and reared their young. When the river was high they were crowded to high ground and we would frequently take a trip to look after them and often captured some.

On one occasion we were passing down the northeast side of the Sand Mound where there is a strip of timber now standing. There was no levee then; the water was up among the trees, and on about every tree two or more large snakes could be seen, also in great number along the bank of the pond. We soon armed ourselves with suitable sticks for killing them, and when we quit had dispatched about 300, that would average three feet each, making nearly 900 feet in all. This is of course a snake story, but if the quantity is doubted we will refer you to G. D. Magoon, as we are the only survivors.

We frequently took fishing trips in the night. We would go over on the Island, or in the bottom, and get some rough hickory bark, tie it up in a bundle to make a torch. When it became dark we would take a canoe ann go over to the fourth slough, and stationing someone in the forward end with a spear, another close behind him with the lighted torch, and one in the back end to paddle, we frequently caught quite a nice mess of very fine fish. It was no uncommon thing, if the fish got crowded or frightened, to have them jump into the boat. I recollect at one time catching a very large black bass in that manner.

Many a time we went to the big timber or on Blanchard's Island to hunt and gather hickory nuts. George was the big boy; he did the climbing and knocking them off; we, my brother and I, would do the picking up.

One winter we took a notion to cut steamboat wood on Blanchard's Island. Each of us built a cabin and each had a man chopping for a while. We hauled over some of the wood on the ice, and banked some for boating. Some of it was washed away without banking. I don't think we made much out of it, but it kept us busy during the winter.

In the winter of 1846 my brother and I moved down to our old farm near the Sand Mound, and George moved to town. We were then young men; George was 21 years old and I was 20. We did not meet so often after that, but nevertheless we took a good many jaunts together for a year or two, George frequently coming down to spend Sunday and preserve the acquaintance.

After George came to town he worked at carpenter work for, or with his brothers-in-law, the Martins, and associated with the young men of the city and joined the brass band. He played the biggest horn in the lot. I have forgotten the leader's name; it was the first band of the town, long before Unger's or Eichoff's were organized.

Early in the season of 1852, George went to California where he remained for about four years when he returned to our city and commenced the building business.

On Sept. 27, 1860, he married Miss Joanna Kincaid, a daughter of the late Col. Kincaid. They have one son, Eddie, born Dec. 26, 1864, who is now working at the carpenter trade for his father and uncle, W. M. Kincaid.

George D. Magoon was a native of Ware, Mass., born Feb. 11, 1825; in 1827 was taken to Ohio; in 1837 to Warsaw, Ills.; in 1840 to Bloomington, now Muscatine. His education was acquired, some in Ohio, some in Illinois, and lastly, in a log school house on the south side of Third street, west of Cedar, about the east line of the hay market, probably taught by John A. Parvin. When the war of the rebellion broke out, he volunteered in the 11th Iowa Infantry, and was commissioned lieutenant in the Pioneer Corps. He served some three years and was mustered out Dec. 6, 1864. Although 74 years of age he continues in business.

HISTORICAL RECOLLECTIONS OF

The Moscow Canal.

Published in the Muscatine Saturday Mail Feb. 11, 1899; written by J P. Walton.

No. 105.

If any one will take the trouble to refer to page 531 of "The Statute Laws of the Territory of Iowa," an act will be found to incorporate the Bloomington and Cedar River Canal Company. The act was approved Jan. 12, 1839, and was passed while the legislature was in session in Burlington; it is a long act, occupying some nine pages with twenty-six sections. It fixed the capital stock at $200,000 with the shares at $100 each. According to section three, Joseph Williams, John Vannata, Adam Ogilvie, Charles Alexander Warfield, Suel Foster, William Gordon, Harvey Gillet, William D. Velie, Stephen Long, James W. Talman and John G. Foy were the commissioners to receive subscriptions of stock. Each subscriber was to pay one dollar a share and when $35,000 was paid in, the subscriptions were to be turned over to a board of directors with the money received. Section 5 allowed the capital stock to be increased to $500,000. section 6 for the construction of a navigable canal from Bloomington to Cedar river, section 7 for the right of way and paying for the same, section 8 for collecting toll and also for borrowing any sum of money needed. Several sections were devoted to the protection of the canal and the penalties for violation of the provision. Section 21 provided for the commencement of the work which was to be within three years and the completion within ten years. Section 22 is rather an uncommon section, it authorized the company to loan money on bonds, notes, drafts, bills of exchange, and other securities at a rate of interest not exceeding twelve per cent per annum, and limits its amount to two hundred thousand dollars. I guess this meant to borrow money at twelve per cent, or in other words, to bond the canal for $250,000, twelve per cent bonds. This would look like an enormous interest to pay, but I think it is no larger than many of the railroads are paying at the present time if we consider the water used in the construction. Section 23 provided for the transfer of the canal to the state of Iowa after the state should be admitted to the Union. It also provided "that in case the congress of the United States shall make an appropriation or donation either in land or money in aid of the construction of the work, this act authorizes the right to the same shall be vested in the state." The corporations were authorized to apply to congress for such an appropriation in money or lands

I am inclined to think that the last feature was the main inducement for building a canal— that is to say, getting an appropriation from congress. The same scheme was worked about that time on the Des Moines river for slack water navigation, the appropriation was made, but the slack water navigation never did much good.

I don't know who were the schemers in the Bloomington and Cedar River Company. I have understood that Suel Foster claimed his name was put on without his knowledge or consent. I have been told that a survey was made previous to the action of the legislature. There was another incentive that may have had an influence on this conception, the state of Illinois was about constructing the lake Michigan canal and also trying to build railroads. The state of Indiana had also taken the same fever, and so had Ohio; they had both been or were building canals more stupendous than the Cedar river canal. Why not Bloomington have one? if it answered for nothing more than an advertisement. The canal question laid dormant from 1839 to 1865—26 years—when a few of our citizens concluded to have it surveyed. A party consisting of Captain A. Kennedy, Hon. J. A. Parvin, Hon. John Mahin, Mr. J. G. H. Little, myself and others went out and made a preliminary inspection of the grounds. A sufficient sum was raised by subscription and a corps of engineers headed by Capt. Kennedy put on the work. His report was made in October, 1865, and embodied the following items:

The fall of water from Cedar river at Moscow to the river at Muscatine was 84 feet.

ESTIMATE OF COST,

Excavation and embankment from Stat. 0 to 460..........$324,000 00
Excavation for tunnel from

Stat. 0 to 460	95,000 00
Masonry for tunnel	231,840 00
Excavation and embankment east end of tunnel	76,300 00
Timber waste way at Sugar Creek	5,000 00
Raising Moscow Dam 5 feet, including gate	6,400 00
Rip-rap at entrance Sugar Creek, Mad Creek, etc.	4,000 00
Reservoir Dam	1,860 00
Engineering etc.	5,600 00
Total	$750,000 00

Excavation and embankment, 16 to 30c per cubic yard.

Excavation in tunnel $1,00 per cubic yard.

Masonry of tunnel $12.00 per cubic perch.

Masonry at Dam (Moscow) $8.00 per cubic perch.

Rip-raps $2.00 per cubic yard.

You will see that Mr. Kennedy figured the excavation at 16 to 30 cents per cubic yard. With the improved methods of handling earth in big cuts, like the Chicago drainage canal for instance, earth can be moved for one-half or a little more, than it could when Kennedy made his estimation. At the present time it is quite probable that by the same method the tunnel could be abandoned, hence little or no stone or brick work will be needed, thus shortening up the estimate on the masonry at least $200,000. I have little or no doubt that $300,000 or $350,000 will bring all the water we want from Cedar river at Moscow to Muscatine.

We have a Commercial Club that have done about all the good things this city has had done since they have been in existence, so the secretary says. The Club is a good thing for the city and is now moving in this canal matter. We hope they will be successful in their efforts. If they are, in our estimation, it will be their best work.

A word as to the fall of the river, in Vol. 2 of White's Geology of Iowa, page 410, is found the survey of the Rock Island railroad. By it the surface of Cedar river at Moscow is 75 feet above the surface of the Mississippi river at Davenport. The surface of the river at Muscatine is probably 9 feet lower than at Davenport, making a fall of 84 feet between Moscow and Muscatine. This verifies the Kennedy survey of 84 feet. The Rock Island surveys were made at low water in the rivers. The figures of the United States show a fall of 12 feet from the old bridge at Davenport and Muscatine, making the fall from Moscow 87 feet.

A HISTORY OF THE OLDEST CONTINUOUS WEATHER RECORD IN THE MIDDLE WEST,

With Paper Read to the Academy of Science in Muscatine, Iowa, February 13th, 1899.

Published in the Muscatine Saturday Mail Feb. 18, 1899; written by J P. Walton.

No. 106.

On July 4th, 1838, Hon. T. S. Parvin, now of Cedar Rapids, landed in Iowa; it was on the birthday of Iowa; he came as private secretary for Hon. Robert Lucas, the first governor of the new territory of Iowa. Mr. Parvin stopped for a while at Burlington, but soon came to Bloomington, now Muscatine. He was a young unmarried man, and what induced him to keep a weather record is more than one can imagine at the present time. He probably commenced on the 1st day of December, 1838, and may have kept his record in his diary, as he transcribed none before the first day of January, 1839, which he most likely did in 1841, when he got his blanks printed. The blanks were lithographs supplied by a Hartford, Conn., company. He made a record of the thermometer readings three times a day, also of the clear, viriable and cloudy days, and also the days that it rained or snowed. In 1847 he seems to have had blanks from the Smithsonian Institute at Washington, D. C. He did not make any record of the barometer until 1850. The following story was going the rounds about Parvin's barometer (which I now have.) The common way of transporting mercurial barometers was to pack them in a leather case with straps on it and carry on one's back like a gun. When Parvin wanted a barometer his friends, Dr. C. O. Waters and H. D. LaCossit, who had been down to Washington to look after some public office, offered to bring him one. So they started with the barometer on their backs; when they got Buffalo, N. Y., they went to a hotel to stay over'night; they found the hotel crowded. LaCosset in the lead walked up to the desk and registered the names of H. D LaCossit, Lt., U. S. A., and Dr. C. O. Waters, Surg., U. S. A., and asked the clerk if he could give them a room; he said he could not, all he would do was to give them cots in the office. LaCossit turned around and said, "Surgeon, what will we do with this instrument, one of us will have to stay up and watch it." The clerk glanced at the names and titles and said "gentlemen, I guess we can arrange a room for you," and he did.

In October, 1860, Mr. Parvin moved to Iowa City and gave his instruments, blanks, etc., to Rev. John Ufford, who continued to take observations until April, 1863, when he gave his instruments, records and blanks to Josiah P. Walton, who has since continued them. Shortly after that time, while in Iowa City, Mr. Parvin gave all the back records he had to me. I have taken the observations or had them taken for more than thirty-five years. This record with those received from Mr. Parvin and Rev. Ufford, makes a continuous record for more than sixty years. We hardley think when Mr. Parvin started this record that he thought it would be kept up as long as it has been.

A PAPER READ BEFORE THE MUSCATINE ACADEMY OF SCIENCE, FEB 13, 1899.

Weather is the state of the atmosphere with respect to heat or cold, wet or dryness, calm or storm, cloudiness or clearness, or any other meteorological phenomena, as warm weather, cold weather, wet weather or dry weather, calm or tempestuous weather. In fact, we are subject to all kinds of weather, especially in this locality.

We, as enlightened people, are dependent for our subsistence mainly on agriculture, which in turn is dependent on the condition of the weather for its success. The question for the agriculturalist is to know how to take advantage and make the most of the weather study although the records are not very continuous. We are told than on one occasion it rained forty days and forty nights, and this was followed by fair weather. We are not told when the next rain occurred or whether another similar rain will occur again, but as all general rules may have an exception, we conclude that the forty days' rain was an exception and will not occur again, unless similar conditions occur, which is not considered very probable.

Ever since the forty days' rain man has been dependent on the generosity of the weather for his subsistence, yet no records have been kept of importance with the exception of a few severe droughts until quite recently. Within the present century great strides have been made in the manner of keeping weather records. We had occasion to look up the age of the meteorological records, and found but two or three in the land that reached back into the last century. We found that there had been spasmodic efforts made to keep a record at various places, but none were continuous. Here let me say that the whole northwest should rise up in a body and thank Hon. T. S.

Purvin, now of Cedar Rapids, for his (then said to be useless) weather record, which he commenced on January 1st, 1839. This record has been kept up continuously to the present time. By the use of it we are enabled to tell what has occurred, and what has followed those occurrences. Of course such a record would be useless for such prophets as Foster, Hicks or Mansil, who have some law for their prophesies not known by the common student, and possibly not by themselves.

For the past year or two we have consulted these records and have found that one month is an index for what the next one is quite likely to be. We have been very fortunate in our predictions made on these data. In making predictions, we don't claim to know what laws make the conditions— all we use is the results that are liable to follow.

The past January, 1899, had but .38 of an inch precipitation. By consulting our records we find there have been 10 Januarys in fifty years that had less than one inch of water fall, which we will consider. January, 1853, was dry and was preceded by a December that after its first day was dry. The February and March that followed were dry. The April was exceedingly wet. 11.80 inches of water fall. May, June and July were wet. January, 1854, was dry. February had more than the average water fall. March and April were dry. May was wet. June and July were not excessively wet.

January, 1859, was dry, with the preceding December about the average. February, March, April, May and June were wet. July was dry.

January, 1865, had less than one-half inch of water fall. The preceding December about the average, with April wet, May and June dry, July wet.

1867. January dry, the December before wet, February wet, March and April dry, May and June wet, July average.

1868. January quite dry, December preceding quite dry, February dry, March, April, May and June wet, July dry.

1872. January had but .03 of an inch of water fall, the dryest on record. The December before was wet, February, March and April were dry, May and June were wet, July dry.

1875 January dry, preceded with an average December, February, March, April, May and June were dry, July was wet.

1878. January dry, preceded by a wet December, February, March and April about the average, May wet, June and July average.

1882. January dry. The preceding December was about the average, February, March and April about the average, May and June wet, July about the average.

These figures show that there were ten dry Januarys with less than one inch of precipitation; also, of the Februarys that followed 6 were wet, of the Marches 3 wet, 3 average, 4 dry; of the April 6 wet and 2 average, and but 2 dry; of the Mays 8 were wet, 1 average, and but 1 dry; of the Junes 5 were wet, 4 average, 1 dry; of the Julys 6 were wet, 3 average, 1 dry. They also show that as a whole the ten dry Januarys have been followed by an average increase of precipitation in every month to and including July. April and May show the largest. Also, that there has been in the ten years but one year that April or May have not been excessively wet.

Now, to the application. We have three important crops grown in this locality, corn, oats and grass. The seasons very frequently do not suit all these crops. For instance, corn requires but a limited amount of rain until July, but after the ploughing is done and shooting begins, then it will stand any amount, while oats and grass prosper better with April, May and June wet, and July dry for harvesting.

In December, 1898, we had but .51 of precipitation, while the average is 1.70 in., more than three times the amount we had. In January, 1899, we had but .38 in,; the average precipitation is 1.66 in.

If we conclude that the next six months are not going to be an exception to the former ones with similar precipitation in January, we can look for a better season for grass and oats than for corn.

We conclude the chances at least are eight out of ten to have May very wet, and if April should prove dry, the chances are 9 out of 10 for a wet May.

In other words we consider the chances for a fine season for oats and grass are very good, while we don't see but 2 out of ten chances for a choice corn season, with one or two more fairly good chances. We presume there will be corn raised, as there is every year, but we hardly expect to see the crop up to an average.

There is another condition that will help the corn and not materially injure the oats and grass. That is the excessive deep freezing. The ground is very dry to a great depth, and packed together, so much so that many of the forest trees are dying from drought. The deep frost will separate or pulverize the ground and make it accessible for excessive rain falls, and will store the water away for future need, thus leaving the surface in a tillable condition. This deep frost will go far in preventing excessive floods after the frost is out of the ground, while a deep snow followed by a heavy rain before the frost is out of the ground might make a flood.

Recollections of

PROMINENT MEN OF BLOOMINGTON---A. O. and CHAS. A. WARFIELD.

Published in the Muscatine Saturday Mail Feb. 25, 1899; written by J. P. Walton.

No. 107

There have been three or more biographical works published of this city and county. They as a rule contain the biographies of the subscribers and but few if any others. These are usually written to suit the subscriber and very brief. In many cases but little of the man is told. Such is the case of Major Asbury O Warfield, who was one of the pioneer settlers of our town. In the Biographical Album on page 297 we find a brief account of his earlier days. He was born in Carroll county, Md., on November 16, 1811; he came to Burlington, Iowa, on a steamboat in November, 1837, the boat being frozen in the ice he and his cousin, David R. Warfield, footed it to Bloomington, or in other words, they bought a horse and rode turn about. One would mount the horse and ride for a while, then would tie the horse and walk on a head; when the other who had been following came up he, would mount the horse and ride some distance in advance of the first one, then tie the horse and walk on again. By this scheme each one got to ride half of the way and they gained time. (Can any one figure out how much time they gained?)

In 1838 Asbury and his cousin David R. erected a saw mill, probably they commenced sawing in 1839. High water in the creek washed out their dam, it was rebuilt and washed out several times; finally Asbury got tired of the venture and sold out to his cousin David, having dropped some $6,000 or $8,000 in it. Peter Jackson in one of his addresses to the old settlers describes this mill thus:

"David R. Warfield a man of horses, dogs and guns, kept bach on the classical banks of Mad Creek with Benjamin Matthews as master of ceremonies and enjoyed frontier life hugely, but in an evil hour tried to confine its waters by a dam to run a saw mill, which the creek resented by washing out the dam. In connection with this mill I will mention an incident to show how primitive our city was at that time. One afternoon I had been up at the mill to see about getting some lumber sawed and returning home in the evening an emigrant with a one-horse covered wagon overtook me as I walked along and asked me how far it was to Bloomington. I answered that we were just then on the public square. This emigrant was Hiram Matthews, who had a fashion of opening his eyes very wide, and how they did bung out among those woods where no houses could be seen. There was then a few houses near the steam boat landing. I recollect of three cabins east of Pappoose—one where Mr. Brannan now lives, one near where Mr. Peter Musser lives, and one on block 30 occupied as a blacksmith shop by a Mr. Walmsey."

After disposing of his interest in the saw mill Asbury Warfield went to Antwerp, Cedar county, an early town some three miles west of Tipton. (I don't think there is any town there now) and opened a store. After a couple of years stay he returned.

John McGreer in his Recollections of Drury's Landing says: "Major Asbury Warfield started a general store at Drury's Landing and sold it out to two brothers named Neienburg, one of them committed suicide and Warfield had to take the store back." How long he kept the store at the Landing John does not say.

If I recollect aright Asbury Warfield helped some of the city merchants most of the time after closing out his store. I have been told he kept books for Jos Bennet until the autumn of 1855 when he was appointed the agent for the Mississippi & Missouri railroad, now the Chicago, Rock Island & Pacific. His office was in the first story of the Ogilvie House, now the Commercial Hotel. He remained there until the old wooden ticket offiice was built at the foot of Linn street. The railroad bought an old two-story frame building that was first built for a farmer's mercantile shipping company in 1843, it stood below Broadway and was moved up near the foot of Linn street and used it for a freight house previous to the wooden station house being built. The major had supervision over the freight department till 1891—36 years.

A word about the major as a railroad man, he was remarkably attentive, he would fret himself nearly to death if there was a likelihood of the railroad company losing a dollar. He always collected all his bills whether they were just or not. If a man came with a little claim for damages or over payment the reception was not a cold one—far from it. It was more likely to be the reverse, as a very hot place would likely be mentioned. If the applicant ment business and would wait until Asbury got over his pet he would receive very courteous treatment. I have no doubt but that hundreds of dollars of just claims have gone unsettled and the good will of the railroad suffered by the bluff reception the applicant received. I don't think that I am telling an untruth when I say that hardly a day for many years passed that some one did not receive an insult in some manner from the major's impetuosity. That is if the man was at all sensitive or did not understand the major's habits. The wonder was why the railroad company kept him so long. The only reasonable solution was his capacity, his correctness and interest in the company's welfare. He succeeded in getting two of his nephews in the railroad's employ—George in the freight house, and Charlie in the ticket office: both of them occupied these places for a long time.

Asbury Warfield never took a vacation of over one day or so at a time, then he would go on a short hunt with Charley Draper, Alf. Brown or some other high toned hunter. Almost our first acquaintance with him was on his hunts with J. R. Bennett. The two would get in a buggy and go down on the Island, locate themselves on a pond and keep up a complete cannonade at the geese and ducks before they would get within gun shot. Of course they killed but few, they were more successful with plovers which were abundant and tamer than anything else. They would kill some quails but that kind of game did not require much hunting in early days, all a hunter had to do was to go along the banks of the river in the autumn and as often as every quarter of a mile a covey could be found.

A. O. AND CHAS. WARFIELD.

Recollections of Prominent Men of Bloomington, Concluded.

BY J. P. WALTON.

No. 106

After Asbury Warfield got older he gave up the hunting and devoted his attention more closely to the railroad company. On one occasion the shippers had a rest for six or eight weeks, it came about in this way. Asbury in going his rounds to look after the shipping clerk or something managed to run his foot down into a hole that had been allowed to come in the floor and broke his leg. This accident compelled him to rest for a while, but he survived it and soon got out again. While laid up with the broken limb he boarded with Auntie Olds, at whose house he had lived for many years, where he received the best of attention. On one occasion it was necessary to call in outside help to set up with him at night; a gentleman of our acquaintance responded to a call and got along so nicely that Asbury said he took better care of him than any woman ever did. This of course was true, as Asbury was not a married man.

Asbury had a small circle of intimate friends, but these he enjoyed greatly. He did not care to have more. During the later years of Charles Draper's residence in Muscatine, Asbury could be found there every Sunday. He sometimes attended the Episcopal church although not very regularly. I think he paid rent for a pew. Many of his chums are dead, for instance, Dr. George Reeder, H. W. Moore and Charles Draper, and others. There is one, however, W. R. Stone, who is not. Some five or six years ago while Mr. Stone was visiting here he met Warfield at the hotel, and seeing that he was not recognized he accosted Warfield as a book agent offering to sell him a book and insisted on taking his name, the book would be issued very soon. Warfield as usual blessed the book agent emphatically, declined to purchase, but Stone became more persistent in wanting his name for the book, after Warfield's introductory declination. Warfield asked who was the author of the d——d book, when Stone replied without a smile that it was W. R. Stone, of Duluth. Warfield looked at the agent and recognized him as his old chum W. R. Stone. We presume the book agent set them up. It was no uncommon thing to hear of some game of a similar nature being played on Warfield, but with all his peculiarities he was a kind hearted man. He was a fussy old fellow; on one occasion Dr. Reeder gave a party while Warfield was boarding with Auntie Olds. Reeder's mother-in-law. Warfield of course was invited; he got his toilet made in good order and just as he was coming down stairs it occurred to him that he had forgotten his perfumery, so he went back and pulled out his dresser drawer, got the bottle and put some on his hand and handkerchief, and after putting some on his face he concluded to smell it and much to his disgust he found it to be sweet oil.

Warfield was a stickler on honor, and followed the southern rule of not allowing any one to call him a liar without resenting it. On one occasion one of our shoe houses in the city had some misunderstanding about freight rates and one of the partners went down to get the difficulty adjusted; he being a New England man was not familiar with the southern rule and being a little excited he told Warfield he lied. Warfield at once knocked him down. The shoe dealer gathered himself up and returned to the store. The other partner asked him if he had adjusted the matter. His reply was he thought he had, for he told Warfield that he lied and had got knocked down for doing it.

In an early time the railroad company furnished an old-fashioned sheet iron safe to keep their money in. One night some one broke in and robbed the safe of some $400 or $500. Warfield expected to pay for it and he sent a friend of some influence with Mr. Kimball the superintendent, to inquire about it. Kimball informed the friend that as Warfield had been such a good, trusty man they would not bother him about it.

On page 296 of the Biographical Album is a portrait of Major A. O. Warfield; it is very fine, but there is only one fault with the picture—that is he has no cigar in his mouth. Warfield could at all times of the day be found with a stump of a cigar in his mouth, it was never lighted, hence one would last him a long time but it was his habit to have it there, so much so that it was noticed by every one acquainted with him, and it became part of the man.

After Auntie Olds stopped taking boarders Warfield went to the Commercial Hotel to board; he always stood in with the steward, and any particular dish he wanted he would generally provide the material and they would cook it for him. He would buy fruit for his own special eating at meal times, he would have a table by himself and boarders eating at other tables would wonder how he managed it.

When the Warfields came to Bloomington they brought several colored men here—old Ben. Matthews, his brother and other relatives. While the Warfields came by boat Ben and his brother Ed came by land and drove their teams. After Ben. became so old as not to be able to support himself, the Warfields helped him in his emergencies. Major Asbury Warfield died October 17, 1894, at the age of 83 years.

Major Asbury O. Warfield had an older brother here. I think about the time or perhaps before he came, by the name of Charles Alexander Warfield. He was a large land operator. He purchased many fine tracts of land near the town. If I recollect aright he was the agent for a Baltimore Land company, and I presume made many purchases for them. He purchased what was the Chester Weed farm that went into J. B. Hunt's hands and was afterwards purchased and converted into the southeast part of Park Place. Chas. A. Warfield built the old frame house with a huge chimney in 1839 and moved his family there and lived there three or four years. In the year 1840 he had a large herd of cows, he having brought here the first Durham bull I ever saw. It was quite large and weighed 1600 or 1800. I don't know why Chas. A. Warfield moved away; he was quite a prominent man in our early city affairs. A portion of the city plat laid off on his claimed lands is known as Warfield's division. The claim titles were all right and respected by every one but the United States government of whom the land had to be bought to make a perfect title. When the land came into market in November, 1838, the different claimants held a meeting and selected a number of persons to go and enter the lands. Chas. A. Warfield was selected to enter what was known as the upper town and to deed to the town the streets and alleys, and to the individual lot owners their lots, they paying all expenses and allowing him twenty-five cents on each lot for his trouble. He gave security of $6,000 for the faithful performance of the agreement which he did satisfactorily.

When the town wanted a ferry an application was made to the legislature while in session in the winter of 1837-8 at Burlington and a charter was granted to Chas. A. Warfield and Jos. Williams. When the Bloomington and Cedar river canal was incorporated Chas. A. Warfield was one of the commissioners appointed to receive subscription of stock.

Chas. A. Warfield left at so early a date, not later than 1844 or '45, that but few persons now living here recollect him. I am satisfied from what I have known of him that he was one of the prominent men of our town. When last heard of he was in Texas. I think in the cattle ranching business. Not to exceed five or six years ago I talked with Asbury O. Warfield, who was my authority about his brother Chas. A. Warfield.

SWINE BREEDING.

PAPER READ AT THE MUSCATINE COUNTY FARMERS' INSTITUTE WILTON, IA., MARCH 4, 1899, BY J P. WALTON, OF MUSCATINE, IOWA.

We think there is some mistake in alloting us such a subject as "Swine Breeding." While we are the owner of several acres of farming lands and are interested in a limited way in cattle raising, we have given swine but little attention. In fact we might say none at all.

When we were young, say a half century ago, we had considerable experience in what we then called raising hogs Then the hog was a free commoner. He run on the commons most of the time. Then the strife was not to keep him in the pen, but to keep him out of the cornfield. We then used common split rails to build our fences. We used the small ones at the bottom, taking great care to prevent "hog holes."

Our fences were what were called "worm fences," made of 10-foot rails and of course had a "fence corner" (so often talked about) every eight feet. These shady fence corners were the most desirable places the hog could find.

On a hot day it would root a hole along the bottom rail and stretch out at full length and take his afternoon siesta. This afternoon bed was freshly dug over every day, and should a "hog hole" develop under the bottom rail, which was quite frequent, when the hog got up from his snooze he almost always found himself on the wrong side of the fence, of course making himself and the farmer much trouble.

The hog had to be gotten out; that was the job for the boy, who would let down the bars and try mild and persuasive means to induce the hog to return to his former status of a hog on the common.

There was an old story that ran about this way: "An evil spirit entered into the hogs and they ran down a hill and were all drowned." We used to think that the story was not correctly rendered. We did not think they were all drowned, for of all contrary things to drive a hog was the worst. We had a friend to call on if need be, in the person of a dog, who would usually work the charm, frequently at the expense of a hog's ear. After the hog or hogs were out we would have to go around and find and stop the "hog hole."

If the hog got a taste of the corn in the field he managed by some means to get in almost every day thereafter.

After the new corn got hard enough in the fall to feed, the hogs intended for market were usually put in a pen and fed until near the holidays. If a farmer had but a few hogs they were killed and hauled to market.

If the farmer or his neighbors had any considerable number, they were driven to market. Fifty years ago it was no uncommon thing to see a drove of one or two hundred head of fat hogs being driven to market. They could by hard driving make from five to eight miles a day. They were frequently driven a distance of 30 or 40 miles. taking a week or more.

The farmer would load several wagons with corn, perhaps keeping one for crippled hogs, and start out on the road, stopping to feed as often as he thought proper. When their destination was reached, they had no corn; their wagons were usually filled with crippled hogs.

Hogs in those days usually brought from $1.50 to $2.00 per hundred on foot.

If the farmer was so located that his hogs could run in the timber or bottom lands he was not usually annoyed so much in the summer or autumn.

We had the advantage of the "Big Timber" on Muscatine Island for our hog range. We would mark our hogs in the ears, and as soon as the river was down within its banks, we would turn our hogs down in the timber, and give them but little or no attention until taking-up time in the early winter. Of course the young hog was quite wild. We always kept two or three old sows, some of them may have been six or eight years old, as leaders. In the Big Timber they had a range of say one by three miles. Of course it was sometimes quite difficult to find them.

When it came to taking-up time we would find their beds or where they were feeding and put corn there for them and frequently lay a train of shelled corn for them to follow to the feed. As soon as the old sows got a taste of the corn they would come up to the farm for more corn, bringing a lot of the others with them. If they did not bring as many as we thought they should we fed them and let them go back to their beds for the night. The next day they would usually return with more young hogs.

In the Big Timber there were a great many oak and hickory trees. The hogs would usually get fat on the acorns and nuts.

We raised a large, coarse hog in appearance, not unlike the Chester White but slow to mature. We never considered them fit for market until eighteen months or two years old.

In the year 1846 we had a hog disease, called the cholera. I recollect getting over 100 good-sized hogs up out of the timber. During the winter we lost over seventy, having but thirty to start with in the spring.

There were but few persons in our neighborhood that were cranky enough to advocate keeping up the hogs the year round. We were not among that number. When the vote for restraining hogs and sheep was taken we voted against it and when it carried we went out of the hog business. Don't apprehend for a moment that the vote was the cause. It really had nothing to do with it.

Our last personal exper'ence was in 1851. We brought one of those coarse hogs up from our farm and enclosed it in a pen in the city, expecting to feed and fatten it on the slops from our kitchen. We kept it until killing time, gave it the slops and fed it four times as much corn as it was worth, and endured the flies and smells peculiar to a pig-pen and then sold the pig to S. O. Butler, and bought hams. Since then we have had no practical experience in "Swine Breeding."

INDEX.

Abernethy, W D, 257
Adams, Miss F, 300
Additions, 258
Agricultural College, 254
Agricultural Society, 225
Allen, B F, 251
Allen, J S, 274
Anderson, Capt, 251
Appel, Michael, 154

Ball, Dan, 6
Bank—Dutton & Co, 12, 13
" Cook, Musser & Co, 14, 35, 207
" First National, 14
" Garrettson, 14, 149
" Green & Stone, 249
" Hershey State, 14
" Merchants Exchange, 14
Banks, A T, 274
Banks, L, 245
Battelle, T S, 27, 290
Barklow, Mr, 22, 191, 258
Baptist Church, 354
Baptism, Public, 232
Barrows, Miss M E, 300
Bartlett, M, 24, 27, 163
Beach, Col Ben, 238, 317
Becke Bros, 222
Beaham, Tom, 300
Binz's Brewery, 162
Bennett, Joseph, 27, 165, 225
Berry, Nicholas, 49
Bevard, William, 133
Bierman, August, 155
Berkshire, M M, 176, 192, 303
Berkshire, John, 154, 307, 318
Bilkey & Fessler, 72, 75
Bitzer, Martin, 288
Blackman, F E, 317
Black Hawk Purchase, 257
Blades, Dr, 106, 189, 227
Blanchard, A, 212
Block, M, 27, 35, 173, 320
Bloomington, 66, 210, 278
Bonds for R R, 257
Book Business, 41
Brannan, Hon W F, 13
Brent Bros, 56, 163, 169
Breese & Higinbotham, 257
Brewster, W C, 14
Bridgman, Jos, 22, 273, 303
Bridgman, Fred, 317
Brown, A B, 153
Brown, Thomas, 323
Brownell, W A, 210
Broomhall, A, 317
Burditt, Thomas, 190

Burdick's Mill, 149
Burns, Christ, 191
Burnett, R M, 308
Butler, Jacob, 13, 267, 312
Butler, S O, 10, 243
Butler, A G, 14

Cadle, Cornelius, 31, 121, 164
Cadle, Richard, 169
Cadle, Mulford & Co, 17, 172
Campaigns of 1840-'48, 253, 256
Campbell, Harry, 221
Carpenters' Union, 19
Casey, James W, 190, 253, 263
Cemeteries, 197
Chambers family, 51, 274
Chambers, John & Co, 164, 258
Champion Hose Co, 14
Champ, John, 262
Chaplin, Chas, 290
Chippewa Lumber Co, 210
Clark, A, 320
Clark, B, 256
City finances, 278
City name, 66
Clothing business, 44
Coe, J E, 43, 317
Coe & Wells, 134, 162
Cohn, Sam, 46
Coleman, J G, 272
Commercial Hotel, 69
Commissioners' quarters, 83
Compton, H S, 72, 290
Comstock, S C, 191
Conner, O P, 212
Cook & Sargent, 249
Cook, S B, 14, 194
Couch, M, 257, 263
Couch, Ed, 318
Court House, 84
Covel, Dr, 189
Cracker, Andrew, 154
Cullen, Bob, 188, 197
Dana, Mrs, 264
Deshler, J G, 138, 211
Darlington, B, 141
Daut, Fred, 24
Davenport, Col G, 83, 190
Davenport firemen, 238
Davis, James, 109
Davis, Isaiah, 109
Day, I C, 28, 281
Daymude, J L, 323
Dean, Henry Clay, 40, 124, 231
Demorest, A F, 43, 194
Democratic Enquirer, 26, 30
Denison, G B, 303, 311

Denison, Miss, 308, 319
Dillaway, G W, 185
Diamond Joe Line, 297
Dinner Party, 38
Doctors, 187, 275
Dougherty, J B, 8, 183, 216, 320
Dougherty, Col J B, 8, 325
Drury, W A, 28
Drury's Landing, 29
Dunsmore & Chambers, 165
Dunsmore, A, 314
Dunn, S C, 31, 238
Durkee, W R, 186, 229
Drug business, 8

Early preachers, 124
Earl, Irving, 155
Early days at Geneva, 108
Eaton, Rev E, 232
Eichelberger, Santa, 260
Erb, Jacob, 141
Ewart, Will, 153
Excursions, 224
Eyrie, the, 31

Fahey, J, 186
Fales, Mrs, 224
Farnam, Mr, 190, 256, 263
Farley, Dr, 245
Farnsworth, 192
Fairchilds, Kate, 38, 65
Fay, Pliny, 8, 9, 65, 273
Fimple, A J, 335
Fire department, 15
Fisch, Jacob, 55
Fish, Chas H, 198, 213, 257
Fish, W B, 4, 213
Fisher, A H, 157
Fisher, Miss E, 299
First Germans, 34
First landlord, 105
First owners of Muscatine, 256
First settlers in county, 258
First jail, 116
Fitch, Dr and Mrs, 187, 221
Fletcher, J E, 285
Foster, Suel, 38, 83, 106, 252
Fulton, M, 167
Fox, Chas R, 194, 200, 205
Freeman, J P, 304, 307
Franklin, Mrs, 258
Fry, Capt William, 107, 279
Fry, Abial, 307, 334
Fullerton, W H, 161, 165
Fulliam, Dr G W, 183, 219, 276
Funck, Henry, 5, 14, 24, 34, 235

Gambling, 96
Garlock, J S, 164
Garner, Col, 243
Gas Works, 24, 48
Garrettson, G A, 320
Geneva, 108

Gilbert, Sam, 190, 258
Gillett, Harvey, 68, 108, 197
Goodno, Dr D H, 300, 322
Gordon, Major W 257, 263
Gordon, William, 341
Gordon, J G, 1, 13, 225
Graham Bros, 8
Grange Movement, 20
Grant, Hon James, 32
Green, Hon J A, 7, 176, 243, 307
Greenwood Academy, 323
Grocery licenses, 20, 279
Grossman, Mr and Mrs, 183
Grindstone Bluff, 250

Hallock, N, 27
Hatch, Gen Ed, 282
Hatch, James, 161
Hatch, C U, 173
Harness making, 71
Hardware and stoves, 54
Hastings, Hon S C, 106, 179, 253
Headley, 192, 230
Hershey, Ben, 148
Hill, S G, 141, 172
Hill, S B, 307, 314
Hine, L C, 257
Hine, H H, 273
Hobson, S P, 160
Hoch, Ed, 35, 161, 191
Holden, M, 165
Hoopes, J J, 158, 173, 218
Hoopes, W H, 63, 320
Hotel Grand, 221
Hotels, early, 101, 144, 272
Horton, Dr J S, 219
Humphreys, G W, 27, 39, 217, 274
Hutchinson, Z W, 209
Huttig Bros, 167

Indian Dance, 269
Ingalls, M, 308, 319
Irwin, J C, 303
Irvine, Thomas, 149
Isett, T M, 12, 106, 140, 221, 253
Islands in the river, 98

Jackson, James, 24
Jackson, Peter, 14, 39, 272
Jackson, A, 71, 307
Jail, first, 116
Jennison, H Q, 64, 328
Jerusha got married, 91
John, A, 69, 238
Johnson, Dr D P, 147
Johnson, Tom, 220

Kane, J M, 71
Kaiser Bros, 142
Kessinger, E M, 171
Killers, The, 267
Kincaid, Col G W, 326, 330
Kincaid, William, 173, 341

Kinney, Robert, 5, 51, 105, 144, 227, 262
Kinson, E B, 4
Kimball, A, 245
Kleinfelder, 161
Knopp, John, 169

Lafferty, Mrs, 178
Langridge, W B, 26, 42
Laurent, Rev, 221, 236
LaCossitt, H D, 16, 352
Leland & Co, 243
Lewis, Daniel, 322
Lewis, Frank R, 327
Lewis, S F, 341
Lemp, John, 6
Light Guards, 238, 243
Leindecker & Co, 161
Linfield, Rev G F, 233
Lillibridge, A, 192
Lockwood, Mrs, 223
Lowe, Gov R P, 211, 269
Lost Creek, 177
Loffland, Harry, 72
Lucas, Gov Rob, 269, 326
Lucas, J W, 13, 327
Lumber business, 51, 137, 165
Lumpe, Fred, 169
Lyon, Miss M M, 299, 311
McCormick, J A, 6, 26
McCormick, Rev Father, 221
McCrow, Mr and Mrs, 222
McDermid, D S, 169
McGreer, John, 259
McKey, Dr Lewis, 106, 188, 259
McKibben, Sam, 140
McNutt, Sam, 20, 308, 319
Magoon, G D, 138, 172, 334
Mahin, Hon John, 125
Manlove, M D, 160
Martin Brothers, 327
Meason, Hon Geo, 317
Matthews, H, 216, 229
Matthews, M, 137, 224
Metcalf, D, 282
Meterological, 37
Merrill, Miss, 309
Mellvine, Thomas, 74
Merchandise, 1, 22, 27, 64, 68
Middleton, W, 214
Mikesell, Miss H, 300, 344
Miller, Fred, 103, 141
Millar, William, 225, 326
Milk and Vegetables, 61
Military spirit, 2, 281
Minnesota Packet Co, 297
Missouri War, 112
Molis, Henry, 34
Moore, H W, 14, 54, 199, 320
Moscow Canal, 348
Moscow in 1838, 93
Mulford, Joseph, 169
Munroe, J H, 12

Muscatine, first owners, 256
Muscatine Sash and Door Co, 163, 193
Musserville, 160
Musser Lumber Co, 144, 164
Musser, Richard, 199
Musser, John, 204
Musser, Peter, 199
Musser, P M, 169, 194, 200
Musser, Drew R, 205
Musser, C R, 194

Narvis, Chas, 186, 254
Name of Muscatine, 258
Names of boats, 291
Nealley, J W, 257
Nealley, Chas, 307, 315
Negroes in the schools, 320
Neidig, B, 238
New school ticket, 321
Newcomb, Mr, 191
Northern Line Packets, 297
Nye, Ben, 256, 258

Oat Meal Factory, 141, 167
O'Connor, Henry, 303, 307, 315
Ogilvie, A, 22, 38
Old Ladies' Home, 207
Old Settlers' address, 271
Old churches, 215
Olds, Dr B S, 189
Ononwa, 249

Packing houses, 243
Page, Chas, 320
Palmer, Mr, 43
Pappoose Creek, 177
Parmer, Capt Jim, 144
Parvin, Josiah, 144
Parvin, J A, 6, 68, 211
Parvin, William, 313
Parvin, T S, 178, 211
Parmlee, James, 155
Parkhurst, Capt L, 291
Patten, J S, 171
Patterson, A O, 13
Payne, Miss D E, 300
Pepper, Miss, 309
Percell, A, 218, 313
Pettibone, G, 257, 274
Pettibone, J, 261
Petrican, P, 212
Photographers, 118
Phelps, C L, 290
Pickel, Jacob, 171
Pickler, J A, 245
Pioneer doctors, 275
Plummer, Deacon, 231
Politics in Iowa, 127
Porter, George, 326
Porter, G W, 327
Porter, J W, 207
Pound, Thad C, 142
Pres. Old Settlers' address, 271

—364—

Railroads, 32, 241, 244, 248
Rodman, Gen, 246
Ray, John, 194
Reynolds, Dr Eli, 187, 275
Reynolds, Addison, 190
Reeder, Dr George, 8, 106, 189
Records, city, 174
Reese, H, 180, 257, 307.
Rescue Hose Co, 15
Richards, Wm, 154
Richardson, Jos, 3
Richman, J S, 106
Richman, J W, 253
Richie, W S, 247
Roach, W L, 194
Robbins, Rev A B, 216, 304
Rublemann, J, 30, 72
Reuling, Adam, 288

Sames, W H, 190
Sash and door business, 167, 193
Satterlee, George, 238
School houses, 86, 298, 320, 323
School teacher's story, 87
School teachers, 36, 302
Seeley, Rev J W, 227
Sells, Luke, 290
Sherfey, 192
Shanghigh Row, 6
Sidewalks, 235
Silverman, Jacob, 45
Sixtieth anniversary, 234
Skunk war, 282
Smalley's p ark, 77
Smalley, A, 161, 171
Smalley, S, 320
Smith, T D, 23, 43
Soda Fountain, 16
Sons of Temperance, 29
Springer, Mr, 307, 318
Spring, Cyrus and William, 6
Standard, A, 191
Stark, Mrs, 261
Steamboat landing, 2, 4, 283
Stewart, S W, 93, 144, 275
Stein, Iohn G, 14, 26, 144
Stein, S G, 144, 164, 313
Steinberger family, 233, 326
Stocker, Rev John, 29, 91, 216
Stone school house, 323
Stone, F H, 8, 39, 64
Stone, G C, 9, 14
Stone, Chas, 55, 165
Stone, William R, 55, 238, 354
Stoves and tinware, 54

Swine breeding, 359
St John, William, 68, 180
St Louis and Keokuk Packet Co, 297

Tavern license, 278
Teller, Capt, 240
Thornton, Err, 86
Thurston, F, 304, 312
Tillard, Robert, 184
Trevoli, the, 224
Tuttle, A B, 307, 315
Turner, J H, 185

Ufford, Rev John, 323
Underwood, John, 42
Union Lumber Co, 142, 163

Vannatta, John, 51, 83, 198, 256, 263, 265
Van Name, 142
Van Nostrand, W H, 73
Viele, S D, 13

Wallace, J H, 225, 238, 241, 320
Walton, J P, 174, 180, 215, 234, 247, 256, 274, 337
Warfield, C A, 23, 257, 354
Warfield, A O, 106, 137, 333, 354
Warfield, D R, 106, 192, 332
Ward, J C, 31
Ward, Myron, 274
Washburn, Zeph, 80, 274
Washburn, L H, 81
Washburn, Parse, 223
Washburn, C C, 164
Washingtonians, 80
Waters, Dr C O, 8, 106, 352
Waters, O P, 62, 238
Wells, Prof D F, 299
Weed, Dr James, 22, 189, 225
Weed, Chester, 13, 119, 240, 253
Weed, Mrs Cora, 25, 31
Wenther Record, 351
Whicher, Stephen, 28, 212, 266, 317
White Hawk, 261
White Collar Line, 297
White, Mr, 258
Wholesale business, 65
Wood chopping, 2
Wilkinson, Mr, 157
Williams, Hon Jos, 211, 273
Williams, Miss Mary, 300
Wilton, 249

Ziegler, John, 161

www.ingramcontent.com/pod-product-compliance
Lightning Source LLC
Chambersburg PA
CBHW031424230426
43668CB00007B/427